THE THREE PILLARS OF LIBERTY

In this landmark study, a thorough audit of British compliance with international human rights standards is carried out. The book identifies 42 violations and 22 near-violations or causes for concern. It provides an up-to-date description of law and practice with respect to freedom of information; freedom of expression; freedom of assembly and public protest; freedom of association and trade unionism; state surveillance; the right to life and liberty; and the right to vote and stand in elections.

This study measures political freedom in the United Kingdom specifically against a unique Human Rights Index, specially constructed from international human rights laws and jurisprudence by the authors. The Index is an important new tool for monitoring human rights around the world. It is already being used to monitor new legislation in the UK.

The Three Pillars of Liberty is the first-ever analysis of both the political and legal systems for securing political freedom in the UK as a whole. It is the most rigorous and systematic review of those systems yet published – and finds them wanting. It strikes at the heart of the historic traditions of government and the rule of law in this country. This book will be essential reading for all those interested in their rights and the rights of others.

Francesca Klug is a Fellow of the Human Rights Centre, University of Essex, and a policy consultant for Charter 88. She is author of *A People's Charter*, Liberty's acclaimed Bill of Rights for the UK, and was Director of the Civil Liberties Trust. **Keir Starmer** is a barrister at Doughty Street Chambers, London, specialising in human rights cases. He is editor of *Justice in Error*, an in-depth analysis of the criminal justice system, and sat on the independent inquiry into the West Midlands Serious Crimes Squad. **Stuart Weir** is Director of the Democratic Audit and Senior Research Fellow at the Human Rights Centre, University of Essex. He edited the *New Statesman* from 1987 to 1991 and is founder of Charter 88.

The Three Pillars of Liberty

Political Rights and Freedoms in the
United Kingdom

Francesca Klug, Keir Starmer and Stuart Weir

The Democratic Audit of the United Kingdom

London and New York

First published 1996
by Routledge
11 New Fetter Lane, London EC4P 4EE

Simultaneously published in the USA and Canada
by Routledge
29 West 35th Street, New York, NY 10001

Typeset in Baskerville by
Florencetype Ltd, Stoodleigh, Devon

Printed and bound in Great Britain by
TJ Press (Padstow) Ltd, Padstow, Cornwall

British Library Cataloguing in Publication Data
A catalogue record for this book is available from the British Library

Library of Congress Cataloguing in Publication Data
Klug, Francesca.
  The three pillars of liberty : political rights and freedoms in the
United Kingdom / Francesca Klug, Keir Starmer, and Stuart Weir.
    p.   cm. – (The democratic audit of the United Kingdom)
  Includes bibliographical references and index.
  1. Political rights–Great Britain. 2. Civil rights–Great Britain.
I. Starmer, Keir. II. Weir, Stuart. III. Title. IV. Series.
JN906.K58 1996
323'.0941–dc20   96–12070

ISBN 0–415–09641–3
      0–415–09642–1 (pbk)

To Tania
who was born while this book was being written,
hoping you inherit a better world

Contents

List of Figures, Tables and Boxes

Foreword

This is one of two companion volumes which between them seek to audit the quality of democracy and political freedom in the United Kingdom. Both books are part of an ongoing project, entitled the Democratic Audit of the United Kingdom (henceforth, 'the Democratic Audit'). The goal of the Democratic Audit is to establish an account of the current state of democracy and political freedom in the United Kingdom on systematic and objective foundations. This volume audits political rights and freedoms in the UK; the companion volume, to be published in 1997, audits democratic institutions and practice.

For this purpose, we have developed two related indices as auditing tools: a set of 'democratic criteria', against which we can for the first time measure the democratic institutions of the United Kingdom; and the *Human Rights Index* of 'evolving international human rights standards' to audit the protection of political and civil rights in this country. These indices are designed both to allow us to carry out these audits in a systemic and transparent way – and to be replicable both in the United Kingdom and other countries. The intention is that the two companion volumes will provide a substantial 'benchmark' for regular audits in the future to measure whether Britain is becoming more or less democratic, and whether people's freedoms are more or less secure. The plan is to review and update both Democratic Audit volumes for the year 2000 and to publish the first set of follow-up volumes the following year.

These indices were constructed on three basic principles. They had to be based on clear and defensible ideas of democracy and political freedom. Second, they had to be specific indices, against which it was possible to measure significant aspects of Britain's political, legal and social life. Third, they had to be applied through a systematic and impartial set of procedures.

The appeal of democracy comes from the idea that ordinary people rule – the original Greek, δημοκρατια (*demokratia*), literally means 'people power'. We took the view that two universal principles underlie the implicit contract that representative democracy makes between the modern state and its people or peoples. In such a democracy, people do not – and cannot – rule directly, but through a representative system in which they have the final say. If that system is to keep the 'promises' that it makes to the public, it must seek to satisfy two basic goals – the first is that of *popular control* over the political processes of decision-making within their society; the second is that of *political equality* in the exercise of that control.

This book is the audit of political freedom in the United Kingdom – that is, of the political rights and freedoms which are constitutive of representative democracy, and which contribute directly to realising the Audit's two basic goals. Appendix 1 describes the Democratic Audit's aims more fully and sets out the 30 'democratic criteria' which the Democratic Audit has drawn from the two goals of popular control and political equality. Five of these criteria (DCs 19–23) provide the broad background against which the authors, along with their contributors, evaluate the quality of political freedoms, how well they are protected and how readily citizens can secure them in the United Kingdom.

But this study goes further. Francesca Klug and Keir Starmer have used these criteria to inform the construction of the international Index of political and civil rights standards described above. The Index is based on the world's major human rights instruments, including the UN International Covenant on Civil and Political Rights (Appendix 2) and the European Convention on Human Rights (Appendix 3). Other instruments and documents on which the Index draws are described in Appendix 4. Britain's system for protecting political and civil rights, and equality in the pursuit of these rights; the freedoms of information, expression, assembly and association; protection against state surveillance, arbitrary arrest, detention, torture and ill-treatment, and extra-judicial killing in time of emergency; the rights to vote and stand for election; all these matters are audited against these evolving international standards for human rights. The Human Rights Centre, at the University of Essex, maintains and develops the Index in association with the authors. It is our view that this is a valuable resource which can be put to many more uses in this and other countries.

This dimension makes this book an innovative and unique enterprise. Most studies of human rights in the United Kingdom stand squarely within an indigenous 'civil liberties' tradition. It is an honourable and influential tradition, and often very eloquent (as in the six editions of *Freedom, the Individual and the Law* since Harry Street's first edition in 1963). But these studies have not drawn upon a systematic set of objective criteria against which to measure 'the state of civil liberties in Britain'. Second, they have tended to draw only upon the values and ideas, law and practice, of the United Kingdom; international conventions are rarely employed as benchmarks.

This study is squarely based on the new world-wide tradition of *positive* human rights, created in 1945 after the horrors of Nazi Germany had shown the need for international protection of human rights. There is now a well-established body of international, and European, standards, case law, reports and observations which gives this study a systemic and empirical base from which to audit conditions in the United Kingdom. The authors argue that it also gives their findings a wider moral force than exists within purely 'British' traditions. But their findings, which may seem severe, are by their nature relative, not absolute. The Democratic Audit does not regard democracy and political freedom as all-or-nothing constructs, which a country like the United Kingdom either has or does not have. Both are living processes of change and adaptation, as are the international standards against which the authors audit political freedom in this country.

All authors must thank the scholars, colleagues and others who have made contributions, direct and indirect, to their work. In the case of the two companion books – this audit of political rights and freedoms and the forthcoming audit of democratic institutions – we have worked within an unusually close network of scholars, journalists and others, all of whom are associates of the Democratic Audit. The Audit aims to be a collegiate enterprise; our base is at the Human Rights Centre, but already 24 academics from 15 other universities or academic departments have contributed to our work, as well as journalists, MPs, civil servants, lawyers and others.

The authors make their own specific acknowledgements below. On behalf of the Audit, I must mention members of the team who helped us to develop the idea of the 'democratic audit' into the fully-fledged enterprise on which we are now embarked. All these colleagues are listed at Appendix 1. Collectively, the authors and I owe thanks to the Joseph Rowntree Charitable Trust and the members of its Democratic Panel, past and present, and especially Grigor McClelland and David Shutt, successive chairs of the Panel, and Professor Trevor Smith (whose brainchild we are). Thanks, too, to Anthony Barnett, who drafted the original bid to the Rowntree Trust; and to Professor David Beetham, of the University of Leeds, for his generous gift of the concept of the 'democratic criteria' and his advice and encouragement on this book.

Professor Kevin Boyle
Academic Editor

Acknowledgements

We are grateful for the advice and support of a number of individuals who have specialist knowledge of human rights and democratic practice. Jonathan Cooper, of Doughty Street Chambers, and Jo Oyediran, now working as a human rights monitor in the West Bank, contributed significant and innovative work on equalities (Chapter 7). Andrew Puddephatt, now director of Charter 88, gave ideas and original material for most chapters in Part 3; John Wadham, recently appointed director of Liberty, and Jane Winter, of British Irish Rights Watch, gave us useful comments on them all. Sheldon Reader, of the Department of Law, University of Essex, commented on Chapter 11 (freedom of association) and Ivor Crewe, of the Department of Government, Essex, and Martin Linton, of the *Guardian*, commented on Chapter 14 (voting).

Nicholas Bratza, vice-chair of the British Institute of Human Rights, contributed detailed advice on Francesca Klug's research into the impact of the European Convention on Human Rights on the British courts. Françoise Hampson and Bill Watts, of the Department of Law, University of Essex, provided incisive comment on early drafts of Part 2; Tony Barker, of the Department of Government at Essex, Phillippa Kaufmann, of Doughty Street Chambers, and Paul Hirst, of the Department of Sociology and Politics, Birkbeck College, advised on later drafts of Part 2. Bill Bowring, of the Law Department, University of East London, gave valuable advice on the methodology. The Index also benefited from debate at the European Consortium for Political Research Workshop on Indices of Democratisation in Leiden in 1993, to which Francesca Klug presented an early paper on auditing civil and political rights (Klug 1993).

Kevin Boyle, director of the Human Rights Centre, University of Essex, and academic editor on the Democratic Audit project, gave continuing advice and comment throughout. David Beetham, Department of Politics, Leeds, gave informed advice on the history of rights along with the 'democratic criteria' which provided the first foundations of the book. Trevor Smith, vice-chancellor of the University of Ulster, commented valuably on the book's conclusions.

Wendy Hall, research officer of the Democratic Audit, unfailingly provided meticulous research and compiled numerous complex tables. Seth Weir researched the passage of the Criminal Justice and Public Order Act 1994 (Chapter 5) and produced tables to rival Wendy Hall's.

Librarians at the British Institute of International and Comparative Law, Doughty Street Chambers, the University of Essex, the House of Commons, Liberty, and the London School of Economics (in alphabetical order) were all very helpful. Caroline Wintersgill and Caroline Cautley, our publishers at Routledge, have been unfailingly enthusiastic and patient. Special thanks are also due to Ann Scott, who has copy-edited and proofread this book with meticulous care.

We all owe a great debt of gratitude to Keir Starmer's colleagues and staff at Doughty Street Chambers for releasing him to work on the book for far longer than they can have imagined. Finally, we must express our appreciation of partners, children and close friends who gave us ideas and encouragement in return for years of neglect.

Francesca Klug, Keir Starmer and Stuart Weir
December 1995

List of Abbreviations and Acronyms

ACTSS   Association of Clerical, Technical and Supervisory Staff (previous title of ACTS, the clerical branch of the Transport and General Workers' Union)
AEA   Atomic Energy Authority (state agency)
APEX   Association of Professional, Executive, Clerical and Computer Staff (previously an independent trade union; now affiliated to the general trade union, GMB)
BBC   British Broadcasting Corporation (public service)
BMA   British Medical Association (trade association)
CAAT   Campaign Against the Arms Trade (pressure group)
CAJ   Committee for the Administration of Justice (pressure group in Northern Ireland)
CAT   Committee Against Torture (UN committee)
CBI   Confederation of British Industries (interest group)
CEDAW   UN Convention on the Elimination of All Forms of Discrimination Against Women
CERD   UN Convention on the Elimination of All Forms of Racial Discrimination
CHAR   Campaign for the Homeless and Rootless (pressure group)
CJPO (Bill or Act)   Criminal Justice and Public Order Bill or Act 1994
Cmnd   Non-statutory report to Parliament
CND   Campaign for Nuclear Disarmament (pressure group)
CPT   Committee for the Prevention of Torture
CRE   Commission for Racial Equality (statutory agency)
CSCE   Conference on Security and Co-operation in Europe (a loose association of states with human rights concerns)
DTI   Department of Trade and Industry
ECHR   European Convention on Human Rights
ECmHR   European Commission of Human Rights
ECtHR   European Court of Human Rights
EPA(s)   Northern Ireland (Emergency Provisions) Act 1991
ERO   Electoral Registration Officer
ESC   European Social Charter
GCHQ   Government Communications Headquarters
HC   House of Commons
HC Deb   House of Commons Debates (followed by Hansard reference)
HC Deb (WA)   House of Commons Written Answer (followed by Hansard reference)

HC SCB	House of Commons Standing Committee 'B' (on CJPO Bill 1994)
HMSO	Her Majesty's Stationery Office
HL Debs	House of Lords Debates (followed by Hansard reference)
HRC	Human Rights Centre, University of Essex
IBA	Independent Broadcasting Authority (private sector regulator)
ICCPR	International Covenant on Civil and Political Rights
ICESCR	International Covenant on Economic, Social and Cultural Rights
ICM	ICM Research Limited (a London opinion poll company)
ILO	International Labour Organisation
INLA	Irish National Liberation Army (terrorist organisation)
IRA	Irish Republican Army (terrorist organisation)
ITC	Independent Television Commission (private sector licensing and regulatory body)
MI5	The domestic security services (government agency)
MI6	Secret intelligence service (government agency)
MORI	Name of London polling organisation
OPCS	Office of Population Censuses and Surveys (government body)
PACE	Police and Criminal Evidence Act 1984 (also used as shorthand for police powers and rules established under the act)
PCA	Police Complaints Authority (statutory agency)
PIIC	Public Interest Immunity Certificate
PSI	Policy Studies Institute (independent policy agency)
PTA(s)	Prevention of Terrorism Act(s) (temporary statutory instrument renewed annually under a continuation order)
QC	Queen's Counsel (designates senior barrister)
RPA	Representation of the People Act (1867–1990)
RRA	Race Relations Act (1965, 1968 or 1976)
RUC	Royal Ulster Constabulary (police force in Northern Ireland)
SACHR	Standing Advisory Committee on Human Rights (statutory body active only in Northern Ireland)
SCOPE	Voluntary mental health organisation (formerly the Spastics Society)
SDA	Sex Discrimination Act 1975
TASS	Technical, Administrative and Supervisory Staffs (formerly part of the Amalgamated Engineering Union)
TUC	Trades Union Congress (national body of affiliated trade unions)
TULCRA	Trade Union and Labour Relations (Consolidation) Act 1992
UDA	Ulster Defence Association (terrorist organisation)
UVF	Ulster Volunteer Force (terrorist organisation)
UN	United Nations
UNHRC	United Nations Human Rights Committee (established to oversee ICCPR, see above)
UNCAT	United Nations Committee Against Torture
UNESCO	UN Educational, Scientific and Cultural Organisation
UNPPE	UN Principles on the Effective Prevention and Investigation of Extra-Legal, Arbitrary and Summary Executions
WRP	Workers' Revolutionary Party

How to Use This Book

The book is divided into four parts. Part 1 – the Introduction – is divided into Chapter 1 on the tradition of political freedoms in the UK and Chapter 2 which describes the *Human Rights Index* and methodology which we use to audit political rights and freedoms in the rest of the book.

Part 2 audits 'the British system' – the legal, cultural and political arrangements for protecting and securing political rights and freedoms in the United Kingdom. Chapters 3 to 6 assess the combined roles of government and Parliament, public opinion and the 'culture of liberty', the common law and the courts in protecting rights. Political equality is vital to modern democracy, but no constitutional right to equality exists in the UK. Chapter 7 analyses the effect of this general absence, considers anti-discrimination measures and assesses how far rights and freedoms are equally available to all citizens and groups.

Part 3 consists of a series of audits of the key political rights and freedoms – the 'democratic rights' which are constitutive of democracy (see **pp. 10–12**) – in turn. The analogy with a financial audit is apparent in this split between Parts 2 and 3. While Part 2 first examines Britain's broad system of 'protections' against agreed indicators set out in the Human Rights Index to see whether any inadequacies can be explained by the structure as a whole, Part 3 evaluates practice within the system for each right at a given moment (mid-1995).

Chapters 8 to 14 audit the key 'democratic' rights and freedoms in turn: freedom of information and expression; freedom of assembly, including the right of public protest; freedom of association, including trade union rights; surveillance of citizens by the security and police forces; the right to life and liberty, including police powers to stop, search and detain individual citizens, ill-treatment and torture in detention, and extra-judicial killings in Northern Ireland; and the right to vote and stand for election.

The chapters generally follow the same basic format (see Chapter 2 for fuller information). Each begins with the appropriate international standards drawn from the Human Rights Index (see Chapter 2). The next section briefly presents the raw data for audit: largely, the common and statute law governing the right in question and how the law is applied. This is in effect a neutral survey of law, policy and practice. The third section is the audit: by applying the Index standards to the data, it determines how far law, policy and practice in the UK meet or violate international standards. Each chapter ends with a conclusion.

The chapters in Part 2 deviate somewhat from this general approach. Chapters 3, 4 and 6 share a common Index section and Chapter 7, which examines issues of equality and discrimination, has its own Index. These chapters do not have separate conclusions. Instead, Chapter 5 analyses the passage of the Criminal Justice and Public Order Act 1994 as a test case, revealing the political system for safeguarding rights in operation; and Part 2 ends with a common conclusion, 'The British way of doing things', auditing the political and legal system for protecting political rights and freedoms in the UK against the claims which are made for it as well as against international standards.

Part 4 finally audits as a whole both the British system for protecting and ensuring political rights and freedoms (Part 2), and the UK position on the individual rights and freedoms (Part 3). It presents the Democratic Audit's findings both on the system and individual rights. It is the first systematic balance sheet on political freedom in the United Kingdom.

PART I

Introduction

1   The British Tradition of Constitutional Rights

Political freedom in the United Kingdom

Citizens of the United Kingdom believe they are among the freest people in the world. The idea that this country has a unique propensity to individual liberties, going back to the ancient resistance of the Anglo-Saxons to the 'Norman yoke' and the Magna Carta, is buried deep in the national psyche. For example, on its 750th anniversary in 1956, Lord Denning celebrated Magna Carta as 'the foundation of the freedom of the individual against the arbitrary authority of the despot'. More recently, Mrs Margaret (now Lady) Thatcher lyrically described how the belief in freedom has been jealously guarded 'on this island of ours':

> 'That was always our glory – not our wealth, although that was great; not our Empire – although that was the greatest ever seen; but our constant commitment to the fundamental liberties which alone allow the human spirit to grow and a free nation to be governed with tolerance, decency and compassion.'
> (Speech in Birmingham, 19 April 1979)

Inherent in this belief is the idea that the country's political and legal institutions are perfectly suited to protecting individual liberties and require no fundamental change. That while the United Kingdom has ratified all the major international and regional human rights instruments, none are really needed by the British people. In 1995, Lord Donaldson, formerly Master of the Rolls, recalled that, as a judge, he had been referred to the European Convention on Human Rights from time to time, but could not remember it ever being suggested that there was 'any inconsistency whatsoever' between the common law and the Convention (HL Deb, 25 January 1995, c1154).

But this belief also inspires a strong popular attachment to 'rights', which is one of the sturdiest elements in the reactive civil society of the United Kingdom. Indeed, for two-thirds of the population, 'living in a free country' is one of the two most important aspects of democracy (ICM 1994). Civil society in Britain is notable for the variety of expert and skilful organisations committed to human rights and democracy. In July 1995, the UN Human Rights Committee reported that the evidence from 'a wide range' of such bodies during its hearings on the UK human rights record 'not only greatly assisted the Committee, but [was] also a tribute to the democratic nature of UK society' (CCPR/C/798/Add. 55, para. 3).

Yet the British tradition of ancient 'constitutional rights' is a double-edged legacy. This tradition conflates ideas of 'strong' government and public order with civil

The historical legacy

liberties, and the first two are usually paramount in the minds of the country's rulers. Thus, citizens may deploy the claim to 'rights' against state power on their own behalf, or that of oppressed or excluded groups. But the idea may equally well be used by those in power against threats from below or outside. The defence of liberty – uniquely 'English' or 'British' – has frequently served as a defence against democracy and protest. It is further employed to inhibit scrutiny of the traditional arrangements through which the state protects human rights. Any idea that these arrangements might benefit from thoroughgoing review is likely to provoke unease or accusations of disloyalty; any criticism from outside – as, for example, in the European Court's judgment in 1995 on the deaths of three IRA terrorists in Gibraltar – can ignite passionate cries of rejection, not least from another symbol of English tradition, Number 10 Downing Street.

The purpose of this book is to provide that thoroughgoing review. There is ample evidence from the Rowntree Reform Trust's 'State of the Nation' opinion polls of the depth of public concern about the erosion of democracy and civil liberties in this country (Rowntree Reform Trust 1991, 1995). This book tests how thoroughly political rights and freedoms are protected in law and practice in the United Kingdom. The intention is to do so in a systematic and objective way, which is described in detail in this and the following chapter.

Ideas of individual freedom and political rights in Britain

This country's contribution to the idea of individual rights and freedoms has been a distinguished one. Magna Carta is a universally significant document as it represents one of the first practical challenges to the idea of absolute rule. From it derive the concepts of natural justice and trial by jury which characterise the English legal system to this day. The 1689 Bill of Rights, the first modern document of that name, set out certain rights and liberties which English subjects could henceforth claim against the king. Prohibitions against 'excessive bail or fines' and 'cruel and unusual punishment', which are common to modern human rights instruments, stem from this Bill. Neither is of course a human rights document in the modern sense. Their main purpose was to share power between monarch and the propertied classes. They did not establish a comprehensive set of rights for the people as a whole and they reinforced existing inequalities and discriminations. For example, Magna Carta singled out Jews for discriminatory treatment; the Bill of Rights secured special rights for Protestants (who alone were allowed to bear arms).

It was not until the Enlightenment that the concept of human rights in a more modern sense began to take root. This was a European movement, in which the English philosopher, John Locke (1632–1704), played a significant part. Locke's theory of a social contract between the rulers and ruled remains influential to this day. He argued that people gave up their natural freedoms in return for protection by their ruler of their life, liberty and property (Locke 1963). This was a persuasive early argument for the now established view that one of the first duties of the state is to protect the rights and freedoms of its citizens. Ideas of individual rights and equality inspired the French Declaration of the Rights of Man (1789) and the

American Bill of Rights (1791). But the French Revolution and the European wars which followed created a divide between the English and European traditions. Thomas Paine, the English radical who played a part in both the American and French Revolutions, published a pamphlet, *The Rights of Man*, in 1791, arguing the case for democracy and the ideas of the French Revolution (Paine 1791). His pamphlet became a bestseller, but the British government indicted Paine for seditious libel; while Paine undoubtedly sowed the idea of natural, or human, rights among the population at large, the authorities met demands for popular sovereignty and a Bill of Rights with severe repression.

Paine's contemporary, Edmund Burke (1729–1797) was in fact to have far more influence on British political thought. Burke, a Whig politician, ridiculed ideas of 'natural rights' as meaningless abstractions, as Jeremy Bentham and the nineteenth century Utilitarians were also to do. Burke counterposed his own abstract vision of ordered progress in an organic society, in which rights and customs evolved naturally over time, and argued forcefully for a concept of representation by able and independent gentlemen in Parliament. It is not easy to over-estimate Burke's continuing impact on British political life. He influenced the way in which nineteenth and early twentieth century Britain gradually accommodated the extension of the franchise. He is generally regarded as the father of modern conservatism in the UK, but the late Labour minister, Richard Crossman, once called him 'not the philosopher of British conservatism, but of British political life from Right to Left' (Arblaster 1984: 225). Another enduring proponent for the British way was to follow – Professor A.V. Dicey (1835–1922), a constitutional theorist who argued that individual liberties were more effectively protected by parliamentary sovereignty, the unwritten constitution and the common law than by continental systems with their constitutional codes and catalogues of rights. Inherent in the British system, he maintained, was the unwritten assumption that every subject is free to do that which is not forbidden by law: what are generally known as 'negative rights'. Precisely because rights were *not* written down, but were upheld by judicial rulings or the common law, it was actually more difficult for governments to take away or reduce the liberties of the people (Dicey 1885). Dicey's arguments remain the rock on which is based the continuing adherence of governments in Britain to the long-established indigenous system of 'negative' rights, built into the common law, as opposed to the model of 'positive' rights, defined in entrenched Bills of Rights and constitutions and in international rights instruments.

The development of universal human rights

The end of the second world war marked a new era in the quest to develop and protect human rights. Until the 1930s, the way a country treated its inhabitants was (in the consistent tradition of international law) exclusively the affair of that country's government. There was almost no scope for legitimate criticism, let alone intervention, from outside. The wholesale abuse, torture and slaughter of millions of citizens in Europe and the rest of the world by Nazi Germany and its allies stirred the conscience of the international community. The people who were murdered were

Human rights

singled out because of their religion, ethnic origin, political opinion, sexual orientation or disability. The doctrine of national sovereignty was morally discredited. It was recognised that states could no longer agree not to interfere in the internal affairs of countries where atrocities were taking place.

The League of Nations, the precursor of the UN, had drawn up narrowly defined treaties in an effort to protect minorities, mainly in eastern European countries. The failure of these treaties persuaded the United Nations that the broad protection of human rights should take its place among the founding principles in the UN Charter. It is from this decision that a set of universal standards for human rights came to be born. In 1948, the UN General Assembly agreed the Universal Declaration of Human Rights, which was intended to establish 'a common standard of achievement for all peoples and all nations'. This common standard rested on empirical evidence of the barbarism which can and does break out in nation states. In human societies, it was recognised, the interests and views of rulers are always likely to differ to some degree or another from those of the ruled, and especially minorities. There was always the danger that states would resort to state or majority tyranny. States would still adopt their own laws. But these laws, in turn, ought to conform to agreed international standards on human rights and freedoms (Sieghart 1986: 40).

At the time, the Universal Declaration seemed to be largely declaratory, but it has since acquired increasing legal significance. There remains plenty of room for neo-Benthamite scepticism. The world may have established common standards for the protection of human rights; and even a new theoretical base for their protection. But all the instruments and covenants in the world have not protected millions of people from human rights abuse, torture and mass slaughter. International agencies, most obviously the UN itself, and individual states remain reluctant and often incompetent to intervene in the internal affairs of the most brutal states. The 'promise' of 1948 has not been fulfilled. But there now exists an evolving set of common standards which have been signed by nearly all the states in the world and against which their actions can be objectively judged. In particular, the UN International Covenants on Civil and Political Rights and on Economic, Social and Cultural Rights came into force in 1976 to develop the broad standards that the Universal Declaration established in greater detail and to turn them into enforceable rights. Two supervisory bodies – the UN Human Rights Committee and the UN Committee on Economic, Social and Cultural Rights – were established to monitor and encourage compliance with the Covenants. Other international and regional instruments have drawn on the Universal Declaration to create binding human rights.

The most significant regional instrument for the UK is the European Convention on Human Rights. This country was one of the 15 European states which, as founding members of the Council of Europe, resolved to take what they described as 'the first steps for the collective enforcement' of political and civil rights set out in the Universal Declaration when they signed the Convention in 1950. The Convention – which came into force in 1953 – is often said to be alien to British political and legal traditions. Yet its Articles enshrine rights and freedoms which are part of a common European heritage and a former legal adviser to the Home Office was the principal drafter of key parts of the text (Lester 1993: 1–3). But the revolutionary ideas of collective enforcement and the right of individual petition to independent outside bodies – the European Commission and Court of Human Rights – have undoubtedly proved unwelcome to British governments. The United Kingdom has refused to incorporate either the European Convention or the International Covenant on Civil and Political Rights into domestic law. (Of the 31 European nations which have now ratified the Convention, only four – the UK, Ireland, Poland and Norway – have refused to incorporate.) It was not until 1966 that the United Kingdom finally allowed British citizens to invoke the European Convention against their own government and courts, and they still have no right of individual petition to the UN Human Rights Committee, the enforcing authority of the International Covenant (see **p. 58**).

Thus modern Britain retains its own domestic arrangements for protecting and enforcing rights, yet now forms part of the European and international systems for protecting rights. It is a curious duality: aggrieved citizens may first of all seek to secure their rights in domestic courts, which follow a 'non-positive' approach; and if unsatisfied, may take the 'positive' road to the European Commission and Court in Strasbourg. The two systems never overlap. The Court regularly considers cases referred from the United Kingdom and has to date found 37 violations of the Convention (Table 3.1). In such cases, the government is obliged, if relevant, to change the domestic law. The government does not respond by introducing a new positive right, but simply deals with the specific problem identified by the court. In 1995, the UN Human Rights Committee, deprived of jurisdiction in individual British cases, unanimously concluded that the whole system for protecting and securing political and civil rights in the UK 'does not ensure fully that an effective remedy is provided for all violations of the rights contained in the Covenant' (27 July 1995: CCPR/C/79/Add. 55). This audit considers how far those arrangements do protect and secure political and civil rights – or more particularly 'democratic rights' – in this country, and how effective the remedies are for individual citizens whose rights are violated.

The auditing tool – the Human Rights Index

To carry out this audit, we have developed a *Human Rights Index*, drawn from international and regional human rights instruments, such as the International Covenant and European Convention, and the interpretations given to them by supervisory bodies, like the UN Human Rights Committee and the European Commission and Court of Human Rights.

The Index is fully described in Chapter 2; it consists of an original set of criteria establishing the evolving international human rights standards for civil and political rights and freedoms. In that chapter, we also discuss the obvious difficulties of carrying out an audit of 'negative' arrangements for protecting rights using criteria drawn from a 'positive' model (see above). In general, however, we reject the idea that such instruments represent an 'alien' tradition. The United Kingdom contributed to the development of both the International Covenant and European

Human Rights Index

Convention in the 1950s and both draw on 'a common heritage of political traditions, ideals, freedoms and the rule of law' (Lester 1993: 1).

We start from the assumption that any democratic political system is capable of protecting human rights, according to the international standards set down in human rights instruments. Neither the International Covenant nor the European Convention prescribes a particular system to be adopted to protect human rights. Contracting states like the United Kingdom may employ their own arrangements for protecting and securing the rights that they set out. The two instruments do, however, require that these arrangements should be effective and lay down certain principles – for example, the right to an effective remedy for breaches of rights – which must be satisfied if a given political system is to protect the human rights of its citizens adequately. Nor are 'positive' continental or international systems necessarily superior to Britain's way of protecting rights. The European Convention, for example, seeks only to provide a set of minimum standards for human rights on which member states can build higher standards. It is well known that its enforcing authorities are willing to make compromises between democratic rights and the needs of states. Libertarians in Britain have complained that none of several *causes célèbres* of the 1980s – the GCHQ trade union ban, media restrictions on reporting Northern Ireland and the long police ban on CND marches – were even found admissible by the European Commission on Human Rights (Gearty 1995: 10).

Political and civil rights may, therefore, be equally well, or better, protected and practised in the United Kingdom than in most continental countries. The point is that we require the most objective set of standards possible by which to measure the protection of political freedoms in the UK. As a signatory of the two most significant instruments – the European Convention and the UN International Covenant – the United Kingdom is already committed to meeting international standards; and the British government has stated in four successive reports to the UN Human Rights Committee – in 1977, 1984, 1989 and 1994 – that the British system meets the standards established under the International Covenant (see also Chapter 3).

Our commitment to the international framework is not only empirical and legal. It has a moral dimension too. All those states which value the political freedoms of their own citizens have a moral duty to ensure that they meet the world's common standards for human rights. For their explicit recognition by states all over the world contributes to raising the standards of other states and raising the expectations and morale of societies and communities which are vulnerable to human rights violations and persecution. That concern for human rights in tyrannical states too often takes second place to strategic goals, regional security considerations and trading opportunities is a shame which stains the conduct of the great majority of democratic and supposedly civilised states.

The links between democracy and human rights

The Human Rights Index has been constructed to audit 'democratic rights' – that is, political and civil rights which are constitutive of democracy. Our position is that human rights of all kinds are best protected by effective political democracy which, in turn, cannot function properly if the political rights and freedoms we audit in this book are not secured.

The links between democracy and human rights are explicitly recognised in the preamble to the European Convention on Human Rights:

> those Fundamental Freedoms which are the foundation of justice and peace in the world . . . are best maintained on the one hand by an effective political democracy and on the other by a common understanding and observance of the Human Rights upon which they depend.

The Statute of the Convention's founding body, the Council of Europe, specifically links individual freedom, political liberty and the rule of law as the basis of 'all genuine democracy' (Council of Europe 1993: 2). The UN instruments do not make the same explicit links, but the International Covenant confirms the right to take part in public affairs and vote in free elections (Articles 21 and 25).

In reality, the links between democracy and human rights are not quite as simple as statements of principle make them seem. From Alexis de Tocqueville and John Stuart Mill onwards, political philosophers have expressed the concern that majority rule is inherently threatening to civil, and especially minority, rights. Such observers have argued that a Bill of Rights, constitutionally protected from political interference and enforced by the courts, is required as an external check on majority rule and elected parliaments (Martin 1993: 173).

A 'human rights' view of democracy seeks to give substance to the argument that democracy cannot be equated simply with majority rule and that processes which protect minorities and give them an effective voice are essential to democratic practice (Rosas and Heligesen 1990: 18; Beetham and Boyle 1995). However, our view that basic rights, such as freedom of expression and assembly, are constitutive of democracy itself is not solely a matter of protecting minorities. Democracy does not genuinely exist, even though governments and MPs have been elected in more or less free elections, unless voters as a whole have had access to the information they need to make 'knowledgeable choices rather than manipulated responses' (Dworkin 1990: 33). Citizens must be able to participate in government between elections through informed and free debate. For this to happen, government and Parliament have to be constrained by citizen's rights which are established in law and not easily tampered with by politicians, bureaucrats or others. They should become part of the fabric of society. It is the task of the courts, or any other body charged with their protection, to establish a specific interpretation of those rights with which to assess and rule unlawful legislation or decisions which violate them. It is often said that this process makes their provisions too 'rigid'; but, in practice, as the continuing interpretation of the European Convention has shown, human rights evolve as society evolves – in the same way as the common law itself adapts over time.

This audit starts from the position elaborated by international human rights instruments. The European Court of Human Rights set out this position in a landmark case in 1981:

Democratic links

> Although individual interests must on occasion be subordinated to those of
> a group, democracy does not simply mean that the views of a majority must
> always prevail: a balance must be achieved which ensures the fair and proper
> treatment of minorities and avoids any abuse of a dominant position.
>
> (*Young, James and Webster v UK*, 1982)

From this perspective, not only are human rights best protected in a political system
based on 'the will of the people'; but for that will to be freely debated and expressed
in ways which give everyone the chance to be involved, certain fundamental human
rights must be protected. A majority decision is democratically legitimate only if it
is a majority within a society of equals.

The democratic rights to be audited

It is widely agreed that the exercise of a vote in parliamentary elections every four
or five years barely scratches the surface of what is meant by democracy:

> Elections of themselves do not constitute democracy. They are not an end
> but a step, albeit an important and often essential one, on the path towards
> the democratisation of societies and the realisation of the right to take part
> in the government of one's country ... democracy implies far more than
> the mere act of periodically casting a vote, but covers the entire process of
> participation by citizens in the political life of their country.
>
> (1991 Report of the Secretary-General of the UN; A/46/609)

This is not simply a remote formal view. Some two-thirds of the British people, for
example, agree with these sentiments. They told ICM pollsters that the right to vote
periodically does not satisfy their own democratic aspirations, and say that they
would like to exercise more power between elections (ICM 1994).

To satisfy our own principles of popular control and political equality, individual
citizens in a democratic state must possess certain legal rights. The United Nations
has listed a set of 'pre-requisite rights' for ensuring that free elections are carried
out in accordance with international standards and that they reflect 'the free expression of the will of the electors'. The rights identified are free opinion, expression,
information, assembly and association. In addition, elections cannot be fair if equal
participation is not assured through non-discriminatory measures (UN 1994).

Citizens can hardly exercise effective control over elected representatives without
access to information about their policies and programmes. They must possess
the rights to express their views on political issues and to gain access to information about their government's policies and actions and issues in their society. They
must be able freely to form political parties and other associations and to demonstrate their political views publicly through protests and demonstrations. The
principle of political equality cannot be satisfied if some citizens live in fear of the
authorities or of others, or are deterred by arbitrary interference by the state – by
being stopped and searched by the police, or put under surveillance, or even detained

and imprisoned, for engaging in lawful political activity. Equality before the law and anti-discrimination measures are essential to make a living reality of the principle of political equality.

For the purposes of the Democratic Audit, these political and civil rights are important components of democracy. Their fundamental importance lies in giving individuals protection from state coercion. But they also protect and energise the very actions which have a public and collective significance. They thus enable individual citizens to influence policies and politics through the control they can share and exercise over elected decision-makers and public servants.

This emphasis not only governs the rights we choose to audit, but determines what aspects of those rights we assess. For example, the combined rights of access to official information and free expression matter for democracy because they enable people to be informed about and comment on issues of public concern. It is essential to informed and pluralistic debate. But we leave aside certain aspects of freedom of expression, like pornography and moral censorship – important though they are – because they are not central to our concerns. In the area of privacy, we examine only the effects of state surveillance on the right to a private life; important issues such as, say, domestic pressures on political participation are not assessed – largely because relevant data are simply not available. Of course, we recognise that every right and every aspect of social life are relevant to the quality of democracy and political freedom. But limits of time, resources and space force us to confine the audit to rights, and aspects of those rights, which are most directly relevant.

The same constraints have obliged us to omit social and economic rights. The great majority of ordinary citizens believe such rights – to secure housing, health care and work – belong in a Bill of Rights (Rowntree 1991–1995). There is ample evidence that poor housing and unemployment, for example, have an enduring impact on people's ability to develop and play a citizen's part in public life (Donnison 1991: 24–41; Townsend 1979). Major inequalities in wealth and resources create major differences in political equality, as they demonstrably confer more political control on their holders than poor or disadvantaged citizens possess. The British public believe that a measure of social equality is a significant component of demo-cratic life (ICM 1994). We treat the question of social and economic differences as an issue in the companion audit volume. The Democratic Audit intends to devise a second Human Rights Index to incorporate economic and social rights, as we believe that the disparity of regard between these rights and political and civil rights is damaging (Beetham 1995: 1–9 and 41–60; Boyle 1995: 79–95). But we cannot apply the civil and political rights index, developed for this volume, to social and economic rights.

Throughout, the aim is to provide an audit of the position in the United Kingdom. However, different laws apply in different parts of the United Kingdom and we are not able to cover the whole systematically. The audit focuses on the legal system in England, Wales and Northern Ireland. We indicate where special laws or practice exist in Northern Ireland, especially in Chapter 3 (on the governance of Northern Ireland) and Chapter 13 (the deprivation of liberty). But we do not pretend to give a comprehensive guide to law and practice in Northern Ireland. Nor has it been

Democratic rights

possible to include Scotland's separate legal and judicial system in the audit; Scottish criminal justice is as distinct from the system in England and Wales as that in France. The intention is to include Scotland in the follow-up audit for the year 2000.

Terminology

On occasions, we use the terms 'national', 'British', 'Britain' and 'this country' informally, largely to smooth the narrative, not as a derogation from our intention to provide a UK survey. We frequently use the term 'citizen' which has both legal and political meanings in the UK. Since 1983, British Citizenship has been a legal category which confers certain rights on those who have this status, such as the right to vote and (subject to the Home Secretary's discretion) to possess a British passport. It is also a word which is used in contrast to British subject, a term still used to denote the relationship between the monarch and the UK population. Only for very few rights do international human rights instruments distinguish between 'citizens' and other individuals. We use the word 'citizen' in this higher meaning to evaluate British standards of political freedom. That is, how far do political rights belong to all individuals who live in the United Kingdom, regardless of their formal status? We also use 'citizen' in a broad political sense. For the idea of active participation forms a backdrop to the evaluation throughout this audit.

To remove any risk of confusion between the institutions of the European Union and the Council of Europe's human rights structure, we always write the 'EU European Commission' or the 'European Court of Justice' in full, to distinguish them from the common usages, 'European Court' and 'European Commission', which, throughout, refer to the European Court of Human Rights and the European Commission of Human Rights. In legal references to reports and judgments from Strasbourg we use the abbreviations 'ECtHR' and 'ECmHR' to distinguish between the European Court and Commission.

Timing

Most of the manuscript was delivered to the publishers in December 1995. Apart from a few findings from the Scott Report and minor amendments, it has not been posible to take into account developments in law and practice which have occurred since that date.

2   Auditing Political Rights and Freedoms

The Human Rights Index

It is not immediately obvious how to audit political freedom in the United Kingdom. No domestic yardsticks exist in the form of a written constitution or a Bill of Rights. No official body is charged with the duty of monitoring the position of human rights in the UK, nor does the government effectively assess the effects of intended legislation on its international obligations under human rights treaties like the European Convention on Human Rights.

The Democratic Audit began at the level of broad principle, by defining the two basic principles on which democracy rests – popular control and political equality – and then creating 30 'democratic criteria' for assessing how far any democratic country satisfies these two principles (Beetham 1993). These criteria are set out in full in Appendix 1. The two main criteria for measuring the quality of political and civil rights are:

● How clearly does the law define the political and civil rights of citizens, how effectively are they protected, and how accessible are the remedies where they are violated?
● How secure are citizens in the exercise of their political and civil rights, and the remedies available to them when they are violated, and how far do they enjoy equal treatment of those rights and remedies?

These criteria are valuable for creating a broad framework for auditing political freedom in the United Kingdom, but they are not specific enough as instruments for a rigorous and specific audit. Nor, as we discuss below, do previous models for assessing the state of political freedoms and rights offer a satisfactory methodology. Therefore, we decided to adopt the *Human Rights Index*, which we described briefly in Chapter 1. The principles underpinning the two major human rights instruments which comprise the greater part of the Index – the International Covenant of Civil and Political Rights and the European Convention – fit squarely with the two criteria of the Audit set out above.

There is a common idea that instruments like the European Convention are too broadly phrased themselves to be of practical value; Roy Hattersley, when Labour's shadow Home Secretary, once declared that 'you could drive a coach and horses' through the provisions of the Convention. In fact, the Convention, International Covenant and other instruments have given rise to a rich 'jurisprudence' – nearly half a century of court judgments, authoritative comments and interpretation. From

Auditing criteria

the instruments and their interpretation we have compiled a specific and detailed Index, against which civil and political rights in this country can be systematically audited. This entails not only examining the quality of individual rights in the United Kingdom, but also the system for protecting them (just as a financial auditor would check the internal systems of any organisation under audit).

Previous attempts to audit human rights

The analogy of the audit suits us well. Like all other auditors in practice, we are 'looking through the books'; our intention is to bring to bear rigorous inspection and verification processes. Neither of the two general approaches which dominate previous human rights studies – the quantitative and the qualitative – are suitable for our purposes.

Several American studies have sought to measure human rights performances by using statistical data – the quantitative approach. They tend to be comparative. Usually, they award unrefined or raw scores to each country on the basis of its human rights record and then rank the countries assessed against each other. Inevitably, the actual scoring methods vary a great deal (Jabine and Claude 1992).

The annual *Comparative Survey of Freedom*, carried out by Freedom House, an American foundation, is the best-known of the quantitative studies. Freedom House categorises any given society as 'free', 'partly free' or 'not free' on the basis of a checklist for both political rights and civil liberties (Freedom House 1994). The index used to evaluate liberties is very broad and is only partially based on international human rights standards. Typical questions are 'Is there open public discussion and free private discussion?' and 'Is there freedom of assembly and demonstration?' These terms are not explained or clarified. Consequently, much is left to the judgment of the independent 'experts' charged with answering these questions.

The Charles Humana *World Human Rights Guide* employs a more elaborate check-list for its periodic surveys of the human rights performance of 120 countries. Humana circulates a questionnaire to informants in each country, 'concerning 40 human rights, all of which are drawn from the articles of the major United Nations treaties' (Humana 1986: 1). Humana himself makes the final assessments, covering issues such as freedom from torture or coercion by the state, the presumption of innocence and the independence of the courts, on the basis of completed question-naires, data gathered from human rights organisations and secondary statistical sources. In the 1992 edition, the UK achieved an unqualified 'yes' on 33 of the 40 rights examined, and a qualified 'yes' on the remaining seven. This produced a score of 93 per cent.

The Humana *Guide* is obviously less impressionistic than the Freedom House surveys. But it still fails to explain the links between the broad categories of rights chosen and how they are measured in practice. How, for example, is the independence of the courts to be judged in such a way as to give a meaningful score? In common with Freedom House, Humana provides very little detail on his coding protocol.

Quantitative approaches to human rights evaluations are open to criticism on several fronts (see, for example, Goldstein 1986). The raw counts of human rights violations do not distinguish between different types of violation. So, for example, in giving the United States the highest score in the world for both political rights and civil liberties, the *Comparative Survey of Freedom* provides no means of differentiating between an impressive performance on open government and a less impressive record on prison conditions and the length of detention for prisoners on death row. Raw scores do not permit distinctions to be made between the treatment of different groups within the population. The disproportionate use of stop and search powers by the police against Afro-Caribbeans in the UK (see **p. 251**), for example, would not emerge in a quantitative study. So political equality is left out of the equation (Lopez and Stohl 1992).

In fact, there is no scope at all for qualitative assessment. Simply to quote the number of demonstrations banned by a government without reference to the prevailing level of political activity in the country in question can be misleading. For example, if citizens fear reprisals, and do not hold demonstrations, the government has no need to ban them and gains unmerited points. Incidents of torture vary widely between severe interrogative techniques to physical beatings and extreme practices: they cannot be interpreted by undifferentiated statistics alone.

Finally, the apparent objectivity of the scores hides a considerable degree of selectivity which becomes apparent when the different guides are compared. For example, the Humana *Guide* ranks the United Kingdom higher than the United States from 1983–87 by a score of 94 per cent to 90. Freedom House showed the UK falling behind the US in the 1980s; by 1991, the UK scored 1 for political rights and 2 for civil liberties, whereas the US scored 1 on both counts. Such differences go unexplained in the guides. Unsurprisingly, critics have asked themselves whether a trained external analyst, following Freedom House's procedures, could replicate any of their surveys – and answered with a resounding negative (Scoble and Wiseberg 1982).

At the other end of the spectrum are qualitative studies which use first-hand observation, press reports and anecdotal information to assemble a picture of the human rights performance of a given country. These studies are far more common. Amnesty International's reports are the best-known and most reliable. But Amnesty International specifically disavows any intention to grade or evaluate governments according to their record on human rights: its brief is to try to end specific and identifiable violations of human rights.

Other qualitative studies are marked by selective use of data and the absence of objective indices against which to test the data. For example, the US State Department's Country Reports recorded that UK prison facilities in 1992 were 'generally good'. Yet only one year earlier, the specialist European Committee for the Prevention of Torture and Inhuman and Degrading Treatment had reported that prison conditions in the UK violated Article 3 of the European Convention. Similarly, the US State Department's 1993 report asserted that 'the right to privacy is generally respected in both law and custom'; in fact, Britain has no law of privacy (see Chapter 12) and the tabloid press is notorious for its flagrant disregard for the privacy of famous and ordinary citizens alike.

Auditing human rights

These are not isolated criticisms of otherwise reliable studies. The American Lawyers Committee for Human Rights publishes an annual critique of the State Department's Country Reports. The problem is that purely qualitative studies inevitably reflect the perspective of those who compile them, for good or ill. By their very nature, they too are not replicable.

Most British studies take a 'civil liberties' standpoint. In 1963, Harry Street revived a tradition of qualitative accounts with a classic study, *Freedom, the Individual and the Law*. Street's objective was to write an authoritative modern account of the legal basis for various executive interferences with the liberties of British citizens (Robertson 1989: 8). Numerous civil liberties text-books and case-books have since followed in the similar tradition, although most recent publications now adopt an international human rights perspective (for example: Robertson 1989; Ewing and Gearty 1990; Bailey, Harris and Jones 1991; Feldman 1993; Fenwick 1994; McCrudden and Chambers 1994; Stone 1994). These are invaluable books and they have, to varying degrees, helped to inform this book. Where they differ from our approach is that none set out to establish criteria against which they evaluate civil and political rights in the UK. They tend not to highlight the positive as well as the negative aspects of the record of successive governments.

How the Human Rights Index works

We seek the best of these two worlds – the quantitative and the qualititative. Our analysis convinces us that to achieve a universal and reliable assessment that may be replicated requires both clear indices for assessing the state of rights and freedoms *and* analysis of relevant data, case studies and description (see Klug 1993). At the heart of our approach is the *Human Rights Index* described above; an original set of criteria compiled from international human rights instruments and texts. This body of internationally recognised human rights standards is continually being evolved by comments, decisions and judgments of the various supervisory authorities which monitor and (in some cases) enforce the instruments. The Index is intended to be a snapshot of these standards in 1995: or, more precisely, an attempt to extract from these human rights standards, the common elements which currently apply to each of the political rights and freedoms we audit here. These are our 'performance indicators'.

Our starting point is the Universal Declaration of Human Rights adopted by the UN General Assembly in 1948 as 'a common standard of achievement for all peoples and all nations'. The Declaration has great moral authority and growing political influence – it is the well from which most subsequent instruments and treaties have drawn their basic principles. We quote from it at the beginning of each section of the Index throughout the book. But since it is broadly framed at the level of principle, we draw on the human rights instruments, treaties and texts which are more detailed and specific than the Declaration for the Index itself.

Since the focus of this audit is political rights and freedoms, the International Covenant on Civil and Political Rights and the European Convention on Human Rights feature most heavily in the Index. The full UN structure within which the

International Covenant operates is set out in the panel and diagram, *'The United Nations Human Rights Umbrella'* (see **pp. 26–30**). The Covenant, which came into force in 1976, is the backbone of the UN human rights programme. It forms part of the International Bill of Human Rights (together with the Universal Declaration and the UN International Covenant on Economic, Social and Cultural Rights). The Covenant is supervised by the UN Human Rights Committee – an expert body of judges and legal specialists – which scrutinises reports filed by each contracting state every five years, and issues reports on their performance, publishes 'General Comments' on implementing the Covenant and (where states have specifically agreed to the procedure) hears complaints from individuals who allege that their rights under the Covenant have been violated.

The European Convention came into force in 1953. It shares its underlying philosophy and much of its language with the International Covenant. The structure within which it works is set out in the panel and diagram, *'The European Human Rights Umbrella'* (see **pp. 31–33**). The Convention covers a narrower range of rights than the International Covenant, but the provisions for interpreting and enforcing those rights go much further. A permanent Commission and Court of Human Rights, based in Strasbourg, exist specifically to provide collective enforcement of the Convention. Governments of states which have ratified the Convention may refer to the Commission alleged breaches by other contracting states. More importantly, individual citizens and associations may complain to the Commission about alleged violations – a provision, now voluntary, which will shortly become compulsory for all signatory states. The Commission can investigate and report; and it can refer cases to the Court (provided that the state has recognised the Court's jurisdiction). The Court's judgments are final and signatory states undertake to abide by them.

We also draw on a wide range of specialist human rights instruments and texts, dealing with issues such as discrimination, torture and freedom of association. These are set out in Figures 2.1 and 2.2, with their arrangements for oversight and enforcement. Certain texts, not ratifiable by individual states, have been agreed by the UN or Council of Europe, dealing with (for example) the use of force and fire-arms by law enforcement agents (UN 1990). As no supervisory body exists to develop the standards in such texts, we draw on the texts themselves. Where they are relevant, the Index also draws on the UN International Covenant on Economic, Social and Cultural Rights and the European Social Charter, both of which protect social and economic rights.

In compiling the Index, we have usually relied on primary materials: that is, the text of the relevant human rights instrument itself, together with the comments, decisions and judgments of the supervisory bodies. We have taken particular advantage of the reports of the European Commission, European Court judgments and the detailed commentaries of the UN Human Rights Committee as an aid to the proper interpretation of the two main instruments. This has been very important where the meaning attributed to a provision in either of them has changed over time.

But we also draw on secondary sources, particularly the leading academic works where it has not been practicable to examine primary materials – for example, the periodic reports sent to the UN Human Rights Committee by more than 100 states

Sources

(other than the UK), individual complaints from those states to the Committee and the preparatory texts of both the International Covenant and the European Convention. Two works, those of Manfred Nowak and Dominic McGoldrick, have been indispensable (Nowak 1993; McGoldrick 1991). Every citation in the Index is fully referenced to make it clear where we have drawn on primary or secondary sources.

Reconciling conflicts between instruments and rights

In general, human rights instruments reinforce and complement each other. But the individual rights protected in different human rights instruments are not always articulated in the same language. In places, the rights protected in one instrument appear to conflict with the rights protected in another. For example, there is clearly a tension between the right to freedom of association in the UN International Covenant and the requirement for a ban on all organisations promoting racial discrimination contained in the UN International Convention on the Elimination of All Forms of Racial Discrimination. Both are universal UN human rights instruments. Different instruments may set out rights in identical terms, but then allow different restrictions to be imposed on them. For example, the UN International Covenant, ILO conventions and the European Convention all protect the rights of free association and trade unionism, but the European Convention contains more grounds for restricting them.

We resolve such conflicts in the following way. As a general rule, we give precedence to the International Covenant and the European Convention. These instruments have achieved a special status in the global protection of human rights and their supervisory bodies have developed and explained their meaning more extensively than any other supervisory body. In particular, the European Court of Human Rights has decided over 300 carefully-argued cases over the past 30 years. Signatory states are bound to change their law in the face of adverse findings and its judgments are respected throughout the world. The UN Human Rights Committee is not a court, but it has made numerous General Comments on the interpretation of the International Covenant and it can, of course, receive complaints from individuals under an optional protocol.

Where the conflict is not between different rights, but in the standards of their protection between instruments, we apply the higher standard in compiling and using the Index (but not without drawing attention to important differences). This approach is justified by the instruments themselves. Most stipulate that their own standards are not to be read as limiting or derogating from any rights and freedoms guaranteed by other agreements to which contracting states are bound (in particular, see Article 5(2) of the International Covenant and Article 60 of the European Convention). The Index, therefore, embodies 'best practice' in the protection of human rights.

The Index also draws on texts which are not ratifiable treaties. It therefore includes, but does not represent, international law. This is a considered decision. The Index is intended to be a 'snapshot' of evolving international standards as of

1995. This necessarily includes standards which have been agreed or promulgated at international level, but which have not (yet) achieved the status of international law. Our aim is not to second guess international law, but to carry out the audit according to current standards. In addition, an index of international human rights *standards* rather than international *law* is better able to incorporate the jurisprudence of important bodies such as the European Court of Human Rights, which, in strict international law, only binds member states in the Council of Europe. Finally, the Index is intended to be universal. In other words, it is hoped that, with some adjustments, it could be used to audit other countries at some future date. Very few of the international human rights instruments are universally binding, whereas, as noted above, the Index is intended to represent a dynamic and universal code of 'best practice'.

This approach does not unfairly disadvantage the United Kingdom. Although we draw on texts which are not treaties, treaties to which the UK is a signatory dominate the Index. Even where they are not treaties, the UK has actually agreed to most of the texts employed in the Index.

Compiling and presenting the data for audit

Each chapter in Parts 2 and 3 contains a summary of the relevant law, practice and policy relating to the political right or freedom which is under audit – the 'data'. This is a neutral summary. We begin with the framework of statutes and case-law (including, where relevant, European Union law) which form the legal basis of protection for the right or freedom in question. Since political rights in the UK tend to be 'negative' rather than 'positive' in nature (see **pp. 37–40**), this framework may seem cumbersome in places – attempting, as it does, to depict what is left of each political right when the law has spoken.

But the formal legal position would be a poor and limited guide on its own. Therefore, where empirical evidence on the effect of the law in practice is available we have included it. To ensure that the data are reliable, we restrict ourselves to official and respected non-official sources. If necessary, we have also included case-studies to illustrate how laws are applied in practice.

Finally, only governments make law, but organisations and individuals can be responsible for human rights violations. This is not just an academic point. Many activities which have a direct bearing on the political rights and freedoms audited here are in private hands – escorting prisoners and deportees, running prisons, maintaining sensitive personal information in databases, patrolling housing estates, residential areas and shopping malls. Our approach is consistent with international human rights law which requires governments to take such measures as are necessary to give effect to their human rights obligations. This requires them to provide the necessary legal and practical framework to prevent violations by private actors as well as by public bodies. In other words, it is the government's record alone that we audit, but that record includes a duty to protect the rights of citizens against private encroachments.

Carrying out the audit in practice

In each chapter in Part 3 we evaluate the extent to which the law, policy and prac-tice set out in the data section conform with standards set out in the human rights index. Inevitably, there are difficulties in applying standards based on codified 'posi-tive' rights to the 'negative' way in which individual rights are protected in the United Kingdom. The rights of citizens in this country are 'negative'; that is, they are for the most part protected *from interference* by others, rather than positive rights to behave in a particular way. To take an example, no one has the *right* to join an association, but everyone is *free* to do so unless the law says otherwise. By contrast, international human rights instruments confer positive rights and then list exhaust-ively the circumstances in which those rights can legitimately be curtailed. Auditing negative rights by reference to a framework of positive rights has not always been easy. In most cases we adopt a two-stage approach:

- First, we evaluate whether the negative freedom to engage in political activity – such as joining an association – falls short of the positive right enshrined in international human rights standards
- Then we consider whether the common law and statutory restrictions on that political activity correspond, both in type and extent, with the restrictions permitted by those standards.

This second stage is fundamental to the audit. Since restrictions qualify nearly every right in the international instruments, questions of their use and interpreta-tion become paramount. As one authority has noted, 'the key issue in disputes on human rights (whether in the courts or in public controversy) is not about the exis-tence of a basic human right or its source but is about the validity of the limitation imposed on its exercise' (Costello 1992: 177). In determining whether common law and statutory restrictions on political rights in the UK comply with international human rights standards, we have taken our lead from the three-part test derived from the International Covenant and the European Convention; and subsequently developed extensively by the European Court of Human Rights (see **Box A**).

Regulating restrictions on rights

According to the three-part test, a government must show that any restriction on civil and political rights is:

- 'prescribed by law'
- justified by one of the grounds recognised under the International Covenant or European Convention
- 'necessary in a democratic society'.

As **Box A** makes clear, the three tests provide strict checks upon any state's ability to manipulate the restrictions set out in the instruments themselves.

BOX A   THE THREE-PART TEST

Restricting rights

Formal recognition of civil and political rights is not enough. It is essential that any restriction of all rights recognised by both the International Covenant and the European Convention be closely scrutinised. The two instruments set out a strict three-part test:

1.   Any restriction on civil and political rights must be 'prescribed by law'
2.   The restriction must be justified by one of the aims recognised under the International Covenant or European Convention
3.   The restriction must be shown to be 'necessary in a democratic society'.

This test is of fundamental importance. For governments rarely seek generally to ignore or curb a right or freedom recognised under either instrument in all situations. Rather they tend to restrict rights and freedoms in particular circumstances − as the United Kingdom has done, for example, in Northern Ireland. So whether they pass the three-part test when they do so goes to the very heart of international protection of human rights. For that reason, we deal with the test in some detail here:

The test in detail

1. 'Prescribed by law'

This first part of the test involves two key questions. First, can ordinary citizens readily discover that the restriction exists? They must have an indication that is adequate in the circumstances of the legal rules in a given case. Second, if so, is the law, or rule, formulated clearly enough to enable citizens to regulate their conduct? The test does not demand absolute clarity but citizens, broadly speaking, should be able to foresee, if necessary with appropriate advice, what activity would infringe the law (*Sunday Times v UK*, ECtHR, 1979).

2. Does it comply with recognised aims?

If the restriction passes these first two questions, it must then meet one of the aims recognised under either instrument as a legitimate ground for the restriction of civil and political rights. With one or two minor variations, these aims are for the protection of the rights and freedoms of others, national security, public safety, or public health and morals; and for the prevention of public disorder or crime. This list is intended to be exhaustive − there is no scope for states to infer grounds for restriction which are not explicitly stated (*Vagrancy Cases*, 1971; *Golder v UK*, ECtHR, 1975). In addition, there is a rule of strict interpretation. Not only may the listed criteria alone justify

Discretion for states

any restrictions; these criteria, in turn, must be understood in such a way that the language is not extended beyond its ordinary meaning (*Sunday Times v UK*, ECtHR, 1979).

3. 'Necessary in a democratic society'

To satisfy the final test a state must show both that the restriction fulfils a pressing social need and that it is proportionate to the aim of responding to that need. A state cannot merely assert that a particular restriction is 'necessary in a democratic society', to protect national security or public order. It has to provide concrete evidence that there is a genuine and serious threat, perhaps from a terrorist organisation, which has to be dealt with; and that it is not over-reacting to that threat (see *Alba Pietroroia v Uruguay*, UNHRC No. 44, 1979; *Sunday Times v UK*, ECtHR, 1979; *Autronic AG v Switzerland*, ECtHR, 1990).

The bodies which interpret the tests – the UN Human Rights Committee and the European Court and Commission of Human Rights – have framed their notion of 'democratic society' in terms of such concepts as 'pluralism, tolerance and broadmindedness'; and have made it clear that although the term 'necessary' is not synonymous with 'indispensable', it does not simply mean 'reasonable' (*Handyside v UK*, ECtHR, 1976).

Discretion for states

Assessing restrictions on political rights according to the three-part test raises a related – and knotty – problem: the doctrine of the *margin of appreciation*. This doctrine arises out of the interpretation of the European Convention by the European Court of Human Rights. In essence, it refers to the discretion which states are permitted in their observance of the Convention. Signatory states are primarily responsible for securing the rights and freedoms provided for in the Convention, but they are free to decide how this should best be done (Article 1). As the European Court stated in a historic case, 'The national authorities remain free to choose the measures which they consider appropriate in those matters which are governed by the Convention' (*Belgian Linguistics Case (No. 2)*, 1979–80). The Court thus allows a 'band of reasonableness' – which varies from right to right, being narrow for example in the case of sexual discrimination (*Abdulaziz, Cabales and Balkandali v UK*, 1985). A choice which falls within this band will not be held by the Court to be contrary to the Convention on the basis that it is not a choice which the Court thinks would have been best in the circumstances. In other words, the Court will defer to states in certain areas of political rights and will not intervene unless the national authorities have stepped outside the band of reasonable options (their 'margin of appreciation').

The margin of appreciation is thus a doctrine of judicial self-restraint (Jones 1995: 431). Our difficulty, as auditors, has been to decide whether or not we should exercise the same or similar restraint. After considerable thought, we decided against doing so for two reasons. First, the purpose of this audit is to subject political rights and freedoms in the UK to close scrutiny. The margin of appreciation can (and often does) amount to a presumption in favour of a state when challenged by an individual citizen. Such a presumption is inconsistent with close scrutiny. Second, the European Court has laid down very little guidance about when and how the doctrine of the margin of appreciation can properly be employed. This has led to widespread criticism of the doctrine. Professor Rosalyn Higgins, formerly the British member of the UN Human Rights Committee and now a judge of the International Court of Justice, has even gone so far as to contend that the doctrine is 'objectionable as a viable legal concept' (Higgins 1976–77: 281). Judge Ryssdal, the President of the European Court, has acknowledged the criticism, 'to some extent' (Ryssdal 1992: 129). Without clear standards for its use, we concluded that it would be almost impossible for us to take the doctrine into account in this audit.

Where the doctrine has been employed, therefore, we do not simply replicate it in our evaluation. Instead, we look at the broad standards which have been developed by human rights authorities to make our own evaluation of the law or practice in question. The audits are not, it is worth emphasising, attempts to second guess bodies like the UN Human Rights Committee or the European Court. We use the standards they have developed to make our own independent assessments.

The role of derogations and reservations

Derogations, reservations and interpretations are special measures available to any state which enters a treaty (whether it concerns human rights or not). At any stage before it ratifies a treaty, a state may express 'reservations' about it (unless the treaty itself forbids or restricts this). By its reservations, a state effectively withholds or limits its consent to being bound by some specified provision, or group of provisions, in the treaty. A state may also express an 'interpretation' – its understanding of how certain provisions of the treaty will be applied. The state agrees to be bound, but only on its own interpretation. Finally, most human rights treaties, including the International Covenant and the European Convention, allow states to 'derogate' from – that is, to cease to uphold – their obligations under the treaty in certain prescribed circumstances, by declaring that they intend to do so.

The United Kingdom has made use of all three measures. For example, the UK has entered a blanket reservation covering immigration and nationality in relation to Article 12(2) of the International Covenant, which provides that 'no-one shall arbitrarily be deprived of the right to enter his own country'. As the UK also refuses to ratify the Optional Protocol granting individuals the right to petition the Human Rights Committee (see **p. 58**), successive governments have prevented any real test of UK immigration policy under the Covenant.

The United Kingdom has lodged a derogation from the guarantee of liberty and security of the person under both the International Covenant and the European

Discretion for states

Convention. The government did so in 1988 following the adverse finding of the European Court of Human Rights in a case involving the arrest and detention of five men under the Prevention of Terrorism Act 1984 (*Brogan v UK*, 1988; see **pp. 255–256**). By its derogation, the government chose to retain the power to detain people for up to seven days without charge under the renewed version of the act in 1989 – even though this power violates the European Convention and almost certainly the International Covenant as well.

In this audit, we have tried to adopt a clear and defensible approach to derogations, reservations and interpretation, consistent with our overall objective – to evaluate how far political rights and freedoms in the UK conform to international human rights standards. We do not, therefore, take the UK's reservations to and interpretations of human rights treaties into account. The Index is intended to be both objective and universal; representing a 'best practice' code (see above, **pp. 16–19**). As such, it cannot be state specific. We are only interested in whether the UK conforms with a set of relatively fixed world-wide standards, not whether it conforms with such of those world-wide standards as it chooses to be bound by.

However, the circumstances in which a state can derogate from its obligations under both the European Convention and International Covenant are clearly defined. A state's derogation can also be challenged (indeed, in 1993, the European Court rejected a case brought specifically to challenge the UK's derogation following the *Brogan* judgment (*Brannigan and McBride v UK*, 1993). In certain respects, therefore, a lawful derogation can be seen as a legitimate restriction on political rights and freedoms under the International Covenant and European Convention. We decided, therefore, that in principle we should take derogations into account, though that does not mean that we would accept them at face value. In fact, only the derogation in respect of the PTA legislation features in this particular audit (**pp. 255–256**).

Conclusions

Our aim in devising the methodology described above was to create an audit of political rights and freedoms which is reliable, replicable and universal. Ultimately, it is for others to judge how well we have succeeded.

Our view is that we have established reliable criteria for the audit by basing the Index on widely-recognised international standards and their interpretation by supervisory bodies. We believe that a similar base would make comparative studies more reliable and less open to the charge that the criteria they use for assessment are based on Eurocentric, or American, standards (which means that western countries always come top; Scoble and Wiseberg 1982). Of course, it is not possible to eliminate bias both in the selection of data and their use in the process of evaluation. But the Index itself can be investigated, criticised and, if necessary, improved and the criteria are less subjective and more detailed than those used in the Freedom House and Humana exercises. Moreover, the process of audit is open to scrutiny. The separation throughout the book of the audit sections from the Index and data sections of the chapters gives readers the opportunity to judge how reliably the authors are evaluating the UK's performance against clear criteria. By stripping all comment and analysis from the Index and data sections and confining our findings (which inevitably are more subjective) to the final and separate audit section, our readers can follow – and therefore accept or reject – the basis upon which we have carried out the audit.

We hope that the open description of the compilation of the Index and the detailed extracts from it throughout this book will make it possible for future auditors to replicate our study in the knowledge that the criteria used to evaluate rights remain relatively constant (except insofar as international standards themselves evolve and develop). This would allow for a study over time of a country's human rights record – a project that the Democratic Audit intends to accomplish for the United Kingdom. But the standards set out here are universal. Thus we believe that the same Index, adapted to embody standards set in regional instruments, could be applied to any country in the world; either simply to evaluate its own human rights record, or to compare it to other countries.

Supervision and enforcement

THE UNITED NATIONS HUMAN RIGHTS UMBRELLA

International Convention Committees

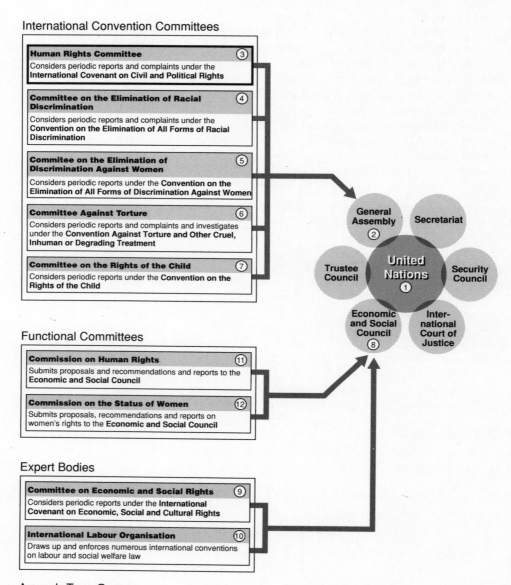

Human Rights Committee ③

Considers periodic reports and complaints under the **International Covenant on Civil and Political Rights**

Committee on the Elimination of Racial Discrimination ④

Considers periodic reports and complaints under the **Convention on the Elimination of All Forms of Racial Discrimination**

Commitee on the Elimination of Discrimination Against Women ⑤

Considers periodic reports under the **Convention on the Elimination of All Forms of Discrimination Against Women**

Committee Against Torture ⑥

Considers periodic reports and complaints and investigates under the **Convention Against Torture and Other Cruel, Inhuman or Degrading Treatment**

Committee on the Rights of the Child ⑦

Considers periodic reports under the **Convention on the Rights of the Child**

General Assembly ②

Secretariat

Trustee Council

United Nations ①

Security Council

Economic and Social Council ⑧

Inter-national Court of Justice

Functional Committees

Commission on Human Rights ⑪

Submits proposals and recommendations and reports to the **Economic and Social Council**

Commission on the Status of Women ⑫

Submits proposals, recommendations and reports on women's rights to the **Economic and Social Council**

Expert Bodies

Committee on Economic and Social Rights ⑨

Considers periodic reports under the **International Covenant on Economic, Social and Cultural Rights**

International Labour Organisation ⑩

Draws up and enforces numerous international conventions on labour and social welfare law

Artwork: Tony Garrett

The institutions above are all numbered. The notes which follow explain the functions of the committees and bodies above.

THE UNITED NATIONS HUMAN RIGHTS UMBRELLA

1. The United Nations Charter is a multilateral treaty binding all UN member states. Its preamble proclaims the determination of the peoples of the UN, 'to reaffirm faith in fundamental human rights, in the dignity and worth of the human person'. One of the purposes the Charter sets out is 'promoting and encouraging respect for human rights and for fundamental freedoms for all, without distinction as to race, sex, language or religion'.

2. The General Assembly is the plenary organ of the UN and has broad competence under the UN Charter to consider issues of human rights. It has adopted a significant number of international human rights instruments:

    ■ The Universal Declaration of Human Rights (1948)
    ■ The International Covenant on Civil and Political Rights (1966). (See Appendix 2 for basic text)
    ■ The International Covenant on Economic, Social and Cultural Rights (1966)
    ■ The Convention on the Elimination of All Forms of Racial Discrimination (1969)
    ■ The Convention on the Elimination of All Forms of Discrimination Against Women (1979)
    ■ The Convention Against Torture and Other Cruel, Inhuman or Degrading Treatment (1984)
    ■ The Convention on the Rights of the Child (1989).

    All reports on the implementation of these instruments go ultimately to the UN General Assembly.

3. The UN Human Rights Committee supervises the implementation of the International Covenant on Civil and Political Rights. It is composed of 18 members who are nationals of the parties to the International Covenant and 'persons of high moral character and recognised competence in the field of human rights'. When appointed, members of the Committee must make a solemn declaration to perform their functions impartially and conscientiously.

    ■ The International Covenant and its First Optional Protocol provide one mandatory and two optional mechanisms to enable the Human Rights Committee to supervise the states parties' obligations.

    ■ Each state which has ratified the Covenant must submit a report every five years to the Human Rights Committee on the legislative and other measures it has adopted to give effect to the rights the Covenant recognises. The Committee studies each report and sends the state involved a list of questions. The state's representatives then make a presentation to the Committee at a public hearing to deal with questions and any matters arising. The Committee

Supervision and enforcement

then makes comments and observations which the state is obliged to make public.

■ Contracting states which have agreed to be bound by the optional inter-state procedure may bring each other before the Human Rights Committee where they believe they have violated the Covenant.

■ Under the First Optional Protocol, individual citizens from a contracting state can directly petition the Human Rights Committee if they consider that their rights have been violated under the Covenant. The Committee will investigate any case which is admitted (i.e., which broadly satisfies certain procedural requirements, such as the petitioner must have exhausted all domestic remedies) and then presents its 'views' on the allegations made. Strictly speaking, these views are not legally binding and there is no enforcement machinery. However, they possess great authority since all states are under a duty to comply with the obligations established by the Covenant and the Human Rights Committee has exclusive competence to rule on compliance.

The United Kingdom has not agreed to either of the optional mechanisms.

From time to time, the Human Rights Committee issues 'General Comments' to assist member states to fulfil their obligations under the International Covenant. These comments draw their attention to general deficiencies in state reports, suggest improvements and interpret particular provisions of the Covenant.

4. The Committee on the Elimination of Racial Discrimination supervises the Convention on the Elimination of All Forms of Racial Discrimination (CERD 1969). It consists of 18 experts who are elected by participating states, but who serve in an independent capacity. States report periodically to the Committee in the same way as they do to the Human Rights Committee under the International Covenant on Civil and Political Rights. There is provision under CERD for a right of individual communication – an optional procedure which the United Kingdom has not agreed to.

5. The Committee on the Elimination of Discrimination Against Women supervises the Convention on the Elimination of All Forms of Discrimination Against Women (CEDAW 1979). It consists of 28 experts who are elected by participating states, but who serve in an independent capacity. Again, the Committee's supervision is based on periodic reporting as under the International Covenant and CERD. Observations on the reports studied by the Committee go to the UN Commission on the Status of Women.

6. The Committee Against Torture (CAT) supervises compliance with the Convention Against Torture and Other Cruel, Inhuman or Degrading Treatment (1984). The Committee consists of ten members who are elected by participating states, but who serve in their individual capacities. The mechanisms of supervision are

periodic reporting, and optional inter-state and individual complaints procedures. Again, the United Kingdom has not agreed to these optional procedures. However, CAT may also decide to investigate a state's conduct on its own initiative when it receives reliable information that torture is being systematically practised within the state.

7. The Convention on the Rights of the Child is supervised by the Committee on the Rights of the Child which has ten members on the same basis as CAT. The main method of supervision is periodic reporting.

8. The Economic and Social Council is a political organ of the United Nations, consisting of 54 members. The Council makes recommendations for the promotion of respect for human rights and fundamental freedoms, and their observance by states, and submits draft conventions to the General Assembly. It also receives reports from specialist agencies such as the Committee on Economic and Social Rights and the International Labour Organisation and co-ordinates their activities.

9. The Economic and Social Council also formally supervises the International Covenant on Economic, Social and Cultural Rights (1966). But in fact the UN Committee on Economic, Social and Cultural Rights, which was created in 1985, carries out this work. It mirrors the Human Rights Committee, with 18 expert members elected by contracting states who serve in their individual capacities. The Committee considers periodic reports from the states and forwards its observations to the Economic and Social Council, the Commission on Human Rights (see below) and other specialist UN agencies concerned with economic, social and cultural rights.

10. The International Labour Organisation pre-dates the United Nations, having been founded in 1919 by the Treaty of Versailles. It became a specialist UN agency by agreement with the Economic and Social Council. The objectives of the ILO were re-stated in the Declaration of Philadelphia in 1944. The ILO has since promulgated numerous Conventions and recommendations which together make up a comprehensive international labour code. Among the most important ILO instruments are the Freedom of Association and Protection of the Right to Organise Convention and the Right to Organise and Collective Bargaining Convention.

Supervision under the ILO constitution takes a number of forms:

■   State parties must submit periodic reports on the measures which they have taken to give effect to the ILO Conventions to which they have agreed. These reports are examined by a Committee of Experts consisting of 18 independent members

■   If an association of employers or workers makes a representation to the ILO that a state has failed to observe the standards set down in any ILO

Supervision and enforcement

convention to which it has agreed, the Governing Body of the ILO may communicate the complaint to that state. A hearing then takes place before a special committee which in turn reports back to the Governing Body

- An inter-state complaints procedure allows a contracting state to make a complaint about another ILO state

- A special Committee on Freedom of Association, established in 1951, acts as the ILO watch-dog on issues of freedom of association. The Committee examines complaints and submits a report to the Governing Body with findings and recommendations.

11. The Commission on Human Rights was established by the Economic and Social Council in 1946 to deal with outstanding human rights issues which could not be resolved during the original drafting of the UN Charter. The Commission now consists of 43 members serving as governmental representatives. The Commission submits proposals, recommendations and reports to the Economic and Social Council on a wide range of human rights issues.

12. The Commission on the Status of Women, comprising 32 members serving as governmental representatives, was also established by the Economic and Social Council in 1946. The Commission makes reports and recommendations to the Economic and Social Council on the promotion of women's political, economic, civil, social and educational rights in general, and additionally recommends action by the Council on urgent problems requiring immediate attention.

The Commission played a major role in drafting the Convention on the Political Rights of Women (1953), the Declaration on the Status of Women (1967) and the Convention on the Elimination of All Forms of Discrimination Against Women (1979).

THE EUROPEAN HUMAN RIGHTS UMBRELLA

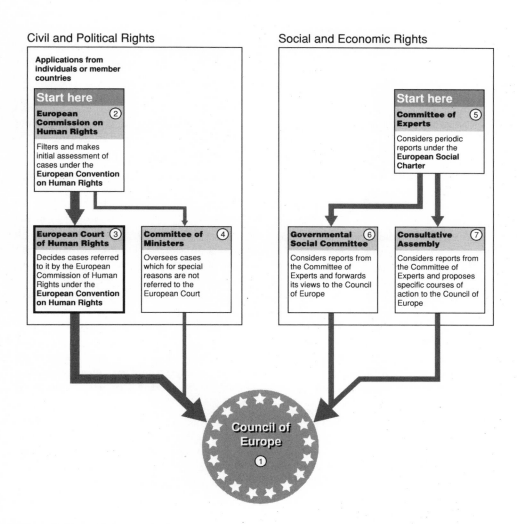

Civil and Political Rights

Applications from individuals or member countries

Start here

European Commission on Human Rights ②

Filters and makes initial assessment of cases under the **European Convention on Human Rights**

European Court of Human Rights ③

Decides cases referred to it by the European Commission of Human Rights under the **European Convention on Human Rights**

Committee of Ministers ④

Oversees cases which for special reasons are not referred to the European Court

Social and Economic Rights

Start here

Committee of Experts ⑤

Considers periodic reports under the **European Social Charter**

Governmental Social Committee ⑥

Considers reports from the Committee of Experts and forwards its views to the Council of Europe

Consultative Assembly ⑦

Considers reports from the Committee of Experts and proposes specific courses of action to the Council of Europe

Council of Europe ①

Artwork: Tony Garrett

Supervision and enforcement

THE EUROPEAN HUMAN RIGHTS UMBRELLA

1. The Council of Europe was created at the end of the second world war to promote European unity, to protect human rights and to facilitate social and economic progress. It is quite separate from the European Union (formerly European Community). The Council of Europe has expanded rapidly since 1989 and now has 38 members. The Council has two main bodies – the Committee of Ministers and the Parliamentary Assembly.

    The Council's most significant achievement is the creation of the European Convention for the Protection of Human Rights and Fundamental Freedoms and of two agencies for its collective enforcement – the European Commission of Human Rights and the European Court of Human Rights. The main text of the Convention is set out in full in Appendix 3.

2. The European Commission of Human Rights is the first port of call for all complaints under the European Convention. It consists of individuals of 'high moral character' who either possess the qualifications required for appointment to high judicial office or who are recognised as having special competence in national or international law. The main functions of the European Commission are:

    ■   To investigate alleged breaches of the European Convention and to filter out and reject inadmissible complaints
    ■   To arrange, if possible, a friendly settlement of the complaint with the state involved
    ■   Where a friendly settlement is not possible, to draw up a report expressing its opinion as to whether a violation has occurred and to refer the matter either to the European Court of Human Rights or the Council of Ministers.

3. The European Court of Human Rights is composed of a judge from every member state of the Council of Europe. Judges of the European Court must fulfil the same qualifying conditions as members of the European Commission (see above). The European Court hears and determines cases referred to it by the European Commission and gives advisory opinions to the Committee of Ministers on request.

4. The Committee of Ministers consists of one minister from each member state of the Council of Europe. The Committee possesses a limited role within the European Convention process and deals with any case which the European Commission does not refer on to the Court. In general, the Committee only handles straight-forward cases, including those where the state concerned has implicitly acknowledged a violation of the European Convention by taking steps to amend its domestic law. The Committee rarely departs from the view of the European Commission.

5. Member states of the Council of Europe signed the European Social Charter in 1961 *(which is not to be confused with the EU 'Social Charter')*. This Charter is intended to protect economic and social rights. It is supervised by a Committee of Experts, consisting of seven 'independent experts of the highest integrity and recognised competence in international and social questions'. The Committee considers two-yearly reports from member states and sends the reports with its conclusions to the Governmental Social Committee and to the Consultative Assembly.

6. The Governmental Social Committee is composed of government representatives who consider the material sent by the Committee of Experts and in turn submit views to the Council of Europe.

7. The Consultative Assembly is composed of delegations of elected members from the legislatures of member states. It is intended to ensure a degree of democratic influence on the activities of the Council of Europe. It too considers the material sent to it by the Committee of Experts and submits its views to the Council of Europe.

PART 2

The UK Framework for Protecting Rights

Introduction   The Three Pillars of Liberty

The system

The United Kingdom possesses no 'system' for protecting human rights in the sense of a specific political and legal structure designed for that purpose. There is no fundamental constitutional law nor fundamental rights enjoying special constitutional and legal protection against interference by Parliament or the courts. Even the idea of a 'system' seems alien to a tradition of civil liberties which is seen to have grown organically. Thus, what has come to be understood as the 'system' for protecting human rights in this country is a set of constitutional arrangements which, whatever their historic purpose, protect human rights in practice.

These arrangements differ from those found in most other countries, where the rights of individual citizens are usually set out in broad terms in a Bill of Rights or other constitutional document. The United Kingdom has no Bill of Rights of this kind. The 1688 Bill of Rights and the Claim of Right of 1689 (its Scottish equivalent) contain some important clauses designed to safeguard personal liberty. But they are essentially declarations about the relationship between Parliament and the Crown.

Human rights are protected by the ordinary law of the land – a diversity of specific rights are established by a combination of the common law and express Acts of Parliament, each with an accompanying remedy. Thus, to secure an individual's freedom from unlawful or arbitrary detention, the law provides specific and detailed remedies such as *habeas corpus* and an action in damages for false imprisonment. Unusually, the law makes no fundamental distinction between 'public law', governing acts of the state and its agents, and 'private law', regulating the relations between private citizens (at least as regards rights and remedies). Except in the case of certain Crown privileges, ordinary people can sue the state, or state officials, where their rights have been violated, just as they can sue private individuals.

The rights of ordinary people in the United Kingdom are for the most part 'negative' – that is, rights to be protected *from interference* from others, rather than positive rights, say, to publish a controversial article or to join a protest march. These rights can be modified or abolished by Parliament, whether they are founded in the common law or created by statute. For Parliament possesses the absolute power to make or un-make any law. Legally, individual citizens have no fundamental rights and no minimum standards apply. Liberties are what is left after the law has spoken. Equally, in theory at least, individual people are free to do as they like so long as they don't break the law or infringe the rights of others.

The human rights treaties or conventions which the United Kingdom has signed – such as the European Convention on Human Rights and the UN International

Negative rights

Covenant on Civil and Political Rights – have not become part of the domestic law. Individual citizens have no remedy here in the United Kingdom for violations of these instruments, unless the rights and freedoms set out in them are already recognised in common or statute law. In the case of the European Convention, citizens can pursue a grievance to the European Court of Human Rights in Strasbourg, once they have exhausted the remedies open to them in this country. Parliament could incorporate international human rights instruments into domestic law by an Act of Parliament, but successive governments have chosen not to. In contrast, European Union law derived from the Treaty of Rome, as modified by the Maastricht treaty, becomes domestic law under the European Communities Act 1972. All the rights and duties provided for by EU law are given legal effect in this country. Accordingly, such fundamental rights as are recognised by the European Court of Justice can follow an oblique route into domestic law.

The supremacy of Parliament leaves the courts with a far lesser role than in other countries. Basically they have three tasks. They interpret and apply the legislation passed by Parliament. For this purpose they have devised principles, or 'presumptions', which they believe assist them in ascertaining Parliament's will. They exercise control over the administrative acts of ministers, public bodies and officials, through a process known as 'judicial review'. The supremacy of Parliament remains intact: judicial review assumes that when it confers powers on ministers and officials, Parliament does not intend them to exceed the powers they are given or to act perversely. Third, the courts created the common law; judges continue to develop, modify and even 'fundamentally re-direct' it through the courts. The common law is in this sense 'a lawyer's law' (Scarman 1974: 2).

Ultimately, the practical protection of human rights relies heavily on the good sense of Parliament – or in effect, of ministers and elected politicians. This may seem a very fragile basis for securing basic human rights. However, it is argued that, for all its undoubted powers, Parliament acts under two significant constraints. First, ministers are ruled by unwritten 'conventions' which, though unenforceable in law, deter them from violating civil liberties. More significantly, the force of public opinion itself is seen as a major safeguard. Early in the nineteenth century foreign observers, such as Alexis de Tocqueville, identified a 'culture of liberty', making it unthinkable that the British public would live under any but 'a free government', which is said to have matured in the course of the nineteenth century.

The absence of rights inscribed in law has generated fierce debate for the past quarter century. In 1974, Lord Scarman, then a law lord – that is, a member of the supreme UK court, the House of Lords (acting in its judicial capacity) – argued the need for a legal declaration of inviolable human rights to restrain the legislative powers of Parliament (Scarman 1974). Yet the system has been highly recommended for more than a century. In 1885, A.V. Dicey, the founding authority on constitutional law in this country, established its canons in *The Law of the Constitution*:

> where the right to individual freedom is a result deduced from the principles of the constitution, the idea readily occurs that the right is capable of being suspended or taken away. Where, on the other hand, the right to

> individual freedom is part of the constitution because it is inherent in the
> ordinary law of the land, the right is one which can hardly be destroyed.
>
> (Dicey 1885: 197)

Dicey's principles survive intact in modern statements in defence of the 'British way of doing things'. For example, Peter Lloyd, a former Home Office minister, argued in 1991 that

> the rights and freedom of the individual and their protection lie at the heart
> of our constitutional practices. Over the years, they have developed prag-
> matically in response to society's needs and perceived problems and in
> keeping with the British tradition.
>
> (HC Deb, 17 May 1991, c582)

Moreover, it is argued that the UK's flexible arrangements have a big advantage over rigid legal codes of rights; as Lloyd added, 'Our system continues to allow us to adapt and change where change appears necessary'.

Governments of both colours have consistently agreed that Britain's flexible system not only encompasses all the aims of international human rights instruments, but is actually superior to positive rights models. Thus, Baroness Blatch, a Home Office minister, spoke forcefully against Lord Lester's Human Rights Bill (which aimed to incorporate the European Convention into domestic law):

> Our present arrangements already provide for our commitments under the
> convention to be taken into proper account in our governmental, legislative
> and judicial systems.
>
> (HL Deb, 25 January 1995, c1164–5)

This fundamental belief was rejected in July 1995 by the UN Human Rights Committee, the authoritative body of legal experts which enforces the International Covenant. After its fourth review of human rights in this country, the Committee held that, far from being superior, the British system failed to secure the basic civil and political rights protected by the International Covenant (27 July 1995: CCPR/C/79/Add. 55). (We shall come back to the Committee's detailed findings at various points in this audit.) On behalf of the government, Baroness Blatch robustly rejected the Committee's findings (HL Deb, 26 October 1995, c1188).

The purpose of this book is in one sense to adjudicate between the findings of the UN's legal experts and the government's view. In Chapter 2, we described the *Human Rights Index* of internationally recognised standards for human rights, against which any system for protecting human rights can be objectively gauged. In Part 2, we use this Index to audit the system for protecting political and civil rights – or 'democratic' rights – in the United Kingdom. In Part 3, we audit the protection of those rights individually. The absence of a codified system obviously makes the task of auditing democratic rights in the light of international standards more difficult than in a country which does inscribe its rights in an entrenched legal document or constitution. But we do not start from any preconceived notion that this absence means that the arrangements for protecting rights in the United Kingdom are any less, or more, likely to meet these standards.

The main pillars of the Index are the European Convention and the UN International Covenant. Both have been signed by the United Kingdom and are therefore binding on UK governments as a matter of international law. The basic requirement of both instruments is that every state committing itself to the rights they seek to protect should first and foremost ensure those rights to its citizens by its *own* law and practice. International intervention ought only to arise when signatory states fail to honour this primary obligation. To comply with its international obligations, the United Kingdom must give all people under its jurisdiction an *effective* remedy in *domestic* law when their rights or freedoms are violated; and must ensure that everyone is entitled, without discrimination, to the equal protection of that law.

The purpose of Part 2 is to determine whether British arrangements for protecting political rights and freedoms fulfil these two fundamental duties. But we are obliged, so to speak, to conduct a 'double audit'. For we must assess how effectively Britain's own arrangements for the protection of democratic rights meet the claims made for them. *The Law of the Constitution* still remains the theoretical starting point for most analysis of these arrangements. Dicey identified three pillars of liberty and the rule of law – Parliament, public opinion and the courts. So we consider how Parliament, public opinion and the courts join to protect and secure political rights and freedoms, and give citizens an effective remedy against violations of their rights. First, Chapter 3 examines the role of government and Parliament's ability to scrutinise draft legislation and to call the executive to account in defence of democratic rights; the chapter also assesses the quality of governance of Northern Ireland. We then assess the power of the public to bolster Parliament's defence of liberties and restrain the dominant legislative and executive powers of government (Chapter 4). Chapter 5 is a case study of the enactment of the Criminal Justice and Public Order Act 1994 – an act with important implications for democratic rights – which illustrates these two protections in action.

Chapter 6 deals with the power of the courts to protect democratic rights. It assesses each of the three functions ascribed to the judiciary in turn: the interpretation of legislation, judicial review and the deployment of the common law. In this chapter we also examine the impact of international human rights standards on judicial decision-making and assess the impact of membership of the European Union on the protection of human rights in this country. Chapter 7 examines how far the UK meets international standards on equal access to democratic rights and the prevention of discrimination. The importance of equality in and before the law pervades all internationally recognised human rights standards and is fundamental to the notion of democracy which underpins them. Part 2 ends with a short overall assessment of the system for protecting human rights in the United Kingdom.

Index   Ensuring and Securing Democratic Rights

The system

Both the International Covenant on Civil and Political Rights and the European Convention on Human Rights require member states to *ensure* or *secure* the rights set out in each instrument to all citizens within their jurisdiction (ICCPR A.2; ECHR A.1). These obligations are both absolute and immediate. They are *not* affected by the prevailing circumstances or limited resources of member states; and each member state is bound to take the necessary steps to secure the rights in question from the moment that they ratify the instrument (Sieghart 1983: 57). The rights to be ensured and secured are wide-ranging. In this book, we concentrate on 'democratic rights' – those rights which are clearly integral to the democratic process.

Neither the International Covenant nor the European Convention require their terms to be incorporated directly into domestic law. Each instrument leaves it to member states to decide for themselves how best to implement the rights in question. What is important is not the means chosen by a state to implement these rights, but the desired result: the effective protection of those rights and the provision in domestic law of effective remedies against violations. Yet the International Covenant requires states to take the legislative or other measures, 'in accordance with its constitutional processes', necessary to give effect to rights it recognises where they are not provided for by existing laws or other measures (Article 2.2).

To some extent, this statement simply reflects a well-established principle of international law. In 1925, the Permanent Court of International Justice emphasised that 'a State which has contracted valid international obligations is bound to make in its legislation such modifications as may be necessary to ensure the fulfilment of the obligations undertaken' (*Exchange of Greek and Turkish Populations*, Advisory Opinion). The same requirement has been included in the American Convention on Human Rights and the African Charter on Human and Peoples' Rights and is implied in the European Convention. However, the wording of Article 2.2 clearly contemplates measures other than legislation alone. The UN Human Rights Committee, which supervises compliance with the International Covenant, has emphasised this wider duty in a General Comment:

> implementation does not depend solely on constitutional or legislative enactments which in themselves are often not *per se* sufficient ... the obligation under the Covenant is not confined to the respect of human rights ... State parties have also undertaken to ensure the enjoyment of these rights to all

individuals under their jurisdiction. This calls for specific activities by the State parties to enable individuals to enjoy their rights.

(GC 3/13, 28 July 1991)

The UN Committee's observations on Britain's failure to meet its obligations under the Covenant recommend specific measures which illustrate this wider duty (see **p. 307** above). They range from a major campaign against racial and sexual discrimination and education for judges, lawyers and police officers on violence and discrimination against women to the closure of an individual detention centre (CCPR/C/79/Add. 55, 27 July 1995). The Committee generally attaches great importance to public education in human rights. Its 1991 General Comment went on to observe that 'it is very important that individuals should know their rights under the Covenant ... and also that all administrative and judicial authorities should be aware of the obligations which the State party has assumed under the Covenant'.

The obligation to ensure or secure the rights set out in the International Covenant and European Convention to all citizens is reinforced by the further requirement that anyone whose rights or freedoms are violated must have an *effective* remedy in domestic law, notwithstanding that the violation has been committed by public officials (ICCPR A.2.3.a; ECHR A.13). To be effective, the remedy must involve the determination of the complainant's claim and must also provide for redress (*Klass v Germany*, ECtHR, 1978). A domestic process for adjudicating upon arguable claims is therefore required, even if that process finally finds that no violation of the complainant's rights has occurred. However, the European Court has conceded that the effectiveness of remedies can vary according to the subject-matter; and, for example, tends to accept weaker remedies where state security and police surveillance are involved.

Restricting rights

Formal recognition of civil and political rights is not enough. It is essential that any restriction of all rights recognised by both the International Covenant and the European Convention be closely scrutinised. The two instruments set out a strict three-part test:

1. Any restriction on civil and political rights must be 'prescribed by law'
2. The restriction must be justified by one of the aims recognised under the International Covenant or European Convention
3. The restriction must be shown to be 'necessary in a democratic society'.

This test is of fundamental importance. For governments rarely seek generally to ignore or curb a right or freedom recognised under either instrument in all situations. Rather they tend to restrict rights and freedoms in particular circumstances – as the United Kingdom has done, for example, in Northern Ireland. So whether they pass the three-part test when they do so goes to the very heart of international protection of human rights. For that reason, we deal with the test in detail in **Box A, pp. 21–22.** Here, broadly, the tests require that ordinary citizens can readily discover what legal restrictions to any right exist with enough clarity for them to be able to regulate their conduct. Any restrictions must then meet one of the aims recognised under either instrument as a legitimate ground for the restriction of civil and political rights. With one or two minor variations, these aims are for the protection of

- the rights and freedoms of others
- national security
- public safety
- public health and morals
- and for the prevention of public disorder or crime.

This list is intended to be exhaustive. States may not introduce other restrictions or stretch the meaning of the criteria listed above to add others. Finally, states must show both that the restriction fulfils a pressing social need and that it is proportionate to the aim of responding to that need. They cannot merely assert that a particular restriction is 'necessary in a democratic society', but must provide concrete evidence of a genuine and serious threat.

The bodies which interpret the tests – the UN Human Rights Committee and the European Court and Commission of Human Rights – have framed their notion of 'democratic society' in terms of such concepts as 'pluralism, tolerance and broad-mindedness'; and have made it clear that although the term 'necessary' is not synonymous with 'indispensable', it does not simply mean 'reasonable' (*Handyside v UK*, ECtHR, 1976).

3   Parliamentary Scrutiny of the Executive

Government and Parliament

Every year, tens of thousands of people benefit from the ability of 'their' Member of Parliament to intervene on their behalf. Many MPs encourage constituents to bring their complaints or problems to their 'surgeries', which are frequently weekly – at least during the parliamentary session. The problems can range from the trivial to social security or housing troubles, an immigration case, consumer law, serious illness. Of course, MPs vary greatly in their interest in this welfare work and in their ability to perform it well. A larger claim, however, is made for MPs collectively. They are said to be the defenders of the civil liberties of the population as a whole, through the democratic power of parliamentary sovereignty. Their role is to improve the protection of people's rights and liberties through legislation, to scrutinise government legislation so that it meets the public's needs and to hold government accountable face-to-face in the political cockpit of the nation – the chamber of the House of Commons. This chapter assesses how well Parliament performs these tasks to uphold the liberty of the subject in the United Kingdom.

The role of Parliament

The protection of liberty in the United Kingdom rests primarily not with the courts and rights inscribed in law or the constitution, but on the sovereignty of Parliament. This is held to be more democratic and more flexible than systems in which the judiciary is supreme. Political and civil rights are inherent simply in being a member of British society. Citizens need not rely on unelected and unaccountable judges to uphold their rights and freedoms. Instead, they may seek to protect or improve their civil liberties through laws made by their elected representatives in Parliament. The government gave examples of measures of this sort in the United Kingdom's third periodic report to the UN Human Rights Committee in 1989 – from laws abolishing slavery and the exploitation of children in the nineteenth century to the equal opportunities legislation of the 1970s (para. 3).

If it is necessary to restrict rights in the interests of society as a whole, this can only be done 'by a democratic decision of Parliament' (Charles Wardle, Home Office Minister, to Graham Allen MP, 6 April 1993). Parliament's power to make or unmake any law, which alarms some outside observers, is actually part and parcel of its ability to protect human rights:

> Citizens' rights are protected by the fact that Parliament is not bound by decisions made by previous Parliaments. If we get something wrong, as we often do, we can rectify it the following year.
>
> (Bill Walker MP, HC Deb, 9 February 1993, c826)

If citizens are dissatisfied with Parliament's discharge of its duties, they have the sanction of the ballot and may replace their MPs with more satisfactory representatives. By the same token, a government will be vigilant in its protection of civil liberties, either because it truly reflects the aspirations of its citizens, or for fear of being voted out of office. If a Bill of Rights or written constitution replaced this democratic system, John Patten, the Conservative former minister, warned that 'power would, in effect, flow not to the citizen, but from Parliament to the courts' (Patten 1991).

Parliament also has the ability to protect its constituents' rights through its powers to scrutinise and amend legislation. Governments may propose, but Parliament ultimately disposes; while governments in reality prepare and present nearly all legislation in Parliament, members of both Houses fulfil an important legislative role through these powers, both to uphold the quality of legislation and to make sure that it respects the liberties of the voters.

This is not the place for a detailed exposition of the legislative process (see Silk and Walters 1995). Suffice it to say that legislative business dominates both Houses. Public bills (i.e., those which seek to alter the general law of the land) are debated in principle by both chambers and then go for detailed scrutiny into standing committee (in the Commons) and a committee of the whole House in the Lords. Major bills – especially those, like the European Communities Act 1972, which raise constitutional issues – are usually taken in committee by the whole of the House of Commons. Bills also go through report stage in both Houses. The House of Lords, in which the Lord Chancellor and law lords sit, is regarded as the defender of constitutional principle. It has the power to insist on amendments and if these are rejected by the Commons, the House may delay legislation for 13 months (after which it becomes law unamended).

Ministerial responsibility to Parliament

Finally, ministers and public servants are of course obliged to conduct government business in accordance with the law. But Parliament's third function is to exercise a complementary political control over government, ministers and civil servants through the doctrine of ministerial responsibility to Parliament. This doctrine has the force of convention, not law. Under it, cabinet ministers first of all share a collective responsibility to Parliament for the conduct of national affairs; and Parliament can on a vote of confidence remove a Prime Minister and cabinet. Individual ministers are also responsible to Parliament for their own decisions and actions and for those of their departments and officials. The conventions of ministerial responsibility are set out in a Cabinet Office document:

Ministerial responsibility

> [ministers] have a duty to explain in Parliament the exercise of their powers and duties and to give an account . . of what is done by them as ministers or by their departments. This includes the duty to give Parliament, including its select committees and the public, as full information as possible about the policies, decisions and actions of the Government, and not to deceive or mislead Parliament and the public
>
> (*Questions of Procedure for Ministers*, 1992, para. 27)

These rules thus give MPs formal powers to call ministers to account through Parliamentary Questions, select committee inquiries, and 'reasonable' individual requests for information. In extreme cases, Parliament may oblige ministers to resign. While it is recognised that ministers have shown an increasing reluctance to re-sign over their own, or their officials', errors (Woodhouse 1993), nevertheless the doctrine is still held to provide a measure of political control by Parliament over the executive.

The belief in ministerial responsibility as a safeguard against the abuse of human rights is strong at official level. In the case of a mentally ill offender who was protesting against the absence of judicial review of his detention, the government argued before the European Court that the doctrine of ministerial responsibility, together with other extra-judicial methods of holding ministers to account, prevented them from exceeding their statutory powers and ensured conformity with the European Convention (*X v United Kingdom*, ECtHR, 1981).

Parliament as a pillar of human rights

Parliament's three functions for the protection of human rights, then, are said to lie in its immediate capacity to legislate to protect the democratic rights of ordinary citizens who elect members of the Commons; in its ability to scrutinise and amend government legislation; and in its power to call ministers and departments to account. It performs the first function more democratically than unelected judges could because it is accountable through the ballot.

Clearly, Parliament does pass laws to establish and protect civil and political rights which are usually, but not invariably, initiated by government. For example, laws against race and sex discrimination are solely the creation of statute. The criminal law is now predominantly statutory, and not only provides for the protection of basic human rights, such as the right to life, but establishes a framework of enforcement through the police, courts and prison. This is not to say that statute law, either civil or criminal, does adequately protect civil and political rights. But criticisms usually focus on defects in the laws themselves, or the policy or practice of the police and courts in enforcing them. It is rarely suggested that statutory laws are the wrong instruments for defining and securing fundamental civil and political rights.

However, government and Parliament have chosen a piecemeal approach to enacting individual rights, treating them in isolation and ignoring some altogether. Contrast this with the approach of most other countries which enshrine the full range of human rights in legislation – usually through a Bill of Rights or written constitution. In some territories and former colonies, the United Kingdom was actually responsible for inscribing human rights in the law or constitution. Very recently, the British government arranged for the UN International Covenant on Civil and Political Rights to be permanently incorporated into Hong Kong law before China took over the territory.

In the absence of entrenched human rights laws, legislation is a double-edged sword. The sovereignty of Parliament establishes, in practice, the political supremacy of the government of the day; and that government, through Parliament, has the same powers to pass laws, or even to issue statutory instruments, which restrict and violate civil and political rights, as it has to make laws which improve and protect them. In the absence of a written constitution or legally entrenched Bill of Rights, there exists no legal restraint on the powers the executive can obtain for itself through majority party grasp of parliamentary sovereignty.

This is not solely a theoretical proposition. As Table 3.1 shows, no fewer than 24 of the 37 violations of the European Convention determined by the European Court between 1975 and 1995 were the work of Parliament, either by way of primary (15) or secondary legislation (nine). The list includes legislation on 'closed shops', corporal punishment, prisoners' rights, child-care, immigration rules, arrest and detention under emergency powers in Northern Ireland, and the detention of the mentally ill. These are findings of violations in cases which actually reached the European Court. Other legislative lapses have been dealt with at other stages of judgment in the process of appeal to Strasbourg – reports by the European Commission of Human Rights and decisions of the Committee of Ministers. The most notorious example is the Commonwealth Immigrants Act 1968, which flagrantly violated the Convention (**pp. 55–56**); the government retreated at the Commission stage to avoid politically embarrassing judgments in the Court. These cases are not simply examples of Parliament's failure to check legislation which violates the Convention. As Table 3.1 shows, the Court found that Parliament had also *failed to legislate* to protect rights of free expression and privacy in certain areas (leading, for example, to the Contempt of Court Act 1981, the Interception of Communications Act 1985, and the Security Services Act 1989). Parliament evidently is not always the flexible friend of civil liberties. The European Court has also found the United Kingdom to be in violation of the Convention more often than any other country (Table 3.2).

This record demonstrates that the system for protecting rights in this country frequently fails, though it cannot 'show' (as some argue) that this country is worse than other countries. In part, the fact that the UK has received more adverse judgments than any other member state is a by-product of the failure to incorporate the Convention into British law; so there is no 'internal filter' in the British courts. It is also a sign of the democratic quality of British political culture. Liberty (formerly the National Council for Civil Liberties) is probably the most active non-governmental organisation on human rights in west Europe and is more alert to cases which might breach the European Convention than its counterparts in other European nations.

Yet, arbitrary as it may be, the British record at Strasbourg represents strong *prima facie* evidence of the failure of the British government and Parliament to play

Table 3.1 UK violations of the European Convention: European Court findings up to September 1995

The United Kingdom ratified the European Convention on 8 March 1951 and allowed individuals to petition the Commission from 1966. The dates of the origin of the violations are given in the brief synopses below

Date	Applicant	Articles violated	Background	Category	UK government action
21 February 1975	Golder	**6** Access to court **8** State interference with correspondence	Under the Prison Rules, consolidated by Statutory Instrument in January 1964, the Home Secretary refused a prisoner access to a solicitor	Delegated legislation	Prison Rules amended in 1972 and 1976
18 January 1978	Government of Ireland	**3** Freedom from torture	Interrogation techniques introduced in Northern Ireland in 1971, including 'hooding' suspects, caused public outcry	Police or military action	Gave undertaking not to use the prohibited five techniques which were officially abandoned in 1972
25 April 1978	Tyrer	**3** Inhuman or degrading punishment	The parents of a juvenile offender objected to the use of the birch under the Summary Jurisdiction (Isle of Man) Act 1960	Statute (Isle of Man)	Executive Council of the Isle of Man gave undertaking to stop corporal punishment
26 May 1979	*Sunday Times*	**10** Freedom of expression	In 1972, under the then strict law of contempt, the courts banned the *Sunday Times* from exposing the reluctance of Distillers, manufacturers of the deforming drug Thalidomide, properly to compensate their victims	Common law	The Contempt of Court Act 1981 liberalised the law
13 August 1981	Young, James and Webster	**11** Freedom of association	The Trade Union and Labour Relations Act 1974 allowed employers to dismiss workers who refused to join a trade union (except on grounds of religion). The aim of the legislation was to protect the 'closed shop'	Statute	Law changed to make firing non-union members unfair dismissal (1980 and 1982)

Table 3.1 continued

Date	Applicant	Articles violated	Background	Category	UK government action
22 October 1981	Dudgeon	**8** Right to privacy	Long-standing Stormont legislation made private homosexual acts illegal in Northern Ireland. A draft Order-in-Council (27 July 1978) proposed to decriminalise such acts in line with 1967 legislation in England and Wales (and 1980 in Scotland). In July 1979, the government suspended the order	Statute	A new order in 1982 decriminalised homosexual activity between consenting adults in NI
5 November 1981	X	**5** Freedom from arbitrary detention	Under the Mental Health Act 1959, the Home Secretary possessed wide, and virtually non-justiciable, discretionary powers to decide whether or not mentally disordered offenders should be discharged from detention	Statute	Law changed in 1982 to give powers of review to independent tribunals
25 February 1982	Campbell and Cosans	**Protocol 1, Art. 2** Parents' right to have children educated in conformity with their religious and philo-sophical convictions	The parents of two children caned in a state school protested that it was contrary to their wishes and their beliefs about how they should be educated	State practice	Legislation prohibiting corporal punishment in state-funded schools passed – by one vote – in 1986
25 March 1983	Silver and others	**6** Access to courts **8** Right to privacy **13** Right to an effective remedy	Silver and six other prisoners lodged complaints against the government's refusal of access to a solicitor; wide discretionary powers to censor their correspondence; and the 'prior ventilation' rule (they had to raise and settle complaints internally before consulting a legal adviser)	Quasi-legislation	Substantial changes to Prison Standing Orders in 1982

Table 3.1 continued

Date	Applicant	Articles violated	Background	Category	UK government action
28 January 1984	Campbell and Fell	**6** Right to a fair trial **8** Access to legal advice **13** Right to consult legal adviser in private; absence of effective remedy for violations of other rights	Prisoners refused legal representation during disciplinary proceedings; and denied privacy for solicitor's visit	Delegated legislation	Regulations were amended during conduct of case. Changes in practice of prisons tribunals introduced (right to legal aid and publicity)
2 August 1984	Malone	**8** Right to privacy	In 1979, a police officer giving evidence in a theft case in court quoted extracts from a tapped telephone conversation. The defendant challenged the lawfulness of the government warrant authorising the tap in the High Court. The judge was shocked by the absence of legal safeguards, but regretted that the court had no power to intervene	Police practice	The Interception of Communications Act 1985 introduced guidelines for surveillance
24 November 1984	Gillow	**8** Respect for privacy and family life	The Housing Authority of Guernsey refused to grant a licence for applicant to occupy his home, after a period of living abroad during which time the housing law had been amended resulting in Gillow no longer having a residence qualification; applicant also prosecuted for unlawful occupation	Local authority rules	Damages and legal costs paid. The rules were not in breach, rather their application in Gillow's case
28 May 1985	Abulaziz, Cabales and Balkandali	**8** Right to family life **14** Discrimination on the grounds of sex **13** Absence of effective remedy against breaches	New Immigration Rules in April 1980 contravened the findings of the European Commission in a previous case by reintroducing a rule preventing non-British husbands from joining their wives in the UK. Within a few months, women lawfully settled here challenged the rule	Delegated legislation	Perverse response – rules were amended so that both female and male spouses were refused right of entry

Table 3.1 continued

Date	Applicant	Articles violated	Background	Category	UK government action
2 March 1987	Weeks	**5** Freedom from arbitrary detention	The Criminal Justice Act 1967 gave the Home Secretary the ultimate discretionary power to refuse parole to mentally disordered offenders serving life sentences. Note parallel with X case above	Statute	Issued a statement that future imposition of life sentences in similar case would be 'unlikely'
8 July 1987	O, H, W, B, R (5 separate judgments)	**6** Right to a fair and full hearing by an independent tribunal **8** Respect for family life	Child-care law, consolidated in the Child Care Act 1980, gave local authorities wide discretionary powers to take children into care, to deny access to their parents and to exclude them from their decision-making processes. Parents were also denied the right to independent legal review of the decisions	Statute	New code of practice issued in 1983 allowed parents access to court review of decisions on care
27 April 1988	Boyle and Rice	**8** Right to legal advice	Another case, similar to that of Silver, restricting a prisoner's access to legal advice in which the Prison Rules and Standing Orders in Scotland were wrongly applied	Delegated legislation	Government apologised for misapplication of rules and undertook to ensure correct application in future
29 November 1988	Brogan *et al.*	**5** Freedom from arbitrary arrest	Brogan (and three others) were held in detention for periods from four days six hours and more, under the seven-day detention provisions of the Prevention of Terrorism Act 1984	Statute	Government lodged derogation in relation to the operation of the law in question
7 July 1989	Gaskin	**8** Respect for private life	The applicant was refused access to childhood records held by social services; government regulations issued in 1983 under the Local Authority Social Services Act 1970 allowed the disclosure of future care records to clients, but not past records	Delegated legislation	Granted damages and legal costs. Legislation to be introduced

Table 3.1 continued

Date	Applicant	Articles violated	Background	Category	UK government action
7 July 1989	Soering	**3** Protection against inhuman punishment	UK government decided to extradite German national to USA to face murder charges in state with death penalty (Virginia), rather than to Germany, after seeking assurances that the death penalty, if passed, would not be carried out. Soering claimed the assurance received from USA was not satisfactory	Executive decision	UK informed US government of the Court's decision. The US government agreed that Soering would not face capital punishment if he were found guilty of murder and the applicant was extradited
23 March 1990	Granger	**6** Right to a fair trial	The Legal Aid Committee of the Law Society of Scotland refused Granger's application for legal aid for representation at a hearing of appeal against a conviction for perjury	Delegated legislation	Scottish legal aid system reformed; courts required to act *ex officio* to review refusals to grant legal aid for certain appeals
30 August 1990	Fox, Campbell and Hartley	**5** Freedom from arbitrary arrest	Fox and others were arrested under the Northern Ireland (Emergency Powers) Act 1978, and were detained for periods varying from 30 to 44 hours	Statute	Legislation amended to confine powers of search and entry and to limit powers of arrest without a warrant to cases where 'reasonable grounds' for suspicion apply
30 August 1990	McCallum	**8** Access to legal advice	A further case of interference with a prisoner's correspondence, effectively denying access to a solicitor (see Silver and others; Boyle and Rice). The government did not contest this case	Delegated legislation	Prisons (Scotland) Standing Orders amended in 1983 and practices changed in light of the Silver case (see above)

Table 3.1 continued

Date	Applicant	Articles violated	Background	Category	UK government action
25 October 1990	Thynne, Wilson and Gunnel	**5** Freedom from arbitrary detention	Lawfulness of their being detained following release on licence; no judicial review of lawfulness of continued detention	Statute	Criminal Justice Act 1991 amended to place control over discretionary life prisoners with special panels, to require disclosure of relevant information
26 November 1991	*Observer* and *Guardian*	**10** Freedom of expression	Injunctions were granted in July 1986 pending a trial in which Attorney General sought permanent injunctions, restraining the two newspapers from publishing details of the unauthorised *Spycatcher* memoirs. The restrictions remained in force until the trial's conclusion in October 1988	Judicial decisions	Damages and legal costs paid
26 November 1991	*Sunday Times*	**10** Freedom of expression	In contempt proceedings, the courts held that the injunction above also bound other newspapers which had notice of them	Judicial decisions	Damages and legal costs paid
25 March 1992	Campbell	**8** Access to legal advice	A further case of control by prison authorities in Scotland of a prisoner's correspondence with his solicitor and with the European Commission of Human Rights	Delegated legislation	Damages and legal costs paid. Circular also sent to Scottish prisons setting out procedures for control of correspondence
26 October 1993	Darnell	**6** Right to a fair trial	Case concerning the length of civil proceedings (nine years) following applicant's appeal against suspension from duty by Trent Regional Health Authority in 1982	Courts	Damages paid

Table 3.1 continued

Date	Applicant	Articles violated	Background	Category	UK government action
28 October 1994	Boner	**6** Right to a fair trial	Boner was sentenced to long-term imprisonment, and refused legal aid for representation at the hearing of his appeal against conviction (Legal Aid (Scotland) Act 1986)	Statute	Damages paid
28 October 1994	Maxwell	**6** Right to a fair trial	As above	Statute	Damages paid
9 February 1995	Welch	**7** Prohibition of retroactive criminal laws	Applicant arrested in November 1986 for drug trafficking offences. The trial judge imposed a confiscation order retrospectively, under the Drug Trafficking Act 1986 (the relevant section of which came into effect in January 1987) following conviction in August 1988	Courts	Costs and damages paid
25 February 1995	McMichael	**6** Right to a fair trial **8** Right to family life	The applicants' child was taken into care by Strathclyde Regional Council in December 1987. The couple were denied access, and refused documents for the Children's Hearings panel	Local authority action	Damages paid
13 July 1995	Tolstoy	**10** Freedom of expression	Tolstoy was ordered to pay a £1.5 million libel award by a High Court jury in November 1989. The applicant complained that the size of the award was disproportionate to the aim of protecting the rights of the person libelled and was not 'necessary in a democratic society'	Jury decision	Damages paid
27 September 1995	McCann and others	**2** Right to life	In March 1988 SAS soldiers shot dead three members of an IRA Active Service Unit on a bombing mission in Gibraltar	Military Rules of Engagement	Costs paid. The UK government vehemently disputed the finding

Source: Compiled by Wendy Hall and the authors

Absence of restraint

Table 3.2 Court of Human Rights Judgments 1959–1995[1]

State	Ratification	Individual petition[2]	Total judgments	Adverse judgments[3]
UK	1951	1966	60	35
Austria	1958	1958	51	34
Italy	1955	1973	45	32
France	1974	1981	54	28
Netherlands	1954	1960	31	23
Sweden	1952	1952 (1966)	30	21
Belgium	1955	1955	32	20
Switzerland	1974	1974	24	14
Germany	1952	1955	28	12
Greece	1974	1985	9	7
Ireland	1953	1953	8	6
Portugal	1978	1978	10	6
Spain	1979	1981	11	6
Denmark	1953	1953	6	2
Finland	1990	1990	3	2
Iceland	1953	1955 (1958)	3	2
Turkey	1954	1987 (1990)	3	2
Cyprus	1962	1989	1	1
Luxembourg	1953	1958	1	1
Malta	1967	1987	1	1
Norway	1952	1955 (1964)	1	1

Source: Authors

Notes:

1 Complete to 29 September 1995. Table 3.2 shows two fewer violations than 3.1 owing to official delays in recording cases

2 Date upon which the right of individual petition to the European Commission of Human Rights was accepted (Article 25). Where a state has recognised the compulsory jurisdiction of the European Court of Human Rights at a later date (Article 46), this date is given in brackets

3 Cases which give rise to a finding of *at least one* violation

their part in protecting and securing political rights and freedoms. We go on to consider further evidence which suggests, first, that governments are indifferent to, and even ignorant of, their obligations under human rights instruments to which Britain subscribes; and secondly, that Parliament is not a sufficient watch-dog.

Government's indifference to human rights instruments

Richard Crossman, an unusually candid politician, noted in his diary that his cabinet colleagues were aware that the Labour government's Commonwealth Immigrants Bill, which they hurriedly prepared to deal with the Kenyan Asians 'crisis' in 1968, 'would have been declared unconstitutional in any country with a written constitution and a Supreme Court' (Bevan 1986: 81). The bill's second reading was moved at 4pm on 27 February 1968 in the Commons and passed all stages in both Houses in three days.

Government indifference

Only one MP raised an issue of compliance with the European Convention. Five years later, the European Commission of Human Rights found that the 1968 Act violated three separate Articles of the European Convention on Human Rights.

Yet, in 1977, the House of Lords Select Committee on a Bill of Rights held that 'it is probably unlikely that a government would deliberately introduce some Bill which flagrantly went against the Convention on Human Rights'. The peers' complacent view has since been disproved by numerous examples of government indifference to the Convention. Only two years later, the new Conservative government decided to introduce a revised version of the 'husband rule' into the Immigration Rules. It was designed to prevent husbands or fiancés living abroad from joining women resident in the UK who were not born here, and who did not have British ancestry. This discriminatory new rule 'flagrantly went against' the Convention, as the government was repeatedly warned in both Houses by Lord Scarman, the law lord, among others. The Commons Home Affairs sub-committee on race relations and immigration consulted expert lawyers, all of whom agreed that the rule violated the Convention. William Whitelaw, the Home Secretary, refused to confirm that ministers had sought the advice of the Law Officers, claiming that this was privileged information. He advanced the inaccurate proposition that compliance with the Convention was a matter to be decided by the courts, not at the pre-legislative stage. He then ignored the sub-committee report (*First Report of Home Affairs Committee*, HC 434, 1979–80) and pushed the Rules through Parliament in their original form, only for the European Court of Human Rights to declare six years later that they breached the Convention in precisely the ways that the MPs had predicted (*Abdulaziz, Cabales & Balkandali v UK (the ACB case)*, ECtHR, 1985; see also Kinley 1993: 83–88).

MPs and peers were unusually sensitive to the human rights implications of the government's policy on this occasion – largely because a similar provision in the Commonwealth Immigrants Act 1968 had been declared a violation by the European Commission only a few years previously. Generally, even where government ministers expressly recognise that legislation restricts civil liberties – as Roy Jenkins did, for example, in enacting the original Prevention of Terrorism Act (PTA) 1974 – it is rare for MPs to remind them of their obligations under international human rights instruments to which this country is party. Throughout the series of PTA bills in 1974, 1976, 1984 and 1989, only a single MP, Gerald Bermingham, emphasised the necessity of 'having laws which comply with the European Convention on Human Rights' while the 1984 bill was passing through Parliament. His observation was completely ignored by the government (Kinley 1993: 55).

Most violations are inadvertent rather than deliberate, but the implications are equally serious. In 1974, a government green paper claimed that the conformity of UK law to the European Convention was reviewed in 1966 (when the right of individual petition was first allowed) and thereafter when the right of petition was renewed (para. 3.09). The government solemnly assured the UN Human Rights Committee in 1995 that government departments routinely scrutinise draft legislation and proposals for administrative change to ensure that they are compatible with international human rights instruments. It is the case that, in July 1987, the Cabinet Office issued a circular, somewhat negatively entitled *Reducing the Risk of Legal Challenge*, urging departments to 'consider the effect of the ECHR jurisprudence on any proposed legislative or administrative measure, in consultation with their legal adviser'. Departments were asked to include an assessment of this effect, if any, on their proposals in 'all cabinet Committee memoranda on policy proposals and memoranda for Legislation Committee' (paras 4(1) and (2)). The circular fails to refer to other human rights obligations, such as those arising under the International Covenant. No specialist assistance is offered to departments, other than 'ad hoc guidance' from the Foreign and Commonwealth Office in the old (and ineffective) way (Annex II, para. 6). The evidence of frequent violations in past and current legislation suggests that this is an area where performance indicators are long overdue.

David Kinley, an academic lawyer, has provided a measure of the government's sensitivity to the European Convention in a study of 22 cases up to 1991 of legislative violations (Kinley 1993: 41–96). His study reveals the absence of any systematic approach or any effort to monitor the jurisprudence of the European Court to ensure that legislation and practice comply with the Convention. In the case of *X v United Kingdom*, a mentally ill person successfully challenged the absence of independent legal review of a minister's decision to continue his detention (ECtHR,1981; see also Table 3.1). Yet there had been extensive public debate during the 1970s about the unfairness of the Mental Health Act 1959. In 1977, the European Commission issued a report, condemning the absence of judicial review in similar legislation in the Netherlands; the Court concurred two years later (*Winterwerp v The Netherlands*, ECtHR, 1979). Yet the government remained unmoved until it was finally obliged by the Court to amend the legislation. It left unchanged similar weaknesses in the Criminal Justice Act 1967, concerning the detention of mentally ill people found guilty of crimes or recalled to prison after release on licence. Predictably, several people took the government to Strasbourg after the Court's judgment in *'X'* and the Court came to exactly the same basic judgment on exactly the same principles (*Weeks*, 1988 and *Thynne, Wilson and Gunnell*, 1990, see Table 3.1). Kinley comments, 'there existed a distinct line of reasoning, originating in *X* and running through both *Weeks* and *Thynne et al.*' (1993: 50). One lapse may be charitably passed off as happenstance; five in a row looks more like negligence or deliberate policy.

Even where the government receives official warning, it does not necessarily act. In 1984, the official government review under the late Sir George Baker of the operation of emergency powers in Northern Ireland specifically warned that existing powers of arrest contravened two Articles of the Convention (Cmnd 9222, 1984). The government failed to act for three years, even though the protection which these powers enjoyed under a notice of derogation was shortly to be lifted. Meanwhile, three suspects arrested under the unchanged powers lodged complaints at Strasbourg, which the European Court subsequently upheld (*Fox, Campbell and Hartley v United Kingdom*, 1990).

Reluctant participation in international human rights treaties

It seems that governments in Britain have been reluctant participants in international human rights treaties since the beginning. Postwar Labour governments (1945–51) took a major role in establishing both the European Convention and the UN International Covenant. The cabinet discussed warnings from Lord Jowitt, the Lord Chancellor, that, in ratifying the two instruments, the government would be obliged to review UK law and practice, and even introduce legislation 'applying the conditions of the [European] Convention to our domestic law' (Lester 1984: 53). Jowitt wrote to a cabinet colleague, Hugh Dalton, explaining,

> We were not prepared to encourage our European friends to jeopardise our whole system of law, which we have laboriously built up over the centuries, in favour of some half-baked scheme.
>
> (Lester 1993: 2)

Jim Griffiths, the Colonial Secretary, warned that the proposed right of petition to a European Court was 'likely to cause considerable misunderstanding and political unsettlement' in many colonies where most people were 'still politically immature' (Lester 1984: 46ff.). The cabinet finally agreed to sign the European Convention only on the strict understanding that it would not accept the right of individual petition (which the Council of Europe then made voluntary). To subject the common law and statute law to external judicial review was considered intolerable. The 1951 Labour cabinet had similar misgivings about the UN International Covenant and decided to seize any opportunity to delay its conclusion.

In the event, the United Kingdom was the first nation to ratify the European Convention in 1951. It did so under royal prerogative powers without any parliamentary debate. The Wilson government ratified the International Covenant under the same powers in 1976. The decision to accept the right of individual petition to the European Court of Human Rights, eventually taken in December 1965, was not debated in Parliament – or even by the cabinet. Ministers took the decision in interdepartmental correspondence and Parliament was only informed later (Lester 1984: 58–61). Governments have continued to refuse to sign the Optional Protocol to the Covenant, allowing individual citizens to petition the UN Human Rights Committee directly.

This early reluctance to accept the jurisdiction of the two instruments need not be read simply as a sign of insular arrogance. Both instruments were untried and nothing was known of the quality of the new enforcement authorities. Britain's human rights record appeared good (though only if its behaviour in the colonies was set on one side) and its legal system was universally admired. But the need to adjust law and practice to the UK's international human rights obligations is now incontestable. Our record in front of the European Court is clear evidence of that; and the UN Human Rights Committee's comments in 1995 represent a highly respected international verdict on UK law and practice (**p. 39, pp. 306–308, and Box F**). The government's complacent protestations that all is well seem increasingly and foolishly arrogant, even to the citizens of this country (Rowntree 1991, 1995). The government has already been obliged to introduce or amend legislation in response to violations identified by the European Court on 15 occasions. Such responses clearly contribute to the protection of human rights in the United

Kingdom. But the government's attitude towards the European Court is caught by the recollection of Ferdinand Mount, once head of Margaret Thatcher's Policy Unit:

> When Strasbourg issues a finding which reflects badly on English law or the British Government, there is a dignified pause for reflection in London to demonstrate HMG's freedom of action; and then, a little shamefacedly and not without a good deal of grumbling behind the scenes, the finding is complied with.
>
> (Mount 1992: 230–231)

Further, the European Court findings are only one measure of the failure of governments to be sensitive to international standards. Governments pay hardly any attention at all to the International Covenant, which has only ever influenced one legislative provision: the payment of compensation for miscarriages of justice under the Criminal Justice Act 1988. Such indifference is not justified by the UK's performance on human rights.

Grudging compliance under duress

In the limited sense of being required to respond to European Court judgments, British governments are not wholly immune to international human rights obligations. But this is an ad hoc and unsatisfactory means of compliance which relies in the first place on an individual citizen embarking on the long and expensive legal route to Strasbourg. Many violations go unchallenged. For example, four years after the European Court judgment in the *ACB* case overturned a discriminatory immigration rule (**p. 56**), Elspeth Gould, an academic researcher, identified no fewer than 17 further instances of sexual discrimination in immigration laws and rules (cited in Kinley 1993: 88). Enforced statutory adjustments are no substitute for the comprehensive and ongoing review of common and statute law, regulations and practice which all governments have evidently failed seriously to undertake for some 50 years.

Further, legislative changes have usually been at best the minimum necessary to achieve compliance with the European Convention. For example, the government changed the rules governing prisoners' rights to legal advice so slowly and grudgingly that they were found to be in violation of the Convention in five cases from 1975 to 1990 (see Table 3.1). In the case of mentally ill offenders, the government strove to retain a wide measure of the discretionary ministerial powers to which the Court objected (Kinley 1993: 47–50). In another case, the European Commission found that the detention of two terrorist suspects for 45 hours without access to their wives violated Article 8 of the Convention (*McVeigh, O'Neill and Evans v United Kingdom*, 1981). Three years later, in the Police and Criminal Evidence Act 1984, the government enacted new rights of access for people in custody to friends, relatives and legal advisers, but set the maximum limit for which a terrorist suspect may be held alone at 48 hours. The government was not ignorant of the disparity.

Grudging compliance

On occasions, the government has found a means to comply while evading the spirit of the Court's judgment. For example, after the European Court's findings in the *ACB* case (see **p. 56**), the government was placed at once under an obligation to remove the sex discrimination inherent in the 'husband rule'. Rather than give men legitimately married to or marrying women in the UK rights of entry, the government removed women's existing rights of entry.

In some cases, government has satisfied only the main finding of the European Court and ignored ancillary findings. Telephone metering provides a good example. It is not an interception of communication, but it does invade the privacy of individuals, allowing the security services and police to build up a picture of their friends, acquaintances and contacts (see Chapter 12). In 1985, the European Court rejected the government's argument that telephone metering requires no legal oversight since the content of calls is not recorded. The Court noted that metering was not governed by legal rules. The information gained might be released to the police without the subscriber's knowledge or consent. Accordingly, it held that metering, like telephone tapping, was not 'in accordance with law' *(Malone v United Kingdom, 1984)*. Yet the government refused to provide for oversight of metering in the resultant statute, the Interception of Communications Act 1985. In response to the Scottish Council for Civil Liberties in September 1992, the Scottish Office said, 'the question of metering was very carefully considered when the legislation was being prepared and was very fully debated in Parliament during the passage of the Act'. In fact, Hansard records only a single late-night exchange on the subject on 3 April 1985 when the Home Office minister simply reiterated the government's view that metering was fundamentally different from interception (Hilton 1993).

Discharging Britain's reporting obligations

Human rights obligations in the United Kingdom are dealt with as part of Britain's foreign relations under prerogative powers. This means that even the government's reporting duties are exercised very discreetly. For example, the government's periodic reports to the UN Human Rights Committee are not reported to Parliament, let alone debated in either House. Expert statutory bodies, such as the Commission for Racial Equality and Equal Opportunities Commission, are not consulted. The reports are not published by HMSO, do not appear in public libraries and can only be obtained by those who actively seek them out from the Foreign Office. The government stated in its 1995 report that, 'as with previous reports', it would make the text of the report and a summary record of the oral examination by the Human Rights Committee 'widely available throughout the United Kingdom' (fourth periodic report, 1995: para. 8). Justice, a human rights organisation, calculated in 1995 that only about 70 copies were ever printed.

In the early 1990s, Lord Lester QC carried out a spot check on the government's reporting activities towards more specialised human rights authorities, like the Committee on the Elimination of Discrimination against Women, the Committee on the Elimination of Racial Discrimination (CERD) and the ILO Committee of Experts. In the 1994 Sieghart lecture (Lester 1994) he told his audience that:

Apart from the first report to the UN Committee on the Rights of the Child, these reports are not published by HMSO; nor are they routinely placed in the Library of either House [of Parliament]. The Commission for Racial Equality has never been consulted about the contents of the 12 government reports to CERD, and does not possess a complete set of them. Odd copies can be obtained from particular NGOs as a kind of *samizdat*. Eventually, I was able to obtain a copy of the twelfth report to CERD from the Home Office. The other eleven are being kept in a depot in Hayes.

The contents of the reports were often trivial and irrelevant. The first substantive report to the Committee on the Elimination of Discrimination against Women in 1985 gave details of Britain's size and topography, seas, climate, prevailing winds and social habits ('Watching television is the main evening activity for all except young men'). As Lord Lester pointed out:

> What the report omits to say is that Parliament has not been consulted by the Government, that Parliament has not considered or authorised the report, and that Parliament has no idea of what is being reported to CEDAW.

Finally, the refusal of any government to set up any formal system for monitoring compliance with the International Covenant hardly suggests a firm and entrenched belief in the fundamental importance of political rights and freedoms. When we asked the responsible civil servant about this in March 1993, he replied:

> This is not the British way of doing things or what the Foreign and Commonwealth Office is for. The Foreign and Commonwealth Office is about the interests of the UK abroad and presenting a good image abroad.

Parliament's failure to bark

One classic response to such evidence of the behaviour of government is to separate the role of government from that of Parliament. While government cannot necessarily be trusted to respect people's political rights and freedoms, according to Dicey and his disciples, Parliament stands ready to act as a watch-dog against any excess executive zeal. As reported above (**p. 46**), they argue that Parliament provides a forum for relatively independent MPs to scrutinise draft legislation, initiate debates, call ministers to account and generally safeguard the interests and liberties of citizens. Erskine May, the standard authority on Parliament, still describes the role of a Commons standing committee in terms of scrupulous scrutiny, with a view to making any bill 'more generally acceptable' (*Erskine May*, 21st edition, 1989: 494).

Whatever might have been the strength of this contention in 1885, or 1989, it does not stand up to scrutiny in 1995. The proof of the pudding is in the eating. If Parliament had acted as an effective watch-dog against government or executive zeal in the last 30 years, the European Court and Commission of Human Rights would hardly have occasion to criticise the law and practice of the United Kingdom so frequently. If government were minded to listen to Parliament and back off, why are there many examples of ministers ignoring the few MPs or peers who do warn them that their proposed bills or actions are liable to violate the European Convention, and failing to take this advice?

The companion Democratic Audit volume on democratic institutions will contain a full analysis of the role of Parliament in contemporary Britain. Suffice it to say here that it is a commonplace, officially recognised by MPs themselves, that government thoroughly dominates Parliament through the disciplined party system. In 1977, the Commons Select Committee on Procedure acknowledged that:

> The balance of advantage between Parliament and government in the day-to-day working of the Constitution is now so weighted in favour of the government to a degree which arouses widespread anxiety and is inimical to the proper working of our Parliamentary democracy.
>
> (*First Report*, 1977–78, HC 588: para. 1.5)

The roots of executive dominance are equally widely known. Any government is normally drawn from the political party with most seats in the House of Commons; and, given an electoral system which boosts the representation of the leading party in the Commons, almost always has a majority of seats even on a minority of the popular vote. Mrs Thatcher's governments, all of which had substantial Commons majorities, were all returned to power on 42–44 per cent of the vote. A considerable proportion of members of the governing party are nowadays also members of the government itself – in 1995, more than a third of the governing party (112 Conservative MPs out of 326) were on the 'payroll vote' and were thus bound to loyalty. The government of the day therefore controls the legislative timetable, initiates the vast majority of bills and is generally able to secure their safe passage through Parliament. The constitutional doctrine of Crown in Parliament – the very settlement which is said to safeguard individual liberties – gives the executive, not the legislature, effective command over legislation, and thus statute law.

Parliament devotes a huge proportion of its time to scrutiny of a mass of legislation. But it is equally common knowledge that this scrutiny is almost wholly ineffective. In 1992, for example, the all-party Hansard Society for Parliamentary Government published an exhaustive report on the legislative process by a commission, chaired by the former cabinet minister, Lord Rippon. This commission considered the evidence of at least 57 organisations and individuals – including MPs, law lords, other peers, senior civil servants, the BMA, chief police officers, the Consumers Association, academic specialists, the CBI, Equal Opportunities Commission, the Law Society, local authority associations, magistrates, Shelter and the TUC. The Hansard Commission concluded that the legislative process was unsystematic:

> there is usually little prior examination by Parliament of the purposes of a bill, insufficient expert analysis of its content and likely consequences during

its progress through the system, and no formal arrangements for considering what its implementation achieved when put into practice.

(Hansard Society 1993: 47)

The sheer weight of legislation is a problem in itself. This problem is compounded by the absence of clarity in bills, which are often hurriedly prepared and presented 'half-baked' to Parliament, leaving the detail to be worked out and inserted, often late, by way of amendments (Hansard Society 1993: 45). Government amendments tend to be inserted in the Lords and their volume has grown dramatically. Lord Howe has pointed out that, from 1987 to 1989, 2,668 government amendments were introduced annually into the Lords. He denounced such 'policy-making on the hoof' in his 1991 address to the Statute Law Society.

Many bodies which gave evidence to the commission criticised the way Parliament handled legislation. Its scrutiny usually 'did not succeed in improving bills' (ibid.: 68). They blamed MPs for their lack of commitment to 'effective scrutiny'. Professor Norton, a believer in the British way of doing things (see **p. 74**), told the commission that,

> The capacity of the House of Commons to subject bills to sustained and informed scrutiny is limited . . . The House is constrained by a lack of time, information, specialisation and resources from submitting bills to effective scrutiny.
>
> (ibid.: 326)

As for standing committees, they are 'crafted to favour government':

> Their appointment on an ad hoc basis – they are anything but 'standing' – militates against developing any form of specialisation or corporate spirit. The absence of the power to send for papers, persons and records limits what they can consider. The replication not just of party strength on the floor of the House, but more especially the party structure (with ministers and – since 1945 – whips appointed) has meant that committee deliberation has tended to be a continuation of the partisan debate at second reading.
>
> (ibid.: 326)

Further, MPs are overloaded with work – individually and collectively: 'the greater the demands on MPs' time, the greater the threat to their being able to give time and attention to standing committees' (ibid.: 328).

It is, however, widely agreed that the root of Parliament's legislative weakness is buried deep in the executive psyche – postwar governments of either party are determined to get their legislation – or 'business' – through and resist any procedural reforms which would diminish their control of the parliamentary timetable (ibid.: 352). For the greater part, opposition parties cooperate with governments, through 'the usual channels' (i.e., the whips' offices), to deliver their legislation on time, and when they don't, then governments can always use the guillotine to get it through.

Parliamentary scrutiny

There is a ritual party political element in opposition complaints, such as John Cunningham's evidence to the Hansard Commission, that the Conservative government 'steam-rollered' bad legislation through and is too reluctant to accept amendments to many bills; yet his complaints are seen to be objectively correct too (ibid.: 71).

Governments are more willing to accept amendments in the Lords – the revising chamber. But even there, as Lord Waddington, then the government spokesperson in the Lords, told a select committee, the government's business needs are paramount:

> Additional or deeper scrutiny of bills in the Lords which succeeded in 'improving the quality of the legislation eventually passed' . . . would be unacceptable if this added to the overall time taken for the passage of a bill through this House.
>
> (The Committee on the Work of the House,
> HL 35–II, 1991–92: 135)

In evidence to the Lords Committee on a Bill of Rights in 1977, the law lord, Lord Reid, said it was inconceivable that Parliament would enact legislation which ran counter to the European Convention. Giving evidence later, Lord Gordon-Walker commented, 'when judges say "inconceivable", they do not know how Parliament works' (*Minutes of Evidence*, HL Select Committee on a Bill of Rights, HL 81, 1977–78: 130). The weight of the evidence from all manner of experienced bodies and experts, summarised above, lies with the former Labour cabinet minister.

Parliament's powers to control the executive

Parliament's weak control of legislation is echoed by its inability truly to call the executive to account. *The Economist* has summarised expert opinion on the practical value of the doctrine of ministerial responsibility: 'as a basis for the UK's system of control over the operations of the Executive, [it] is now widely conceded to be outmoded and thoroughly inadequate, capable today of providing little more than "technical accountability"' (4 February 1985). Two academic observers described the doctrine in the very title of their study of Parliament and the executive, *The Noble Lie*, commenting that Parliament failed to deliver on 'the promise of accountability for the exercise of public power because a Parliament dominated by the Executive cannot effectively call ministers to account' (Harden and Lewis 1987: 118).

Curiously, the very doctrine of ministerial responsibility to Parliament limits the actual potential of members' control over departments and agencies. Ministers no longer accept personal responsibility for the bad judgment or major mistakes of their officials, while the officials themselves are protected from direct parliamentary scrutiny by the continuing fiction that they have no identity other than through ministers. Moreover, as civil servants are responsible to ministers alone, and not to Parliament nor any notion of the 'public interest', they give account in

Parliament only on ministers', and the government's, terms. Under the government's 'Osmotherly rules', ministers determine exactly what officials may say in evidence to select committees, and may even refuse to let them give testimony. Officials are forbidden to discuss policy issues or options, or to comment on 'questions in the field of political controversy' (Garrett 1992: 94–95). Select committees have raised Parliament's ability to scrutinise the executive. But they have found it impossible to get at the facts in sensitive cases, like the DTI committee's inquiries into the Supergun affair and arms deals. On other occasions they split on partisan grounds, with the majority party members combining to protect government.

The convention that ministers should give Parliament 'as full information as possible' about their policies and decisions is of limited value. In 1993, the government introduced a new 'open government' regime which allows for the public release of official information only at the discretion of officials, and protects all policy decisions and the information leading up to them (Weir 1994: 16–17). Britain's MPs are better placed than the general public, but there are effective limits on what they may be told. A variety of rules limit the scope of Parliamentary Questions. Ministers sometimes give 'holding' answers, with no apparent intention ever to provide an answer, or refuse to answer at all on the grounds of 'disproportionate cost' (Garrett 1992: 150–156). The Scott inquiry revealed that civil servants drafted deliberately misleading answers to PQs to conceal the shifts in the declared policy on arms exports to Iraq and Iran from MPs (Norton-Taylor 1995: ch. 6). It is likely that similar exercises in semantic deceit have occurred in other sensitive areas of government policy.

The evident reality of government power over Parliament tends to obscure a fundamental weakness in the very idea of parliamentary control of the machine of state in modern Britain. It is a truism to observe that the business of government has been vastly expanded in the twentieth century. It is rarely also observed that the idea that a relatively small group of parliamentarians, under-resourced as they are, could possibly hope to render the vast universe of official decision-making of a modern extended state accountable through ministers is absurdly anachronistic; so too is the idea that ministers themselves could possibly discharge this responsibility.

As for protecting human rights, David Kinley's study of the parliamentary processes involved in legislation which ultimately proved to be in violation of the European Convention revealed that Parliament was generally as indifferent to or ignorant of the Convention's provisions as government (Kinley 1993: 41–96). Even in high-profile cases, such as the Prevention of Terrorism Acts, the relevance of the Convention was hardly appreciated, as we have seen. Labour's 1974 'closed shop' Labour Relations bill was hotly challenged in both Houses, but there was not a single mention of the Convention. On occasions, MPs have been outraged by the European Court's decisions, such as that on corporal punishment in the *Tyrer v UK* case (see **Table 3.1**), and have argued in Parliament that Britain should not abide by them (HC Deb, 31 March 1987, c923). In 1995, prominent Conservative MPs protested strongly against the European Court finding against the government, protecting the 'right to life' in the case of the Gibraltar killings of three IRA terrorists (*McCann and Others v United Kingdom*, 1996).

It is true that the government's attitude, when challenged on issues of compliance, hardly encourages members to raise the question of its obligations under human rights instruments. Ministers will ignore well-founded warnings, as in the case of new immigration rules in 1979 (see **p. 56** above), or claim, as a matter of routine, that their bills do not infringe the Convention – or rather, 'any EC human rights obligations,' as the Home Office minister inaccurately put it on the committee stage of the Criminal Justice and Public Order Act 1994 (HC Deb, 21 January 1994, c712). Yet MPs and peers as a whole do not use the European Convention, or other human rights instruments, as a yardstick against which to measure government legislation or actions.

Ministerial powers and delegated legislation

Ministers in Britain possess wide discretionary powers. First and foremost, royal prerogative powers – once the preserve of the Crown – are now at the disposal of ministers and officials. It is not clear what the limits of these powers are. They are of direct importance to Britain's obligations under human rights instruments, however, as international treaties fall within the province of foreign and diplomatic affairs and are dealt with through prerogative powers. Foreign policy is generally conducted by way of prerogative powers in secret. Ministers report to Parliament after the event, as they did in ratifying both the European Convention and International Covenant. This means that government seeks to satisfy its human rights responsibilities at a remove from the parliamentary arena and public opinion.

Royal prerogative powers are significant for human rights in other directions – for example, 'national security' and the civil service are both governed by ministers under their prerogative powers. Mrs Thatcher relied upon prerogative powers to ban trade union membership at GCHQ in 1984, in contravention of ILO conventions; and the government argued that even the courts, let alone Parliament, were powerless to intervene (see **p. 220**).

Ministers are also able to assume discretionary powers through primary and delegated legislation – statutory instruments and Orders in Council – almost entirely unchecked by Parliament. Very often, as Henry Knorpel, then the Speaker's Counsel, informed the Committee on Procedure, ministers sponsoring a bill 'do not know themselves quite what use they intend to make of the powers' they are assuming (*Minutes of Evidence*, HC 350, 1986–87: 9). The combination of ill-defined discretionary powers, often of a quasi-judicial nature, and delegated legislation has serious implications both for parliamentary democracy and civil liberties. The Law Society has pointed out that delegated, or 'secondary', legislation, is not 'secondary' in importance, but is more important in some cases than 'primary' legislation, and 'should therefore be accorded the necessary time for full and detailed scrutiny' (Hansard Society 1993: 286). Of the 37 violations of the Convention found by the European Court, no fewer than nine had their origins in delegated legislation and 'quasi-legislation' – like immigration and prison rules and codes of practice.

But delegated legislation does not receive the scrutiny it is due. It is widely recognised, yet again, that parliamentary control of delegated and 'quasi' legislation ranges from being weak to virtually non-existent (Garrett 1992: 59–65; Byrne 1976: 366 and 375). MPs cannot amend statutory instruments – they must accept or reject them. Some 2,200 flood through Parliament every year, but fewer than 20 per cent – 'affirmative instruments' – actually require members' approval. The rest – 'negative instruments', which are employed, for example, to introduce immigration rules – become law if no MP has objected within 40 days of their being laid before Parliament. Few objections are ever debated, fewer still achieve their objective. The House of Lords Select Committee on the Scrutiny of Delegated Powers concluded in its 1992–93 report that the weight of evidence suggested that parliamentary control over delegated legislation is so tightly limited as to be ineffective (HL Paper 77: para. 29).

'Quasi-legislation' – a dense mass of official codes of guidance, rules and regulations promulgated by government departments – is almost entirely outside parliamentary control. These codes, many of which have a quasi-judicial aspect, vary from internal standing orders for prisons and circulars for prison governors, and unpublished instructions to immigration officers on applying the Immigration Rules, to official guidance on the recognition of state beneficiaries' needs under the Social Fund. Some, like the ministerial instructions to immigration officers, are unpublished. The most MPs can do when they do debate 'quasi-legislation' is to make recommendations which ministers may or may not accept. The legal status of the mazes of 'quasi-legislation' is confused, while the system itself is inconsistent and unsystematic (Ganz 1987: 36).

Parliament's inability to control delegated and 'quasi-legislation' means, in practice, that it cannot control the vast range of discretionary powers which ministers assume for use largely by their civil servants, state agencies, quangos and the armies of officialdom. But the rules they set out govern the behaviour of officials – prison officers, immigration officers, the police, social security staff – who deal with people at the sharp end of state practice in the most sensitive areas of political and civil rights. The United Kingdom's poor record at Strasbourg bears out the case made by the Law Society for effective parliamentary scrutiny of delegated legislation and 'quasi-legislation'.

The rising tide from Europe

Another mass of legislation which Parliament does not deal with effectively is that which comes from Brussels. The Commons undertakes only random and superficial scrutiny of a small proportion of European legislation, which it cannot anyway amend or reject. The Lords has established a select committee which analyses issues rather than directives. The key decisions are taken by ministers and senior civil servants with their counterparts from other member states. Therefore, if the Commons is to have any influence over European legislation, members have to brief themselves well in advance of impending legislation so that they can bring pressure to bear on ministers before they enter into negotiations in the Council of Ministers and require ministers to report back more systematically and fully than at present. For the most part, ministerial accountability consists largely of occasional statements after meetings of the Council or heads of government and twice-yearly debates.

Europol

Yet serious human rights issues are increasingly at stake. At the end of 1995, the government pushed the European Convention establishing Europol, the cross-border police intelligence agency, through Parliament. Europol was originally intended to deal with serious organised crime, but in secret talks among EU governments its remit was broadened to people who are merely suspected of crimes. Its activities raise serious issues of data protection, in particular, since Europol will be linked into a network of Europe-wide databases, including the Schengen Information System which already holds 10 million records (September 1995). A large range of 'suspected' people – 'suspected' illegal immigrants and migrants, 'suspected' public order threats – and extradition and other cases will be affected. The human rights dimensions are clear and a House of Lords inquiry heard evidence on the evident need for 'accountability measures'. However, the House of Commons was obliged to approve its ratification, without debate, while Europol's own shape and role was not finally decided; before it had been debated by the European Parliament; and before the role of the European Court of Justice in its future was resolved. The government pressed the Convention through Parliament under the 'Ponsonby Rules', under a convention, established in 1924, that all international treaties and agreements would be 'laid' before the House for 21 days before being ratified. Such agreements cannot be altered by Parliament, as they fall within the province of the government's pre-rogative powers and are deposited in the Commons purely as a courtesy (see Bunyan, 1995; and *Europol*, Lords Select Committee on the European Communities, HL 51, HMSO 1995).

The significance of constitutional conventions

As we have seen, important political checks on government – such as the doctrine of ministerial responsibility to Parliament – are constitutional conventions. These conventions of behaviour are of great significance in public and political life. They are more flexible than rigid rules or legal constraints and have often been developed to adapt to situations where a degree of discretion is necessary. The idea of convention belongs to the nineteenth century tradition of government through an organic and like-minded establishment, small and coherent enough to work on the basis of trust, and a new meritocratic state bureaucracy, devoted to a consensual view of the public interest and purged of nepotism. Westminster and the new Whitehall were governed, like other institutions such as the City of London, by a 'club ethic'. This ethic underwrote not only the voluntary idea of self-regulation in the 'social constitution', but the unwritten nature of the political constitution (Hirst 1995: 170–171). The interlocking elites of the establishment in government, the City, judiciary, business, the Anglican church, universities, and so on, shared common perceptions and followed broadly similar unwritten codes of conduct.

Such conventions are said to play a significant role in the protection of political rights and freedoms in the United Kingdom. They form an elite part of the 'culture of liberty' which authoritative commentators find throughout British society (see Chapter 4). They are the rules of political practice and, though 'unwritten', undoubtedly have some power to influence government. They are regarded as binding to various degrees by those to whom they apply, but they are not statutory or legal rules enforceable in the courts (Hood Phillips and Jackson 1978: 104–105). Those which are unvarying – for example, the Queen must give her assent to every bill passed by the Houses of Parliament – usually just leave unsaid a political reality which would be rendered in statutory form if it were flouted. Otherwise, the very point of conventions is that they are *not* absolute rules of behaviour, but rather flexible guides which adapt to current conditions. Such guides, like the doctrine of ministerial responsibility to Parliament, are continually being adapted (see **pp. 45–46** above; also Woodhouse 1994).

It is not necessary to enumerate all the constitutional conventions here. However, one convention was recently advanced which is of particular significance to the protection of human rights:

> Once a new form of individual constitutional empowerment is introduced it cannot be reversed. This has been the characteristic feature of the development of rights in the United Kingdom. Once embodied in statute, a civil right is rarely, if ever, reversed.
>
> (Patten 1993: 28–29)

According to this convention, it is claimed, certain statutes, formally no different from any others, have special constitutional status. These include Magna Carta 1215, the Habeas Corpus Act 1641, the Bill of Rights 1688, the Act of Settlement 1700 (which provided for succession to the throne), the Act of Union with Scotland 1707, the Parliament Acts 1911 and 1949, which restricted the powers of the House of Lords, and the 'immutable' right to jury trial. There are other significant conventions which bear upon human rights, such as the presumption against retrospective legislation and government respect for the independence of the judiciary.

The fading powers of political convention

This wider establishment club described above no longer exists. Since the late 1960s at least, social, economic and political turbulences have shaken established institutions in this country to their foundations. Britain's politicians now operate within European, and global, constraints, just as the City and industry are now exposed to global markets. Those in command have changed and the *mores* of Britain's institutions have changed with them. They are no longer governed by a common code of ethics, and traditional 'club' conventions have lost much of their force.

It is always wise to be sceptical of accounts of golden ages in any sphere of life. However, a change in attitudes may be discerned, for example, in Home Secretary Jim Callaghan's cynical postponement of disadvantageous boundary changes in advance of the 1970 general election and in the 1970s Conservative reorganisation of local government in which partisan political advantage was covertly one of the guiding aims. However, lack of respect for conventions became pronounced under recent Conservative governments, which have tended to the view that if rules are not written down, they need not apply. The most dramatic example of this attitude being probably the humbling of local government, which took place even though, as the Widdicombe report on local authority business (Cmnd 9797, HMSO 1986: 45) emphasised, 'the sovereignty of Parliament [over local government] is underpinned by a corpus of custom and convention as to the manner in which that sovereignty should be exercised' (see also Jenkins 1995; Young 1990; Gilmour 1992). The point is that when it comes to conflict between the political needs of the day and the protections offered by convention alone, convention is the likely loser.

If it ever existed, 'Patten's law' (**p. 69**) does so no longer. *Habeas corpus*, a civil right long embedded in statute, could scarcely have been reversed, but it has certainly been reduced in the modern era of emergency terrorist legislation, indefinite detention of the mentally ill (under the now reformed Mental Health Act 1959), and expanded police powers. As we have seen, the European Court is readier than politicians observing political convention to provide protection against arbitrary or indefinite detention (Chapter 13). Similarly, the 'immutable' right to elect jury trial, first articulated in Magna Carta 1215, has proved a moveable feast, having been recently withdrawn for serious offences (not limited to those which bear upon terrorism) in the 'Diplock courts' in Northern Ireland and a host of 'lesser' criminal cases throughout the UK. The Immigration Act 1968 removed rights to residence from thousands of UK citizens; the Nationality Act 1981 abolished the right to British citizenship of those born on British soil – a right which could be traced back to the middle ages. Other conventions of significance, such as the independence of the judiciary, seem to be under challenge from the government – witness the conflict between Home Secretary Michael Howard and the judiciary in 1994–96.

Patten's argument loses yet more persuasive force when it is recalled that the distinguishing feature of the UK approach to human rights is that many 'civil rights' [his phrase] are not precisely inscribed in law. Of the rights audited in this book, no statutes exist which protect general rights to freedoms of expression, assembly and association, privacy, and equality (apart from the limited anti-discrimination laws; see Chapters 7 and 9–12).

As for Parliament's role, ministers have been increasingly unwilling to observe the conventions of ministerial responsibility. This is evident enough in the common reluctance of ministers to resign in circumstances which may well have demanded resignation in the immediate postwar period. But the convention of openness in ministers' dealings with Parliament, enshrined in paragraph 27 of their code of .conduct, has been dishonoured in continual breaches and deceits, the most recent of which have been chronicled at length in the Scott report and inquiry hearings (*Report of the Inquiry into the Export of Defence Equipment and Dual-Use Goods to Iraq and Related Prosecutions*, February 1996, HMSO; Norton-Taylor 1995).

Parliamentarians are often unfairly traduced. But A.V. Dicey's confidence in the 'internal' limits to which parliamentary sovereignty was subject no longer seems convincing (Heuston 1979: 2). MPs as a whole are still 'not usually men of outrageous view': yet no one now could possibly entrust their democratic rights to their good sense, respect for convention, knowledge of the UK's human rights obligations and ability to scrutinise legislation, primary and delegated, and to control the executive. The structures of Parliament are failing MPs, and they are failing the people.

Political and civil rights in Northern Ireland

The government of Northern Ireland raises particular issues for the protection of political and civil rights under the parliamentary umbrella in the United Kingdom. From 1920 to 1972, Westminster gave devolved powers to a Parliament at Stormont, in Belfast, to legislate for the peace, order and good government of Northern Ireland on 'transferred' matters, while retaining control of 'excepted' or 'reserved' matters. Excepted matters were issues of national concern. Reserved matters were to be the preserve of the all-Ireland institutions (which never came into existence). Transferred matters concerned affairs which were other than excepted or reserved – in practice, largely domestic and social affairs, including public order.

In 1972, the Stormont Parliament was suspended. The Northern Ireland Constitutional Act 1973 now provides for direct rule from Westminster. Within this framework, all formerly 'transferred' or 'reserved' matters – with the exception of fair employment legislation – are made by Order in Council: a delegated legislation process, which effectively by-passes the stages that a public bill would go through (see above **pp. 45ff.**). From 1974 to 1991, some 399 Orders in Council were made, covering matters such as criminal law, housing, education, employment and training, social security and sex discrimination. Excepted matters are dealt with by ordinary legislation.

The democratic deficit in Northern Ireland

Northern Ireland has been ruled directly from Westminster since 1972. Much of the process of parliamentary scrutiny, outlined above, applies equally in the province. However, there are a number of particular concerns. Legislation by Order in Council allows for even less effective scrutiny than the ordinary legislative process. The draft Orders laid before Parliament cannot be amended at all and must be accepted or rejected in their entirety. Generally, these Orders are made under the 'affirmative procedure', which obliges the government to allow brief parliamentary time to debate them. The only special provision for Orders applying to Northern Ireland is that an extra hour may be added for their examination, and they occasionally go before the Northern Ireland Committee (Livingstone and Morison 1995: 15–16).

In such circumstances, external advice to the government assumes great importance, especially on the effect of Orders in Council on human rights. In 1973, the government recognised the demand for additional safeguards in Northern Ireland and established the Standing Advisory Commission on Human Rights to advise the Northern Ireland Secretary on the human rights implications of government Orders and policies. The Commission has been an alert and vigorous body. Its report on religious discrimination in employment, for example, influenced the government's decision to introduce the Fair Employment Act 1989, which greatly strengthened anti-discrimination law in this area – though pressure from the US government was probably decisive (Livingstone and Morison 1995: 20).

Another report which was influential but did not sway government was the Commission's 1977 report on a Bill of Rights for Northern Ireland, published after two years' study. The report considered how far existing legislation provided adequate protection for human rights, noting that while

> Parliament must necessarily remain at the centre of our constitutional arrangements ... human rights cannot be always protected by the parliamentary process [and] ... there is a need for human rights to be given further protection in Northern Ireland.

The Commission took the view that all people living in the United Kingdom should so far as possible share the same fundamental rights and freedoms, regardless of the place in which they reside, and recommended incorporation of the European Convention on Human Rights into the domestic law of the United Kingdom (Cmnd 7009, 1977: 75–76). The Commission has subsequently reiterated its support for incorporation and a Bill of Rights for Northern Ireland (SACHR, 17th Report 1992–93, 1992: 3).

The Commission has repeatedly drawn to the government's attention legislative and administrative provisions which it considers violate international human rights standards. Here we give several examples. In 1989, the Commission advised the government that the restriction of the right to silence in Northern Ireland might breach Article 14 of the International Covenant, which guarantees fair trial. In 1990, it advised that the absence of legislation against racial discrimination in Northern Ireland might violate the United Kingdom's obligations under Article 26 of the International Covenant. In 1991, it warned government that the power to arrest suspected terrorists and to question them for up to seven days (under what is now section 14 of the Prevention of Terrorism (Temporary Provisions) Act 1989) violates both Article 5 of the European Convention and Article 9(3) of the International Covenant, and advised government – just as the UN Human Rights Committee (HRC) more recently did in 1995 – that derogation was both unnecessary and undesirable (SACHR, 16th report, 1991: 81–83; HRC, CCPR/C/79/Add. 55, 1995: para. 22). The Commission greatly angered government by filing evidence and submissions, challenging its policies, before the European Commission and the UN Human Rights Committee.

The Commission has long expressed strong concerns about legislation by Order in Council, stating in 1993, for example, that 'without the opportunity for detailed discussion and amendment of the proposed legislation, [the process] is inherently unsatisfactory ... in short, there is a democratic deficit' (SACHR, 18th report, 1993: 7–8).

Overall, the wide range of issues highlighted in the Commission's annual reports reveals fundamental flaws in the ability of the legislative procedure in Northern Ireland adequately to protect political and civil rights. Yet none of the provisions which the Commission has complained about have been repealed or modified on account of its advice or interventions. This is a watch-dog that barks, but government generally ignores its warnings, and on occasion treats it with contempt. The government failed to consult the Commission over such significant decisions as the restriction of the right to silence and the introduction of the 'broadcasting voice ban' (for the ban, see **pp. 183–184**).

The Commission protested that

> The Commission is established by law to advise the Secretary of State on matters relating to human rights in Northern Ireland. This function cannot properly be carried out if new legislation with significant human rights implications is introduced without prior consultation.
>
> (14th report, 1989: 7)

But as the government is not under a duty to consult it, the Commission has to make do with promises of better behaviour in the future. The Commission also declared its concern over well-substantiated reports that the government had deliberately chosen to restrict the right to silence by Order to avoid 'the need for detailed discussion and possible amendment'. It recommended that in future legislation affecting human rights in Northern Ireland should be introduced and processed in the same way as for the rest of the United Kingdom and that all interested parties should be properly consulted in that process.

4   The 'Culture of Liberty'

Political culture

The protection of political values

Apart from the formal political and legal checks upon government, political rights and freedoms in the United Kingdom are said to be further protected by 'the force of public opinion', which the authoritative *Halsbury's Statutes of England* cites as a main protection of 'the liberties of the subject' (1992, vol. 8: 729). These arguments frequently acknowledge the reality of a government's dominance over Parliament. For example, a prominent political scientist, Philip Norton, writing for the Conservative Research Centre in 1992, declared that a government, backed by a parliamentary majority, can basically obtain legislative sanction for whatever it wants:

> Yet government in this country is constrained . . . by a number of checks and balances . . . that are not confined to bodies that enjoy political muscle. Government is constrained by values that are pervasive at both mass and elite levels.
>
> (Norton 1992: 7)

In similar vein, John Patten MP has argued that a written constitution is unnecessary in the United Kingdom because 'Our liberties are firmly entrenched in, and by, our political culture, improved through rolling constitutional change. It is this culture that provides the most effective form of constitutional protection for our liberal and relaxed community, the best way to guarantee our civil liberties' (Patten 1991: 6).

A culture of liberty is, indeed, the basic safeguard of popular liberties. The indigenous culture of liberty is said to encompass not only 'the force of public opinion', but also such intangible, but nevertheless real, features such as the idea of the 'free-born Englishman', the 'weight of history' and 'the British way of doing things'.

Britain was a liberal state long before it became democratic, and the tradition of liberty predates the popular franchise. Writing in the 1830s, the political theorist Alexis de Tocqueville drew attention to the idea of liberty being entrenched in political culture, stating that in the United States and England, there seemed to be 'more liberty in the customs than in the laws of the people', whereas in Switzerland liberty resided 'more in the laws'. In a celebrated aside, he added, 'it is impossible to think of the English as living under any but a free government'.

But it is not difficult to find contemporary praise for the quality of liberty in British society. Perhaps the most authoritative recent tribute was contained in the report of the UN Human Rights Committee, which simultaneously found the British system for protecting democratic rights to be defective and British society democratic:

> The detailed information submitted by a wide range of non-governmental organisations has not only greatly assisted the Committee, but it is also a tribute to the democratic nature of United Kingdom society. These organisations play an essential role in furthering protection of human rights in the country.
>
> (CCPR/C/79/Add. 55, para. 3)

Thus, by means of shared values and expectations, unwritten though they be, politicians, bureaucrats and the public share a historic respect for civil liberties in the United Kingdom. In modern Britain, a host of pressure groups and associations, with widely varying concerns and perspectives – Amnesty, the British Institute of Human Rights, Charter 88, Justice, the Law Society, Liberty, Mind, the National Association of Probation Officers, Statewatch, to name but a few – actively seek to protect and promote political and civil rights. There is a strong liberal element in the legal profession; trade unions actively defend and assert workers' and trade union rights; the media take an active interest in issues of civil liberties and investigative journalists in television and the press frequently uncover abuses (for example, they played a significant part in bringing serious miscarriages of justice in the criminal justice system to public light).

AUDIT

'The force of public opinion'

No one should doubt the basic value to political rights and freedoms of a public culture of liberty. But we are asked to accept that, in the United Kingdom, this public (and elite) culture makes unnecessary auxiliary precautions, such as a Bill of Rights or written constitution. Here, we examine the evidence of the recent past to consider how far 'the force of public opinion' has acted as a major check on inroads by government or the state into the liberties of citizens and inquire into the quality of public opinion as a solid bulwark of such liberties.

It is possible to discern the force of public opinion at work in politics. The most remarkable example was the popular revolt against the poll tax, which contributed to the downfall of a Prime Minister and led to its removal from the statute book. Ministers and political parties constantly check on the state of public opinion in framing policies and taking decisions. It is common wisdom, for example, that the NHS and education services are partially 'protected' by public opinion. But it is hard to identify a single recent instance since the 1939–45 war, when basic civil liberties, which were genuinely under threat, were protected by the culture of liberty.

Yet it is possible to identify occasions when the 'force of public opinion' has proved a poor ally of human rights. In fact, public opinion is more readily advanced as an argument for curtailing and invading the rights and freedoms of individual citizens and minorities than for protecting them. In 1974, Lord Scarman argued the case for constitutional restraint on legislative power to protect individual citizens 'from instant legislation, conceived in fear and prejudice and enacted in breach of human rights' (Scarman 1974: 20). He cited the notorious detention powers which the wartime government assumed by Defence Regulation 18B and the 'retrospective effect' of the Immigration Act 1971, as two examples. Recent history also provides many examples of legislation designed either to placate public 'fear and prejudice', or to exploit it. Such legislation affecting civil liberties is subject to the same legislative procedures as bills on dangerous dogs or street lighting.

Sometimes the parliamentary parties combine in panic and legislation receives even more cursory treatment. The Commonwealth Immigrants Act 1968, for example, was inspired by popular – and elite – panic over the prospect of a mass exodus of Kenyan Asians to this country. The political parties and both Houses united to pander to what they saw as public hysteria and the Act passed through all its legislative stages in three days. The Official Secrets Act 1911 took a day to achieve its parliamentary progress. Not a single MP spoke on the notorious section 2 which managed to 'create more than 2,000 different offences in a few statutory paragraphs' (Robertson and Nicol 1992: 415).

More recently, the Prevention of Terrorism Act was introduced into Parliament by Roy Jenkins, a liberal Home Secretary, in response to the Birmingham pub bombings in 1974 and took just two days to reach the statute book. Jenkins was fully aware of the 'encroachment – limited but real – on the liberties of individual citizens' (HC Deb, 27 November 1974, c634). But was it really required to combat terrorism, or was its real purpose quite different? Sir Robert Mark, former head of the Metropolitan Police, commented in his memoirs that the police were indifferent to the Act and believed it was 'essentially a propaganda measure'; Jenkins, he wrote, 'felt a need to reassure the public of the willingness of the government to take firm measures in the face of Irish terrorism' (Mark 1978: 174). Whatever Jenkins's motive, the PTAs have been renewed and kept in force by Parliament without major protest ever since, in spite of growing doubts about their efficacy.

The varying strands of public opinion

There is no single force of public opinion, just as there is no single public. British society was by no means homogeneous in the time of A.V. Dicey; it is now far more heterogeneous both in composition and interests, and notably so in terms of minorities and differences (for example, ethnic, gender, sexual) which raise modern human rights issues. Richard Crossman, the former Labour minister, crudely distinguished two publics in the wake of 'the real revolt of the masses' which a controversial speech on race and immigration by Enoch Powell conjured up in April 1968. On the one hand, there were the dockers marching and demonstrating against the Race Relations bill outside the Palace of Westminster – 'the illiterate industrial proletariat who have turned up and revolted against the literate'. On the other hand, there was a well-informed and respectable public opinion, which was in favour of the bill:

It's the same problem we've had with the abolition of capital punishment, the repeal of the law against homosexuality and all the other liberal causes where a minority of the well-informed public has leapt well ahead and dragged mass opinion resentfully behind it.

(Crossman 1977: 29–30)

This is a brutally simplistic model, typical of its author. Yet it is possible to discern the influence of the 'well-informed public' and its skilful pressure groups in the 1960s, as it secured limited social and human rights advances. A similar public exists today – known scornfully in some circles as 'the chattering classes'; so do many progressive pressure groups, like those praised by the UN Human Rights Committee. The formation of Charter 88 in November 1988, with the backing of more than a hundred scholars, lawyers, actors, pop stars, scientists, and so on, was in direct response to the perception that liberties were in danger. The rebirth of Liberty (formerly the National Council for Civil Liberties) is another sign of concern among the 'well-informed public'. However, the influence of this public, though hardly spent, has proved unable to prevent further violations of political and civil rights in the 1980s and early 1990s (see Part 3). Attitudes in society and politics have apparently changed from 'permissive' to 'populist anti-reformism' (McConville and Bridges 1994).

Crossman's own example – homosexual law reform – shows how complex the inter-relationship between public opinions and government action on human rights actually is. The original 1967 act applied only to England and Wales. 'Well-informed' groups put governments under constant pressure to extend the reform to Scotland and Northern Ireland, but were opposed by influential forces, largely religious, in both societies. It was not until 1980 that homosexual acts between consenting adult males became lawful in Scotland. It took a European Court judgment to force the government to extend reform to Northern Ireland in 1982 (*Dudgeon v UK*, 1981). In 1976, the Labour government began cautiously to explore attitudes towards reform in Northern Ireland, but a sizeable and well-organised minority, led by Roman Catholics and Presbyterians, complained that it would lower moral standards. The NI Standing Advisory Commission on Human Rights, gay organisations and other groups were in favour. An opinion poll suggested that the general public was evenly divided. In 1979, the (now Conservative) Northern Ireland Secretary bowed to organised pressure and withdrew a draft order introducing reform. (The question of compliance with the Convention was never raised in parliamentary debates on the issue.) Since 1982, the government has forbidden local authorities to promote homosexuality in schools; Parliament has refused (on a free vote) to equalise the age of consent for heterosexual and homosexual relations; and the armed forces have continued to expel gays and lesbians (see Chapter 7).

As for other minorities, skilled and expert pressure groups campaigned passionately for reform of oppressive prison rules and legal rights of appeal against detention for mentally disordered offenders. They won converts in both Houses and warned governments that they were in violation of the Convention. But they failed to bring about the reforms which the European Court finally obliged the UK government to introduce in the wake of adverse findings. If the force of public opinion is in play, it seems that it is not on behalf of the human rights of minorities, but against them.

The shift towards 'populist anti-reformism'

All the evidence suggests that public opinion is not set in concrete, but is a product of a variety of long-term attitudes and shorter-term reactions to events and argument. For example, the *British Social Attitudes* (BSA) surveys measure two sets of underlying value dimensions – left–right and libertarian–authoritarian – both of which have an obvious influence on attitudes towards democratic rights (Heath *et al.*, 1986). Two successive BSA surveys, in 1990 and 1994, provide short-term evidence that British society became 'less libertarian' during the 1990s, especially in attitudes towards crime and punishment (reported in Brook and Cape 1995: 204).

This shift in attitudes is closely linked to political and legislative changes. Up to 1991, there was a broad political consensus on 'law and order' issues and a decade of liberal advances in, for example, the treatment of young offenders. The consensus broke down dramatically as the government took a decidedly 'tougher' attitude. Three Criminal Justice Acts were passed in 1991, 1993 and 1994. The Bail (Amendment) Act was enacted in 1993, the Drug Trafficking Act and the Police and Magistrates' Court Act in 1994. This may not seem surprising in view of the political background described thus in a leader in *The Times*:

> . . . a wave of disquiet about crime . . . The litany of horrific cases – from the death of James Bulger to the sickening torture of Suzanne Capper – has helped to keep the fear of crime consistently high in the list of public concerns.
>
> (18 December 1993)

However, the litany of high-profile cases of miscarriages of justice – such as the Birmingham Six, the Tottenham Three, Stefan Kizsko, and Judith Ward – may well have swayed people against tilting the balance in favour of the police and eroding the rights of defendants. The *British Social Attitudes* polls show that they didn't.

The attitudes of politicians and the media clearly influence public opinion, though it is not possible to assess the degree of that influence – nor how far public attitudes influence politicians and newspapers rather than the other way round. Some observers believe that the breakdown of the 'law and order' consensus was inspired by politically-led moves towards 'populist anti-reformism' (McConville and Bridges 1994). *The Times* editorial, noted above, held that disquiet about crime was 'borne upon a tide of government unpopularity'.

Crossman, writing on the discontents inspired by Powell in 1968, compared the British constitution to a rock,

> against which the wave of popular emotion breaks, and one hopes that after a time the tide will go down and the rock stand untouched. This is the strength of our system that, though in one sense we have plebiscitary demo-

cracy, actually the leadership is insulated from the masses by the existence
of Parliament. Parliament is the buffer which enables our leadership to avoid
saying yes or no to the electorate in the hope that, given time, the situation
can be eased away.

(Crossman 1977: 30)

In other words, Parliament's strength as a pillar of civil liberties depends not, as
A.V. Dicey and others have claimed, on its ability to represent a public steeped in
the culture of liberty, but rather the reverse – in its ability to deny the public what
it wants. In this spirit, the official Conservative opposition of the time changed its
attitude towards the Race Relations Bill, about which Lord Hailsham and others
had misgivings, and took a bipartisan approach. Such well-meaning elitism was no
longer in fashion in the 1990s. The Prime Minister and his Home Secretary declared
their contempt for a well-informed approach to combating crime, for example, and
placed their faith in often expressive legislation, most notably the Criminal Justice
and Public Order Act 1994. It is widely believed that the CJPO bill was designed
to exploit for electoral purposes fear of crime and 'moral panics' (about 'raves',
young offenders, 'bail bandits', 'new age travellers', etc). The way the measure was
first publicly introduced – 'a 27-point plan to crack down on crime' – lends weight
to this belief. The Home Secretary did not present it in Parliament, but in a populist
speech to the Conservative Party conference in October 1993. However fervently
he personally believed that the balance of criminal justice had for 30 years 'been
tilted too far in favour of the criminal', he clearly intended to restore the pro-
Conservative tilt of the political balance on 'law and order' issues. For the Labour
opposition had adjusted its own stance to the prevailing public mood, encapsulated
in its slogan, 'Tough on crime, tough on the causes of crime'. It seems that the
government and opposition parties both calculate in the 1990s on Scarman's 'fear
and prejudice' among the public.

The BSA surveys show that around three people in five (58 per cent) still believe
in the principle that an accused person is 'innocent until proved guilty'. But the
majority who think it worse to risk convicting an innocent person than to acquit a
guilty one has fallen from two-thirds (67 per cent) in 1985. Rather more now think
it worse to risk letting the guilty go free (24 per cent now; 20 in 1985) and many
more are ambivalent (18 as against 12 per cent). Opinion surveys suggest that politicians have influenced public opinion on the associated issue of a defendant's right
to silence. For example, the Rowntree Reform Trust's *State of the Nation* surveys,
carried out by MORI, reveal that, in 1991, 40 per cent believed that a defendant's
right to silence should be protected in a Bill of Rights (17 per cent said it should
be excluded); by 1995, the public was almost evenly divided, 32 to 29 per cent for
inclusion and exclusion. The BSA surveys show that public support for the right to
silence fell sharply from 42 per cent in 1990 to 31 in 1994 (Brook and Cape 1995:
193).

The 1995 *British Social Attitudes* survey also shows that large majorities of people
support police surveillance of suspects, with or without a criminal record, on the
thinnest possible evidence (an anonymous tip). A growing minority (46 per cent now;

37 per cent in 1985) believe that the police should be allowed, without a court order, to tap the suspect's telephone. In 1990, the BSA surveys found 'impressive majorities' in favour of people's rights to engage in three forms of peaceful protest – by way of public meetings, pamphlets, marches and demonstrations – against 'a government action they strongly oppose'. In 1994, 'none of these three rights of protest . . . now attracts the wholehearted support of the British public'. On a more positive note, the principle of anti-discrimination laws for ethnic minorities now captures the support of between two-thirds and three-quarters of the population, even though only one in four want the existing law to be implemented 'more strictly' (Brook and Cape 1995: 196, 199 and 202).

The need for knowledge and understanding

A culture of liberty presumes a public who know and understand their rights. The absence of parliamentary debate when the European Convention and International Covenant were signed and the neglect of the United Kingdom's reports to human rights monitoring bodies point to a political culture which fails to take seriously the need to inform the public. And the government's orchestrated campaign of protest, with ministers, MPs and a xenophobic tabloid press shamelessly rubbishing the European Court's decision in the case of the Gibraltar killings (*McCann and Others v UK*, ECtHR, September 1995), suggests that this culture may yet become more devalued still.

There is also a related but different problem: the extent to which ordinary citizens are able to discern what the law and their rights actually are. Over 150 years ago, Jeremy Bentham complained that the common law was largely unfathomable to lay people and statute law too voluminous, chaotic and technical. Some years later, the Criminal Code Commissioners found similarly that 'the elasticity so often spoken of as a valuable quality [of the common law] would, if it existed, be only another name for uncertainty' (Cmnd 2345, 1879). Lord Jenkins, as Home Secretary, made the same complaint in 1967: 'There are too many archaic principles that have been handed down from precedent to precedent . . . as a result, much of our criminal law is in many areas obscure, confused and uncertain' (Labour Party Conference). The Law Commission has consistently advocated codifying the criminal law to make it accessible, comprehensive and certain, and has prepared a draft code for Parliament. The government so far has taken no notice.

In 1994, Andrew Puddephatt, then general secretary of the civil rights body, Liberty, broadened the complaints, arguing that the absence of a human rights code inscribed in law created another area of damaging uncertainty. He listed three important consequences for a culture of liberty:

> Firstly, as positive rights are not enshrined in the law they cannot be invoked to protect individuals from abuses. The constraints exist but not the counterbalancing rights. Secondly, the boundaries of rights are uncertain and unknown: because they are not written down they are more likely to

be vague, open to interpretation and vulnerable to the exercise of official discretion. Thirdly, such vague and unclear rules cannot represent something that we can respect and fight for, they cannot be taught in schools, or indeed be part of our culture.

(Wadham 1994: xiv)

There is no sign that those who argue the value of a culture of liberty invest much more than rhetoric in its support. Scarcely any effort is made to enlighten the public about their rights. Civil liberties form no part of the national curriculum in schools. Even when major legislation affecting fundamental rights is introduced, little is done to explain the law. Compare and contrast, for example, government expenditure explaining the rights of suspects following the introduction of the Police and Criminal Evidence Act 1984 with its promotion of privatisation share offers. Between 1985 and 1988 the government spent a total of £50,300 on people's rights under the 1984 act as opposed, for example, to £40 million on gas privatisation in 1986 and £86 million on British Telecom flotations in 1984, 1991 and 1993 (HC Deb, WA, 1 December 1993, c626–627; WA 29 November 1993, c334). Similarly, despite UN recommendations that governments take positive steps to ensure that all the electorate have the right to vote and growing concern about the four million or so potential British voters who fail to register, it is estimated that the United Kingdom spends only 1.2p per elector on the national promotion of voter registration (Blackburn 1993: 79).

The net result of such neglect is evident in public responses to the Rowntree Reform Trust's *State of the Nation* surveys. They reveal that the majority of adults in Britain know very little about their rights. Asked in 1995 to estimate how much they knew about their rights as citizens, 6 per cent replied that they knew 'a great deal' and 37 per cent 'a fair amount'; but over half – 55 per cent – said they knew 'just a little' or 'hardly anything at all' (Rowntree 1995: 4). As for the British constitution, 69 per cent considered that they knew 'just a little' or 'hardly anything at all'. Such results hardly reflect a well-informed public capable of routinely and effectively protecting their own political and civil rights, let alone recognising the importance of protecting those of others.

Our judgment is that the complexity of the law, coupled with a general failure to promote human rights in the United Kingdom, raises important questions of compliance with international human rights standards. The UN Human Rights Committee has emphasised that implementation does not depend solely on constitutional or legislative measures which in themselves are often not sufficient. The Committee enjoins signatory states to undertake further 'specific activities . . to enable individuals to enjoy their rights', adding that as part of this process,

it is very important that individuals should know their rights under the Covenant . . . and also that all administrative and judicial authorities should be aware of the obligations which the State party has assumed under the Covenant.

(General Comment 3/13, 28 July 1991)

The United Kingdom has some way to go before it can claim to have achieved these objectives.

Conclusions

Even A.V. Dicey, who promoted the idea that the culture of liberty acted as a restraint on the abuse of civil liberties, found it hard to provide a convincing explanation of how it actually worked, when pushed on the subject. To the question, 'Why did Parliament not command that all blue-eyed babies be killed?', Dicey gave the still conventional reply that parliamentary sovereignty was subject to both internal (conventional) and external (cultural) limits. The internal limit is the fact that Members of Parliament 'are not usually men of outrageous view': the external, the possibility that 'the English electorate would not obey such a statute' (Heuston 1979: 2).

The poll tax controversies in Scotland, and then England and Wales, showed that sections at least of the electorate were prepared not to obey a statute to which they objected. Blue-eyed babies would no doubt be safe in modern Britain. Fundamental democratic rights – like, for example, the right to vote – are probably equally safe. But for most people modern human rights issues are 'somewhat abstract and hypothetical', as Brook and Cape argued in the 1991 *British Social Attitudes* survey:

> Those who are not directly affected may believe that the checks and balances are acceptable, and that 'ordinary people' are able to get on with their day-to-day-lives with no discernible infringement by the state upon their rights as citizens; some encroachment on minority rights is therefore acceptable if it leads to a more stable society.
>
> (Brook and Cape 1991: 182–183)

This it seems to us sets out the fundamental flaw in relying upon 'the culture of liberty' alone for the protection of democratic and civil rights. Constitutional and legal provisions have frequently proved inadequate in the absence of public support for human rights. But they are necessary precautions, especially in a highly-competitive political environment coloured, as British politics are today, by 'populist anti-reformism' and 'the race card'.

5   The Criminal Justice and Public Order Act 1994

Test case

The passing of the Criminal Justice and Public Order Bill 1994 provides a useful test case for analysis of the role of Parliament and public opinion as defenders of civil liberties in the United Kingdom. The resultant Act so severely restricted the 'right to silence' that the UN Human Rights Committee, the adjudicatory authority for the International Covenant on Civil and Political Rights, found that it violated 'various' fair trial provisions in Article 14 of the Covenant. In doing so, the Act also broke 'Patten's law' about the respect shown by convention for long-established rights (**pp. 69–70**); for centuries, the right to silence had been regarded as the cornerstone of criminal justice in this country, based as it is on the presumption of innocence. As John Fraser MP said in committee stage on the bill:

> If we had a written constitution, the right to silence would be part of it. It is a right which has found its way into the constitutions of countries where the British legal system has been copied.
>
> (HC SCB – the House of Commons Official
> Report of Standing Committee B, Criminal Justice
> and Public Order Bill, 1 February 1994, c388)

The Act also imposed new restrictions on the granting of bail, expanded police powers to ban public assemblies and crack down on 'raves' and travellers, set up a national DNA bank data-base and created new police powers to take intimate body samples, tightened sentencing policy and introduced several new offences of trespass.

The government's attitude towards amendments

Throughout all stages in Parliament, opposition MPs and peers expressed concern about the erosion of the right to silence and moved numerous amendments, frequently praying in aid the findings and conclusions of the Royal Commission on Criminal Justice, which recommended that 'adverse inferences should not be drawn from silence at the police station' (Cmnd 2263, July 1993: 54). However, on every occasion, the government simply out-voted any dissent – for example, defeating an amendment requiring that suspects should have had the opportunity of legal advice before their silence could be taken into account in court. Indeed, it is clear that the government was unwilling to accept amendments to the bill, whether from the two opposition parties or eminent law lords, on any of its wide range of proposals.

The bill's passage

There was a single, significant exception. The Lord Chief Justice, Lord Taylor of Gosforth, secured two important amendments to the government's original proposals modifying the right to silence. In a legal lecture, Lord Taylor condemned the provision that an accused who has remained silent should be called on by the court to give evidence as 'an unnecessary piece of ritual' which was likely to produce 'undesirable and unfair results'. The government removed the provision in the Commons. In a detailed speech during committee in the Lords, Lord Taylor asked the government to change by report stage the key clause 34, providing for suspects to be cautioned before their silence could be taken into consideration. Taylor accepted that the caution could be given when people were being questioned, either by police officers or others, before they were taken to a police station. Other peers, including the law lord, Lord Ackner, wanted the process to begin at the police station, to avoid the danger of 'non-verbals'. The government changed clause 34 to reflect only Lord Taylor's view. It is clear that his influence over the final shape of the proposals flowed not from his status as a peer, but from his office and role as spokesperson for the judiciary.

On the proposed refusal of bail to suspects convicted of or already charged with murder, rape and other serious crimes, the government was unable to give a single example of such people wrongly being given bail. Yet ministers steadfastly refused to give way, even to eminent critics like Lord Ackner:

> The risk has been in existence for years and years and years. Yet he [the minister] can give no example of the risk being wrongly taken. He fails in that regard, while seeking to justify interference with judicial discretion.
>
> (HL Deb, 17 May 1994, c182)

and again:

> Where the Executive seeks to interfere with the established discretion of the judiciary, it has a very heavy burden to discharge and the government have not got within miles of doing so on this occasion.
>
> (HL Deb, 15 July 1994, c1234)

Table 5.1 sets out the success rate for amendments in four key areas of the bill, where we took the view that political rights and freedoms under scrutiny in this audit were likely to be at issue. In the four key areas under scrutiny, the time given for debate was arbitrary and frequently brief. Members in both Houses carefully selected those amendments which they actually pressed to division. However, the government refused to accept any and they were all voted down. The House of Lords did in fact pass fundamental amendments to other provisions of the bill which may well breach international human rights standards. For example, the government's secure training units for young offenders could breach the International Covenant's standards for the detention of young offenders (see Article 10.3). None of the Lords' amendments survived the two-day recall of the Commons on 19–20 October 1994. The government majority duly reversed them all.

Table 5.1 The Criminal Justice Bill in Parliament: time for debate on key human rights clauses and amendments

	Bail	Right to silence	Freedom of assembly	Police powers
HOUSE OF COMMONS				
HC Committee Stage:	4hr 48 min	9hr 55min	9hr 51min	26min
Clauses	5	5	11	4
Pressed to division	0	4	0	0
Opposition amendments:				
Moved	3	12[1]	4	1
Withdrawn	3	6	1	1[2]
Pressed	0	6	3	0
Accepted	0	0	0	0
New opposition clauses (debate)	25min	—	—	—
Opposition new clauses:				
Moved	1	0	0	0
Accepted	0	0	0	0
Report Stage:				
HC Committee Stage considered	11min – no opposition	2hr 10min	1hr 5min	1hr 5min
Opposition amendments:				
Moved	0	2[3]	2	1
Withdrawn	0	0	0	0
Pressed	0	2	2	1
Accepted	0	0	0	0
HOUSE OF LORDS				
Committee Stage:	1hr 55min	4hr	7hr 40min	1hr 5min
Opposition and crossbench amendments:				
Moved	5	2	11	1
Withdrawn	5	2	11	0
Pressed	0	0	0	1
Accepted	0	0	0	0
Clauses voted against:	0	1	0	0
Report Stage:	1hr	2hr 40min	1hr 30min	20min
Amendments:				
Moved	5[4]	2	11	1
Withdrawn	2	1	2	2
Pressed	1	1	0	0
Accepted	0	0	0	0
HOUSE OF COMMONS				
HL amendments considered:	—	1hr	—	—
Amendments to LA	0	1	0	0
Speaker additional	0	1	0	0
Pressed	0	0	0	0
Accepted	0	0	0	0

Source: Democratic Audit analysis of Hansard Debates in both Houses and the House of Commons Committee Stage on the CJPO Bill, December 1993–October 1994

Notes:
1 The chairman added 44 further opposition amendments for debate along with those moved. One was pressed to division
2 A 'probing' amendment (i.e., one designed to explore the government's intentions) was moved and withdrawn
3 The chairman added 38 additional non-government amendments for discussion, along with government amendments
4 The amendment was to abolish one of the clauses

The bills's passage

Table 5.2 The Criminal Justice Bill in Parliament: references to Human Rights Instruments

	ECHR	ICCPR	Other
Bail (0)	0	0	0
Right to silence (5)			
Commons	4	0	1[1]
Police 'stop and search' powers (1)			
Lords	1	0	0
Freedoms of protest and assembly (5)			
Commons	4*	0	0
Lords	1	0	0
Secure training units (3)			
Commons (Government)	1*	0	0
Lords	1*	0	1*[2]
Gypsies (7)			
Lords	3	2	1[3]
Commons (Lords amendments)	1	0	0
Age of consent for male homosexuals (2)			
Commons	2*	0	0
Compensation for victims of violent crime (1)			
Commons	1*	0	0
Racially motivated attacks (1)			
Commons	1	0	0
Drug tests for prisoners (1)			
Lords (Government)	1	0	0
New offence of group defamation (1)			
Lords	1*	0	0
Blasphemy (1)			
Lords	0	1*	0
Initial references (28)	22	3	3
Responses (9)	7	1	1

Source: Democratic Audit analysis of Hansard Debates in both Houses and the House of Commons Committee Stage on the CJPO Bill, December 1993–October 1994

Notes:
* Response to original reference from one or more members
1 General reference
2 UN Convention on the Rights of the Child
3 UN Convention on the Elimination of All Forms of Racial Discrimination

The bill's passage

Parliament's role as a forum for scrutiny and amendment is thus easily negated by a government determined to have its way. The only real sanction for opponents is to seek to disrupt the government's timetable. The Lords' amendments did in fact finally delay the bill for several months. But the opposition parties in the Commons shrank from deliberately obstructing the bill, conscious that they would then be portrayed by ministers as being 'soft on crime'. As stated in Chapter 4, one of the purposes of the bill was to regain the Conservative Party's customary advantage on 'law and order' issues. Labour's tactics throughout were constrained by their desire not to be wrong-footed in the public eye. Labour remained silent while Lord Taylor publicly criticised both this bill (and the Police and Magistrates Courts Bill, which threatened to bring the police under direct political control). Labour abstained on the second reading of the Criminal Justice bill, 'adding insult to injury by claiming this as a triumph,' according to the *Observer*, 'because the Home Secretary had been caused a few moments of discomfort' (23 January 1994). (The Home Secretary had to abandon his prepared response to the second reading debate.) In the eye of this *Observer*:

> If it were not for the Lord Chief Justice and some fellow peers, measures which jeopardise judicial independence and go to the heart of the relationship between the individual and the State would be passing virtually without debate.
>
> (23 January)

Awareness of Britain's international human rights obligations

The mini-audit of the bill's passage through Parliament revealed a rather higher level of references to the provisions of the European Convention than in the period studied by the academic lawyer, David Kinley (see **p. 58**). In all debates and stages in both Houses, ministers and members between them drew attention to relevant aspects of the Convention, or discussed its relevance, on 22 occasions. Members further referred to or exchanged views on the International Covenant (three times); the UN Convention on the Rights of the Child (once); and the UN Convention on the Elimination of All Forms of Racial Discrimination (once).

MPs gave several warnings that the government's proposals to restrict the right to silence could be in breach of the Convention and drew comparisons with similar provisions under recent fraud laws. For example, Gerald Bermingham MP drew the government's attention to the case of *Saunders v UK*, challenging the restriction of the right to silence under the Companies Act 1985, which the European Commission of Human Rights had declared admissible just five weeks previously (HC, 11 January 1994, c84). A month later, on 11 February, Stephen Byers MP similarly drew attention to the case of *Murray v UK*, which challenged existing restrictions in Northern Ireland on the right to silence. This case was then to be heard in June 1995 by the European Court of Human Rights (HC SBC, 11 February 1994, c350). Ultimately, the European Court found for the government in *Murray* (judgment in *Saunders* is still outstanding). The government pressed on regardless.

International standards

Lord Lester QC twice drew ministers' attention to the relevance of the International Covenant to the repeal of the duty on local authorities to provide adequate camping sites for gypsies. He warned that, having studied the comments of the UN Human Rights Committee on Ireland's provision for gypsies, repeal might violate Article 26 of the Covenant (HL Deb, 25 October 1994, c484). His warning was ignored and Parliament enacted the provision as drafted. Mrs Edwina Currie MP cited the Convention in support of her own clause to equalise the age of consent between heterosexual and homosexual relationships.

The government was not swayed by any of the references to their international human rights obligations. However, during the Commons committee stage, David Maclean, the Home Office minister, declared that, 'There is a general over-arching requirement that all ministers, including the Home Secretary, obey the European Convention on Human Rights'. His Labour opponent, John Fraser MP, expressed doubt about the sincerity of the statement, shouting, 'Nonsense' (HC SCB, 25 January 1994, c200). The statement by Earl Ferrers, the government minister in the Lords, that 'it is just as much a miscarriage of justice when guilty people go free and untried, as when innocent people are convicted' (HL Deb, 7 July 1994, c1417), appears to bear out Fraser's view.

Complaints about parliamentary process

The Criminal Justice and Public Order Bill originally introduced in Parliament in December 1993 consisted of 117 sections and 112 pages. By the time it received royal assent, it had almost doubled in size to 172 sections and 214 pages. There were 480 government amendments, often introduced late. Very early on, Alun Michael, the Labour spokesperson on the Commons standing committee, complained, 'we have expressed anxiety about the piecemeal way in which matters seem to be reaching us' (HC SCB, 8 February 1994, c527).

In the circumstances, it is inevitable that it should be opposition members who express such concerns. So when the government moved that the standing committee should sit four times weekly for nine weeks, it was three Labour MPs – one of them, Mike O'Brien, a representative of the Police Federation – who protested. Stephen Byers MP said this timetable did not allow time for mature reflection and adequate briefing. The opposition MPs were not serviced by the civil service and relied on voluntary briefings. When a Conservative MP interjected with a taunt about Labour's links with pressure groups, Byers responded: 'Conservative members do not want to hear any arguments, because they are present to be whipped to vote in a particular way'. Ms Ann Coffey MP added that responsibility for examining a bill's clauses 'lay entirely' with opposition MPs, 'while government members remained entirely silent'. O'Brien also argued for more time for research and reflection, saying that he had been 'almost shocked by the sloppiness of consideration' by the standing committee on the previous Criminal Justice Bill. 'Repeated amendments were tabled at the last moment . . . matters were sprung on the opposition at such speed that very little time was left to consider any amendments' (HC SCB, 18 January 1994, c19–22).

There were further opposition complaints in the Lords about procedural short-comings. Lord McIntosh and Lord Harris both complained about debating 'major issues relating to the criminal law' after midnight in an inquorate House. 'There has been inadequate debate, taking place between a handful of people in a deserted chamber,' said Lord Harris; 'it is quite wrong to ask members to sit into the early hours . . . discussing matters of this degree of gravity' (HL Deb, 21 June 1994, c181–182). The government's response was that peers should speak 'a little less'. In reply, Lord Wakeham, Lord Privy Seal, echoed the sentiments of Lord Waddington, quoted earlier (**p. 64**), observing, 'There is always tension between noble lords who wish to debate important issues and their recognition of the ability of the government to achieve their business' (c182). Quite so.

The influence of public opinion

Unlike most bills, the Criminal Justice Bill was widely and hotly debated outside as well as inside Parliament. Highly respectable bodies, such as the Law Society and Justice, published comments and lobbied MPs for amendments. Some bodies, notably Liberty, attended the debates and committee stage, providing briefings on clauses and drafting potential amendments. (So sensitive were Labour members to the charge of the Conservatives that they were in the pockets of pressure groups of a leftish nature that they quoted bodies like the bar, the Law Society, the British Mountaineering Council and the Ramblers' Association, for example, in their arguments, but not Liberty.) Government ministers, MPs and peers were therefore well informed, at least in broad terms, of the issues at stake. A number of Dicey's 'independently-minded' MPs and peers did intervene to try and ensure that fundamental rights were not being eroded. The government's unwillingness to amend the bill hardly inspires confidence in Parliament's role in protecting human rights in the United Kingdom.

It is often argued that the Lords provides extra safeguards in its role as a revising chamber. The quality of debate in the Lords was high and human rights experts, like Lord Lester, law lords and other specialists contributed to the Lords debates on the bill. Yet the Lords' crucial weaknesses – the absence of democratic legitimacy and its consequent subservience to the Commons – prevented them from pressing amendments on the government when they were reversed by majority party vote in the Commons.

Overall, therefore, there is little evidence to support the argument that citizens of the United Kingdom, concerned about their civil liberties, are well served by the existing parliamentary process. Those whose rights were put most at risk by the 1994 bill were those who, almost by definition, could not command a majority in Parliament. In a very real sense, the government had turned the parliamentary 'watch-dog' on them.

6 How the Courts Protect Political Rights

The courts

The principle of parliamentary sovereignty requires the courts to apply any legislation which has been properly passed. Even if that legislation clearly infringes international human rights obligations, the courts are powerless to intervene. They cannot set aside or quash statutes. Yet they play an important role in the protection of the 'rule of law' and human rights in the United Kingdom.

The courts have enjoyed independence from both Parliament and the Crown (or executive) ever since James I and Sir Edward Coke, Chief Justice of the Common Pleas, met at Whitehall one Sunday morning, 10 November 1607. James wanted to take cases from the courts and decide them himself. He had been advised that the common law was based on reason and he was as well qualified to deal with reason as any judge (Heuston 1979: 32). Coke explained that while His Majesty had undoubtedly been bestowed with excellent science and great endowments of nature, cases in the courts were decided not by natural reason, but the artificial reason and judgment of the law. James reluctantly agreed to leave such cases to the judges (*Prohibitions del Roy*, 1607).

The independence of the judiciary is crucial to democracy. There is a strong, jealously guarded tradition of judicial independence from the executive and from politics in the UK. And while the British courts have a lesser role than their counterparts in constitutional courts in countries with written constitutions, they nevertheless perform three vital functions which have an important bearing on the protection of human rights.

First, the courts interpret and apply legislation, often in accordance with principles the courts have themselves developed. Few, if any, statutes are absolutely clear in their meaning and the courts' use of their powers to interpret and apply statute law can be crucial to the protection of human rights. For example, a narrow interpretation of a criminal statute will mean that fewer citizens are likely to be affected by it. A consistent approach to the interpretation of similar statutes assists citizens in knowing what their rights are.

Second, though Parliament confers multitudes of powers on ministers, public bodies and officials, their decisions and acts in the exercise of these powers are not *supreme*. They may be challenged in the courts, usually by way of judicial review proceedings in the High Court. The marked expansion in the number and scope of such cases from 491 cases in 1980 to 2,439 in 1992, and the judiciary's growing readiness to overturn executive decisions and call ministers to account, is a renewed sign of the judiciary's independence; as Hugo Young wrote in 1992, 'For Thatcherite Whitehall, the judges were a curse' (*Guardian*, 30 April). The expansion of judicial review has also inspired a new confidence in the ability of the courts to protect human rights by this means. Higher courts judges, such as Lord Browne-Wilkinson, Mr Justice Sedley and Mr Justice Laws, have openly acknowledged their capacity to act as custodians of fundamental rights and advocated further expansion of this role. Even government ministers, not now immune to challenge themselves, have emphasised the importance of this developing jurisprudence. Charles Wardle MP, former Home Office minister, has claimed that,

> The readiness of the citizens of the United Kingdom to seek judicial review of Government actions, and of the courts to entertain such applications . . . is an important safeguard against the unreasonable exercise of discretion by the Government.
>
> (HC Deb, 27 May 1993, c133)

The third function of the courts is to apply and develop the common law, by making individual remedies available to anyone who can show that a basic interest of theirs has been violated. We have coined the phrase 'basic interest' – in contrast to the term 'rights' – to describe an interest already recognised and protected by the courts. People frequently describe interests protected by the common law as 'rights', but throughout this book we use the term 'rights' to mean rights recognised and protected in the International Covenant on Civil and Political Rights, the European Convention on Human Rights, and other international instruments to which the United Kingdom subscribes. It is crucial to keep these concepts separate when considering the role of the common law in protecting human rights: the basic interests of individual citizens under the common law do not always coincide with their political rights and freedoms in international law.

The distinction between these *concepts* is fundamental to the question of how effectively the courts protect human rights. Unless citizens seeking the protection of the courts can show that their claim can be squeezed into the strait-jacket of judicial review (see **pp. 94–99** below), the courts will only grant a remedy if they can show that one of their 'basic interests' has been violated. If not, the courts are powerless. For example, if a police officer arrests and detains a person out of malice, the courts will be able to provide that person with an effective remedy. But if someone prevents the same person from exercising their freedom of assembly, that person has no remedy in law, no matter how unreasonable or arbitrary the intervention was, if their basic interests have not also been violated in the process. For personal liberty is a 'basic interest'. Freedom of assembly is not.

Judicial interpretation of statute law

The courts have bound themselves to apply Acts of Parliament, whatever view the judges take of their morality or justice. However, the courts do interpret all Acts of Parliament and, in doing so, they have adopted general 'presumptions', or

Interpreting statute law

principles, which, it is claimed, provide a powerful breakwater against statutory encroachment on important rights and liberties.

These presumptions work on two levels. First, the courts must decide exactly what Parliament means by the words it uses in statutes. They look first to a statute itself, and then fall back on their general presumptions. The most important for our purposes concerns the courts' approach to international human rights obligations. According to the House of Lords:

> There is a *prima facie* presumption that Parliament does not intend to act in breach of international law, including therein specific treaty obligations; and if one of the meanings which can reasonably be ascribed to the legislation is consonant with the treaty obligations and another or others are not, the meaning which is consonant is to be preferred.
>
> (*Salomon v the Commissioners of Customs and Excise*, 1967)

This rule has several times been applied to enable the courts to draw on the European Convention on Human Rights. So, for example, in 1974, the House of Lords, the supreme UK court, relied upon Article 7 of the European Convention to conclude that an ambiguous provision in the Immigration Act 1971 should be interpreted so as to avoid the introduction of retrospective penalties (*Waddington v Miah*, 1974).

Once they have decided the meaning of a statute, the courts have to determine how it is to be properly applied. The most important of the secondary presumptions to which they turn is the 'well-known . . . principle that statutes which encroach upon the rights of the subject, whether as regards person or property, are subject to a strict construction' (*AG for Canada v Hallett and Carey Ltd*, 1952). From this, three further presumptions are drawn:

- that Parliament does not intend legislation affecting individual rights to operate retrospectively
- that the courts should interpret inconclusive or ambiguous legislation in such manner as leaves private rights undisturbed
- that individuals are not to be deprived of their property without proper compensation unless Parliament has unequivocally expressed that intention.

The limits on judicial interpretation of legislation

By interpreting statutes in conformity with general notions of fairness and justice, judges can and do operate to strengthen democracy in broad terms by helping to ensure that the powers of government are applied with respect for the legitimate expectations of the governed (Allen 1994: 130). How far the political and civil rights entrenched in postwar human rights instruments can be adequately protected by the same means is less clear. For a start, the courts are obliged to apply any legislation which has passed through Parliament, even if it clearly infringes international human rights obligations. In 1975, Lord Denning, the Master of the Rolls, once briefly flirted with the idea of setting aside statutes which contravened the European

Convention, stating in a case involving the Home Secretary that 'if an Act of Parliament did not conform to the Convention, I might be inclined to hold it invalid' (*Birdie v Secretary of State for Home Affairs*, 1975). A year later he had returned to orthodoxy: that treaties do not become part of the law until made so by Parliament, and that 'if an Act of Parliament contained any provision contrary to the Convention, the Act of Parliament must prevail' (*R v Secretary of State for Home Affairs ex parte Bahjan Singh*, 1976).

In other words, judges may resolve ambiguities in statutes to minimise their impact on rights they regard as particularly important, but political and civil rights can in general be overridden by clear statutory terms or 'necessary implication'. So, for example, Lord Denning was unable in 1982 to order compensation for a worker sacked by his employers because he refused to join a trade union (*Taylor v Co-op Retail Services*, 1982). Denning examined a European Court decision in a similar case which found that the 'closed shop' violated the Convention (*Young, James and Webster v United Kingdom*, ECtHR, 1981) and concluded:

> Mr Taylor was subjected to a degree of compulsion which was contrary to the freedom guaranteed by the European Convention on Human Rights . . . He cannot recover any compensation from his employers under English law because under the Acts of 1974 and 1976, his dismissal is to be regarded as fair. But those Acts themselves are inconsistent with the freedoms guaranteed by the European Convention.

Even where an ambiguity in legislation gives judges the opportunity to bring the European Convention to bear on a decision, the extent to which they do so, the principles that they extract and the weight that they accord those principles vary widely from judge to judge. Consider, for example, the Court of Appeal's use of Article 9 of the European Convention – which protects freedom of religion – to interpret the Education Act 1944 in the case of a dismissed school teacher (*Ahmed v Inner London Education Authority*, 1978).

Ahmed, a Muslim, claimed that he was unfairly dismissed when the education authority varied his contract from five days a week to four and a half because he missed 45 minutes of teaching to attend the nearest mosque on Friday lunch-times. Section 30 of the Education Act 1944 provided that 'no teacher . . . shall . . . receive any less emolument or be deprived of or disqualified from any promotion or any other advantage by reason of . . . his religious opinion or his attending or omitting to attend religious worship'. Lord Denning read this as subject to the phrase 'so long as the timetable allows'. He dismissed Article 9 as 'drawn in such vague terms that it can be used for all sorts of unreasonable claims and provoke all sorts of litigation'. He decided that Ahmed's right to worship was subject to the rights of others, namely the education authority and 'the children he is paid to teach', and concluded: 'I see nothing in the European Convention to give Mr Ahmed any right to manifest his religion on Friday afternoons in derogation of his contract of employment, and certainly not on full pay'. He disallowed the claim. Lord Justice Scarman dissented. As far as he was concerned, 'Today . . . we have to construe and apply

Interpreting statute law

section 30 not against a background of law and society in 1944 but in a multi-racial society which has accepted international obligations and enacted statutes designed to eliminate discrimination on grounds of race, religion, colour or sex.'

The case shows that the use of the European Convention in the courts depends not so much on its precise legal status as an aid to interpretation, but on the willingness of the individual judges to take it into account – and with it, the philosophy and practice behind it (Clapham 1993: 15). Much depends on their own philosophy and practice. Similar problems arose when the Bill of Rights 1688 came to be interpreted in 1981, with equally unsatisfactory consequences for the protection of human rights. A prisoner challenged his detention in solitary confinement for months on end (*Williams v Home Office (No. 2)*, 1981). He relied upon the rule in the Bill of Rights that 'excessive baile ought not to be required nor excessive fines imposed nor cruell and unusuall punishments inflicted'. Both the European Convention and the 1973 UN *Standard Minimum Rules for the Treatment of Prisoners* were put before the judge. But he declined to read the Bill of Rights in the light of modern human right standards. Instead, he determined that the 1688 statute only prohibited punishment which was both cruel *and* unusual, not punishment which was either cruel *or* unusual.

Even where an ambiguity in wording allows judges to consider international human rights obligations, how far they may draw on instruments other than the European Convention is unclear. In theory, the International Covenant has the same status in domestic law as the European Convention. In practice, it is very infrequently cited in argument and even more rarely relied upon in judgments (see below **pp. 105–107**). Second, the government sometimes inserts 'interpretation sections' into statutes, defining the meanings of certain words and expressions for the purpose of the legislation in question, and so prevents the courts from interpreting statutes on their general principles of fairness and justice.

The exercise of judicial review

Parliament confers wide powers on government ministers, departments, local authorities, other public bodies and public officials generally to deal with the affairs of citizens in a wide variety of ways – to name but a few, housing, education, health care, immigration, deportation and extradition, social security, detention in prison, criminal justice, local bylaws and regulations. To ensure that individual officials and public bodies do not exceed their legal powers is obviously of great importance to civil liberties. In the United Kingdom, both Parliament and the courts are given the task of controlling their exercise of the powers conferred on them – Parliament, politically through the principle of ministerial responsibility (see Chapter 3); the courts, legally through proceedings for judicial review.

Unlike the position in many other countries, judicial review in the United Kingdom cannot question Parliament's ability to confer powers on the individuals or bodies concerned, nor does it include a review of the merits of the decision reached by those individuals or bodies. In fact, the only grounds on which government decisions can be controlled are the three grounds described in 1985 by Lord Diplock in the House of Lords (*Council of Civil Service Unions v Minister for the Civil Service*, 1985). These are *illegality*, *irrationality* and *procedural impropriety*:

> *Illegality* underpins the rule that a public body or official must only act for a purpose expressly or impliedly authorised by an Act of Parliament: if not, their decisions or actions are said to be *ultra vires* - 'outside their powers' – and may be quashed or set aside.

> *Irrationality* applies to a decision which is so outrageous in its defiance of logic, or of accepted moral standards, that the court considers that no sensible person who had applied his or her mind to the question in dispute, could have arrived at it. An example is where a minister allowed only four days for objections to be made to a scheme for a comprehensive school (*Lee v Department of Education and Science*, 1967). Irrationality is often known as the test of 'unreasonableness', or the *Wednesbury* principle (after the leading judicial case).

> *Procedural impropriety* covers a failure to act with procedural fairness towards people affected by the decisions or powers in question. For example, the courts overturned a watch committee's decision to dismiss a Chief Constable because the committee failed to give him the chance to put his case to them (*Ridge v Baldwin*, 1964).

These tests all recognise the supremacy of Parliament. For example, the test of illegality assumes that Parliament would not wish public bodies or officials to exceed their powers, or employ them perversely. The criterion of irrationality takes it as given that Parliament would never give them powers to act in defiance of logic or accepted moral standards.

AUDIT

The constraints on the judges' 'constitutional raid'

The ability of the courts to ensure, through judicial review, that public bodies and officials do not exceed the authority given to them by Parliament can, and some-times does, act as an effective brake on the curtailment of civil liberties in the United Kingdom. In particular, the House of Lords, acting in its judicial capacity to review ministerial powers under the Immigration Act 1971, has made it clear that 'anxious or rigorous scrutiny is involved where fundamental human rights are at stake' (*R v Secretary of State for the Home Department ex parte Bugdaycay*, 1987).

Mr Justice Sedley has described the huge postwar expansion of judicial review as a planned and executed 'constitutional raid on the fiefdoms of ministers and public authorities' (Richardson and Genn 1994: 39). Yet there are significant limitations on the role of the High Court in judicial review proceedings. Some are self-imposed. The judiciary are still very reluctant to intervene, for example, in certain areas of government activity, like national security, official secrecy and certain uses of the royal prerogative. The classic example is national security, which the courts still regard as the exclusive preserve of the executive. In January 1984, the then Prime Minister, Margaret Thatcher, had an Order in Council issued banning the staff at the Government Communications Headquarters in Cheltenham (GCHQ) from joining or belonging to trade unions. Six union members at GCHQ applied for judicial review. They claimed that she had been under a duty to act fairly by consulting the staff before issuing the Order. The House of Lords agreed, holding that the decision-making process had been conducted unfairly. But it accepted the Prime Minister's arguments that she was obliged to act as she did on grounds of national security and refused to interfere with the Order (*CCSU v Minister for the Civil Service*, 1985). Subsequently, the International Labour Organisation found that its Convention on Freedom of Association (ratified by the United Kingdom) had been violated and urged the government to reach agreement with the unions. The government declined and in 1988 dismissed the remaining trade union members at GCHQ who had not accepted re-assignment or retirement.

Similarly, several recent attempts to challenge the procedures adopted in decisions to deport people on national security grounds have all failed. The procedures clearly do not comply with normal principles of natural justice – for example, deportees are not allowed to hear and challenge the evidence against them. They may well also fail to meet the standards laid down in the European Convention and the International Covenant. But the courts have ruled that the principles of natural justice are liable to be curtailed where national security is at stake. They take the view that the Home Secretary is in a better position than the courts to decide what national security demands, and to balance its demands against those of individual rights and civil liberties. Therefore, they consistently assume that the decisions of Home Secretaries are not 'unreasonable' (*R v Secretary of State for Home Department ex parte Hosenball*, 1977; *R v Secretary of State for Home Department ex parte Cheblak*, 1991). (The security service case against Cheblak was eventually admitted to be flawed and the government finally set aside its own decision.) As one commentator has noted, 'this sort of executive prerogative, reviewable only for bad faith on the part of the Home Secretary, devalues the notion of judicial protection for rights' (Feldman 1993: 341).

Even where the courts are willing to intervene, further limitations on the effective protection of civil liberties through judicial review often arise. Judicial review examines only the procedure according to which public bodies exercise their powers, not the substantive merits of their decisions. There are obviously good reasons for this – otherwise, non-elected judges could usurp the functions of the officials and bodies to whom a democratically-elected government has delegated power. However, there is a trade-off. So long as the procedure by which a decision is made is lawful, the higher courts will not intervene, whatever the consequences for civil liberties. So, for example, when the Chief Constable of Wiltshire applied to Salisbury district council for a blanket ban on any assembly within four miles of Stonehenge over the summer solstice, the fact that law-abiding druids were prevented from celebrating the most important religious celebration of their year was not sufficient reason for the High Court to overturn or qualify the order in the absence of some procedural defect (*R v Salisbury District Council ex parte Pendragon*, 1995).

Most attempts to introduce international human rights obligations into the balance in determining the procedural requirements of fair decision-making have failed.

The most recent example was the directive issued by the former Home Secretary, Douglas Hurd, prohibiting British television and radio media from transmitting interviews with individuals who represented Sinn Fein and other particular Irish organisations who showed support for them. Lord Lester QC submitted that when a statute confers a discretion on an administrative body capable of being exercised in a way which violated the European Convention, the courts should presume that the discretion should only be exercised within the limits which the Convention imposes. Accordingly, he argued, it was for the Home Secretary to show that the broadcasting ban satisfied the Convention's three-part test (see **Box A, pp. 21–22**). Did it comply with legitimate aims under the Convention? Did his interference with free speech correspond to a pressing social need? Was it 'proportionate' to the legitimate aim pursued? In the Court of Appeal, Lord Donaldson 'unhesitatingly and unreservedly' rejected Lester's submission. In the House of Lords, Lord Bridge admitted that it possessed 'considerable persuasive force', but ultimately rejected the submission:

> When confronted with a simple choice between two possible interpretations of some specific statutory provision, the presumption whereby courts prefer that which avoids conflict between our domestic legislation and our international obligations is a mere canon of interpretation which involves no importation of international law into the domestic sphere. But where Parliament has conferred on the executive an administrative discretion without indicating the precise limits within which it must be exercised, to presume that it must be exercised within Convention limits would be to go far beyond the resolution of ambiguities. It would be to impute to Parliament an intention not only that the executive should exercise the discretion in conformity with the Convention, but also that the domestic courts should enforce that conformity by the importation into domestic administrative law of the text of the Convention and the jurisprudence of the European Court of Human Rights in the application of it.
>
> (*R v Home Secretary ex parte Brind* [1991] AC 696 at 748)

There has been substantial criticism of this reasoning and there have been some attempts to circumvent it. But it remains the binding authority of the House of Lords, the supreme UK court.

The irrationality principle, according to which courts have intervened to quash actions or decisions of public bodies which they consider extravagant, absurd or capricious, may seem to provide fertile ground for the protection of civil liberties in judicial review proceedings. But this has not been the case. According to the High Court, it may be 'unreasonable' to allow only four days for objections to be made to a scheme for a comprehensive school (see above). But it is not necessarily 'unreasonable' to impose a blanket prohibition on gay or lesbian members of the armed forces, or to fail to give international human rights obligations any weight in reaching a decision. In particular, the law lords have determinedly resisted attempts to re-fashion the irrationality principle to require public bodies or officials exercising administrative powers which curtail political rights or freedoms to justify any restriction by the strict three-part test recognised under the European Convention or International Covenant and show that it is 'necessary in a democratic society' – i.e., that it is in proportion to a legitimate aim (see **Box A, pp. 21–22**).

Judges themselves recognise the need for these tests. In the broadcasting ban case, Lord Bridge noted that Article 10(2) of the European Convention spells out and categorises the competing public interests by reference to which freedom of expression may have to be curtailed, but acknowledged that 'in exercising the powers of judicial review we have neither the advantages or the disadvantages of any comparable code to which we may refer or by which we are bound'. Lord Ackner expressed the same sentiments, but in stronger terms:

> The European test of whether the 'interference' complained of corresponds to a 'pressing social need' . . . must ultimately result in the question, 'Is the particular decision acceptable?' and this must involve a review of the merits of the decision. Unless and until Parliament incorporates the Convention into domestic law . . . there appears to me at present no basis upon which the proportionality doctrine applied by the European Court can be followed by the courts of this country.

Lord Bridge himself was keen to point out that the judicial rejection of the proportionality doctrine does not mean that the courts in judicial review proceedings are powerless to prevent infringements of civil liberties. But it is hard to argue that judicial review provides the type of scrutiny and effective remedy required by international human rights obligations. The point is demonstrated by a High Court case in 1995. Three male homosexuals and a lesbian, who were discharged from the armed forces because of their sexuality, challenged the policy of the Ministry of Defence (*R v Ministry of Defence ex parte Smith and others*, 1995). The court explicitly refused to subject that policy to the proportionality test which would be applied by the European Court – i.e., was it 'necessary in a democratic society'? Were the military authorities over-reacting? Under this test, the applicants might well have won. Instead, they lost. The court simply asked itself whether the policy was so unreasonable that no reasonable body would operate it: i.e., in the court's view it was not an *outrageous defiance of logic*. Here lies the nub of the difference: international human rights law only accepts reasonable and defensible decisions, not any decision which is not absurd. Lord Justice Simon Brown expressed 'hesitation and regret' at the outcome and added that:

> I conclude that the decision upon the future of this policy must still properly rest with others, notably the government and Parliament. But I make no secret of this: that my greatest concern in leaving the matter in this way is lest the policy's human rights dimension becomes depreciated once the court's doors are closed. There is little in the papers before us to instil confidence that the fundamental rights of these applicants and others like them will be fully and faithfully recognised elsewhere.
>
> (Queen's Bench Division, High Court, 7 June 1995)

In November 1995, the Court of Appeal refused to overturn the High Court's findings. The Court of Appeal and the High Court both noted that, in a previous case (*Vilvarajah v UK*, 1991), the European Court had held that judicial review proceedings in the UK satisfied the requirement in the Convention that there should be a national remedy to enforce the substance of the Convention in domestic courts. But both were sceptical about the prospect of the MOD policy surviving a challenge in Strasbourg – and thus also questioned the continuing validity of the *Vilvarajah* judgment.

Clearly, judicial review will develop still further. Well-placed commentators, bolstered by its rapid development since 1945, have argued that the higher courts can, and should, carve out for themselves a more robust role in the protection of civil liberties. For example, Mr Justice Laws, a recently-appointed High Court judge speaking extra-judicially, has suggested that in judicial review proceedings judges should develop a variable standard of review according to the importance of the rights in question; 'the greater the intrusion proposed by a body possessing public power over the citizen into an area where his fundamental rights are at stake, the greater must be the justification which the public authority must demonstrate' (*Laws* 1993: 59). In other words, the courts should no longer rely solely on the three traditional grounds for judicial review where basic human rights were at stake.

Other judges, most notably Mr Justice Sedley, have presented similar views in recent cases. But when Mr Justice Laws himself overturned the decision of a district health authority to withdraw funds for the medical treatment of a 10-year-old girl seriously ill with leukaemia, on the ground that a public body exercising a discretion that infringed such rights as the right to life ought not to be allowed to do so without showing substantial objective justification on public interest grounds, his decision was itself promptly overturned by the Court of Appeal (*R v Cambridge Health Authority, ex parte B*, 1995). Clearly, there is still a long way to go.

DATA

The protection of the common law

The common law grows like coral – decisions made by judges in individual court cases create precedents for later cases and, by accretion, establish a firm system over time for the protection of citizens' 'basic interests' (**p. 91**). It is often rightly described as 'judge-made law'. It is a process that has been going on since 'royal' courts were founded after 1066 and established a system of law which was common throughout the land. This law came to be called 'common' by comparison with older local laws. Gradually, criminal law sanctions and private law remedies developed to protect a variety of interests. The four basic interests which the common law came to protect are: personal (physical) integrity; property (and hence freedom of contract); reputation; and fair procedure in matters affecting the individual (see the section on judicial review, above).

The protection of the common law operates at two levels. First, the courts will provide a remedy for anyone who can show that their basic interests have been violated – either by way of compensatory damages, or by some other means, such as an injunction. Second, everyone is subject equally to the law: in Dicey's words,

Common law

'with us every official, from the prime minister down to a constable or a collector of taxes, is under the same responsibility for every act done without legal justification as any other citizen' (Dicey 1885, 1924: 189).

Inevitably, conflicts arise when the courts seek to protect people's basic interests. To resolve them in a fair and uniform way, the courts have developed principles, or 'presumptions', which are also capable of affording a degree of protection to political rights and freedoms. However, it is important to stress that these 'presumptions' are not common-law 'basic interests'. Rather they give limited protection to the legitimate expectations of citizens.

Foremost among them is 'the presumption of liberty', which can be traced back to at least 1765, when a Secretary of State, without lawful authority, issued a warrant to search the premises of a publisher, John Entick, and to seize seditious literature. In court, he sought to justify his action on the basis that the existence and exercise of such a power was necessary in the interests of state. The judge, Lord Camden, rejected his defence and set out the approach that judges should take in such cases. They should, he said,

> see if such a justification can be maintained by the text of the statutes, or by the principles of common law. If no such excuse can be found or produced, the silence of the books is an authority against the defendant.
>
> (*Entick v Carrington*, 1765)

In other words, there is a presumption of liberty in favour of the individual citizen. Those who wish to interfere with that liberty must justify it by law. From this case Dicey derived a proposition of 'residual liberty': that British citizens are free to do as they like, unless they are expressly prohibited by the law from doing so.

Failures of the common law

Insofar as the political rights and freedoms, recognised and protected in the International Covenant, the European Convention and other international human rights instruments, coincide with the basic interests recognised by the common law, they receive full and effective protection in the British courts. Freedom from arbitrary arrest provides a good example.

Personal freedom is a basic interest recognised by the common law. Citizens who are arbitrarily arrested have at least three courses of action open to them. First, they may resist arrest, if need be by the use of force. Second, they may submit to arrest, but then seek their release by applying to the High Court for an order of *habeas corpus*. Third, they may submit to arrest and detention and then, upon release, sue the arresting agency (often the police) in a civil action for damages for wrongful arrest and false imprisonment.

But where 'human rights' and 'basic interests' do not correspond, aggrieved citizens are likely to receive less effective protection, or even none at all. Suppose, for example, their privacy has been invaded. Like freedom from arbitrary arrest, personal privacy is protected in a wide variety of international human rights instruments.

But, unlike personal freedom, privacy is not a basic interest recognised by the common law. Consequently, the courts are unable to protect anyone's privacy against invasion by, say, the tabloid press, unless its invasion overlaps with one of that person's other basic interests. So if the invasion of privacy involves the seizure or release of confidential information, an intellectual property right, the courts can employ the common law to prevent unauthorised disclosure, and later can award damages. But where no basic interests are violated, the courts are powerless to intervene to protect someone's privacy.

A most notorious recent case of the failure of the common law is that of Gordon Kaye, a star of the television series, *'Allo, 'Allo*. Kaye suffered severe head injuries in a car accident and three weeks later, while he was still seriously ill in hospital, a journalist and a photographer from the *Sunday Sport* entered his room without permission, interviewed him and took photographs. He was, according to the medical evidence, not fit to give consent to the interview. Kaye attempted to claim damages for the violation of his privacy, but the courts were powerless, as no property rights were infringed. As Lord Justice Bingham stated in his judgment in the Court of Appeal, Kaye's case highlighted, 'yet again, the failure of both the common law of England and statute to protect in an effective way the personal privacy of individual citizens' (*Kaye v Robertson*, 1991).

Similar inadequacies are apparent, for example, in the protection of prisoners' rights. Four years ago, a prisoner sued the government over the poor conditions in Parkhurst Prison. Conditions in British prisons were generally so appalling at that time that the European Committee for the Prevention of Torture reported that they breached Article 3 of the European Convention on Human Rights (which prohibits degrading and inhuman punishment). But the House of Lords decided that prisoners have no right to sue for false imprisonment in respect of their conditions of confinement. Since they were serving prison sentences, the court deemed their detention lawful. Only if it could be shown that the conditions actually caused injury (and therefore violated the recognised basic interest of personal integrity) was it possible to sue for negligence (*R v Deputy Governor of Parkhurst Prison ex parte Hague*, 1992). As a result, legal challenges to prison conditions are virtually impossible.

Even a principle as basic to human rights standards as equality is not a recognised basic interest under the common law. So the common law could not be developed to prohibit race and sex discrimination. The courts were powerless to assist people who suffered discrimination until Parliament intervened to introduce race relations and sex discrimination laws. Save where statute laws prohibit race and sex discrimination, the courts are still powerless. And the laws fall far short of a comprehensive ban on discrimination. (See Chapter 7.)

In light of such examples, it is difficult to share Dicey's faith that the remedies of the common law are 'for all practical purposes worth a hundred constitutional articles guaranteeing individual liberty' (Dicey 1885, 1924: 199).

Equality

The limits of equality before the law

Dicey saw the principle of equality before the law as the essential underpinning of the common law, but also that equality only extends as far as the basic interests recognised by the common law take it. Equality before the law has no meaning in cases which do not involve one or more of the basic interests. On the contrary, save where judicial review might be invoked (see above), citizens have no remedy for the violation of their human rights if no basic interest is involved, whether that violation is carried out by the lowliest of individuals (for example, the journalist and photographer from the *Sunday Sport*), or by the government itself.

Even where basic interests are at stake, the principle of equality before the law has only a very limited meaning. It simply means that no one is above the law. This was recently emphasised by the House of Lords when it refused to grant Kenneth Baker, then Home Secretary, immunity from contempt of court proceedings when he failed to comply with a court order prohibiting the deportation of a Zairian asylum seeker (*M v Home Office*, 1993). Beyond that, there is considerable scope for discrimination in the law, as the next chapter on equality demonstrates. Nor has the principle of equality before the law ever meant equality of access to the law in the United Kingdom. Even the most obvious prerequisite of such access – the provision of legal aid to enable those otherwise unable to pursue their rights in the courts – is not available for all types of case and has been subject to sharp financial reductions in recent years. Legal aid is not available for inquests, which usually provide the only forum in which families can find out what happened to their relatives who die; nor for employment cases in industrial tribunals (which deal, for example, with unfair dismissal and discrimination at work). And yet an official report in 1989 to the Lord Chancellor concluded that the presence of a legal representative significantly and independently increases the probability that applicants in industrial tribunals will succeed with their case (Genn and Genn 1989).

Citizens cannot get legal aid to initiate or defend defamation actions, which are usually complicated cases reserved to the High Court and can be vastly expensive. Perhaps the most dramatic illustration of the inequality caused by the total ban on legal aid in such cases is the trial between the multi-million dollar McDonald's fast-food chain and two unemployed Londoners, Helen Steel and Dave Morris. McDonald's complained that the couple had handed out leaflets, which it accepted the two had not written, outside their restaurants. The trial took four years to come to court and then became the longest libel trial in legal history, with over 200 days of evidence. Over a hundred witnesses were examined. McDonald's were advised and represented throughout by specialist solicitors and barristers, including leading QCs. Helen Steel and Dave Morris, with a disposable income of £1.57 a week between them, had to represent themselves (never having done so before) and did not have the time or resources to prepare and call key witnesses in their defence.

Overall, eligibility for legal aid, where it is available, has fallen from 79 to 48 per cent of the population (Lewis and Birkinshaw 1993: 215). According to Kate Markus, a former chair of the Law Centres Federation, 'limits have been consistently reduced so that now many people are excluded from the scheme even though they cannot afford to pay lawyers' fees. As a result, many people are effectively excluded from the courts' (Grigg-Spall and Ireland 1994: 184). It is poor and middle-income citizens who are thus disadvantaged in the pursuit and defence of their rights through legal proceedings.

The weakness of the 'presumption of liberty'

In this light, the proposition that citizens are free to do as they like, unless expressly prohibited by the law from doing so, hardly convinces. In practice, citizens are only free to engage in actions which, if challenged, they can afford to defend in court. In any event, the 'presumption of liberty' cannot provide any protection against 'lawful' restrictions on political rights or freedoms. The presumption only applies in the absence of legislation or of the assertion of a basic interest. It generally has very little real value in practice.

Take, for example, freedom of assembly (which is fully considered in Chapter 10). Freedom of assembly has no positive value as it does not qualify as a basic interest; therefore, it cannot be a defence to an action by individuals or a group asserting their statutory or common law rights. Thus, when a group of people picketed an Islington estate agents to protest against a policy which favoured higher-income house-buyers, the High Court rejected the claim in their defence that they were engaged only in peaceful and orderly picketing to express their opinions about a matter of substantial public interest. Instead, the court upheld the estate agents' claim that the protest interfered with their enjoyment of their business premises (*Hubbard v Pitt*, 1976).

It is thus a mistake to place much trust in the idea of 'the presumption of liberty'. The common law rule which requires those who wish to interfere with the liberties of ordinary British citizens to identify the law that justifies their inter-ference may seem to be raising a high hurdle in defence of their liberties. In fact, the hurdle is not high, and is shrinking in size. Two academic lawyers have defined the space in ordinary people's lives protected by the presumption of liberty as 'the *residue* of liberty'. As the courts develop ever more sophisticated means for enforcing the basic interests they do recognise, and as legislation continues to extend into new areas of law, they argue, 'the residue of liberty just gets smaller and smaller, until eventually, in some areas, it is extinguished altogether' (Ewing and Gearty 1990: 9).

Again, freedom of assembly provides a good example. Theoretically citizens are free to gather as they wish. In practice, their ability to do so is strictly hedged about by a combination of common-law restrictions designed to protect the basic (prop-erty) interests of other citizens, statute laws designed to prevent public disorder and innumerable local by-laws. The result is that people cannot even assemble on the highway without committing trespass. Practically all squares, parks and public places are governed by by-laws or similar regulations, under which assemblies can be prohibited and people may generally be ordered to disperse. Generally, public author-ities are not obliged to lease public premises to people wishing to hold a meeting. In fact, so long as no real nuisance is being caused, local authorities generally tend not to assert their rights as land-owners and police officers will tolerate protests. But the general willingness to accept people gathering together in public disguises the fragility of the presumption of liberty as an effective means of protecting the democratic rights of free assembly and public protest. As Chapter 10 shows, for example, on numerous occasions public protest is not tolerated and protesters denied permission to meet in public have no effective remedy.

The flexibility argument

Finally, a few words about the nature of the common law itself. Since it is judge-made, it is capable of change. So, too, is statute law, since a supreme Parliament is not restrained either by pre-determined laws or rigid constitutional rules. The value of these two 'flexible friends' is given considerable weight in the debate about how effectively the existing system in the United Kingdom protects human rights. As the former Home Office Minister, Peter Lloyd MP, said, the pragmatic British system 'continues to allow us to adapt and change, where change appears to be necessary' (HC Deb, 17 May 1991, c582). Bill Walker MP perceived another advantage: 'If we get something wrong, as we often do, we can rectify it the following year' (HC Deb, 9 February 1993, c826).

The system is flexible, to an extent. To take a recent example, a young woman was persistently harassed by her ex-boyfriend who followed her around shouting abuse and pestered her with telephone calls to her parents' house. The Court of Appeal had little hesitation in developing the law of private nuisance to cover the situation (*Khorasandjian v Bush*, 1993).

However, two important caveats are needed. First, judge-made developments in the common law are not driven by any quest for the better protection of human rights. They simply tend to reflect the prevailing view among the judiciary about the issues – and even the parties – before them. When striking miners stood outside collieries in South Wales shouting 'Scab!' at working miners, the High Court judge searched the common law to see if their action was unlawful. There was no obvious law against their behaviour. But he effectively invented a new cause of action under the same law of private nuisance to outlaw their activities (*Thomas v NUM (South Wales Area)*, 1985).

Second, only basic interests already recognised in the common law can be developed. Judges cannot create new foundations, they can build only on what is already present. As we have observed above, privacy may be protected only to the extent that it overlaps with a basic interest such as property rights. Otherwise, as Mr Malone discovered when he sought a declaration that the police had acted unlawfully in tapping his telephone, judges cannot develop the common law into new areas, even when they may wish to do so (*Malone v Commissioner of Police*, 1979). He had to go to the European Court to obtain justice, much later, in 1985.

Overall, the organic, or flexible, nature of the common law does not necessarily lead to the further protection of political and civil rights. On the contrary, it can quite feasibly take the law in another direction altogether. Further, the ability of judges to develop the law creatively, through their judgments, can run counter to the general principle, recognised in international human rights standards, that restrictions on political and civil rights should be 'prescribed by law'. The European Court has ruled that the common law does not necessarily breach this principle simply because it is 'unwritten' (*Sunday Times v UK*, 1979). Yet citizens must have a reasonably adequate indication in law of the legal rules which apply in a given set of circumstances; and those rules must be sufficiently clear to enable them to regulate their conduct.

The influence of international human rights standards

In recent reports to the UN Human Rights Committee, the present government has been keen to emphasise the impact of international human rights standards on the domestic courts. For example, the government's 1989 periodic report claimed that 'the European Commission and Court of Human Rights have increased in influence in domestic courts' (para. 5). This theme is developed in the 1994 report which asserts that 'judgments of the House of Lords have made clear that [international human rights] obligations are part of the legal context in which the judges consider themselves to operate' (para. 5). Here, we briefly consider these claims which are clearly significant to this audit: the more domestic measures and remedies are influenced by international human rights standards, the more likely the United Kingdom is to meet those standards.

Most of the international human rights standards used in this audit – for example, those taken from the International Covenant and the European Convention – are contained in agreements made between states, classified as treaties. But as they have no status in domestic law, they cannot become a source of rights and obligations. To this principle there are a few, very limited exceptions. It is now established that the European Convention on Human Rights can be used to resolve an ambiguity in legislation, including delegated legislation; but if the words of a statute are clear, it must be applied whatever its effect (see above).

The relevance of international human rights obligations to the common law is more complicated. The case of *Malone*, described above, in which the plaintiff sought a declaration that telephone-tapping by the police was unlawful because it contravened the European Convention, is decisive authority for the rule that the common law cannot grant a remedy simply because an international human rights obligation has been breached (*Malone v Commissioner of Police (No. 2)*, 1979). Nonetheless, the European Convention is sometimes cited as 'evidence' of certain common law rights. For example, in the *Spycatcher* litigation, Lord Donaldson reviewed the common law approach to freedom of expression in the Court of Appeal and declared himself satisfied that he could 'detect no inconsistency between our domestic law and the convention' (*AG v Guardian Newspapers (No. 2)*, 1988). Some courts have gone further and used the European Convention to help determine the direction in which the common law should be developed where it is uncertain.

The leading case is now *Derbyshire County Council v Times Newspapers*, 1992. The county council was attempting to sue *The Times* for publishing two articles which questioned the propriety of certain investments. In deciding whether a body such as a county council could sue for libel under the common law, the Court of Appeal looked to Article 10 of the European Convention and concluded that it could not, since it was not 'necessary in a democratic society' and would amount to an unjustifiable restriction on freedom of expression.

However, the case represents a high-point in the courts' willingness to have recourse to international human rights obligations. In 1993, a research project for the Democratic Audit used the Lexis facility (a database containing 91,000 English cases, including every reported case since 1945 and all unreported cases in the High Court, Court of Appeal or House of Lords since 1980) to study all English cases from 1972 to 1993 in which either the International Covenant or European Convention was cited, either in passing or in argument by counsel or the judge. The Convention was cited in only 173 cases (0.2 per cent of the total) – a very low figure, given the wide range of rights protected by the European Convention and the frequency with which such rights are considered by domestic courts.

All 64 cases in which the Convention was cited in the judgment, or by counsel in argument – a third of the total – were selected for analysis in detail. In only 27 cases did the Convention have any real impact. In 11 of these cases, it was used to bolster the reasoning of one or more judges, and in 13 it arguably influenced the majority judgment. But the Convention could be said to have affected the outcome in only three cases (of which the *Derbyshire County Council* case above was one). Notably, 18 of the 27 cases in which the Convention played a role concerned freedom of expression, where, as noted above, the courts have often suggested that the common law and Article 10 of the European Convention on Human Rights are identical anyway. The analysis confirmed that the influence of the Convention varies considerably between judges and provided several examples of a circular judicial argument: judges state that the Convention does not extend rights any further than existing English law, and so there is no need to consider it in their judgments.

The International Covenant on Civil and Political Rights was referred to in ten cases (0.01 per cent of the total) over a slightly longer time-scale (1972–95). Five of the ten were unusual in that they involved compensation for miscarriages of justice following the Home Secretary's 1985 statement in Parliament that he was prepared in future to pay compensation, 'where this is required by our international obligations'. That principle was enacted in the Criminal Justice Act 1988 specifically to give effect to Article 14.6 of the International Covenant. In each of the five cases, the Covenant was used to assist in the proper interpretation of the Home Secretary's statement or of the 1988 Act, but in none was the appeal against the non-payment of compensation successful. In three further cases the International Covenant had no effect on the judgment. Of the two cases remaining, one made reference to the International Convention to bolster the reasoning of one judge – the other was the *Derbyshire County Council* case, where Lord Justice Balcombe treated Article 19 of the International Covenant and Article 10 of the European Convention as identical.

Undoubtedly one of the factors giving rise to the failure of the courts to invoke the International Covenant is the refusal of successive governments to sign the optional protocol allowing a right of petition to the UN Human Rights Committee. According to the present government, ratification is not necessary to ensure the protection of individual rights in the United Kingdom, particularly since citizens have access to the procedures and institutions established under the European Convention (Fourth Periodic Report 1994, para. 6).

Clearly, the International Covenant and European Convention overlap frequently. But there are important distinctions both in the terms of the protection laid down and the interpretation of those provisions by the relevant expert bodies. For example, when employees at GCHQ, deprived of their trade union rights in 1985, lost their case in the House of Lords (see **pp. 220–223** above), they applied to the European Commission, claiming that Article 11 of the European Convention, safeguarding freedom of association, had been breached. The Commission rejected their application, largely because Article 11.2 specifically provides that restrictions may be imposed not only on the police and armed forces, but also on 'members of the administration of the state'. The International Covenant contains no restriction of this kind. Indeed, it prohibits states from 'applying the law' in such a way as to prejudice the 1948 International Labour Organisation Convention on freedom of association and the right to organise. Since the ILO body of experts, the Committee on Freedom of Association, found that the 1948 Convention had been breached, it is highly likely that, had the unions been able to petition the UN Human Rights Committee under the International Covenant, they would have succeeded in establishing that their rights had been violated.

DATA

The protection of European Union law

The European Union wields an increasingly significant curb on parliamentary supremacy. Indeed, it sets at least one court – the European Court of Justice – above Parliament's unfettered legislative powers and confers similar powers on the domestic courts in respect of EU legislation. The European Communities Act 1972 gave existing and future EU legislation the force of law in the United Kingdom. Parliament has no formal constitutional role in this process. It cannot amend EU legislation and is not required to approve it. It may, however, be required to legislate to incorporate it into domestic law, or to take additional measures to ensure that it applies in this country. Thus European Union law prevails over the domestic law. Where the two clash, the courts will not enforce an Act of Parliament.

There was no reference to the protection of fundamental rights in the original Treaty of Rome (1957). But since 1969, the European Court of Justice has made it clear that it will ensure respect for such rights within the legal order of the European Union (*Stauder v Ulm*, 1969). In 1974, the Court determined that:

> international treaties for the protection of human rights on which the member
> States have collaborated, or of which they are signatories, can supply guide-
> lines which should be followed within the framework of Community law.
>
> (*Nold v European Commission*, 1974)

Subsequently, the European Court of Justice has taken the European Convention on Human Rights into account when reviewing Community acts and in determining references from national courts and tribunals (Grief 1991: 560).

EU law

At Maastricht, political recognition was given to the place of fundamental rights by Article F.2 of the Treaty on European Union:

> The Union shall respect fundamental rights, as guaranteed by the European Convention for the Protection of Human Rights and Fundamental Freedoms signed in Rome on 4 November 1950 and as they result from the constitutional traditions common to the Member States, as general principles of Community law.

However, this provision is not part of EU law and is not justiciable by the European Court.

The influence of EU law on domestic rights

European Union law certainly provides some scope for the protection of human rights. Much of the equal pay legislation and case law of the last 20 years has been driven from Europe. Moreover, as commentators such as Nicholas Grief have argued, the European Court of Justice would be competent in certain circumstances to determine the compatibility of a national statute with the European Convention. They maintain that the President of the Court could even suspend a statute insofar as it was inconsistent with principles in the Convention, even though the Convention itself has not been incorporated into domestic law (Grief 1991: 555). In 1983, the European Court considered a British statutory instrument which operated retrospectively on the authority of a Community regulation which was itself retrospective (*R v Kirk*, 1984). The European Court held that retroactive penal legislation infringed a fundamental human right and found the Community regulation – and consequently, the statutory instrument – invalid.

Even where a case is not referred to the European Court of Justice, there is room for the infiltration of fundamental rights through EU law (Browne-Wilkinson 1992: 399). Points of EU law arising in the United Kingdom have to be decided by domestic courts in accordance with the stated principles and relevant decisions of the European Court (*R v Secretary of State for Transport ex parte Factortame (No. 2)*, 1991). If fundamental rights underpin those principles and decisions, domestic courts must take them into account.

However, there are important limitations on the protection of fundamental human rights through EU law. First and foremost, EU law is limited to areas of economic activity; and the European Court of Justice has no power to examine the compatibility with fundamental rights of national legislation lying outside the scope of EU law. The influence of EU law on political rights and freedoms in this country has been confined to certain aspects of equality at work and to freedom of movement. So, while sex discrimination is contrary to the Treaty of Rome, as it has developed, neither the Treaty nor subsequent directives or regulations prohibit racial discrimination. The nearest that the Treaty comes to in addressing the issue is by requiring the free movement of workers (McCrudden and Chambers 1994: 444).

There is also a clear danger that some aspects of EU law and policy, far from protecting fundamental rights, will actually erode or even negate them. For example, the long-standing aim of abolishing internal frontiers has provoked a widespread fear that member states will create a 'Fortress Europe', strictly policing the EU's external frontiers, restricting the influx of non-EU nationals, and significantly increasing internal controls (Spencer 1990). This danger is increased by the range of issues which fall within the domain of 'Third Pillar' affairs, including justice and home affairs. These issues are not subject to control either by the institutions of the Union or by national parliaments or courts, but are determined by inter-state cooperation.

7   Equal Access to Political Rights

Equality

Democracy is diminished if citizens do not possess genuine equality of access to political rights and freedoms and the law. Equal access to such democratic rights is the cornerstone of political equality – one of the two basic principles on which the Democratic Audit's scrutiny of democracy in the UK is based. The more equal the access to democratic rights, the more democratic a country will be; the greater the inequality, the less democratic it is. As such, equality and equal access to democratic rights are fundamental to modern representative democracy.

The absolute relationship between equality and democracy has been a common theme in expressions of democratic rights. For instance, Thomas Jefferson wrote in the 1776 Declaration of Independence that:

> All men are created *equal* [our emphasis]. That they are endowed by the creator with certain inalienable rights; that amongst these are Life, Liberty, and the Pursuit of Happiness. That to secure these rights Governments are instituted among men, deriving their just powers from the consent of the governed.

This is a statement of universal principle, even though Jefferson's demand for equality was made on behalf of white, propertied men seeking independence for the American colonies. Similarly, Article 1 of the Universal Declaration of Human Rights, the fount of postwar human rights instruments, proclaims that 'all human beings are born free and equal in dignity and rights'. The idea of equality, then, is a pillar of evolving human rights standards as well as democracy.

Yet no constitutional right of equality exists in the United Kingdom. Nor are the existing democratic rights audited in this book based on any premise of equality. Democracy in the United Kingdom developed gradually by a process of accommodation with a ruling monarchy and then with those interests which took over the powers of the Crown. At no moment were relations between rulers and ruled re-defined and inscribed in a constitutional document, such as the American Declaration of Independence. Democracy became associated with the processes of lawful government and public order; the country is still ruled in the name of the Crown, not of the people. Historically, individual immunities and liberties existed by grace of the Crown and its servants. The polity is founded, therefore, on a historic, and unspoken, presumption of inequality. The essence of this inequality was described as early as the thirteenth century by the jurist Bracton: 'Subjects cannot be equals of the ruler because he would thereby lose his rule, since equal can have no authority over equal' (Bracton 1968).

Citizens have over time assumed democratic rights, but there has still been no positive assertion of equality. It is not possible in this book to measure the insidious effect on democracy of the failure to give citizens a right to equality. We do highlight particular examples of the absence of a right to equality in the chapters dealing with individual democratic rights. For example, in evaluating the compliance of police 'stop and search' with international human rights standards, we note their disproportionate use against young Afro-Caribbeans (**p. 251**). On the right to vote, we draw attention to regulations which prevent most people who are held in mental institutions from registering to vote (**pp. 276–277**). Such examples demonstrate that, owing to the absence of a constitutional right of equality, not all citizens are able equally to enjoy the same rights even where the United Kingdom formally complies with international standards.

Our focus is broader in this chapter. We aim to evaluate the practical effect of the general failure to guarantee a right to equality on the overall 'system' for protecting human rights in the United Kingdom. We have resisted the temptation to divide the subject-matter up into specific types of discrimination, such as race, sex, sexuality, language, religion and so on. Instead, we have tried to provide an overview of the way in which the institutions, laws and rules comprising the system for protecting human rights deal with equality.

In practice, this means that the Human Rights Index which follows concentrates on the general principles of equality and non-discrimination, as they emerge from the European Convention and the UN International Covenant. Single issue instruments on race, women and disability are included to the extent that they too enunciate these general principles. Broadly speaking, three themes emerge in the index: a general right to equality; the need for anti-discrimination measures; and the role of affirmative action.

We divide domestic law and practice according to these three themes in the data section and the audit which follows. We start with the general difficulties inherent in a system for protecting human rights which is not grounded on the principle of equality. We assess in particular the failure of the common law to deal with discrimination. We then examine the existing framework of anti-discrimination legislation – focusing on sex and race non-discrimination measures in Great Britain and fair employment law in Northern Ireland. Finally, we evaluate existing arrangements for positive action.

International standards

The primacy of equality

All human beings are born free and equal in dignity and rights. (Article 1 Universal Declaration of Human Rights)

Everyone is entitled to all the rights and freedoms set forth in this declaration without distinction of any kind, such as race, colour, sex, language, religion, political or other opinion, national or social origin, property, birth or other status. (Article 2, UDHR)

All are equal before the law and are entitled without discrimination to equal protection of the law. (Article 7, UDHR)

Equality and the prohibition of discrimination are central to the protection of human rights in postwar international instruments. They spring from the Universal Declaration of Human Rights (see above) and run 'like a red thread throughout the International Covenant on Civil and Political Rights' (Nowak 1993: 460). They have inspired special human rights instruments as the world has repeatedly learned the painful lessons of the divisive politics of difference and discrimination over the past half century.

The 'red thread' of equality asserts itself throughout the International Covenant:

- Article 2.1 obliges contracting states to ensure the rights of the Covenant without discrimination to all individuals within their territory and subject to their jurisdiction
- Article 3 guarantees equal rights to men and women in the enjoyment of all rights under the Covenant
- Other articles reinforce these provisions with specific rights of equality – equality before the courts (Article 14) and the equal rights of spouses (Article 23)
- Article 26 expresses the Covenant's commitment to the value of equality by making it an autonomous right: 'All persons are equal before the law and are entitled without any discrimination to the equal protection of the law. In this respect, the law shall prohibit any discrimination and guarantee to all persons equal and effective protection against discrimination on any ground such as race, colour, sex, language, religion, political or other opinion, national or social origin, property, birth or other status.'

The significance of Article 26 of the International Covenant is that it is free standing and independent of the other Covenant rights. It is the strongest possible guarantee of the primacy of equality in international law. Its place is reflected by corresponding proclamations of equality in the UN conventions on the elimination of all forms of racial discrimination and discrimination against women (see **p. 115** below).

The European Convention does not give the same primacy to equality. Article 14 offers people protection against discrimination only in respect of the rights and freedoms it guarantees. In similar terms to Article 2.1 of the International Covenant, it prohibits discrimination 'on any ground such as sex, race, colour, language, religion, political or other opinion, national or social origin, association with a national minority, property, birth or other status'.

For our purposes, the more limited approach of the European Convention to equality is not crucial: the Convention contains all the individual democratic rights audited in this book. However, Article 26 of the International Covenant provides a more satisfactory starting point – as Judge Ryssdal, President of the European Court, has implicitly recognised (Partsch 1993: 571). Article 26 distinguishes between the right to 'equal protection of the law' and 'equality before the law'. Equal protection of the law has two aspects:

- states must refrain from discrimination when enacting and implementing legislation
- states must prohibit discrimination and provide effective protection against it by enacting special laws.

Equality before the law, by contrast, means that the law must be applied in the same manner, no matter who the parties may be. This obligation applies in the courts and to all public officers, such as the police, prison, immigration and customs officers.

In its interpretation of Article 26, the UN Human Rights Committee has stressed that prohibiting discrimination is not sufficient to satisfy its terms:

- 'affirmative action designed to ensure the positive enjoyment of rights' is also necessary (General Comment 4/13 of 1991)
- 'Article 26 . . . prohibits discrimination in law or in fact in any field regulated and protected by public authorities' (General Comment 18/37 of 1989)
- the principle of equality may require states to take affirmative action to diminish or eliminate conditions which cause or help to perpetuate discrimination prohibited by the Covenant (General Comment 18/37 of 1989).

States are thus obliged not only to recognise equality and prohibit discrimination in laws, but also to initiate policies and other practical measures to achieve it as well. They must not only act to prevent discrimination by public bodies, but also to a lesser extent to protect citizens from discrimination by private bodies (Nowak 1993: 476–477). Quite where the line is to be drawn is not clear. During the drafting of the International Covenant, it was repeatedly emphasised that discrimination in private relations was a matter of legitimate personal decision-making. So, for example, individual citizens are free to exclude anyone from a private party. But discrimination in the quasi-public sector such as employment, schools, transportation, hotels, restaurants, theatres, parks and beaches is prohibited (Nowak 1993: 478).

Neither instrument prohibits every difference in treatment as discrimination. The Human Rights Committee has observed that a difference in treatment is justifiable 'if the criteria for . . . differentiation are reasonable and objective and if the aim is to achieve a purpose which is legitimate under the Covenant' (General Comment 18/37 of 1989). Similarly, the European Court of Human Rights has defined two tests for assessing an allegation of discrimination:

- Is there an objective and reasonable justification for the difference in treatment concerned?

International standards

● Is there a reasonable relationship of proportionality between the means employed and the aim sought to be realised? (*Belgian Linguistics Case*, ECtHR, 1968).

But while states enjoy a certain discretion, or 'margin of appreciation' (see Chapter 2), in assessing how far differences in otherwise similar situations justify different treatment, very weighty reasons would have to be advanced to justify a difference of treatment on the ground of sex (*Abdulaziz, Cabales and Balkandali v UK*, ECtHR, 1985).

Neither instrument actually defines discrimination, but the UN Human Rights Committee has approved the following definition which includes

> any distinction, exclusion, restriction or preference which is based on any ground such as race, colour, sex, language, religion, political or other opinion, national or social origin, property, birth or other status, and which has the purpose or *effect* of nullifying or impairing the recognition, enjoyment or exercise, on an equal footing, of all rights and freedoms [our emphasis].
>
> (General Comment 18/37 of 1989)

This definition covers direct discrimination (less favourable treatment on prohibited grounds) and, as our emphasis shows, indirect discrimination (an apparently neutral practice, rule, requirement or condition which effectively discriminates against particular groups).

Both instruments ban discrimination on the grounds set out in the terms above, though the Convention also prohibits discrimination based on 'association with a national minority'. The European Court and UN Human Rights Committee have tended to approach homosexuality from the standpoint of privacy, but the Committee has recently demonstrated a willingness to include homosexuality in the reference to 'sex' in Article 26 (*Toonen v Australia*, 1992).

The words 'other status' in both instruments have not been clearly defined. Decisions and jurisprudence in this area are developing on a case-by-case basis. However, the Human Rights Committee has found that the following grounds constitute 'other status': nationality, marital status, a distinction between 'foster' and 'natural' children, and even differences in funding between public and private schools. The nearest the UN Committee has got to a definition came in a declaration that 'other status' includes membership of an 'identifiably distinct category' (*BdB et al. v Netherlands*, 1989).

Neither instrument expressly protects people with disabilities against discrimination. However, in 1971 the UN General Assembly approved a declaration on the rights of people suffering from mental handicap. The 1975 UN Declaration on the Rights of Disabled Persons made it clear that disabled people in general were protected from discrimination. Disabled people (in the now dated terminology of the time) included:

> any person unable to ensure by himself or herself, wholly or partly, the necessities of a normal individual and/or social life, as a result of deficiency, either congenital or not, in his or her physical or mental capabilities.

But the 1971 and 1975 declarations are without enforcement mechanisms and hence remain largely statements of aspiration. The UN General Assembly subsequently adopted the World Programme of Action Concerning Disabled Persons and, in 1993, issued Standard Rules on the Equalisation of Opportunities for Persons with Disabilities.

In 1965 and 1979, the UN adopted two anti-discrimination conventions to reinforce the International Covenant: the Convention on the Elimination of All Forms of Racial Discrimination (CERD), which came into force in 1969; and then the Convention on the Elimination of All Forms of Discrimination against Women (CEDAW), which came into force in 1981. CERD prohibits discrimination based on 'race, colour, descent or national or ethnic origin' (Article 1) and CEDAW discrimination against women 'in all its forms'. Under CERD (Article 2) and CEDAW (Article 2a & b) contracting states agree:

- to 'engage in no act or practice of racial discrimination' (CERD)
- to ensure that 'all public authorities and public institutions, national and local ... act in conformity with this obligation' (CERD)
- to 'review governmental, national and local policies, and to amend, rescind or nullify any laws and regulations which have the effect of creating or perpetuating racial discrimination' (CERD)
- to 'embody the principle of equality of men and women in their national constitutions or other appropriate legislation if not yet incorporated therein and to ensure, through law and other appropriate means, the practical realisation of this principle' (CEDAW)
- to 'adopt appropriate legislative and other measures, including sanctions where appropriate, prohibiting all discrimination against women' (CEDAW).

Other anti-discrimination instruments include the UN Convention on Political Rights of Women (1952); the Conventions of the Independent Labour Organisation (ILO) on Equal Remuneration and on Discrimination in Employment and Occupation (1951 and 1958); the UNESCO Convention against Discrimination in Education (1960); and the UN Declaration on the Elimination of all Forms of Intolerance and of Discrimination Based on Religion or Belief (1981). In the UN Convention on the Rights of the Child (1990) the principle of equality is again affirmed, though the emphasis is on protection from discrimination.

In summary, what emerges from postwar human rights instruments is not a single and precise definition of equality, but a cluster of concepts including equality before the law, equal protection of the law, non-discrimination and affirmative action. There is no requirement that all people should be treated the same; rather that differences in treatment must be objectively justified and proportional to the achievement of their objective aims. It is in this sense that we employ the term 'equality' in this chapter and book.

The absent right

The general absence of a right to equality

None of the international instruments that guarantee 'equality' (as defined above) or outlaw discrimination have been directly incorporated into domestic law in the UK. In the absence of a Bill of Rights, British citizens have no universal right to equality. No statute nor any aspect of the common law can be challenged because it is unequal. There is no scrutiny of legislation to ensure that it will not be unequal in its operation. On the contrary, as we have seen, Parliament has the right to make or unmake any law whatsoever and the courts are powerless to intervene.

There is a single exception to this general rule. European Union law forbids discrimination on the grounds of sex and nationality (but not race) in its sphere of operation. The European Court of Justice has given a progressive interpretation to these principles of equality and EU law prevails over domestic law (see Chapter 6). Article 119 of the Treaty of Rome provides that 'each Member State shall . . . maintain the application of the principle that men and women should receive equal pay for equal work'. Thanks to Article 119, together with the EU Equal Treatment Directive, radical changes in employment law in the UK have ensued over the last 20 years.

Elsewhere in the law, equality in the United Kingdom means no more than 'equality before the law': i.e., that no one is exempt from the enforcement of the law (**pp. 102–103**). This principle is essential to any democratic society. But it does not and cannot extend to a prohibition of unequal laws. It may constrain racially-biased enforcement of laws, but does not stop racially-biased laws from being enacted. The courts have been unable (or unwilling) to embrace any wider notion of equality through the common law. Equality is not among the 'basic interests' to which the common law gives priority – personal freedom; property (and with it contractual freedom); reputation; and fair procedure in matters affecting the individual (see Chapter 6). Before Parliament passed legislation prohibiting discrimination on the grounds of sex and race, the only protection offered by the common law was to put inn-keepers under a duty to accept all travellers who were 'in a reasonably fit condition to be received' (*Constantine v Imperial Hotels Ltd*, 1944). In the words of Lord Simon:

> The common law before the making of the first Race Relations Act (1965) was that people could discriminate against others on the ground of colour, etc., to their hearts' content. This unbridled capacity to discriminate was the mischief and defect for which the common law did not provide.
>
> (*Applin v Race Relations Board*, 1975)

For any individual people or groups falling outside the scope of the non-discrimination legislation now in force (see below), the position under the common law remains the same. Banning homosexuals from a bar or club, or dismissing them from the armed forces (see **p. 121**), is perfectly lawful in the United Kingdom.

In the realm of public law, inequality *in itself* is not a ground upon which the administrative decisions of public officials or bodies can be challenged by way of judicial review. The courts can only review decisions on grounds of illegality, irrationality and procedural impropriety (*CCSU v Minister for the Civil Service*, 1985; see also **p. 95**). The only challenge to a discriminatory decision has to be under the head of irrationality – that the discrimination in question was so outrageous in its defiance of logic or of accepted moral standards that no sensible person who had applied his or her mind to the question could have arrived at it.

The bizarre effects of the absence of equality

The absence of a right to equal protection of the law is clearly contrary to Article 26 of the International Covenant. Discrimination in the United Kingdom is lawful, unless specifically prohibited by legislation which is disunited and piecemeal – and easily summarised. The Equal Pay Act 1970 and the Sex Discrimination Act 1975, and equivalent legislation in Northern Ireland, forbid sex discrimination throughout the United Kingdom. The Race Relations Act 1976 forbids discrimination on the grounds of colour, race, nationality, or ethnic or national origins – but only in England, Scotland and Wales, *not* Northern Ireland. (Initially the legislation was deliberately kept out of Northern Ireland for fear that Catholics might use it to challenge discrimination: see Lester and Bindman 1972: 115 and 158. It is said now to be in the legislative pipeline.) In contrast, the Northern Ireland Constitution Act 1973 and the Fair Employment (Northern Ireland) Acts 1976 and 1989 forbid discrimination on grounds of religious belief or political opinion only in Northern Ireland, not the rest of the UK. The 1944 Disabled Persons (Employment) Act requires employers in England, Scotland and Wales – but not Northern Ireland – with 20 or more workers to employ a minimum quota (currently 3 per cent) of registered disabled people.

The results are bizarre. In 1994, the government issued its fourth report to the UN Human Rights Committee, the body which supervises compliance with the International Covenant. Justice, the civil liberties organisation, pointed out in its response to the report:

> while it is unlawful to discriminate against a Catholic in Belfast, it is lawful in Glasgow. While it is unlawful to discriminate against a West Indian in Wolverhampton, it is lawful in Londonderry. While it is unlawful to discriminate against a Sikh in both Belfast and London, it is unlawful in Belfast if it is religious discrimination, but not if it is solely ethnic, while in London it is unlawful if it is ethnic, but not if it is solely religious.
>
> (para. 2.1)

No government could seriously suggest that this depicts compliance with international human rights standards on equality.

Individual citizens (or groups of citizens) in the UK may be discriminated against on such grounds as age, health, mental illness or sexual orientation. Homosexuals, for example, receive no protection from discrimination under the law. It is even arguably lawful to incite hatred against people on the grounds of their sexual orientation. It is still against the law for male homosexuals to have sex in many circumstances. Sex between men was a criminal offence, without exception, until 1967. The Sexual Offences Act 1967 Act decriminalised only homosexual acts between two consenting men aged over 21, in private, in England and Wales; they remained illegal in Scotland until 1980 and in Northern Ireland until 1982, where reform came only at the instigation of an adverse judgment in the European Court (see **p. 77**). After impassioned debate, Parliament lowered the age of consent for consenting males to 18 in the Criminal Justice and Public Order Act 1994, while the age of consent for heterosexual sex is 16; and if either or both men are under 18, both commit a criminal offence, regardless of consent.

Even within those categories covered by the existing non-discrimination laws, the prohibition on discrimination is not comprehensive. The law on the employment of disabled people is almost entirely unenforced (see **pp. 128–129** below). Other legislation covers particular types of discrimination in specific and carefully defined circumstances. As a result, substantial gaps exist between United Kingdom law and practice and international human rights standards (see below).

This fundamental flaw seems obvious enough. Yet the government, like most governments before it, simply refuses to acknowledge it. The government's report to the UN Human Rights Committee in 1994 claimed that:

> The Government remains committed to the development of a society in which all individuals have equal rights, responsibilities and opportunities. The Government seeks to ensure that its policies and programmes benefit all sections of society and supports legislation, institutions and policies directed at tackling discrimination and promoting equality of opportunity.
>
> (para. 19)

It then lists a number of legislative or other measures which, it says, demonstrate its commitment to addressing problems of discrimination, but adds the qualification that 'in the United Kingdom's view, *[these] are not measures which are required to give effect to rights recognised in the Covenant*' [our emphasis].

Among the 'legislative or other measures' listed, there are some important initiatives – for example, projects aimed at helping criminal justice agencies gain the confidence of local minority ethnic communities; race and ethnic sensitivity training for judges; and changes to the entry examinations for the police. But 'legislative' measures are notable by their scarcity: six in all. Section 95 of the Criminal Justice Act 1991 requires the government to publish annual information to assist those administering the criminal justice system to avoid discriminating against anyone on the basis of race, sex or any other improper ground. This new duty may pave the way for further measures, but it is hardly in itself a powerful measure of anti-discrimination. Likewise, the Courts and Legal Services Act 1990 makes it unlawful for barristers to discriminate against pupils on racial grounds – an admirable addition to race relations law, but very narrow in its field of application and near impossible to enforce.

Three of the remaining 'legislative measures' listed by the government adjust employment law. They were forced on the UK by adverse findings by the European

Court of Justice. The final measure creates a new offence of 'intentional harassment' (section 154 of the Criminal Justice and Public Order Act 1994). This measure is a public response to concern over the reported increase in incidents of racial harassment and violence, but does not publicly recognise the factor of race at all.

In reality, the current government has done very little to combat existing discrimination and its claims to be tackling discrimination and promoting equality of opportunity ring hollow. Nor has the government shown any inclination to measure up to the principle of equality enshrined in Article 26 of the International Covenant. In its third report to the UN Human Rights Committee in 1989, the government does not refer to Article 26 at all. There is one reference in the fourth report:

> The United Kingdom continues to believe that the right to equality before the law and the entitlement without discrimination to the equal protection of the law are fully recognised in the established tradition of the common law.
>
> (para. 483)

It is a shame that this one reference is both inaccurate and inadequate. As we have shown above, the common law does not and cannot give citizens equal protection under the law, 'without discrimination'. The UN Human Rights Committee, considering the report in July 1995, found the reference inadequate and expressed regret at the failure 'to address adequately issues properly arising under Article 26'. The Committee gave examples of specific concerns about the disproportionate use of police stop and search powers against members of ethnic minorities and about 'the levels of support offered for the protection of cultural and ethnic diversity'. The Committee concluded, 'much remains to be done to effect changes in public attitudes and to combat and overcome racism' (CCPR/C/79/Add. 59: 27 July 1995; para. 18).

The government's third and fourth reports failed to mention the new trend of enacting legislation that discriminates against groups least able to command parliamentary majorities. Section 28 of the Local Government Act 1988, which makes it unlawful for a local authority to 'intentionally promote homosexuality' or to promote the teaching in schools of 'the acceptability of homosexuality as pretended family relationship', provides a good example (see **pp. 177–179**). In a climate of growing intolerance and hostility towards lesbians and gay men, section 28 has rightly been described as 'prejudicial, unnecessary, discriminatory and liable to arouse hatred' (Colvin 1989: 61). It symbolises, and gives legitimacy to, discrimination.

Similarly, changes brought about by the Criminal Justice and Public Order Act 1994 will have – and were intended to have – a discriminatory impact on gypsies and others who adopt a travelling lifestyle. First, the duty on local authorities to provide sufficient caravan sites for the gypsies in their areas was repealed, along with assistance from central government. Second, new powers have been given to the police and local authorities to direct the removal of vehicles and caravans from unauthorised property. At the same time as the Standing Advisory Commission on Human Rights (of Northern Ireland) was publishing a report recommending that anti-discrimination legislation in Northern Ireland be enacted to include protection for 'Irish Travellers' (1992–93 Report: 49), some MPs used the debate on the Caravan Sites (Amendment) Bill 1993 to call for their mass deportation (HC Deb, 5 February 1993, c613–614).

These examples demonstrate that, in the absence of a constitutional right to equality, there is no equal protection of the law in the United Kingdom in the sense that all citizens are equally protected from discrimination. The very mischief that the international requirement of equality seeks to outlaw – the suppression of minority views, cultures and interests – actually flourishes in certain areas, on occasions with the tacit collusion or outright encouragement of government ministers.

The failures of the courts

It might be assumed that, whatever the excesses of Parliament, the judiciary would outlaw arbitrary discrimination by developing principles of equality in the common law. Quite the opposite. Historically, the judiciary have passed up almost every opportunity to protect citizens in the United Kingdom from discrimination. Women's disqualification from exercising public functions, holding civil or judicial office, entering any civil profession and being admitted to any incorporated society was removed only by statute in 1919. Women were only given equal voting rights with men in 1928, again by statute, even though the courts were asked to bring into being an equal franchise as early as 1868 (Robertson 1989: 373).

The refusal of the judiciary to develop broad principles of equality is not only an historic phenomenon. Until Parliament and the European Community intervened from the 1970s onwards, employers openly paid a 'women's rate' for the job and openly refused to appoint women above certain levels or to do certain jobs (Fenwick 1994: 482). The courts patiently observed these practices but refused to prohibit them. The principle that like cases be treated alike was satisfied by uniformly rejecting all applications for equal treatment.

Unlike sex discrimination, generalised racial inequality has not been enshrined in the law itself since the abolition of slavery at the beginning of the eighteenth century. But, as with sex discrimination, until Parliament intervened with non-discrimination legislation in the 1960s, the judiciary was unable or unwilling to develop any general rule, policy, or principle in common law capable of combating racial discrimination. 'English law', wrote one of Britain's foremost legal academics in 1960, 'has very little to say about discrimination' (Griffith 1960: 171). Putting inn-keepers under a duty to accept all travellers 'in a reasonably fit condition to be received' hardly demonstrates an appreciation that discrimination can engender gross human rights abuse and is an affront to human dignity.

No doubt some of the judiciary saw the creation of a comprehensive anti-discrimination code as the province of Parliament, but there is clear evidence that others, even as late as the 1970s, actually sympathised with discriminatory practices. In a 1975 case, for example, a judge was prepared to find a solicitor negligent for taking advice from a wife when a husband was available, on the basis that a sensible wife would expect her husband to make the major decisions (*Morris v Duke-Cohan and*

Co., 1975; see Fenwick 1994: 483). Even in the 1990s, it is nonsense to talk of a constitutional principle of equality, as some academic lawyers do, when magistrates' courts convict homosexual males for kissing in the street on the basis that they had exhibited 'threatening . . . or disorderly behaviour' which heterosexuals might feel insulting and are upheld on appeal in the higher courts (*Masterson v Holden*, 1986).

Even in the realm of public law, where broad principles may be expected to prevail over prejudice, equality as a constitutional principle has had a chequered history. As noted above, inequality in itself is not a ground upon which the decisions of individuals or bodies taking administrative decisions can be challenged by way of judicial review. Discriminatory decisions can only be challenged if they are 'irrational'. Ironically, in some cases the courts have decided that discrimination itself is not 'irrational', but measures taken to combat it are. In a notorious case in 1925, the House of Lords confirmed the view of the district auditor that attempts by Poplar borough council to ensure that the wages paid to their male and female employees were equal lacked 'rational proportion' and were therefore unlawful. Lord Atkinson fulminated against the council for allowing themselves to be guided by 'eccentric principles of socialistic philanthropy, or by feminist ambition to secure the equality of the sexes' (*Roberts v Hopwood*, 1925).

However, the courts have lately appeared much more willing to embrace wider principles of equality, a century after a landmark case (*Kruse v Johnson*, 1898), in which the High Court sowed the seeds of wider principles by suggesting that local byelaws which were partial or unequal in their operation might be unlawful. For example, in 1986 the High Court struck down an immigration rule which allowed only dependent relatives 'having a standard of living substantially below that of their own country' to enter Britain. The rule was held to be 'manifestly unjust and unreasonable' and also 'partial and unequal in its operation as between different classes' and therefore invalid (*R v Immigration Appeal Tribunal ex parte Begum Manshoora*, 1986). Had the same rule been enshrined in statute, of course, the courts would have been powerless to intervene.

It is equally clear that no universal principle of equality can yet be said to underpin the judiciary's approach to judicial review. In the recent case of *R v Ministry of Defence ex parte Smith and others*, 1975, three male homosexuals and a lesbian challenged the Ministry of Defence's policy under which they were all discharged from the armed forces because of their sexuality. The High Court explicitly refused to subject that policy to the tests which would be applied by the European Court of Human Rights; namely, was the aim of the policy legitimate? and, if so, was it necessary in a democratic society? (See **Box A, pp. 21–22.**) Instead, the judges simply asked themselves whether the policy was so unreasonable that no reasonable body would operate it. On that basis the challenge failed (see also **pp. 98–99**). Lord Justice Simon Brown expressed 'hesitation and regret' at this outcome and added that his 'greatest concern in leaving the matter in this way is lest the policy's human rights dimension becomes depreciated once the court's doors are closed . . . There is little in the papers before us to instil confidence that the fundamental rights of these applicants and others like them will be fully and faithfully recognised elsewhere' (7 June 1995). In November 1995, the Court of Appeal upheld the High Court's findings.

Significant inequalities in British life

The absence both of a constitutional and judicial principle of equality simply means that significant inequalities in areas not covered by anti-discrimination laws remain unchecked by the courts in this country. The UN Human Rights Committee also drew attention to the urgent need to take forceful public action 'to ensure that women play an equal role in society and that they enjoy the full protection of the law'; and urged the government to tackle problems of racial and ethnic discrimination in (among other areas) law enforcement (CCPR/C/79/Add. 55, 17 July 1995). The following statistics on the participation of women in public life and of ethnic minorities in the criminal justice system illustrate the scale of the problems the Committee was addressing:

Participation of women in public life, 1994

- Women MPs: 9 per cent (60 out of 650)
- Women councillors: 25 per cent
- Women judges: 7 per cent
- Police women: 13 per cent
- Women appointed to public bodies: 28 per cent (1993)
- Women civil servants in the top four grades: 4 per cent
- Non-industrial women civil servants: 51 per cent
- Women ambassadors: 3 per cent.

(Source: UK Fourth Periodic Report to the UN Human Rights Committee, October 1994)

Ethnic minorities and criminal justice, 1994

- Ethnic minority population in the UK: 5.5 per cent
- Ethnic minorities in prison population (men): 12 per cent
- Ethnic minorities in prison population (women): 14 per cent
- Ethnic minority police officers: 1.5 per cent
- Ethnic minority prison officers and governors: 2 per cent
- Ethnic minority solicitors: 2.3 per cent
- Ethnic minority judges: 1 per cent
- Ethnic minority magistrates: 5 per cent.

(Source: *Race and Criminal Justice System 1994*, Home Office)

The inequalities we examine here concern only the civil and political sphere. We do not seek to assess how far growing social and economic inequalities have placed British governments in breach of international obligations to secure such rights to its citizens (as required by the Council of Europe's Social Charter and the UN International Covenant on Economic, Social and Cultural Rights). However, the severe social and economic inequalities which exist in the United Kingdom are bound to have a profound effect on the exercise of the democratic rights audited in this book (Donnison 1991: Part 1; Townsend 1979). Such inequalities affect Britain's ethnic minorities with especial severity. The black population is still largely confined to the poorest urban areas. Four of the five boroughs with the highest concentration of Afro-Caribbean residents in the country – Lambeth, Hackney, Haringey and Southwark – are in the top ten of Britain's most deprived districts. In 1993, the overall unemployment rate among ethnic minorities was almost double that of white people – 13 per cent compared to 7 per cent. Black and ethnic minority people were highly concentrated in low-paid and casual work (PSI 1993: 112–131). It is not credible to argue that such inequalities do not affect the ability of people in the ethnic minorities to exercise their political and civil rights.

Anti-discrimination laws in the UK

In the absence of a general principle of equality, the scope of the anti-discrimination laws passed by Parliament is crucial to the protection of human rights. We have already indicated the piecemeal nature of these laws and their unequal application throughout the United Kingdom. No comprehensive anti-discrimination code exists in this country. What statutory protection there is outlaws particular types of discrimination in specific and carefully defined circumstances. The most important laws relate to sex and race discrimination in England and Wales.

The Sex Discrimination Act 1975 provides protection from direct and indirect discrimination on the basis of sex or marital status in employment, training, education, the provision of goods and services and the disposal and management of premises. It also aims to protect employees who bring complaints or give evidence under the Act's provisions from being victimised. The 1975 Act covers discrimination by trade unions and employment agencies. Under pressure from the European Court of Justice, it has been widened to cover any aspect of a collective agreement which is discriminatory.

The Race Relations Act 1976, which replaced the Race Relations Act 1965, follows broadly the same approach covering discrimination on 'racial grounds' – 'colour, race, nationality or ethnic or national origins'. The offence of 'incitement to racial hatred', created by the 1965 Act, has now been hived off into public order legislation (see **pp. 176–179**).

Both Acts distinguish between direct and indirect discrimination. The former occurs when a person is treated less favourably than someone of the opposite sex, or of another racial group, would be in the same circumstances (SDA section 1(1)(a); RRA section 1(1)(a)). Motive is irrelevant. The House of Lords has suggested that cases of direct sex discrimination can best be approached by asking the simple question: would the complainant have received the same treatment from the defendant but for his or her sex (*James v Eastleigh Borough Council*, 1990)?

The same test obviously applies to direct race discrimination, but there are two further aspects. First, the Race Relations Act states that segregation on racial grounds is to be regarded as less favourable treatment. Second, discrimination does not necessarily have to be on the basis of the *victim*'s race, as long as it is based on racial grounds: in 1979, the dismissal of a white barmaid who refused to obey an instruction not to serve black customers was held to be unlawful (*Zarcynska v Levy*, 1979).

Anti-discrimination laws

Indirect discrimination is essentially concerned with practices which have the effect, without necessarily the intention, of discriminating against women and certain racial groups, either because of past direct discrimination or existing social conditions. The legal definition of indirect discrimination is complex. Both Acts set out the same test. Someone discriminates against a woman or a person of a particular racial group if they apply to that person 'a requirement or condition' which applies equally to men or people of other racial groups, but

- considerably fewer women or people in the person's racial group can comply with it than men or members of other racial groups; and
- the defendant cannot show that the 'requirement or condition' is justifiable irrespective of the person's gender, colour, race, nationality, or ethnic or national origins; and
- the 'requirement or condition' is to the complainant's detriment because she or he cannot comply with it.

Both Acts provide civil remedies (usually damages) rather than criminal sanctions where discrimination is proven. As a result, the onus is on the private citizen who has suffered from discrimination to bring the action. The unlawful act is effectively categorised as a dispute between individuals, rather than a conflict between the wrongdoer and the state. Some support for the citizen is provided, however, by the creation of two statutory bodies. The Equal Opportunities Commission and the Commission for Racial Equality have responsibility for furthering the aims of the legislation, conducting investigations, and in some circumstances, providing support for individual complainants.

The Sex Discrimination Act 1975 was introduced to reinforce the Equal Pay Act 1970 which prohibits pay discrimination on the basis of gender. In actual fact, since the Equal Pay Act 1970 was not implemented for five years, the two acts came into force at the same time. The underlying principle of the 1970 Act is that a woman can claim equal pay for the 'same or broadly similar work' as a man, or for work which has been 'rated as being equal' by a job evaluation scheme.

European Union law, as we have seen, has also had a huge influence on sex discrimination law and in particular equal pay. Article 119 of the Treaty of Rome governs the principle of equal pay for equal work. This is amplified by the Equal Pay Directive 75/117, while the Equal Treatment Directive 76/207 and the Pregnancy Directive 92/85 govern other aspects of sexual discrimination. These provisions are directly enforceable in domestic courts and many of the positive amendments to sex discrimination law in the last 20 years have been driven by adverse findings in the European Court of Justice against the United Kingdom. For example, following judgment in the case of *Marshall v Southampton AHA* (1993), the government has removed the ceiling of £11,000 compensation which can be awarded by tribunals in cases of sex discrimination with the passage of the Equal Pay (Remedies) Regulations 1993 (a parallel change has been made in the race discrimination legislation).

Save for laws dealing with trade union rights (see Chapter 11), the only other legislation prohibiting discrimination in England and Wales is the Disabled Persons (Employment) Act 1944. As briefly mentioned above, the 1944 Act was based on the belief that people with disabilities have a right to work and require an employment service which will ensure that they secure their fair share of available employment. The backbone of the legislation is a quota scheme by which firms with more than 20 employees are required to ensure that at least 3 per cent of staff they employ are registered as disabled. They are also required to maintain records on the operation of their quota. In addition, certain jobs are reserved to be filled only by people registered as disabled. Contravention of these provisions can make an employer liable to a fine or even a term of imprisonment. (New disability legislation is in the pipeline: see below).

Weaknesses and gaps in anti-discrimination laws

We have already noted the geographical peculiarities and limited nature of British anti-discrimination legislation (**p. 117**). The Sex Discrimination Act and the Race Relations Act do not make sex and race discrimination generally unlawful, but outlaw it only in certain specific situations. The legislation therefore falls far short of international human rights standards. Both Article 14 of the European Convention and Article 2 of the International Covenant prohibit discrimination across the whole range of rights and freedoms set out in each instrument respectively. The overriding international obligation on the United Kingdom is to ensure and secure those rights to its citizens, without discrimination.

Article 26 of the International Covenant goes further. The principle of non-discrimination it contains is not limited to rights provided for in the Covenant (UN Human Rights Committee, General Comment 18/26). In a landmark decision in 1984, the UN Committee held that the denial to married women of social security benefits for which only married men qualified constituted impermissible discrimination under Article 26, even though the International Covenant guarantees no right to social security payments as such (*Zwaan-de-Vries v The Netherlands*, 1984).

Exemptions in domestic anti-discrimination laws lead to further failures to match international human rights standards. Most strikingly, the Race Relations Act is subordinate to other statutes, and even to statutory instruments. Normally where two statutes conflict, or a statute conflicts with *secondary* legislation, the later enactment prevails. However, under the terms of the Act (section 41(1)), any discriminatory practices which occur or arise under any other statute, Order in Council or statutory instrument, *whenever it was enacted*, are lawful. So are discriminatory acts or practices arising from a minister's instructions under any other statute. Even government circulars and ministerial pronouncements concerning matters of nationality and residence are exempted.

At one time, the Sex Discrimination Act was limited in the same way. But after an adverse judgment of the European Court of Justice (*Johnson v Chief Constable of the RUC*, 1986), the Employment Act 1989 effectively nullified statutory provisions violating the 1975 Act's employment and training requirements. No parallel changes were made to the Race Relations Act 1976. The effect is to make lawful any racially discriminatory practices of public officials, such as the police or immigration officers, so long as they are obeying orders. They will often be acting on orders made without Parliament's express knowledge. As the Commission for Racial Equality has pointed out, statutory instruments rarely receive detailed parliamentary scrutiny (see Chapter 3) and ministerial instructions may receive no scrutiny at all. The CRE has argued that:

> The Act should assume the normal status of an Act of Parliament, superior to all earlier Acts and all subordinate legislation. If discrimination is required in any area as a matter of policy, it should be provided expressly in the statute. This would have the valuable effect of requiring each particular discriminatory policy to be examined critically and then defended publicly if it is to be retained.
>
> (*Review of the Race Relations Act*, CRE 1985: 9)

So far as international human rights standards are concerned, no other approach is acceptable. Any distinctions in treatment between different groups of citizens, particularly by or on behalf of governments, are only allowed if they can be objectively justified – by reference to international standards – and if the means employed are reasonably proportionate to the aims. The government's desire for as much flexibility as possible for its activities hardly justifies so wide a series of exemptions from international standards.

The Crown Service and other public bodies may also discriminate in their employment procedures on grounds of birth, nationality, descent and origin. Various public bodies, like the Bank of England, the British Council and the National Army Museum, have taken advantage of this exemption from the 1976 Act (ibid.: 8). In addition, discriminatory actions undertaken to safeguard national security are allowed under both the Race Relations Act and the Sex Discrimination Act. A minister's certificate, confirming that an action was carried out to protect national security, is conclusive proof that the action is exempt. The legality of this exclusion under European Union law was also challenged in the case of *Johnson v Chief Constable of the RUC* (above). The European Court of Justice concluded that the issue of a certificate preventing discrimination claims constituted a failure to ensure effective judicial control of compliance with the terms of the Equal Treatment Directive. As a result, the Sex Discrimination (Amendment) Order 1988 removed employment and vocational training from the national security exclusion.

The reasoning of the European Court of Justice in the *Johnson* case must surely apply to the equivalent exemptions in the Race Relations Act. The court took the view that the requirement of effective judicial control reflects a general principle of law which is inherent in the constitutional traditions of member states of the European Union; and is further required by the European Convention on Human Rights. This view renders the national security exclusion in the Race Relations Act equally deficient. However, the Equal Treatment Directive applies only to sexual discrimination, not racial discrimination, and the European Court of Justice has therefore no jurisdiction. The government has refused to make any changes to the Race Relations Act.

Such public licence to discriminate directly violates the UN Convention on the Elimination of All Forms of Racial Discrimination (CERD). As a contracting state, the United Kingdom has agreed to 'engage in no act or practice of racial discrimination' and to ensure that 'all public authorities and public institutions, national and local . . . act in conformity with this obligation'. CERD does not allow wide-ranging exclusions of this type. The United Kingdom has also agreed to 'review governmental, national and local policies, and to amend, rescind or nullify any laws and regulations which have the effect of creating or perpetuating racial discrimination' (CERD, Article 2(1)(e)). There is no evidence that it has done so; rather the reverse. As the government has refused to recognise the competence of the Committee on the Elimination of Racial Discrimination, the enforcing agency, aggrieved individuals or groups cannot complain to the Committee. Thus, while the United Kingdom clearly violates the Convention, there is little scope for the breach to be directly tested.

The ability of both Acts to combat discrimination has also been severely curtailed by a restrictive ruling of the House of Lords. Both statutes apply to acts done by, or on behalf of, ministers, government departments or statutory bodies, *as they apply to the acts of a private person*. In 1983, a House of Lords interpretation of this phrase narrowed the effect of the Acts. The court ruled that the state activity in question must resemble an act that might be done by a private person, so that exclusively 'public' duties are largely excluded from the ambit of either Act (*R v Entry Clearance Officer ex parte Amin*, 1983). Such duties include the activities of public officials in vitally sensitive public areas such as the administration of justice, police operations, prisons and immigration procedures. The effect can be to deprive those most needing protection from discrimination of a remedy. For example, conscious or unconscious racism by police officers in disproportionately stopping vehicles driven by black men and questioning the occupants is not in itself unlawful. Yet such discriminatory activity is exactly the kind of practice which international human rights bodies have been urging countries which aspire to political equality to protect its citizens against.

The question of when unintentional discriminatory conduct is lawful under the two Acts is obviously of great importance. The circumstances in which a person can justify applying a discriminatory requirement (and can therefore avoid the prohibition on indirect discrimination) have given rise to considerable legal difficulties. Initially, it seemed that the courts were willing to equate justification with necessity (*Steel v Union of Post Office Workers*, 1978). But they then retreated from this position, until, in 1987, the European Court of Justice clarified the scope of the justifiability defence in European Union law. In a landmark decision on appeal from Germany, concerning unequal access for part-time workers – predominantly women – to a company's occupational pension scheme, the court decided that for such a policy to be justified, it must be explained by objective factors unrelated to any discrimination on grounds of sex (*Bilka-Kaufhaus*, 1986).

National courts must now ask themselves, therefore, whether the measures which have caused a complaint correspond to a *real need* on the part of the undertaking; whether the measures are an *appropriate means* of achieving the objective pursued;

and whether they are *necessary* to achieve the objective. Since 1987 courts in England and Wales have followed the guidance provided by the European Court and reverted to a stricter approach (Collins and Meehan 1994: 377) which appears to comply with international human rights standards.

But when it comes to whether an aggrieved person whose rights and freedoms have been violated has an *effective remedy* in British courts, the prospect of a serious violation of international human rights standards looms once again. First, in a case of indirect discrimination, the person who has suffered discrimination will receive no damages if the defendant proves that he or she did not intend to treat the claimant unfavourably on grounds of race or sex (RRA section 57(3); SDA section 66(3)). Secondly, all claims concerning employment must be brought before an industrial tribunal, where legal aid is unavailable. As most commentators agree, 'it is virtually impossible for an employee to enter this procedural minefield and emerge triumphant at the other end with a decision in his or her favour' (Gregory 1987: 75). There is no absolute right under the European Convention to legal aid in civil proceedings. But the European Commission has emphasised that the right 'to a fair and public hearing' under Article 6 requires that everyone who is a party to either civil or criminal proceedings must have a reasonable opportunity to present their case to the court under conditions which do not place them at a disadvantage vis-à-vis their opponent (*X v Federal Republic of Germany*, 1967).

Women may be further denied their right to an effective remedy by the notoriously slow and complex procedures under the equal pay legislation. In more than ten years since the 'equal pay for work of equal value' legislation was introduced, there have only been 23 successful cases, some of which took more than six years to complete. The most significant are still proceeding after seven years and are expected to last several more (Foley 1995: 129). The Equal Opportunities Commission has described the process as 'tortuous, time-consuming and unworkable' and has recently requested the Commission of the European Communities to clarify whether these procedures violate European Union law (EOC Briefing 1993). In 1990 the President of an Employment Appeals tribunal described the legislative provisions as 'scandalous' and amounting to 'a denial of justice' (*Aldridge v British Telecommunications plc*, 1990).

The position of disabled people

Disabled people get very limited protection from discrimination. Throughout its 50 year life, the Disabled Persons (Employment) Act 1944 has been wholly ineffective in providing equal protection of the law to disabled people. Even more than the sex and race discrimination legislation, its field of application is very limited – employment only. Moreover, only one in four firms with 20 or more employees meet the 3 per cent quota of disabled workers. Virtually no firm has ever been prosecuted for non-compliance with the act (Lonsdale and Walker 1984: 6).

A private member's bill, the Civil Rights (Disabled Persons) Bill 1994, aimed at last to give people with disabilities comprehensive rights of non-discrimination. The bill was covertly blocked by government opposition. The government subsequently introduced the more limited Disability Discrimination Bill 1995. This measure contains no enforcement mechanism comparable to the race relations and sex discrimination legislation and confines the protection against discrimination for people with disabilities to a few specific areas – primarily employment and access to goods and services. For the first time, people who believe that they have been discriminated against because of their disability may complain to an industrial tribunal. Defences are provided for employers (for example, unreasonable cost). The Act is undoubtedly a breakthrough. It is only just coming into force, so it cannot be assessed. Generally, in the absence of legislation which seeks fully to give disabled people equal protection of the law, the UK cannot be said to comply with evolving international human rights standards in this sphere. It is true that the only specific instruments protecting the rights of disabled people – in particular the UN Declaration on the Rights of Disabled People 1975 (see Index, **p. 114** above) – are not binding in international law. Yet it is strongly arguable that the category 'other status' in Article 26 of the International Convention includes disability. As explained in the Index, the UN Human Rights Committee has declared that the term includes membership of an 'identifiably distinct category' – a definition which can clearly be applied to people with disabilities. The general trend in human rights instruments is also towards inclusiveness. Among other recent developments, the UN General Assembly adopted Standard Rules on the Equalisation of Opportunities for Persons with Disabilities in 1993. These rules recommended measures covering the full range of circumstances in which discrimination can occur; much like the Civil Rights Bill which the government blocked as too far-ranging.

DATA

Anti-discrimination laws in Northern Ireland

The laws in Northern Ireland governing discrimination on grounds of sex and disability broadly reflect those in England, Scotland and Wales. Therefore we do not propose to deal with them separately here – save to note that similar difficulties arise concerning their scope. The significant difference between Northern Ireland and the rest of the UK is that Northern Ireland has laws prohibiting discrimination on grounds of religious belief or political opinion, but no legislation prohibiting racial discrimination.

A very broad-based prohibition on discrimination on political or religious grounds is contained in the Northern Ireland Constitution Act 1973. Acts by government and public bodies which are discriminatory on political or religious grounds are unlawful and actionable in the courts (section 19(1)). Orders in Council – the main legislative measures for the province – can be challenged too. The 1973 Act also established the Standing Advisory Commission on Human Rights (SACHR), which has the function of advising the Northern Ireland Secretary on human rights issues and in particular:

> on the adequacy and effectiveness of the law for the time being in force in preventing discrimination on the ground of religious belief or political opinion and in providing redress for persons aggrieved by discrimination on either ground.
>
> (section 20)

Northern Ireland

The Commission has produced two detailed and influential reports on religious and political discrimination and equality of opportunity in Northern Ireland. The first, in October 1987, concentrated on employment matters; the second in June 1990 considered other issues, such as discrimination in the provision of goods and services and racial discrimination. Since the first report there have been several significant developments; in particular, the enactment of the Fair Employment (Northern Ireland) Act 1989.

The 1989 Act was passed after a five-year campaign which drew attention to the persistence of large differences between the rates of Catholic and Protestant unemployment in Northern Ireland. An earlier fair employment act in 1976 had failed. The 1989 Act prohibits both direct and indirect discrimination on religious or political grounds, in terms similar to those used in the race and sex discrimination laws (see **pp. 123–125** above). It transferred jurisdiction over individual complaints from the Fair Employment Agency to the Fair Employment Tribunal.

One essential difference between the 1989 Act and non-discrimination laws in England and Wales is that the Northern Ireland measure gives greater emphasis to equality of opportunity. The Act does not impose a positive duty on employers to pursue equality of opportunity, but does require all employers with more than 10 employees to register with the Fair Employment Commission. Registered employers are obliged to review internal employment practices at least once every three years to see if 'fair participation' is provided. All large public and private employers (with more than 250 staff) must submit annual monitoring returns to the Commission. If it considers that a firm is failing to offer 'fair participation', the Commission can require affirmative action.

A patchwork of anti-discrimination law

The absence of legislation prohibiting racial discrimination in Northern Ireland constitutes a clear breach of international human rights standards. The Standing Advisory Commission has made sure that the government is fully aware of its non-compliance. In 1990, the Commission warned that it was clear that 'the various United Nations sponsored covenants and conventions impose a general obligation on the United Kingdom Government to ensure that its legislation provides equal protection throughout its territory against all relevant forms of discrimination' (SACHR, Cmnd 1107, 1990: 22). The Commission reminded the government that the UN Committee on the Elimination of Discrimination was not convinced by the reasons it had given for not extending the Race Relations Act 1976 to Northern Ireland (SACHR, 1990: 23). The government has so far failed to act on the Commission's recommendation that the 1976 Act should be extended (though it is understood that this may now be in the pipeline).

The general prohibition on discrimination on political or religious grounds of the Constitution Act 1973 remains largely unused. The Committee for the Administration of Justice in Northern Ireland suggests that this may be because it is generally assumed – perhaps correctly – that the Act applies only to 'direct discrimination' (Dickson and Scarman 1990: 169). The Standing Advisory Commission has recommended that the 1973 Act be amended specifically to cover indirect as well as direct discrimination (SACHR, 1990). The government's reluctance to clarify the position, and the very real possibility that the Act does not apply to indirect discrimination, means that the United Kingdom fails to satisfy international standards prohibiting discrimination on grounds of religious belief and political opinion in Northern Ireland, let alone the rest of the UK where no prohibitions exist at all.

The Fair Employment (Northern Ireland) Act 1989 undoubtedly improves on the 1973 Act, but it is confined to employment. Again, the Standing Advisory Commission has repeatedly recommended the government to extend the Act in line with the race and sex discrimination laws in England and Wales – that is, to cover the provision of goods, facilities and services (SACHR, 1990). We endorse the Commission's view that 'the maintenance of these major differences in coverage cannot be justified in light of the United Kingdom's international obligations' (1990).

The overall situation in Northern Ireland is particularly unsatisfactory. No comprehensive measures outlawing discrimination exist.

The scope of affirmative action

The very principle of affirmative action is regarded with deep suspicion in the United Kingdom. In most circumstances, affirmative action is actually unlawful. There are only one or two exceptions. The race and sex anti-discrimination laws permit positive action to be taken in England and Wales to encourage members of one sex or of particular racial groups to apply for, or to be specially trained for, work in which they have been under-represented. They may be encouraged, for example, by specific words of encouragement or in the wording of job advertisements. But taking sex or race into account in choosing between applicants goes beyond mere encouragement. So a council which considered only black and ethnic minority applicants for two gardening apprenticeships acted unlawfully (*Hughes and Gissing v Hackney Borough Council*, 1987).

In addition, the Race Relations Act 1976 contains a general rule that people of a particular racial group may lawfully be given facilities or services to meet the special education, training or welfare needs of people in the same group, or to provide them with ancillary benefits. Under the 1976 Act, seats may be reserved for women on elected bodies of trade unions and employers' associations and extra seats may be created for women to secure a 'reasonable minimum number' of women on the body concerned. Finally, the NI Fair Employment Commission can require affirmative action by a firm which does not provide 'fair participation' in its employment practices (see **p. 130**).

The thorny issues of affirmative action

International human rights instruments permit affirmative action 'as long as such action is needed to correct discrimination in fact' (UN Human Rights Committee, General Comment 18/37 of 1989). None of the measures outlined above exceed this limitation and accordingly they satisfy international human rights standards.

Affirmative action

Whether additional measures are required is a thorny issue. The UN Human Rights Committee has repeatedly stressed that Article 26 of the International Covenant requires more than the mere prohibition of discrimination and may entail 'affirmative action designed to ensure the positive enjoyment of rights' (General Comment 4/13 of 1991). Arguably, therefore, member states are under a duty to take positive action wherever significant discrimination exists in their society. The Human Rights Committee also appears keen to endorse transitional action which 'may involve granting for a time to the part of the population concerned certain preferential treatment in specific matters as compared with the rest of the population' (GC 18/37 of 1989).

There is no dispute about the prevalence of discrimination against women and racial minorities in the United Kingdom. Earlier in Chapter 7 we gave graphic examples of the inequalities which severely affect the lives and prospects of the three million people in Britain's ethnic minorities. These inequalities are closely associated with the high degree of discrimination and racism in British society – a fact which the majority of white and black people in this country acknowledge (*Guardian*, 20–22 March 1995). We also gave particular examples of the unequal participation of women in public life and of people from ethnic minorities in the criminal justice system. We could easily multiply such examples – beginning with, perhaps, women's disadvantage in the labour market where, despite fair pay laws, their wages are still, on average, 28 per cent lower than men's (Labour Force Survey, Spring 1993; New Earnings Surveys).

The persistence of these patterns of discrimination, despite the various anti-discrimination laws, raises the question of whether the government is doing enough to comply with its international obligations on positive action. The UN Human Rights Committee raises the question with some impatience in its official comments on the United Kingdom's human rights record in July 1995. The Committee acknowledges the government's efforts to combat racial and ethnic discrimination, for example. But its members urge the government 'to take further action to tackle remaining problems of racial and ethnic discrimination and of social exclusion'; and recommend 'forceful action . . . to ensure that women play an equal role in society and that they enjoy the full protection of the law' (CCPR/C/79/Add. 55: para. 26).

Conclusions: 'The British Way of Doing Things'

The system

Governments in the United Kingdom rely heavily on an unexamined belief that existing arrangements – the three pillars of parliamentary sovereignty, a public culture of liberty, and the rule of law – fully protect political rights and freedoms in this country. They along with some judges assert that protections in statute and common law are sufficient to meet the requirements set out in the international human rights instruments – and especially the European Convention – to which the United Kingdom is party.

Official complacency is compounded by the extraordinary degree of informality in the 'unwritten' constitutional and political system in Britain. The flexibility which is said to be the great virtue of this system often allows for arbitrary and even careless conduct at all levels of government. It also means that while the United Kingdom shares most of the values of liberty which are enshrined in the International Covenant on Civil and Political Rights, and the European Convention on Human Rights, the codified nature of such instruments is 'alien' to the British culture of government.

Thus, while the 1976 green paper on incorporation of the Convention into British law categorically states that its conformity with British obligations under the Convention is regularly reviewed, and the UK's periodic reports to the UN Human Rights Committee assert British compliance with the Covenant, it is clear from Chapters 3 and 7 that whatever reviews take place are superficial and flawed exercises (see, for example, **pp. 118–119**). Governments are largely indifferent to their obligations under the instruments they have ratified; as we have seen, they will pass and operate legislation, primary and secondary, which they know is in breach, or likely to be, of these obligations (for example, see Chapter 7). They are negligent in their duty to ensure that legislative proposals do not violate their terms, and deficient in carrying out their reporting and educational responsibilities. This is in part because Britain's responsibilities under international treaties are ordered by the Foreign Office under prerogative powers, and tend therefore to be handled in a way which is traditionally 'ring-fenced' from parliamentary or public view.

The role of Parliament

One of Parliament's prime roles is said to be the protection of individual rights against encroachment by the state, either by way of legislation or administrative action; entrenching positive rights in legislation is rarely seen as falling within that role. But government's dominance of the House of Commons, through its

Parliament

disciplined party majority, has neutered the Commons' ability properly to fulfil even this rather limited role. The House of Lords lacks the democratic legitimacy to challenge government, however pertinent its views and amendments to legislation may be (Chapters 3 and 5). Under normal circumstances, the governing party's majority is sufficient to carry all government legislation and to protect the government and ministers from parliamentary sanctions. The government's overwhelming desire to get its 'business' through Parliament means that it is not amenable to amendments, however well-intentioned or expert, and certainly not from opposition members. The committee stage on bills, which is supposed to subject intended legislation to close scrutiny, actually represents the continuation of partisan political battle, not disintererested deliberation.

Certain MPs and peers on all sides of the political divide distinguish themselves by their skilled devotion to issues of individual liberties, democratic practice and executive abuse. Such members are rarely linked to the hierarchies of power in the government, or opposition, parties and are liable therefore to be labelled as 'maverick' and consigned to the margins of political influence. But members of both Houses generally are too overworked and under-equipped. Few have a thorough knowledge of the terms and standards of international human rights instruments or even an interest in such matters (Chapter 3).

Besides which, the actions of government, ministers and departments, and public bodies generally, are far removed from effective parliamentary oversight. Ministers possess wide discretionary powers – which are in effect at the service of the whole bureaucracy – to drive the machinery of government. Parliament lacks the will, and as currently constituted, the means too, adequately to check the mass of secondary legislation which passes through it annually and confers yet more powers on the executive. Through a variety of such instruments, 'quasi-legislation' and statutory and non-statutory codes and guidance, violations of the European Conventions occur and are identified by the European Court (Table 3.1). Other violations go unchecked, and yet have real impact on the lives of people whose rights are most vulnerable to administrative decision – prisoners, state beneficiaries, police suspects, and others. All government activity is supposed to be accountable to Parliament through the doctrine of ministerial responsibility. It is a commonplace that this doctrine, if anything, limits genuine accountability to Parliament (Chapter 3). As the pivot of democratic accountability to the people's representatives in Parliament for the universes of decision-making of a complex extended state, it is a fiction. Parliament is an unreliable pillar for the protection of political rights and freedoms. There are obvious reforms which would strengthen Parliament against the executive, many of which have been advanced by Commons committees. The simple fact is that government has no interest in making a rod for its own back and has blocked the great majority of reforms.

The role of public opinion

Halsbury's Laws of England states that public opinion is a mainstay of the 'liberties of the subject'. A culture of liberty is indeed the ultimate safeguard of popular rights

– and in the absence of public support for democracy and freedom, constitutional guarantees, however firmly entrenched in law, can save neither. But public opinion can also sanction, or even encourage, violations of basic political rights and freedoms, or politicians will enact 'instant legislation, conceived in fear and prejudice' in anticipation of the public view (see Chapter 4). In a mixed and pluralistic society like modern Britain there is no single public, but rather a shifting set of public views and values. While long-term attitudes are discernible, majority opinion is not a constant given. The evidence of opinion surveys, and in particular the *British Social Attitudes* surveys of 1990 and 1994, suggests that public opinion as a whole has moved in a less tolerant and 'anti-reformist' direction; that fear of crime has diminished concern for traditional protections, such as a suspect's right to silence; and that the 'race card' (playing on racial prejudice) is a potent political instrument. 'Well-informed' opinion is clearly disturbed by current political trends, as is evident in the formation of Charter 88, the high profile of constitutional issues in the quality media, and the judiciary's concern about executive interference in the sphere of the courts. Yet for most people human rights issues, and particularly minority rights, are 'somewhat abstract and hypothetical' matters which do not affect their everyday lives. The public are poorly educated in such matters, anyway, and are prepared to admit it. No doubt, to take Dicey's notorious example, people would still refuse a command to kill blue-eyed babies. But there must be considerable doubt whether they would intervene positively to protect the rights of minorities or formal safeguards of liberties; while the record shows that public opinion has endorsed violations in both respects. Proper constitutional and legal safeguards are vital precautions, not only to reinforce popular support for liberties, but also to safeguard political rights and freedoms when public opinion is inflamed or neglectful.

The role of the courts

The courts are independent of the executive, but in many respects subordinate to it through the practical effects of the overriding rule of parliamentary sovereignty. They are thus bound to apply any legislation which has passed properly through Parliament, even if it clearly violates political rights and freedoms, as measured either by domestic values or by this country's international obligations. Yet they perform three vital functions which bear on the protection of such rights. They interpret and apply legislation; they have the power to review executive actions; and they protect 'basic interests' through the common law (Chapter 5).

However, their actual powers to protect fundamental human rights and to control the executive are constrained by legal and procedural limits. They cannot review the contents of legislation nor consider the merits of executive actions. The vast expansion of judicial review is still channelled through three conduits, *illegality*, *irrationality*, and *procedural impropriety*, which confine it almost wholly to questions of process, not substance. *Irrationality*, for example, is not sufficiently robust (to the dismay of some judges) to outlaw the blatant discriminatory practice of the military authorities in dismissing homosexuals serving in the armed forces, entirely irrespective of their conduct. Since the International Covenant and European Convention

The courts

have not been incorporated into domestic law, judges cannot apply their provisions and prohibit violations. Thus, they are also unable to apply the strict three-part test and standards of 'proportionality' developed under such instruments in judicial review of executive action. Moreover, the judiciary imposes further restrictions on itself, most notably in cases involving national security.

The common law protects 'basic interests' rather than 'positive rights'. These interests are a poor fit with modern political rights and freedoms, as defined by international human rights standards. Thus, while the right to life and liberty is protected as a basic interest under the common law, other rights – such as free speech and assembly – are protected only in the negative sense, that people are entitled to do as they wish, so long as they do not break the law or infringe the rights of others. Notoriously, people have no right to privacy, unless someone who violates their privacy infringes a basic interest too. Political rights, like that of public protest for example, are so hedged about by statute and common-law protection of other interests that they barely exist in the sense that they can be positively claimed and exercised. International standards require that restrictions on such rights should be strictly limited and clearly laid down in law; and that people have remedies in law where they are denied. The law in the UK fails to provide such protection.

Human rights instruments are nevertheless said to have a gathering influence in the domestic courts. There is little evidence to support this view. The European Convention has occasionally been called upon to resolve uncertainties in statute law; but where the law is clear, it must be applied, regardless of whether it breaches international standards. Almost every attempt to import broad human rights principles into judicial review proceedings has been blocked by the judges. Under common law, the courts have refused to introduce new rights and obligations derived from international human rights instruments, nor can they grant a remedy solely because an international human rights obligation has been violated. Our own research shows that they are rarely relied upon in judicial decision-making. The International Covenant has only been cited in ten cases in the higher court (0.01 per cent of the total from 1972 to 1995) and the Convention in 173 (0.2 per cent from 1972–93). Taken together, they affected the actual outcome in only four cases. Thus, their influence is negligible.

Questions of equality

The Race Relations and Sex Discrimination Acts introduced in the UK in the 1960s and 1970s represented a significant step forward. The courts had failed to develop any meaningful concept of equality through the common law and Parliament had until then done nothing to prevent open discrimination on grounds of race and sex in all walks of life. Advances since then have chiefly occurred in the field of sex discrimination in employment, largely as a result of adverse rulings by the European Court of Justice with which the UK is bound to comply. In Northern Ireland, fair employment legislation has been strengthened, in part in response to US pressure. The only other significant legislative development has been the new Disability Discrimination Act which will provide strictly limited protection in this sphere.

We have demonstrated the narrow remit of the race, sex and disability anti-discrimination laws, concentrating as they do on employment and the supply of goods and services; the significant statutory and judicial limits on that remit; and the restricted nature of the remedies they offer. These laws do not even apply uniformly throughout the United Kingdom: religious, but not racial, discrimination is prohibited in Northern Ireland; racial, but not religious, discrimination in the rest of the UK. Even in relation to race, sex and disability, there is no protection against discrimination in the UK on many of the grounds covered by the European Convention (such as in the right to privacy, free association or free assembly). The United Kingdom provides no protection against discrimination in other significant areas, including age, health (where HIV-positive people are especially at risk) and sexual orientation. Incidents of direct discrimination abound in these spheres.

At the root of this arbitrary, variably effective patchwork of legislation lies the absence of a general right to equal protection of the law. This right to equality is explicitly required by Article 26 of the International Covenant. In its absence, major categories of people in need receive no protection against discrimination at all from the law, and even those who do receive only partial protection.

Equality before the law is one of the proudest canons of the law in the United Kingdom. All laws, it has been claimed from Dicey onwards, are applied equally, regardless of status or creed. But public bodies, officials and ministers are specifically allowed to take discriminatory actions which would be against the law if performed by private individuals. Restrictions on the types of cases and legal forums in which legal aid is available, and the low qualifying financial criteria for eligibility, devalue equality before the law for most people in most circumstances. Thus, the proposition that citizens are free to do as they wish, unless expressly prohibited by the law, is of dubious currency. In practice, they are free only to engage in actions which, if challenged, they can afford to defend in court.

The systemic failure

This analysis of the role of the three pillars of British liberties reveals that, separately as well as in combination, they fail adequately to protect political rights and freedoms in the United Kingdom. Each part of the 'system' – Parliament, public opinion and the courts – requires the additional support of a consistent set of civil and political rights, secured in law or practice, if they are to play their role in protecting liberties effectively – individually or in combination. Such a resource could strengthen Parliament against the executive; would provide additional support to public opinion; and could give the courts constitutional legitimacy and established standards and tests for the interpretation of statute, judicial review and the development of common law. The precise legal or institutional safeguards require full public debate; we discuss some possibilities later (**p. 304**). But a full set of rights, however secured, could for the first time introduce the democratic principle of equality into United Kingdom law and practice; and provide aggrieved citizens with remedies in the domestic courts, instead of at the end of the long and costly process of appeal to the European Commission and Court.

CONCLUSIONS

Systemic failure

Above all, adequately protected rights could provide a constitutional 'fail-safe' mechanism which is now missing. An executive with a large majority in Parliament possesses almost unchallengeable powers over people's lives. There is an urgent need for restraint of government-in-Parliament, especially at times of panic about enemy spies, terrorism, rising crime – or even football hooligans or 'dangerous' dogs. In the absence of constitutional safeguards for democracy and liberty, the role of judges, peers and concerned citizens is reduced to that ascribed to Parliament by Austin Mitchell MP – 'heckling the steamroller' (Garrett 1992: 16).

Against all the disadvantages, the principal advantage of the current system is said to be its flexibility. Both statute and common law are adaptable. Statute law is in theory infinitely flexible; in practice, it is constrained by political realities only. Common law is less so, because only basic interests it already recognises can be developed. Thus, the common law has failed to protect privacy or prevent most discrimination – the only resort, therefore, has been to statute law. The development of the common law is further constrained by the prevailing views of the judiciary. In neither case does this flexibility necessarily lead to the further protection of political rights and freedoms. On the contrary, it can take the law in other directions altogether. We now turn in Part 3 to audit individual political rights and freedoms against evolving international human rights standards.

PART 3

Political Rights and Freedoms – The Audit

8   The Ascendancy of Official Secrecy

Freedom of information

The freedoms of information and expression are inter-connected. Both are recognised as essential to democratic society by global institutions and governments around the world. At its first session in 1946 the UN General Assembly declared:

> Freedom of information is a fundamental human right and . . . the touch-stone of all the freedoms to which the United Nations is consecrated.

In 1982, the Committee of Ministers of the Council of Europe, adopting the Declaration on Freedom of Expression and Information in 1982, held that 'the principles of genuine democracy, the rule of law and respect for human rights form the basis of [European] cooperation, and that . . . freedom of expression and information is a fundamental element of those principles'.

This chapter assesses freedom of information in this country, as logically it comes first. Here, we cover access to information held by the government, court hearings and documents and the use of injunctions to prohibit disclosure of information. We examine issues of freedom of expression in the next chapter. The press and broadcasting media operate under the same laws which apply to the population at large, and their role is discussed, as appropriate, in this and the following chapter.

The basic principles of democracy which govern the Audit, popular control and political equality, require ready access by all citizens to all relevant information and the ability to exchange opinions about the society in which they live, the way it is governed, and changes which might (or might not) be made. In the United Kingdom, however, government information is regarded as the property of the Crown. Until 1989, the unauthorised release of any state information, however trivial, was regarded as a breach of the draconian Official Secrets Act 1911. The Official Secrets Act 1989 modernised the 1911 Act, retaining criminal sanctions for the release of information of certain types. In 1994, the government introduced a voluntary code of practice for the release of official information. This is a discretionary scheme which does not provide a public right of access to official documents. Various western democracies, including some with 'Westminster model' constitutions, have introduced 'right to know' regimes, which confer a qualified right of access on their citizens.

International standards for freedom of information

> *Everyone has the right to freedom of opinion and expression; this right includes freedom to hold opinions without interference and to seek, receive and impart information and ideas through any media and regardless of frontiers.*
>
> (Article 19, Universal Declaration of Human Rights)

Freedom of expression ranks as one of the most highly-prized human rights. Article 19 of the International Covenant on Civil and Political Rights – expressed in similar terms to the same article of the Universal Declaration – has become a world-wide symbol and benchmark of that right. Article 19 guarantees freedom of expression and affirms the right of everyone to 'seek, receive and impart information and ideas of all kinds'. Thus, Article 19 makes freedom of information an integral part of freedom of expression.

Article 19 guarantees both freedoms, regardless of frontiers, 'either orally, in writing or in print, in the form of art, or through any other media of his choice'. Every communicable type of subjective idea and opinion, of value-neutral news and information, of commercial advertising, arts works, political commentary, pornography, etc., is protected under Article 19 (Nowak 1993: 341). The equivalent Article 10 of the European Convention is expressed in broadly similar terms, but does not specifically include reference to seeking information and ideas. However, it is widely assumed to protect this right implicitly. The European Court has drawn on the text and drafting history of the International Covenant to apply Article 10 widely (*Müller v Switzerland*, 1988; *Groppera Radio AG v Switzerland*, 1990). The preamble to the Council of Europe's Convention on Transfrontier Television (which entered into force in May 1993) states that the 'continuous development of information and communication technology should serve to further the right, regardless of frontiers, to express, to seek, to receive and to impart information and ideas, whatever their course'.

Freedom of information is protected from interference by public authorities *and* private interests. An Indian motion to insert the words 'without government interference' into Article 19 was defeated at the drafting stages because the majority of delegates decided that private interests and media monopolies were as harmful to the free flow of information as state censorship (see generally, Nowak 1993: 344–345). This *horizontal* effect is fully recognised under the European Convention. In 1992, the European Commission observed in a case challenging the Austrian government's broadcasting monopoly, that 'Article 10 is based on the idea that a pluralism of ideas must be safeguarded' (*Informationsverein Lentia v Austria*, 1992).

The European Court has consistently made clear that the European Convention's protection of freedom of expression rests in significant measure on the public's 'right to know' (*Thorgeirson v Iceland*, 1992); and that the right to receive information 'basically prohibits a government from restricting a person from receiving information that others may wish or be willing to impart to him' (*Leander v Sweden*, 1987).

Restricting rights

Formal recognition of civil and political rights is not enough. It is essential that any restriction of rights recognised by both the International Covenant and the European Convention be closely scrutinised. The two instruments set out a strict three-part test:

1. Any restriction on civil and political rights must be 'prescribed by law'
2. The restriction must be justified by one of the aims under the International Covenant or European Convention
3. The restriction must be shown to be 'necessary in a democratic society'.

    This test is of fundamental importance. For that reason, we deal with the test in detail in **Box A, pp. 21–22**. Here, broadly, the test requires that ordinary citizens can readily discover what legal restrictions to any right exist with enough clarity for them to be able to regulate their conduct. Any restrictions must then meet one of the aims recognised under either instrument as a legitimate ground for the restriction of civil and political rights. These aims are:

● the protection of the rights and freedoms of others
● national security
● public safety
● public health and morals
● the prevention of public disorder or crime
● the protection of the reputation of others
● the prevention of disclosure of information received in confidence
● maintaining the authority and impartiality of the judiciary.

This list is intended to be exhaustive. States may not introduce other restrictions or stretch the meaning of the criteria listed above to add others. Finally, states must show both that the restriction fulfils a pressing social need and that it is proportionate to the aim of responding to that need. They cannot merely assert that a particular restriction is 'necessary in a democratic society', but must provide concrete evidence of a genuine and serious threat.

    The bodies which interpret the tests – the UN Human Rights Committee and the European Court and Commission of Human Rights – have framed their notion of 'democratic society' in terms of such concepts as 'pluralism, tolerance and broad-mindedness'; and have made it clear that although the term 'necessary' is not synonymous with 'indispensable', it does not simply mean 'reasonable' (*Handyside v UK*, ECtHR, 1976).

Evolving human rights standards

The evolving human rights standards for freedom of information can now be said to incorporate the following features:

International standards

- The right to 'receive information' does not confer a specific duty on the state to provide a general right of access to information through, for example, freedom of information laws, where a government or official is unwilling to release that information (*Leander v Sweden*, 1987, ECtHR).

- Nevertheless the trend is towards a general presumption of access to information held by the state. The European Committee of Ministers adopted the *Recommendation on the Access to Information Held by Public Authorities* in 1981, which calls on member states to grant

    Everyone within their jurisdiction ... the right to obtain, on request, information held by the public authorities other than legislative bodies and judicial authorities ... subject only to such limitations and restrictions as are necessary in a democratic society for the protection of legitimate public ... and private interests.

    (Rec. No. R (81) 19)

- In 1982, the Council of Europe reaffirmed the importance in a democratic society of freedom of information and access to information in the public sector in particular. The participating states made known their intention to protect the right of everyone to 'seek and receive information and ideas, whatever their source, as well as to impart them under the conditions set out in Article 10 of the European Convention' (*Declaration on the Freedom of Expression and Information*, 29 April 1982).

- In addition, the state's obligation not to interfere with the communication of information is particularly strong where the information is of vital concern to the recipient's private or family life (*Gaskin v UK*, 1989, ECtHR).

- In earlier cases, the European Commission of Human Rights refused to rule out the possibility that in certain circumstances, Article 10 of the European Convention includes a right of access to documents which are not generally available (*X v Ireland*, 1980; *Behrendt v Germany*, 1981).

- The trend towards a general presumption of access to information held by the state in Europe has been shadowed in the United Nations Human Rights Committee – but less clearly. The preparatory papers of the International Covenant indicate that the word 'seek' was selected over 'gather' only to endorse active and investigative journalism in the public interest. Recently, a Human Rights Committee member has suggested that the phrase 'seek, receive and impart information and ideas of all kinds' is open to a much more dynamic approach in terms of such issues as the openness of local and national government, access to official records, access to personal information and accessibility of the media (McGoldrick 1991: 470).

- There is some authority for the argument that information on human rights forms a special category of information to which the public are entitled. In 1990, the participating states of the Conference on Security and Cooperation in Europe, including the UK, committed themselves to 'respect the right of everyone, individually or in association with others, to seek, receive and impart freely views and information on human rights and fundamental freedoms; including the rights to disseminate and publish such views and information' (*Document on the Copenhagen Meeting of the Conference on the Human Dimension of the CSCE*, 1990).

■ Although certain categories of officials (for example, military service staff) owe an obligation of confidence in relation to information concerning the performance of their duties, official secrets – including classified military information – do not fall outside the scope of international protection of freedom of expression (*Hadjianastassiou v Greece*, 1992, ECtHR).

■ States are generally afforded a wide latitude in determining when national security is threatened. However, it is clear that national security should only be invoked when the threat is to a state's territorial or national integrity, not merely to a given government (International Centre Against Censorship, 1993a: 114).

■ Even where national security is involved, it cannot outweigh the interests of the press and public in imparting and receiving information once that information has been published elsewhere (*The Observer and Guardian v UK*, 1991, ECtHR).

■ Access to court hearings and documents is integral to freedom of information. The media must not overstep the bounds imposed by the proper administration of justice, but they have a duty to impart information and ideas concerning matters that come before the courts, just as in other areas of public interest, and the public has a right to receive them (*Sunday Times v UK*, 1979, ECtHR).

■ However, access to court hearings and documents may legitimately be regulated under both Article 19 of the International Covenant and Article 10 of the European Convention in order to protect 'the rights ... of others' or to maintain 'the authority and impartiality of the judiciary'.

■ The paramount 'right of others' which requires protection is the right to a fair trial (Article 14 of the International Covenant; Article 6 of the European Convention). While both treaties recognise the right to a 'public hearing', they also provide that the press and public may be excluded from all or part of the trial for a number of listed reasons, including: to safeguard the interests of morals, public order, national security and juveniles, to protect the private lives of the parties and to prevent prejudice of a fair trial.

■ Defendants in criminal proceedings have a right of access to information and, in particular, documentation (under Article 14(3)(b) and (e) of the International Covenant and Article 6(3)(b) and (d) of the European Convention, which provide that they should have 'adequate time and facilities' for the preparation of a defence and the right to 'examine, or have examined' witnesses for the prosecution).

- Article 10 of the European Convention does not prohibit censorship by way of prior restraints on publication (*The Observer and Guardian v UK*, 1991, ECtHR); but it is not clear whether censorship by 'prior restraint' is acceptable under the International Covenant (the preparatory papers suggest that the drafters considered it justified in exceptional circumstances only).

- Nonetheless the European Court has emphasised that 'the dangers inherent in prior restraints are such that they call for the most careful scrutiny on the part of the court'. According to the minority view in the same case, prior restraint should only be imposed on the press 'in very rare and exceptional circumstances' (*The Observer and Guardian v UK*, 1991, ECtHR).

Open government

The United Kingdom is one of the few countries in western Europe which does not have a freedom of information statute for central government. In UK law, unpublished information in the possession of central government, created, received or used for official business, is the 'property' of the Crown (Birkinshaw 1990: 1). In addition to the ordinary criminal law of theft, governments may invoke the Public Records Acts, the Official Secrets Acts or the law of confidence or copyright to protect the information in its possession.

However, in 1993, an Open Government white paper (Cmnd 2290) paved the way for a voluntary code of practice 'extending access to official information, and responding to reasonable requests for information, except where disclosure would not be in the public interest' (Open Government: Code of Practice on Access to Government Information, para. 1). Part 2 of the code sets out 15 'categories of information' which are exempt from the commitment to release official information. The code retained the 30-year embargo on the release of public records (see below) and contemplated the retention of many of the 200 or so statutory provisions prohibiting disclosure of official information (Cmnd 2290: paras 1.18 and 1.19).

The latest version of *Questions of Procedure for Ministers* also commits ministers to open government. Revised by John Major after his election victory in 1992, *QPM* identified as one of the facets of ministerial accountability to Parliament 'the duty to give Parliament, including its select committees, and *the public* [our emphasis] as full information as possible about the policies, decisions and actions of the Government, and not to deceive or mislead Parliament and the public'. However, in response to the Nolan report on standards in public life, the government has proposed that the simple principle, recommended by Nolan, that ministers 'must be as open as possible with Parliament and the public', should be qualified by the following addition, 'withholding information only when disclosure would not be in the public interest, which should be decided in accordance with established Parliamentary convention, the law and any relevant Government Code of Practice' (HC Deb, 2 November 1995, c456).

Public records

Before 1959, the public possessed no right of access to public records whatsoever. Even now, the Public Records Acts of 1958 and 1967 prevent their disclosure for 30 years (the so-called '30-year rule'). At the request of individual departments or ministers, and with the approval of the Lord Chancellor, this period can be extended for up to 100 years for any documents, if required 'for administrative purposes or [if they] ought to be retained for any other special reason'. The criteria for retention have recently been reviewed and now cover:

- exceptionally sensitive records containing information which, if disclosed, would harm the country's defence, international relations, national security, law and order, or the economic interests of the UK and its dependent territories
- documents containing confidential information, the disclosure of which would or might constitute a breach of good faith
- documents containing information about individuals which, if disclosed, would cause substantial distress to them or their descendants, or put them in danger.

In each case it is also a condition of retention that the actual harm by disclosure should be identified (Open Government, Cmnd 2290, HMSO 1983).

The public have access to much local government information and personal records. Local council and committee meetings are open to the press and public, unless certain information falling into special categories recognised by statute is to be discussed – in which case, the council must state in advance the reason for secrecy (Local Government Act 1971). The press and public also have a right to inspect a wide range of local authority documents. Pollution records and much local environmental information are also open to the public under the Environmental Protection Act 1990 and the Environmental Information Regulations 1992.

The Access to Personal Files Act 1990 gives individuals access to housing and social services files held on them by local authorities. The Access to Health Records Act 1990 gives patients the right of access to records held on them by their doctors and the health authorities.

Official secrecy

The Open Government white paper lists over 200 statutory provisions prohibiting the disclosure of official information (Cmnd 2290: annex B). Only the main controls over freedom of information in relation to official secrecy, contained in the Official Secrets Acts 1911 and 1989, are considered here. The 1989 Act repealed most of the notorious 1911 Act, which passed through Parliament in a day. But section 1 survives and prohibits certain activities undertaken for purposes prejudicial to the interests of the state – approaching, being near or being in a 'prohibited place', or gathering or obtaining or communicating information, such as sketches, plans or notes which may be of use to an actual or potential enemy. 'Prohibited places' are usually military establishments, but could include any place of military significance or of interest to an enemy state. Unusually, the accused must establish the absence of any prejudicial purpose, reversing the normal burden of proof.

The 1989 Act replaced the 'catch-all' section 2 of the 1911 Act which made the unauthorised disclosure of any official information at all a criminal offence. In theory, to reveal how many cups of tea were consumed each day in the MI5 canteen was a criminal offence (Robertson 1989: 132). In practice, two men were prosecuted for disclosing details of army clothing contracts in 1919 even though this information had no military significance whatsoever (*R v Crisp and Homewood*). Criticism of section 2 became widespread. In 1985, a jury refused to convict civil servant Clive Ponting for passing on classified information about the sinking of the Argentinian warship *Belgrano* to Tam Dalyell MP in 1985 and made reform inevitable.

It remains a criminal offence to disclose state secrets. The 1989 act sets out six main categories of information in respect of which disclosure is controlled: security and intelligence, defence, international relations, information obtained in confidence from other states or international organisations, crime and law enforcement, and communications intercepted under the authority of a warrant (for example, telephone tapping). It is an offence for a Crown servant or government contractor to make an unauthorised disclosure of information in any of these categories. However, subject to the exceptions dealt with below, the disclosure must also be shown to be 'damaging' to the state's interests. For these purposes, damaging means: causing damage to the work of the security and intelligence services; damaging the capability of the armed forces, causing loss of life or injury, or seriously damaging equipment; endangering the interests of the UK or its citizens abroad or seriously obstructing the protection of interests; and impeding law enforcement.

The Act imposes two absolute bans. It is always an offence to disclose intercepted communications. Staff in the secret services and people 'notified' under section 1(1) of the Act are guilty of a criminal offence if (without authority) they disclose *any* information, document or other article relating to security or intelligence. No damage needs to be shown. The secretary of state can have a notice served on anyone carrying out work connected with the security and intelligence services if he or she believes its nature is such that the interests of national security require it.

Confidence and copyright

The law of confidence and copyright is based on the notion that information is property. Broadly speaking, breach of confidence is a civil remedy affording protection against the disclosure or use of information that is not publicly known and that has been given in circumstances imposing an obligation not to disclose that information without the authority of the person who gave it (Robertson and Nicol 1992: 173). This area of law largely developed in the field of employer–employee relationships. But since about 1975, the Attorney-General has invoked it to restrain publication of government information: for example, to try to prevent the publication of the memoirs of the former secretary of state, Richard Crossman, and, more recently, to try to prevent newspapers publishing the contents of Peter Wright's book *Spycatcher* (see below).

Confidence and copyright

The law against breach of copyright, in brief, gives the owner of any work the right to stop others reproducing it without permission. The Copyright Act 1988 creates several categories of 'work' in which copyright can exist. Under section 163, any work of an officer or servant of the Crown in the course of their duties qualifies for copyright protection and the Crown is the first owner of any such copyright.

Public access to government information

The trend in international human rights standards is towards open government and a presumption in favour of disclosure of government-held information. Many western European countries are introducing some form of freedom of information legislation or practice in line with this trend. Commonwealth countries, like Australia and New Zealand, influenced though they are by the Westminster style of government, have adopted 'right to know' laws (Birkinshaw 1990: 1). The UK government refuses to pass similar legislation, remaining in its own words 'opposed to [a] general statutory right of access to information on the internal workings of government'. The argument is that 'ministerial accountability to parliament would be undermined by appeals on release of information to the courts or some form of Information Commissioner' (Third Report to the UN Human Rights Committee, 1989: para. 256). In the Commons debate on the Scott report, the President of the Board of Trade rejected the 'legalistic approach' of freedom of information regimes, arguing that they were 'inflexible in . . . application and much more expensive' for users (HC Deb, 26 February 1996, c595).

This argument is closely associated with the classic statements advanced by ministers signing public interest immunity certificates to prevent the disclosure of official documents to the defence in the Matrix Churchill case in 1992 (see **pp. 160–162** below):

> It would . . . be against the public interest that documents, or oral evidence, revealing the process of providing for Ministers honest and candid advice on matters of high level policy should be subject to disclosure or compulsion.
> (Norton-Taylor 1995: 161ff.)

The ultimate focus of the 1996 Scott report is on the duty of ministers, set out in *Questions of Procedure for Ministers* (see **p. 146**), to give Parliament and the public as full information as possible to make a reality of the principle of ministerial accountability to Parliament (*Report of the Inquiry into the Export of Defence Equipment and Dual-Use Goods to Iraq and Related Prosecutions* (the Scott report), vols I to XI, HMSO 1996: paras K8.1–16). The report lists numerous examples of the failure of ministers to discharge this duty, and of 'designedly' misleading or inaccurate information being given instead, in public statements, parliamentary answers and letters to MPs. Former ministers, ministers and senior civil servants advanced a variety of reasons for this absence of candour, but Lord Justice Scott concludes:

> Having heard various explanations of why it was necessary or desirable to withhold knowledge from Parliament and the public of the true nature of

the government's approach to the licensing of non-lethal defence sales to Iran and Iraq respectively, I have come to the conclusion that the overriding and determinative reason was a fear of strong public opposition.

(Scott report, para. D4.42)

Scott accepts that there are circumstances in which government information may legitimately be withheld, but argues that the public interest in full disclosure ought to be 'a constant heavy weight' in holding the balance between disclosure and the other public interests which may be adversely affected by disclosure. However, he found that over the period 1984–90,

in circumstances where disclosure might be *politically or administratively inconvenient* [our emphasis], the balance struck by the government comes down, time and time again, against full disclosure.

(para. D1.165)

Lord Howe unapologetically told Scott that 'there is nothing necessarily open to criticism in incompatibility between policy and presentation of policy' (D4.52). He agreed that government 'knew best' and argued that disclosure was often not possible in view of the 'extremely emotional way in which such debates [over arms sales] are conducted in public' (D4.52). Senior civil servants informed the inquiry that is was acceptable for a public statement to disclose only 'half a picture' (D4.55). They also played a significant part in concealing the true nature of policy on the sales of defence equipment to Iraq from Parliament and from the public (see, for example, D2.35 and 36).

Most 'right to know' regimes protect sensitive policy advice and decision-making at the highest levels. But the UK government withholds 'low level' documents and 'technical' information, for at least 30 years in the normal run of things. Even in the Matrix Churchill case, in which three men may have wrongly been gaoled, ministers and civil servants insisted in their Public Interest Immunity Certificates that whole classes of documents had to be withheld from defence lawyers. Such secrecy was 'necessary for the proper functioning of the public service', even if (in Lord Justice Scott's own words) 'documents which are low level are getting swept in because of an abundance of caution or excessive caution' (Norton-Taylor 1995: 178). Andrew Leithead, the assistant Treasury Secretary responsible for public interest immunity certificates, admitted to Scott that they were often used 'for administrative convenience'. The Attorney-General argued that disclosure was 'unhelpful' for decision-makers. Secrecy was necessary to prevent ill-informed criticism. Scott replied, 'As to being ill-informed, the more information there is, the less likelihood there is of it being ill-informed' (Norton-Taylor 1995: 161, 178–179).

There are examples of official concealment of significant information which should be in the public domain under governments of all colours. When records for the year 1957 were disclosed in January 1988, they revealed that the then prime minister, Harold Macmillan, had ordered the suppression of information on an accident at the Windscale nuclear plant (since re-named Sellafield). The level of radioactivity released made it the worst-known nuclear accident before Chernobyl, but the affected public were given no inkling of the risks they were allowed unknowingly to run (International Centre Against Censorship 1991: 337). In the 1940s, and again in the 1970s, Labour governments committed this country to developing nuclear weapons in total secrecy.

Liberalising the regime of secrecy

The Code of Practice adopted in 1994, which followed the Open Government report, is a step in the right direction. It relaxed the rules for retaining documents after 30 years, committed the government to the release of more information and created a mechanism for investigating complaints through the Parliamentary Commissioner (or Ombudsman) when requests for such information were not satisfactorily met.

However, apart from the retention of the 30-year rule and all other statutes prohibiting disclosure of official information noted above, it suffers from a number of serious shortcomings. First and foremost, the code is not legally binding. In addition, there is the extensive list of categories of information exempt from the code including that dealing with: international relations; defence; national security; communications with the royal household; law enforcement; legal proceedings; individual privacy; immigration issues; Whitehall 'internal discussion and advice'; effective management of the economy; incomplete research and commercial confidences. These categories are drafted widely enough to justify almost any decision to refuse access should the need arise. Finally, only 'information', not 'documents' is released. In other words, the public will get an answer from the government to a request for information, but will not be able to check that it is a full and accurate answer.

Moreover, it is clear from the extensive findings of the Scott report and the government's reaction to demands for a more open regime that the Code of Practice is likely to be interpreted in a highly restricted way. If the government decides to withhold 'low level' documentation from the defence in a criminal trial, it is not likely to make information drawn from similar documents available to the general public. Further, any information which is likely to prove 'politically or administratively inconvenient', to use Lord Justice Scott's words (see above), or which is politically sensitive, will probably be withheld.

The government is now seeking to liberalise the public records regime. A steady stream of documents previously held for more than 30 years – for example, on the German occupation of the Channel Islands, the Rudolf Hess and Roger Casement papers – has been released since the government invited historians to identify important documents held for longer than the usual 30 years. Yet old habits die hard and every year on 1 January – the date on which 30-year-old files are opened up – sensitive documents are still held back. Many of these documents are likely simply to be embarrassing to government, like a false and damaging police report on 1930s hunger marches which was clawed back into the restricted category shortly after its release in 1977. The authorities retrieved it on the pretext that a marcher named in it was still alive. In fact, he had no objection to the release of the information (Robertson and Nicol 1992: 441). In addition, there is little evidence that the authorities are influenced by international standards on access to information when deciding what to release or withhold after 30 years. Until recently any document which as much as mentioned MI5 or MI6 was withheld (Michael 1982: 185).

Britain's record on open government

Official secrecy for specific purposes is not contrary to international human rights standards (for example, on genuine national security grounds). But it is clear that the 30-year rule is anything but a careful and considered application of these standards. In reality, little or no consideration is given to the real dangers of disclosing the huge bulk of information withheld – which occupied 85 miles of shelving at a recent count! If a document falls within a category usually withheld, it is generally put on the shelf for at least 30 years without reference to its specific contents. The point was demonstrated in the mid-1970s when the government tried to stop publication of Richard Crossman's memoirs on the ground that they concerned cabinet discussions (*A-G v Jonathan Cape*, 1976). Official records of these discussions are automatically subject to the 30-year rule. However, the Lord Chief Justice read the memoirs and decided that it was not possible to show that harm would flow from their disclosure. The same would presumably apply to the official records of the same meetings, yet they remain secret.

The key question is, of course, whether the 30-year rule passes the test posed by international instruments – is it 'necessary in a democratic society'? This seems highly unlikely, particularly since it has been repeatedly emphasised by the European Court that the adjective 'necessary' implies the existence of a 'pressing social need' (*Sunday Times v UK*, 1979). At an international conference organised by the Freedom of Information campaign, Justice Michael Kirby, President of the New South Wales Court of Appeal, described how the introduction of freedom of information legislation was greeted in Australia:

> Various extravagant claims were made, namely that this act would result in: the fall of the Westminster system of government as we know it; the loss of frankness and candour amongst public servants; the inability of government to function properly when its every action was open to public scrutiny; and the imposition of inordinate costs and the ultimate triumph of lawyerly concern with the process rather than the outcome of administrative action. None of these dire prognostications has been borne out.
>
> (FOI conferences, 8 February 1993)

This statement has considerable bearing on the government's arguments for the 30-year rule in the UK. Obviously withholding some documents may legitimately come within the recognised notion of 'necessary in a democratic society' (all freedom of information legislation recognises categories which remain exempt from disclosure). But the blanket operation of the 30-year rule offends this principle – particularly since there are alternatives. When Channel Island dossiers documenting collaboration with the Nazis during the second world war were eventually released, individual names and identifying details were simply blacked out, revealing belatedly vast amounts of important historical detail for the first time (Robertson 1993: 2).

Protecting national security

National security is recognised in international human rights instruments as a legitimate ground for restricting disclosure of information. Section 1 of the 1911 Official Secrets Act, which has survived into the 1989 Act, is designed to prevent spying on behalf of enemy states and therefore accords in principle with international standards. But, in practice, it is also used to restrict activities which clearly do not amount to spying or the disclosure of state secrets. Yet the courts have been unwilling to scrutinise government claims that the national security is at stake.

In 1964, members of the Campaign for Nuclear Disarmament planned to enter an air base occupied by the US air force and to disrupt its operation by sitting on the runways, etc. They were charged with conspiracy to commit an offence under section 1 (i.e., of approaching or entering a 'prohibited place' for a purpose prejudicial to the safety of the interests of the state). They argued that their purpose was to try to rid the country of nuclear weapons, which was in the interests of the UK. The House of Lords upheld their convictions and sentences on the basis that, in matters of national security, the interests of the state are synonymous with the interests of the government of the day (*Chandler v DPP*, 1964).

It is unlikely that the European human rights authorities or the UN Human Rights Committee would adopt quite such a 'hands-off' approach. It is clear from their jurisprudence that national security should only be invoked when the threat is to a state's territorial or national integrity, not merely to a government or its policies (International Centre Against Censorship 1993a: 114). However, the section has not been used in cases not concerning espionage or related activities since the so-called 'ACB' trial in 1978, where two journalists and a soldier were acquitted on charges of publishing information which was already in the public domain.

On the face of it, the 1989 Official Secrets Act appears to comply with international standards. But three features of the Act warrant special attention. First, it does not provide for any form of 'public interest' defence for unauthorised disclosure of information where the existence of crime, abuse of authority or other misconduct are revealed. The significance of this in terms of its potential impact on democracy is highlighted by two well-known examples: the Colin Wallace affair and the background to the *Spycatcher* saga.

Colin Wallace, a former senior information officer at British Army Headquarters in Northern Ireland, has repeatedly claimed that in the 1970s he was instructed to spread disinformation to denigrate elected politicians, including former prime ministers Edward Heath and Harold Wilson, through an operation code-named 'Clockwork Orange'. Wallace claimed that this operation was organised by MI5, with the approval of Army Intelligence in Northern Ireland. In May 1987, the government issued statements denying Wallace's allegations but refused to carry out a full public inquiry. In February 1990, the then prime minister, Mrs Thatcher, told the House of Commons that she and Parliament had been 'misled'. However, the ensuing inquiry was limited to the circumstances of Wallace's dismissal.

Similar allegations provided an important backdrop to the publication of *Spycatcher* (which is dealt with in more detail below). Peter Wright, a senior officer in MI5 from 1955 to 1976, made a series of allegations of improper, criminal and unconstitutional conduct on the part of MI5 officers. These included very serious allegations – for example, that MI5 was guilty of routine burglary and 'bugging'; that (contrary to its guidelines) MI5 diverted its resources to investigate left-wing political groups in the UK; and also (like Wallace) that MI5 plotted to disgrace Harold Wilson, the Labour leader and Prime Minister. In the mid-1980s Wright tried to persuade the government to institute an independent inquiry into these allegations before deciding to publish *Spycatcher*. But the government refused, even after prominent members of the 1974–79 Labour government called for an inquiry in 1987. Instead, the government sought to suppress *Spycatcher* when it was published.

In the absence of any mechanism for independent inquiry into (and government will to investigate) the Wallace and Wright allegations, it is difficult to sustain the argument that the absence of a 'public interest' defence in the 1989 Act is 'necessary in a democratic society'. To so do elevates the protection of national security from its proper position as a legitimate ground for restriction in some circumstances to a doctrine that can override democratic process. As the European Commission reminded the government when the *Spycatcher* cases were before it:

> Freedom of expression constitutes one of the essential foundations of a democratic society, in particular freedom of political and public debate. This is of special importance for the free press which has a legitimate interest in reporting on and drawing the public's attention to the deficiencies in the operation of government services, including possible illegal activities. It is incumbent on the press to impart information and ideas about such matters and the public has a right to receive them.
>
> (*The Observer and Guardian v UK*, 1991)

The government rejected an amendment to the 1989 Act which was inspired by similar reasoning. The amendment would have allowed disclosure in the public interest by a whistle-blower who had reasonable cause to believe that he or she was revealing the existence of crime, fraud, abuse of authority, neglect of duty, serious misconduct or a threat to public safety. The government argued that the 'public interest' could be taken into account in deciding whether to prosecute (Birkinshaw 1990: 46). On the evidence of the government's conduct in cases such as the 'ACB trial', Clive Ponting and others, this is akin to leaving the keys to the hen-coop in the possession of a fox. Certainly, it is not the reliable safeguard against abuse of civil and political rights envisaged by international human rights instruments.

The second feature that warrants attention is more technical. It is hard to see how information falling within the category of 'international relations', disclosure of which is an offence, necessarily comes within the ambit of national security. Obviously, some material within this category will do so; equally, not all of it would.

In so far as this category is too wide, it violates both the International Covenant and the European Convention.

Finally, there is no defence to a charge of disclosure under the 1989 Act that the material disclosed is already in the public domain. This is a particularly onerous burden for members of the security services, who carry a lifelong duty of confidentiality under the Act. It is doubtful that it complies with the requirement, derived from international human rights standards, that measures restricting freedom of expression be proportionate to the legitimate aim pursued. In the *Spycatcher* case, the European Court of Human Rights decided that restrictions on newspapers publishing the allegations from Wright's book could not be justified under Article 10 of the European Convention, as it had been circulated widely elsewhere (see below).

Confidentiality and the *Spycatcher* case

It now seems established under the European Convention that states can protect confidential information which passes into the hands of their servants or agents, so long as they comply with the requirements of 'necessity' and proportionality (*Hadjianastassiou v Greece*, 1992, ECtHR). However, the limits of this doctrine are unclear. In the cases heard so far, there has been a clear overlap between confidentiality and national security. Moreover, unlike the European Convention, the International Covenant does not specifically list the prevention of disclosure of information received in confidence as a legitimate ground for restricting freedom of expression (although, it could presumably be subsumed into the ground permitting restrictions to protect the rights of others).

The *Spycatcher* litigation in this country is of great significance to the role of the law of confidence. While the British government was seeking to prevent the publication of Wright's memoirs in Australia in June 1986, the *Observer* and *Guardian* published two short articles on Wright's allegations about the plots and other misdeeds of MI5 officers (see above). The government conceded that both reports were factual and accurate accounts of matters of public interest, but four days later brought proceedings for breach of confidence against the two newspapers. Government lawyers argued that both knew, or ought to have known, that the material from Wright had been divulged in breach of his duty of confidence to the Crown. They obtained temporary injunctions to prevent the publication of any other information derived from Wright.

Extracts from *Spycatcher* were published in the *Washington Post*. Viking Penguin announced plans to publish the book in the United States and in 1987 sold the UK serialisation rights to the *Sunday Times*. The government issued yet further proceedings against the *Sunday Times* when the newspaper published the first extract in July 1987, again for breach of confidence, and obtained an injunction to stop publication of further extracts.

The three newspapers all appealed against the temporary injunctions imposed on them. By the time their appeals were heard by the House of Lords on 30 July 1987, *Spycatcher* had been published in the United States and Canada. But the court refused to remove the injunctions – a decision which was ultimately considered in detail by

Spycatcher

the European Court of Human Rights in 1991. *Spycatcher* was then published in Australia and Ireland in 1987 and by the end of the year more than one million copies had been sold around the world. Eventually, at a full hearing of the cases against the newspapers in October 1988, the House of Lords decided that the *Observer* and *Guardian* had not in fact acted in breach of confidence because the public interest in publishing serious allegations outweighed national security concerns. However, the *Sunday Times* was deemed to have breached confidence, because the serialisation of *Spycatcher* was *indiscriminate* (i.e., it would involve publishing matters which the House of Lords did not think outweighed national security considerations as well as those that did). It was made to account for its profits. The court, however, refused to grant further (and permanent) injunctions against any of the three papers.

The principles applied by the House of Lords in October 1988 have not been tested before the European Court. However, the 1991 *Spycatcher* case heard by the Court (which concerned the 1987 House of Lords decision) makes it clear that confidentiality is not a legitimate ground for restricting publication when the information at issue has already been published elsewhere. From this it is questionable whether confidentiality can be regarded as a legitimate ground for making the *Sunday Times* account for its profits, which, although clearly not *prior restraint*, is nevertheless a form of *subsequent restraint*. If not, the principles enunciated by the House of Lords may well violate international standards on freedom of expression.

By contrast, the United States has a long tradition of outlawing prior restraint, as a leading Supreme Court judgment stated firmly in 1931 (*Near v Minnesota*). The significance of this tradition was reflected in the 1971 Pentagon Papers case. The US government attempted to restrain the *New York Times* and *Washington Post* from publishing classified papers called History of the US Decision-Making Processes on Vietnam Policy. The Supreme Court refused to grant an injunction. According to Justice Black:

> In the First Amendment . . . the Government's power to censor the press was abolished . . . so that the press would remain forever free to censor the government. The press was protected so that it could bare the secrets of government and inform the people.
>
> (*New York Times v US*, 1971)

Court hearings and documents

As a general rule, courts in the UK are open to the public and any case can be reported in full. There are a number of exceptions. Contempt of court laws may prevent publicity about the early stages of many cases and even the actual trial of others; the public and press may be denied access to some cases or reporting may be restricted; and, for the parties, even during the course of a trial, key documents may be withheld.

Contempt of court

The law on contempt of court is intended to protect the fair and impartial administration of justice. It is particularly concerned with preventing juries from being
exposed to prejudicial comment. The modern law is now largely found in the
Contempt of Court Act 1981, which was passed after criticism of existing UK law
by the European Court of Human Rights in the *Sunday Times* case (see below).

The 1981 Act makes it an offence to publish anything which creates a substantial risk that the course of justice in any particular case will be substantially impeded
or prejudiced. This rule covers any speech, writing or broadcast addressed to the
public and applies when any proceedings are 'active' (or *sub judice*). Criminal proceedings are active from the time when someone is arrested, or an arrest warrant or a
summons has been issued. Civil proceedings are active from the time when a date
for trial is set.

In parallel to the Contempt of Court Act, some common law offences still survive
– for example, deliberate contempt, which consists of publishing information *with
the intention* of prejudicing or interfering with court proceedings. Prosecution of this
offence does not require the Attorney-General's consent. The accused cannot claim
that they published the information in the public interest or innocently and the prosecution only has to prove a real risk of prejudice – not a substantial risk of prejudice.

Open justice and reporting restrictions

The practice of making the courts open to the public was established in the middle
ages and later elevated to a fundamental precondition of justice. In 1913, Lord
Halsbury proclaimed, 'Every court in the land is open to every subject of the King'
(*Scott v Scott*, 1913). However, important qualifications of this principle exist. In the
Scott case itself, Lord Halsbury accepted that the public and press could be refused
access to a case under the common law if 'the administration of justice would be
rendered impracticable by their presence'. This has remained the position ever since
(though any restriction should be kept to a minimum). So, for example, if disorder
breaks out in the court, the public can be excluded; but journalists who take no
part in the disruption should be allowed to stay (*R v Denbigh Justices ex parte Williams
and Evans*, 1974).

Various statutory rules also restrict access to cases. Courts must sit in private in
cases involving mental patients, guardianship and adoption proceedings, and may
sit in private in other cases involving children, families, confidential information or
national security. During the trial of offences under the Official Secrets Acts, the
public can be excluded if the court considers that publication of the evidence would
be prejudicial to national safety (Official Secrets Act 1920). Finally, the public and
press are routinely excluded from hearings relating to divorce, bail (in the Crown
Court), applications for injunctions and eviction orders.

Court hearings in public may normally be reported. The Contempt of Court Act
1981 gives an express right to publish in good faith a fair, accurate and contemporaneous report of public legal proceedings. However, again, there are exceptions

(for example, victims of sexual offences may not be named in most circumstances). A court may also postpone reporting to avoid a serious risk of prejudice, either to the case being heard or to some other pending or imminent case.

Magistrates' court orders restricting access to court or postponing reports can be challenged by proceedings for judicial review. However, nothing related to a trial on indictment (i.e., jury trial in the Crown Court) can be judicially reviewed and until 1988 there was very little that journalists could do to challenge such orders. This led them to complain to the European Commission of Human Rights (*Hodgson v UK; Channel 4 v UK*, 1987). When their case was admitted by the Commission, the government implemented an appeal procedure to the Court of Appeal in the Criminal Justice Act 1988.

Public interest immunity

Access to all relevant documents by the parties to a case is fundamental to a fair trial. In the United Kingdom, this is provided for by rules regulating the duties of disclosure. In criminal proceedings, the prosecution must disclose any documents which they intend to rely on and also any other documents in their possession which have or might have 'some bearing on the offences charged' (Archbold and Richardson 1995). Generally speaking, the defence does not have to disclose documents before trial (but there are currently government proposals to modify these rules.) In civil proceedings, a process known as 'discovery' takes place, under which each party has to disclose any relevant documents to the other before trial. A court order for discovery is only required if the parties do not volunteer the information themselves. The rules governing disclosure and discovery are complex and we are unable to provide a thorough analysis here. We have therefore focused on one aspect because of its potential effect on the democratic process: public interest immunity.

Public interest immunity allows government ministers to contend that certain documents should not be disclosed because to make them public would harm the public interest. It may be harmful to disclose the contents of a particular document, or even a class of documents which must be withheld to safeguard 'the proper functioning of the public service'. The rationale for the second ground is said to be 'the need to secure freedom and candour of communication with and within the public service, so that government decisions can be taken on the best advice and with the fullest information' (HL Deb, 6 June 1956, c742–743).

If the question of public interest immunity arises, the judge has to balance the public interest in non-disclosure and the public interest in the fair administration of justice. If he or she decides that non-disclosure is more important, the documents will not be disclosed no matter how relevant or crucial they might be to the case being tried.

AUDIT

Public access to court hearings and documents

The Contempt of Court Act 1981 was passed as a direct result of the UK losing the *Sunday Times* case in the European Court of Human Rights in 1979. The

European Court acknowledged the need to maintain the authority of the judiciary and to protect the rights of litigants under Article 10 of the European Convention. Britain's old common law rules on contempt of court were not 'necessary in a democratic society' because they gave too much weight to the litigants at the expense of freedom of expression (*Sunday Times v UK*, 1979).

The 1981 Act has gone a long way towards compliance with international requirements. It is only an offence to publish anything which creates a *substantial risk* that the course of justice in any particular case will be substantially impeded or prejudiced. However, once that degree of risk is shown to exist, liability is strict. No room is left for the balancing exercise between the rights of the litigants and the freedom of expression envisaged by the European Court (unless the publication is made as part of a discussion in good faith of public affairs or matters of general public interest).

More significantly, the courts have interpreted the 1981 Act very widely, undermining freedom of expression. In December 1987, the Court of Appeal prevented Channel 4 TV from broadcasting a contemporaneous re-enactment by actors of highlights of the 'Birmingham Six' appeal then going on against their 1974 convictions for IRA bombings in Birmingham (they were subsequently released after a further appeal in 1991). The Court of Appeal ordered that the broadcast be postponed until after the case had been decided, even though the appeal was being heard by senior judges who, unlike juries, are not normally considered to be subject to influence by the media.

The Lord Chief Justice reasoned that the broadcast was 'likely to undermine public confidence in the administration of justice' if shown during the appeal, but not if it was shown immediately afterwards. Such reasoning hardly reflects the priority which should be afforded to freedom of expression and information according to international human rights standards. Moreover, the decision has had a 'chilling effect' on other programmes. In June 1990, Ulster TV declined to relay a four-hour drama-documentary, which was carried in other regions, on the alleged 'shoot-to-kill' policy of the security forces in Northern Ireland, citing fear of contempt of court proceedings – again, despite there being no possibility of a jury ever determining the issues involved.

Finally, when the government failed to prevent the publication of *Spycatcher* in Australia in March 1987, the *Independent* and other newspapers published a summary of the main allegations from the book. The government issued proceedings against them all for criminal contempt for having violated the spirit of the injunctions against the *Observer* and *Guardian* (see **pp. 155–156**). In 1989, the High Court imposed fines of £50,000 on each newspaper and two years later the House of Lords upheld the findings of contempt (but quashed the fines in light of the novelty of the theory on which liability was based). The House of Lords thereby sanctioned the invention of a new species of contempt law, with no evident regard for the internationally recognised requirement that restrictions on freedom of expression and information be 'prescribed by law' – meaning, that citizens should be able to foresee, if necessary with appropriate advice, what activity would infringe the restriction (*Sunday Times v UK*, 1979).

Openness of courts

Open justice and reporting restrictions

The absence before 1988 of any right of appeal against orders restrict access to the courts, or reporting of cases, was a serious infringement of international standards on freedom of information and expression – particularly since, in the words of the former Master of the Rolls, Lord Donaldson, 'the media are the eyes and ears of the general public' (*AG v Guardian Newspapers (No. 2)*, 1988)). Even now, the procedure under section 159 of the Criminal Justice Act 1988 is far from satisfactory. There is no *right* of appeal, leave must first be obtained from the courts. There is no appeal to the House of Lords, the highest court in the land; and appeals against secret hearings on national security grounds, or for the protection of a witness's identity, are determined without a hearing.

Otherwise, the laws governing the circumstances in which orders restrict access to or reporting of cases broadly conform to international requirements. However, there is growing concern that in practice unnecessary orders are being made. For example, the grounds upon which the Court of Appeal agreed in 1991 to hear some applications in respect of the Polly Peck collapse in secret – namely, that banks, building societies and other financial institutions might suffer damage – were 'fanciful' (Robertson and Nicol 1992: 313). More generally, there seems to be no justification in international human rights terms for the practice of hearing bail applications secretly in the Crown Court – particularly since the equivalent applications in magistrates' courts are routinely heard in open court.

The use of public interest immunity certificates

The withholding of relevant official documents from any party in a criminal or civil trial in the public interest is obviously a controversial issue in a democracy. The right to a fair trial is a fundamental democratic right. Judicial authorities clearly state that other public interests – for example, the acquittal of the innocent and the conviction of the guilty in a criminal trial – outweigh 'the public interest considerations in non-disclosure' (the Scott report, paras K6.1–18). The Scott inquiry provided a great deal of evidence of the 'catch-all' and routine nature of claims for public interest immunity (see **pp. 149–151**) and the final report may bring about significant changes. Whether international standards on freedom of information will become the yardstick for disclosure in practice remains to be seen.

At a fairly early stage in the prosecution of the three Matrix Churchill executives for allegedly exporting machine tools to Iraq for arms manufacturing, it became clear that their defence would rely on evidence of government complicity or acquiescence in the exports. First, it would be alleged that the government, through trade minister Alan Clark MP, had encouraged exporters to be less than frank when applying for export licences. And second, that government anyway had known that the machine tools were intended for the manufacture of munitions and yet had remained willing for the machine tools to be exported. These lines of defence were reinforced by the fact that one of the accused, Paul Henderson, had been supplying information about Iraq to the British intelligence agencies.

Thus, Customs and Excise officers carrying out the investigation and the three departments of state involved in the export licensing process (the DTI, the Foreign and Commonweath Office and the MOD) were aware that the defence would call for the disclosure of documents relating to the government's policy towards exports to Iraq and its operation and Henderson's contacts with the intelligence services. Early on a decision to resist requests for disclosure was taken. The resistance included the procuring of public interest immunity certificates signed by four government ministers – Kenneth Clarke (then Home Secretary), Malcolm Rifkind (then Defence Secretary), Michael Heseltine (then President of the Board of Trade) and Tristan Garel-Jones (then Foreign Office minister). These certificates objected to the disclosure of the documents they respectively covered on the ground that disclosure would cause serious damage to the public interest. However, the trial judge decided to grant defence applications for the certificates to be set aside and the large number of government documents disclosed to the defence provided the basis for a sustained cross-examination of two DTI officials and Alan Clark. The thrust of the cross-examination was to establish both lines of defence and the prosecution took the view that their case was no longer tenable. The jury were directed to return 'Not Guilty' verdicts.

The judge's decision to override the certificates signed by the four ministers had turned a run-of-the-mill prosecution into a high-profile prosecution with significant political implications. At the heart of the controversy was the allegation that the government's attempts to prevent disclosure of the documents were motivated by a desire to cover up its own misdemeanours and to avoid embarrassment, notwithstanding the risk that without access to the documents innocent defendants might suffer conviction and prison sentences. One of Lord Justice Scott's tasks was to examine and report on the decisions taken in the Matrix Churchill case by those signing public interest immunity certificates (HC Deb, 16 November 1992, c76).

Having reviewed every step in the Matrix Churchill prosecution, Scott concluded that the making of public interest immunity claims was not the only factor impeding the disclosure to the defence of the relevant departmental documents. He specifically noted that the government attitude to disclosure was 'consistently grudging' (the Scott report, G18.37). Scott suggests that the approach ought to have been to 'consider what documents the defence might reasonably need and then to consider whether there was any good reason why the defence should not have them'. Instead, the actual approach for all documents 'seems to have been to seek some means by which refusal to disclose could be justified'. As a result, 'no attempt was made to distinguish between documents that would be of obvious assistance to the defence and documents of only peripheral significance, nor . . . to distinguish between documents with genuine sensitivity and run of the mill documents of which no more could be said than that they were attended by some degree of confidentiality within Government' (G18.37).

As for public interest immunity certificates (PIICs), it emerged during the inquiry that the routine practice of the Treasury Solicitor was to claim privilege from disclosure of any document referring to government policy at any level – even 'piffling' or 'low level' information which, in other circumstances, ministers and civil servants

PII certificates

felt able freely to release. Furthermore, when Heseltine initially refused to sign a PIIC in the Matrix Churchill case, he was advised by Sir Nicholas Lyell, the Attorney-General, that he was under a legal duty to do so and that he was not entitled to exercise any judgment as to whether the damage that might be caused to the public interest by disclosure of the contents of the documents to the defence was of sufficient gravity to justify withholding them. Scott sharply criticised this advice which he considers to be based on a 'fundamental misconception' of public interest immunity law (G18.54). For this reason, Scott rejected claims that the four ministers deliberately sought to deprive the defendants of their right to a fair trial to cover up government wrongdoing.

The official attitude to and practice of the disclosure of government documents in criminal and civil trials exposed by the Scott report hardly reflects the scrutiny and careful balancing of competing interests envisaged by bodies such as the European Court and Commission of Human Rights. Equally alarmingly, the Prime Minister had to concede in answer to a House of Commons written question that he could not say how many certificates had been signed since 1974 because 'no central record is held of the number involved' (HC Deb, WA, 25 November 1992, c673).

Scott questioned whether 'class' or wide-ranging public interest immunity claims should be made at all in criminal cases. Where the liberty of an individual is at stake, democratic principles and judicial authorities cited in the Scott report both argue that the requirement of a fair and public hearing outweighs any otherwise legitimate restriction on access to information. After all, the prosecution always has the option of discontinuing the case where disclosure would genuinely jeopardise national security.

More generally, the need for non-disclosure of whole categories of documentation without reference to their particular contents is highly questionable. It also appears to be a rather flexible tool: when contempt of court proceedings were brought against Kenneth Baker in 1992, the Home Office took the view that notes of his meetings with their officials should be disclosed to the court, even though they fell into a class of documents for which public interest immunity from disclosure would usually be claimed (*M v Home Office*, 1993).

There is another issue to be resolved before there can be full compliance with international standards. To what extent do the security services withhold documents from civil servants making the key decisions about disclosure? When Messrs Randle and Pottle were prosecuted for helping the spy George Blake to escape, they made numerous requests for further documents from the prosecution. At one stage, leading counsel for the prosecution stated in open court that no documents in his file would assist the defence. It subsequently transpired that MI5 had documents that were central to the case, but had not been given to the prosecuting authorities (see John Wadham, *The Law Society's Gazette*, 18 November 1992).

The use of injunctions

We have examined the laws relating to freedom of information on the assumption that the courts consider the relevant principles of law involved before imposing any restrictions. This is not always the case. In many cases, 'temporary' injunctions to prevent disclosure or publication are requested and granted without full consideration of the law.

Any party to civil proceedings can apply at once (within a few hours if need be) for an injunction to prevent the other party from disclosing or publishing information. All that the person or body applying needs to show is an arguable case and that their interest in preventing disclosure or publication of the information in question outweighs any interest the other party may have: the so-called 'balance of convenience' test. Often the evidence before the court considering the issue is incomplete and the court is required to make a hasty decision. Equally significantly, by the time the case comes to be heard in full, the information in dispute has frequently lost all newsworthiness.

In general, temporary injunctions are rare in defamation cases, but quite common in cases concerning breach of confidence or of copyright. The courts argue that publication pending trial in these latter cases can irreparably prejudice a party. They are therefore very willing to grant an interim injunction to preserve the status quo pending a full court hearing (International Centre Against Censorship 1993b: 186). Permanent injunctions can be granted after the full hearing of a case, but this rarely happens. In particular, it is now clear that publication of confidences owed to the government will only be restrained permanently if the government proves that the public interest would otherwise be harmed (*AG v Guardian Newspapers (No. 2)*, 1988; see also **pp. 155–156**).

A backdoor route to prior restraint

The imposition of temporary injunctions in the United Kingdom raises fundamental problems of compliance with international human rights standards which go well beyond freedoms of information and expression. International standards set out clear rules which must be satisfied if any political or civil right is to be restricted. First, priority must be given to the right in question. Any restriction must then be scrutinised for compliance with the well-known three-part test: namely, it must be 'prescribed by law', imposed for a legitimate purpose and 'necessary in a democratic society' (see further, **pp. 21–22**). The European Court has emphasised that in evaluating any such restriction, it is faced 'not with a choice between two conflicting principles, but with a principle of freedom of expression that is subject to a number of exceptions which must be narrowly interpreted' (*Sunday Times v UK*, 1979).

In contrast, the British courts merely apply the 'balance of convenience' test in hearing injunction cases and require the person or body seeking the injunction to show they have an arguable case. In this balancing exercise, the traditional 'negative right' of free speech can easily be outweighed by positive commercial or property rights. The judge must balance the commercial or property right of the plaintiff in controlling the information against the value of the defendant's right of free speech, but as two experienced lawyers have commented, 'for many judges brought up in a world that accords pre-eminent value to rights of property, this may seem like balancing hard cash against hot air' (Robertson and Nicol 1992: 21).

On occasion the UK approach leads to the right result in international human rights terms, but more by luck than judgment. Just as often, it leads to the wrong result. The ruling of the European Court of Human Rights in the *Spycatcher* litigation demonstrates the point (see **pp. 155–156**). The European Court approved the temporary injunctions imposed on the *Observer*, *Guardian* and *Sunday Times* before July 1987. However, the continuation of these injunctions after *Spycatcher* was published outside the UK was held by the Court to have violated Article 10 of the Convention. Yet the domestic courts had in fact applied the same test throughout. Therefore, although the European Court did not go so far as to rule that the 'balance of convenience test' itself infringes Article 10, that is the strong inference from its judgment.

Conclusions

Access to information is essential to the effective working of a democracy. Yet, unlike many European and Commonwealth countries, the United Kingdom has refused to introduce a Freedom of Information regime, giving a public right of access to government documents. The code of practice for open government, introduced in 1994, is purely voluntary and relies on the discretion of officialdom. It fails to address the inadequacies in the existing law and practice when evaluated against international human rights standards. For example, the routine non-disclosure of most public records under the '30-year' rule cannot be justified; the offences under the 1989 Official Secrets Act are too tightly drawn; and the Contempt of Court Act 1981 fails adequately to take into account freedom of expression.

The law of confidence and copyright is not in itself a cause for concern in international human rights terms. But its wide application by the courts is. In particular, the use of temporary injunctions, such as those criticised in the *Spycatcher* litigation, often fails to conform with international human rights standards. This is a general problem caused by the disparity between the 'balance of convenience' test applied in UK courts before imposing an injunction and the stricter three-part test insisted on by the European Court of Human Rights, according to which *any* restriction must pursue a legitimate aim, fulfil a pressing social need and be proportionate to the aim pursued.

The use of public interest immunity certificates in criminal proceedings raises major concerns. The evidence is that ministers signing certificates frequently fail to scrutinise or question their contents (though the Scott inquiry revealed that some, like Michael Heseltine, took their responsibilities seriously). But not even the government's law officers, let alone ministers or senior civil servants, seem to have undertaken the careful balancing exercise between the public interest in non-disclosure and the administration of justice that is required under international human rights instruments.

9   A Freedom Too Governed by Law

Freedom of expression

It is in the nature of any state to wish to restrict freedom of expression. This has been evident in this country from the state's control of printing presses in the seventeenth century to the vain attempts to suppress *Spycatcher* in the twentieth. Britain has no equivalent to the First Amendment to the American Constitution, creating a constitutional guarantee of freedom of expression for all. The 1689 Bill of Rights – the last major statement of rights in this country – guaranteed freedom of speech only to Members of Parliament.

British citizens have a 'negative right': they are free to say anything that is not prohibited. As the House of Lords pointed out in 1936, 'free speech does not mean free speech: it means speech hedged in by all the laws against defamation, blasphemy, sedition and so forth' (*James v Commonwealth of Australia*, 1936). Since then new laws and principles restricting freedom of speech have been introduced. Old restrictions are rarely repealed. As two lawyers with a special interest have explained, 'by and large, Parliament and the judiciary have taken the view that free speech is a very good thing so long as it does not cause trouble' (Robertson and Nicol 1992: 1).

In this chapter we examine various constraints on the freedom of expression – the law of defamation; blasphemy, obscenity and public morals; racial hatred and public order offences; and finally restrictions on the open discussion of homosexuality. We dealt with freedom of information in the previous chapter. We do not deal separately in this book with the related freedoms of conscience and opinion – of which freedom of expression is the public manifestation. The press and broadcasting media operate under the same laws which apply to the population at large and their role is analysed both in this and the previous chapter. But in recognition of the special role of the media, this chapter also briefly examines the status, ownership and control of the media. (Their political role is considered more fully in the companion Democratic Audit volume on democratic institutions.)

Human Rights Index: freedom of information

Freedom of expression is not an absolute right anywhere, but it ranks as one of the most highly regarded human rights. Although by no means the first articulation of that freedom, Article 19 of the International Covenant on Civil and Political Rights has now become the world-wide benchmark for its protection (see also the Index on freedom of information, **pp. 142ff.**). Article 19 guarantees freedom of expression and affirms

International standards

the right of everyone to seek, receive and impart information and ideas of all kinds, regardless of frontiers 'either orally, in writing or in print, in the form of art, or through any other media of his choice'. Every communicable type of subjective idea and opinion, of value-neutral news and information, of commercial advertising, arts works, political commentary, pornography etc., is protected (Nowak 1993: 341). Article 10 of the European Convention is expressed in broadly similar terms, but does not specifically include reference to seeking information and ideas (see further **p. 142**).

Freedom of expression is protected against interference by public authorities and private interests under the Covenant and European Convention (see generally, Nowak 1993: 344–345). In 1992, the European Commission observed, in a case challenging the Austrian government's broadcasting monopoly, that 'Article 10 is based on the idea that a pluralism of ideas must be safeguarded' (*Informationsverein Lentia v Austria*, 1992).

Restricting rights

Formal recognition of civil and political rights is not enough. It is essential that any restriction of all rights recognised by both the International Covenant and the European Convention be closely scrutinised. The two instruments set out a strict three-part test:

1. Any restriction on civil and political rights must be 'prescribed by law'
2. The restriction must be justified by one of the aims under the International Covenant of European convention
3. The restriction must be shown to be 'necessary in a democratic society'.

This test is of fundamental importance. For that reason, we deal with the test in detail in **Box A, pp. 21–22**. Here, broadly, the test requires that ordinary citizens can readily discover what legal restrictions to any right exist with enough clarity for them to be able to regulate their conduct. Any restrictions must then meet one of the aims recognised under either instrument as a legitimate ground for the restriction of civil and political rights. These aims are:

- the protection of the rights and freedoms of others
- national security
- public safety
- public health and morals
- the prevention of public disorder or crime
- the protection of the reputation of others
- the prevention of disclosure of information received in confidence
- maintaining the authority and impartiality of the judiciary.

In the case of freedom of expression specifically, the International Covenant requires, and the European Convention permits, restrictions on the advocacy of national, racial and religious hatred. In addition, the European Convention specifically declares that Article 10 does not prevent states from requiring the licensing of broadcasting, television or cinema enterprises.

This list is intended to be exhaustive. States may not introduce other restrictions or stretch the meaning of the criteria listed above to add others. Finally, states must show both that the restriction fulfils a pressing social need and that it is proportionate to the aim of responding to that need. They cannot merely assert that a particular restriction is 'necessary in a democratic society', but must provide concrete evidence of a genuine and serious threat.

The bodies which interpret the tests – the UN Human Rights Committee and the European Court and Commission of Human Rights – have framed their notion of 'democratic society' in terms of such concepts as 'pluralism, tolerance and broadmindedness'; and have made it clear that although the term 'necessary' is not synonymous with 'indispensable', it does not simply mean 'reasonable' (*Handyside v UK*, ECtHR, 1976).

Evolving human rights standards

The evolving human rights standards which apply to restrictions on freedom of expression are as follows:

- The general rule is that free expression must be protected. Restrictions are the exception. It is the interplay between the principle of freedom of expression and such restrictions which determines the actual scope of the individual's freedom of expression (UN Human Rights Committee, General Comment 10/19, 27 July 1983).

- Article 10 of the European Convention does not require a balance between freedom of expression and permitted restrictions. They are not competing principles of equal weight – exceptions must be strictly interpreted and the need for them must be convincingly established (*Sunday Times Case*, 1979, ECtHR).

- Restrictions by governments of the exercise of freedom of expression may not put in jeopardy the right itself. The restrictions may not be applied so that the dissemination of an opinion in a particular matter is completely suppressed (*Handyside v UK*, 1976, ECtHR).

- In assessing the grounds for the justification of restrictions on free expression, different standards may apply to different categories of people (for example, civil servants, soldiers, the police, publishers, journalists and politicians) (*Handyside* and *Sunday Times Case*; see above).

- The mere fact that a potential restriction belongs to one of these categories does not provide sufficient reason for its imposition; it depends on the person's actual duties and responsibilities. Even so, restrictions have to be 'necessary in a democratic society' (*Glasenapp v Germany*, 1986, ECtHR).

- Although one of the grounds for permitting restriction of freedom of expression is respect for the rights and reputation of others, the requirement that an accused must prove the truth of an allegedly defamatory opinion infringes his or her right to impart ideas, as well as the public's right to receive ideas (*Lingens v Austria*, 1986, ECtHR; *Oberschlick v Austria*, 1991, ECtHR).

International standards

- Where a value judgement is based on facts, it should not be considered defamatory so long as the facts are reasonably accurate, relayed in good faith and the value judgement is not intended to imply a falsehood, even if a falsehood is possible (*Schwabe v Austria*, 1992, ECtHR).

- The European Court has even suggested that a speaker or publisher is protected by Article 10 so long as his or her claims are based upon public opinion, do not disparage specific named individuals and are primarily intended to promote a positive aim, such as institutional reform (*Thorgeirson v Iceland*, 1992, ECtHR).

- The limits of acceptable criticism of politicians are wider than for private individuals, and criticisms of government are to be accorded even greater protection than criticisms of politicians (*Lingens v Austria*, 1986, ECtHR; *Castells v Spain*, 1992).

- Any claim for defamation is weaker if the allegedly defamatory statement was made in response to a statement that itself was provocative or inflammatory (*Oberschlick v Austria*, 1991, ECtHR).

- However, judges and 'judicial officers' do not have to tolerate the same degree of scrutiny as other government agents (*Barford v Denmark*, 1989).

- States enjoy a 'margin of appreciation' in deciding what is necessary to protect morals, but this discretion is not unlimited. Freedom of expression is one of the essential foundations of a democratic society and applies to the expression of ideas that offend, shock or disturb, so restrictions must be proportionate to the aim pursued and reasons for restriction must be relevant and sufficient (*Handyside v UK*, 1976, ECtHR; see also the Human Rights Committee Minority Report in *Hertzberg v Finland*, 1979).

- State-imposed restrictions on free expression should allow for a *changing* conception of 'public morals' (*Müller v Switzerland*, 1988, ECtHR; and again the UN Human Rights Committee in *Hertzberg v Finland*, 1979).

- Advocacy of national, racial or religious hatred that constitutes incitement to discrimination should be prohibited by law (ICCPR A.20).

- The UN Human Rights Committee has held Article 20 of the ICCPR (which prohibits propaganda for war and the advocacy of national, racial or religious hatred) to be fully compatible with freedom of expression under Article 19, which carries with it special duties and responsibilities (HRC General Comment 11(19) 1983).

- The dissemination of ideas based on racial superiority or hatred, incitement to racial discrimination, assistance to racist activities and participation in organisations which promote and incite racial discrimination should be made criminal offences (International Convention on the Elimination of All Forms of Racial Discrimination, Article 4).

The law of defamation

The protection of reputation in the UK is dealt with primarily by the law of defamation. This is a civil wrong committed whenever anything is published about a person which lowers him or her 'in the estimation of right-thinking members of society generally' (*Sim v Stretch*, 1936). It is divided into 'slander' (for the spoken word) and 'libel' (in published or broadcast form). Generally, a jury decides whether a statement is defamatory. The motive of the author is irrelevant. Apparently harmless statements can be defamatory by innuendo to those in possession of extra information. The person who is suing must prove that the statement was defamatory and referred to him or her. But the burden of proof lies largely on the defendant, who must establish one or more of the recognised defences – or risk an award of damages.

The main defences are truth (sometimes called 'justification'), fair comment or privilege. Truth is a complete defence. The difficulty with it is not legal, but practical: assembling admissible evidence sufficient to persuade a jury that a serious defamatory statement is true can be very hard, especially for a defendant of limited means. Legal aid is not available for defamation cases in any circumstances, either for the plaintiff or defendant.

'Fair comment' only arises if the statement complained about expresses an opinion rather than states a fact. For example, to describe someone as a 'bad singer' is comment; to say that they are 'untrained as a singer' is fact (Stone 1994: 288). To be 'fair', the facts on which a comment are based must be true and the comment itself must be in the public interest. Although establishing the truth of the facts does raise problems, it is relatively easy to satisfy the requirement of public interest. The behaviour of people in public life will be of public interest, as will anything which is published to the public (Stone 1994: 289).

'Privilege' arises from the law's recognition that, on particular occasions, it is important for there to be open communication, even if this openness is achieved at the cost of damage to someone's reputation. 'Absolute privilege' is a complete defence; 'qualified privilege' is a defence unless the statement in question was made with 'malice'. The exact limits of privilege are still being explored. However, it is now clearly established that absolute privilege is confined to proceedings in Parliament or in the courts. It will be extended to reports of these proceedings that are fair, accurate and contemporaneous. Qualified privilege, on the other hand, applies where the person who publishes the words has a duty or interest in communicating them and his or her audience has a duty or interest in receiving them. For example, the communication of a public grievance to the proper authorities.

The arcane offence of 'criminal libel', created in 1275 to protect 'the great men of the realm' against discomfiture from stories that might arouse the people against them, remains – but is rarely used (Robertson and Nicol 1992: 100). Truth is not a defence, unless the defendant can convince a jury that publication is for the public benefit.

Defamation concerns

The law of defamation is one of the most effective restraints on free speech in the UK. It has its origins in the eighteenth century state's resolve to stifle the freedom of those who wished to argue the issues raised by the French Revolution: libel law, along with sedition, was the legal mechanism used to suppress dissent. Its most important features have remained unchanged since the early nineteenth century. Liability is absolute. Unlike most other civil wrongs, it makes no difference that those involved in communicating a libellous statement have acted in perfect good faith, have no intention of harming someone else's reputation, or don't even know what it is they are publishing. By contrast, establishing that reasonable care was taken is a complete defence to killing someone in a car accident.

This rigidity in British law runs counter to the trend in international human rights standards, which seek to give wider protection to freedom of speech. In recent years, the European Court has suggested that opinions should not be considered defamatory so long as the underlying facts are *reasonably accurate*, that the opinion was expressed in good faith and that the person expressing it had no intention to defame (see **pp. 167–168**). This trend is likely to continue. Unless the domestic law of defamation is radically overhauled, the gap between it and international standards will soon become unbridgeable.

Rigidity of the law is not the only problem in the UK. The good reputation of the person suing is presumed: no actual loss need be proven. In most cases, the plaintiff need only demonstrate that the words complained of have a defamatory meaning. The outcome then rests entirely on the defendant's ability to prove truth or fair comment. As noted above, the difficulty is a practical one. It takes time, resources and money to prove that a statement is true. Legal aid is not available in any circumstances, whatever the means of the defendant – yet if he or she fail in the task of proving truth, huge damages can be awarded, resulting ultimately in bankruptcy.

This has a huge impact on freedom of expression. Even major newspapers and broadcasting organisations shrink from making statements which they know to be true, if their legal advisers consider that they may give rise to the cost and trouble of defending defamation cases. This legal advice is frequently based as much on the litigious nature of an organisation or individual concerned as it is on the facts of the case; the question for the lawyers is rarely whether a claim for defamation could be successfully defended, but simply whether a writ will be issued. For example, media lawyers take especial care with any information on the pharmaceutical industry. The Police Federation are ever ready to protect the reputations of their members and the late media tycoon, Robert Maxwell, was notorious for his readiness to unleash libel writs. And there is always the danger of massive awards, which may subsequently prove to have been unwarranted, as in the case of Sonia Sutcliffe's £600,000 damages award against *Private Eye* in May 1989 (later reduced to £60,000 in a settlement). The highest award was made against a private individual, Nikolai Tolstoy, who had written a pamphlet about forcible repatriation of Cossacks and Yugoslavs at the end of the Second World War. In November 1989, he was ordered to pay £1.5 million damages to Lord Aldington. These sums stand in stark contrast to the recommended level of damages for personal injury; for example, the judicial studies guide recommends £15,000 for the loss of an eye. In July 1995, the European Court of Human Rights delivered a judgment which will have considerable repercussions on libel law in the UK. The Court accepted Tolstoy's argument that the size of the libel damages awarded against him, taken in conjunction with the state of the UK law, violated his right to freedom of expression under Article 10 of the European Convention (*Tolstoy Miloslavsky v UK*, 1995).

The trial between multi-million dollar instant food chain, McDonald's, and two unemployed people from North London, Helen Steel and Dave Morris, is testimony to the patent inequality caused by the total ban on legal aid for defamation cases (see also **p. 169** above). McDonald's claimed that the two young people were handing out defamatory leaflets (which it accepted the two had not written) outside its restaurants. The trial took four years to come to court, over a year to be heard, involved the examination of over 130 witnesses, and has now become the longest civil trial in history. McDonald's were advised and represented throughout by specialist solicitors and barristers, including leading QCs. Helen Steel and Dave Morris, with a disposable income of £1.57 a week between them, were forced to represent themselves (never having done so before) and did not have the time or resources to prepare their case fully and call some of the key witnesses in their defence.

It cannot be said that every failure to provide legal aid necessarily breaches international human rights standards. Howeyer, the European Commission of Human Rights made it clear in 1976 that a fair hearing meant that anyone who was party to either civil or criminal proceedings should have a reasonable opportunity to present their case to the court under conditions which do not place them at a disadvantage against their opponent (*X v Germany*, 1976, ECmHR).

Far from reconciling freedom of expression and the protection of the rights and reputations of others, the law of defamation for the most part protects neither. Only very few people – the wealthy or well-patronised – can sue in practice. Most people have no redress, even when a story about them may be quite deliberately false. In effect, the defamation law is deployed to conceal information and stifle comment rather than to protect people's reputations.

Our audit of the law of 'criminal libel' for compliance with international standards has been carried out for us by Lord Diplock in a 1980 House of Lords case *Gleaves v Deakin*. Lord Diplock began his speech with the following observations:

> The examination of the legal characteristics of the criminal offence of defamatory libel as it survives today ... has left me with the conviction that this particular offence has retained anomalies which involve serious departures from accepted principles upon which the modern criminal law of England is based and are difficult to reconcile with international obligations which this country has undertaken by becoming a party to the European Convention.

His words have not provoked any change in the law.

Public morals

Blasphemy, obscenity and the protection of public morals

Blasphemy

Blasphemy is a common law offence which protects the Anglican faith against exposure to 'vilification, ridicule or indecency'. It applies whenever 'there is published anything concerning God, Christ or the Christian religion in terms so scurrilous, abusive or offensive as to outrage the feelings of any member or sympathiser with the Christian religion' (*Whitehouse v Lemon*, 1978). A defendant has no 'public good' defence and cannot argue that the published material is in the interests of science, literature, art or learning (which is a defence to a charge of obscenity: see below), or some other worthy interest.

The crime of blasphemy was originally employed in the defence of 'national security', for the established church was regarded as part of the trinity which sustained the state. It was used vigorously to imprison free-thinkers and publishers in the nineteenth century, but fell into disuse. There has only been one successful prosecution for blasphemy since 1922; the private prosecution by Mary Whitehouse against the publishers and editor of *Gay News* in 1979. The offending item was a poem called 'The Love That Dares to Speak its Name' about the alleged homosexual relationships of Jesus Christ. The editor was given a suspended sentence of nine months' imprisonment, quashed on appeal (*Whitehouse v Lemon*, 1978). In 1985, the Law Commission recommended that the crime be abolished, but the offence of blasphemy remains in force. An attempt in 1989 to extend the law to cover Islam by an opponent of Salman Rushdie's novel *The Satanic Verses* failed (*R v Bow Street Magistrates' Court ex parte Choudhury*, 1991).

Obscenity

Obscenity law is now mainly governed by the Obscene Publications Act 1959, under which it is a criminal offence to publish an obscene article or to possess it for publication for gain. The maximum penalty on conviction in the Crown Court is three years imprisonment or an unlimited fine. An article is regarded as obscene if it has a tendency 'to deprave and corrupt persons who are likely, in all the circumstances, to read, see or hear the matter contained or embodied in it'. The 1959 Act has never been extended to Northern Ireland, where the common law applies a broadly similar law of obscene libel with the same test of whether the material in question has a tendency to 'deprave or corrupt'.

The precise meaning of deprave and corrupt is not clear. There seems to be general agreement that it does not cover articles which are merely shocking or offending (*R v Martin Secker & Warburg Ltd*, 1954). However, although the House of Lords has emphasised that 'corrupt is a strong word', it has given little real guidance on its full meaning, other than that the effect of publication must go beyond immoral suggestion or persuasion and constitute a 'serious menace' (*Knuller v DPP*, 1973).

The law of obscenity extends beyond sexual material: books dealing with drug-taking have been classified by the courts as obscene (*John Calder Publications v Powell*,

1965). In 1968, while allowing the appeal of the publishers of *Last Exit to Brooklyn*, the Court of Appeal said that the encouragement of brutal violence could come within the test of obscenity.

The 1959 Act introduced the 'public good' defence that publication (in the case of magazines and books) is 'in the interests of science, literature, art or learning, or other objects of general concern'. A similar, but rather narrower defence (the interests of drama, opera, ballet or any other art, or of literature or learning) applies to plays and films. The use of this defence was demonstrated in the first major case under the 1959 Act when the publishers of D.H. Lawrence's novel, *Lady Chatterley's Lover*, were acquitted at the Old Bailey in 1960.

Public morals

The concept of indecency is contained in a number of statutes creating specific offences and also exists at common law. The common theme is the prohibition of public displays of offensive material. Such prohibition is aimed at protecting persons from the shock or offence occasioned by encountering certain material, rather than at preventing moral deterioration (Fenwick 1994: 167). Indecency is easier to prove than obscenity because there is no defence of public good, there is no need to consider the article as a whole and there is no need to satisfy the 'deprave and corrupt' test.

At common law, prosecutions can be brought for conspiracy to corrupt public morals. Consequently, a directory of prostitutes and their services was condemned by the House of Lords on the basis that the law conferred a general discretion to punish immoral conduct which could injure the public (*Shaw v DPP*, 1962). Closely allied to conspiracy to corrupt public morals is the common law offence of outraging public decency, which the House of Lords decided was appropriate to punish the publishers of homosexual contact advertisements (although, in fact, their appeal succeeded because of a misdirection by the trial judge: *Knuller v DPP*, 1973). Both offences were preserved by the Criminal Law Act 1977.

Laws on public morality under scrutiny

The publishers and editor of *Gay News* failed to persuade the European Commission of Human Rights of the merits of their case. But it is difficult to see how the law of blasphemy can survive close scrutiny for compliance with international human rights standards. Not only does it clearly discriminate between faiths (and therefore necessarily between citizens observing those faiths); it also fails the test of 'necessity' – it cannot be said that its retention is necessary in a democratic society because it deals with some pressing social need. As long ago as 1949 Lord Denning said of the law of blasphemy:

> The reason for this law was because it was thought that a denial of Christianity was liable to shake the fabric of society, which was itself founded on Christian religion. These is no such danger to society now.
>
> (Denning 1949: 46)

Blasphemy and obscenity

Similarly, the Law Commission advised in June 1985 that the deficiencies of the law 'are so serious and so fundamental that it ought not in our view to remain as it is, and no measure short of abolition would be adequate to deal with these deficiencies' (Report No. 145). To date that advice has been ignored.

The law of obscenity has at least been reconsidered and redefined this century by the Obscene Publications Act 1959. The 1959 Act was tested before the European Court in 1976 (*Handyside v UK*, 1976). Handyside had published a book entitled *The Little Red Schoolbook* which was aimed at schoolchildren aged 12 and above. Alongside advice on education, teachers, pupils, etc., it gave sex advice on, for example, masturbation, orgasms, homosexuality and abortion. The book was seized under the 1959 Act. The European Court took the view that the procedure under the 1959 Act was 'prescribed by law' and that the government's aim was the protection of morals, which was legitimate by international standards. On the more difficult question of whether the seizure was 'necessary in a democratic society', the Court relied on the (much criticised) doctrine of the 'margin of appreciation' (see **pp. 22–23**) in dismissing the claim. In other words, questions of morality were essentially for member states to determine without the Court's intervention.

The impact of the *Handyside* case may not be as wide as it first appears. The Court's stress on the responsibilities of publishers suggests that the result would have been different if the book had not been intended for children (Robertson and Merrills 1993: 152). The lack of clarity over the meaning of 'deprave and corrupt' might prove difficult to defend in relation to adult publications. Since 1976, it has become clear that international standards require that citizens should be able to foresee, if necessary with appropriate advice, what activity would infringe the law. The notion that a publication must constitute a 'serious menace', introduced in the *Knuller* case, might well fail this test, since the House of Lords has declined every opportunity so far to define what it means by this phrase. In a broader context, the Williams Committee appointed to examine and report on obscenity and film censorship commented in 1979 that:

> The law is scattered among so many statutes, and these so often overlap with each other and with the various common law offences and powers which still exist in this field, that it is a complicated task even to piece together a statement of what the law is, let alone attempt to wrestle with or resolve the inconsistencies and anomalies to which it gives rise.
>
> (Cmnd 7772, para. 2.29)

In a later case, the European Court has stressed that state-imposed restrictions on freedom of expression should allow for a changing conception of public morals (*Müller v Switzerland*, 1988).

The indecency laws raise similar problems, but they run deeper than those for the law on obscenity. Their aim is to protect people from the shock or offence occasioned by encountering certain material, rather than to prevent moral deterioration. Yet the European Court was at pains to stress in the *Handyside* case that 'freedom of expression is one of the essential foundations of a democratic society and applies to the expression of ideas that offend, shock and disturb'. So far as corrupting public morals is concerned, in the *Shaw* case mentioned above (**p. 173**), Lord Reid dissented from his colleagues' decision in the House of Lords because the laws of indecency offended against the principle that the criminal law should be certain. In the circumstances, it is difficult to see how the laws of indecency can be said to conform to internationally recognised human rights standards.

Racial hatred laws

Offences of inciting or stirring up racial hatred were introduced in the Race Relations Act 1965. However, the aim has always been to protect public order rather than to prevent people from expressing offensive views. This emphasis was endorsed when the offences were re-enacted and expanded within the framework of the Public Order Act 1986. There are now three principal offences. In each case, the person charged must have intended to stir up racial hatred, or the circumstances must be such that racial hatred is likely to be caused. The offences are the use of threatening, abusive or insulting words; publishing or distributing written material which is threatening, abusive or insulting; and possessing racially inflammatory material (including videos), which is threatening, abusive or insulting, if it is for display or distribution.

Racial hatred means 'hatred against any group of persons . . . defined by reference to colour, race, nationality (including citizenship) or ethnic or national origins' (section 17). Prosecutions can only be brought by or with the consent of the Attorney-General, who, in practice, consults the Director of Public Prosecutions (Bailey, Harris and Jones 1991: 613). The maximum penalty is two years' imprisonment. The law in Northern Ireland is very similar, save that religious belief is protected as well (Public Order (NI) Order 1987).

A public order approach

The United Kingdom's position on legislation to restrict the expression of racist ideas stands half-way between that of the United States and western Europe. The traditional US position, with its strong commitment to freedom of speech, only regards restrictions as legitimate insofar as they guard against a likely breach of the peace. United Kingdom law will restrict racist speech if it is *likely to stir up racial hatred*; on the grounds that racial hatred can in the long run lead to a breakdown in public order. But in contrast to France, Italy and Austria, the UK does not go so far as to criminalise the expression of views which 'merely' insult or vilify racial groups, except in certain very limited circumstances (see Oyediran 1992: 245).

When the UK ratified the International Covenant of Civil and Political Rights, it entered reservations on the way Article 20 dealt with national, racial and religious hatred. The UK stated that it interpreted the article consistently with Articles 19 and 21: that is, in the spirit of freedom of conscience and expression. Having legislated in the interests of public order, it reserved the right not to introduce any further legislation. The UK made a declaration to similar effect when it ratified the UN

Racial hatred

International Covenant on the Elimination of All Forms of Racial Discrimination (CERD). The claim to full discretion in determining what measures are necessary to fulfil international obligations has been criticised by several members of the CERD Committee (UN Doc. A/30/18, 1975, para. 144).

The UK fails to comply with international standards in three ways. The first two are straightforward and reflect deliberate political choices by successive UK governments. CERD demands that dissemination of ideas based on racial superiority and hatred, or incitement to discrimination, should be made criminal offences (Article 4a). The International Covenant is less strict, requiring that advocacy of national, racial or religious hatred be 'prohibited by law' (Article 20). The UK only criminalises the expression of views which insult or vilify racial groups if they stir up racial hatred or are likely to do so. Further, except in Northern Ireland, protection is not afforded to groups on the basis of their religious beliefs (as required by Article 20 of the International Covenant).

The third failure is more complex. The United Kingdom is under a duty to ensure that laws against the dissemination of racist ideas and incitement to discrimination are effectively enforced. But the government's 1994 report to the UN Human Rights Committee (which specifically asked for the information), showed that in the past four years only 15 people were prosecuted under the 1986 Act (from April 1987, when it came into force, to May 1994). Yet the Commission for Racial Equality received 494 complaints about printed material alone in just four years between 1986 to 1990 and recommended prosecution in 55 cases. The government's record makes a poor showing in the context of an estimated 70,000 racists attacks a year (Oyediran 1992: 248). In 1990, the Home Affairs Committee of the House of Commons expressed dissatisfaction with the UK government's explanations for so few prosecutions and condemned the Home Office's weak monitoring of the Act's effect (First Report of the Home Affairs Committee Session 1989–90 – Racial Attacks and Harassment, 1990, para. 32). The UN Human Rights Committee responded to the government's 1994 report by noting that 'many persons belonging to minorities frequently feel that acts of racial harassment are not pursued by the competent authorities with sufficient rigour and efficiency'; it recommended a major campaign against racial discrimination (CCPR/C/79 Add. 55, 27 July 1995).

Public order, treason and homosexuality

Laws restricting freedom of expression are scattered throughout various statutes and statutory instruments as well as the common law. It is impossible to list and consider every such restriction here. What follows, therefore, is an examination of three more significant restrictions which touch on the expression of political ideas in the broadest sense.

Public order offences

Only three public order offences primarily involve speech rather than actions. The original purpose of the three offences was supposedly to outlaw racial abuse, harassment and violence, although the terms of the three clauses which create these offences under the Public Order Act 1986 are widely framed and make no reference to race (sections 4, 4A and 5). All three require the use of threatening, abusive or insulting words or behaviour and that:

- the words or behaviour are aimed at a particular individual and the intention is either to cause that person to believe that unlawful violence will be used against him or her (or anyone else present for that matter) or to provoke violence from him or her (section 4) or
- the words are aimed at a particular individual, with the intention to cause that person (or someone else) harassment, alarm or distress (section 4A, introduced by the Criminal Justice and Public Order Act 1994) or
- the words or behaviour are used within the hearing or sight of a person likely to be caused harassment, alarm or distress (section 5).

It will be seen that the third offence has a much lower threshold and covers words or behaviour which need not be aimed at anyone in particular (under section 5).

Promotion of homosexuality

Section 28 of the Local Government Act 1988 provides that local authorities shall not 'intentionally promote homosexuality or publish material with the intention of promoting homosexuality' or promote the teaching in any maintained school of the acceptability of homosexuality as a 'pretended family relationship'.

Treason and sedition

Since feudal times, actions which constitute a breach of the subject's obligation of allegiance to the monarch have been punishable as treasons. As defined and extended by statute, treason includes imagining the death of the Queen and her eldest son and violating the Queen's eldest daughter before her marriage or the wife of the Queen's son. Related offences extend criminal liability to words and publications (Feldman 1993: 674).

Sedition was used historically to stifle criticism of government policy, potentially including all democratic debate and party-political activity, since it encompassed almost any political opposition to the government of the day (Feldman 1993: 676). Although there is considerable uncertainty about the precise definition of sedition today, more recent cases have stressed that the speaker or publisher must intend to provoke violence aimed at disturbing the government by force.

AUDIT

Different ways to restrain free expression

The European Court has frequently made it clear that the Convention protects not only information and ideas which are favourably received, but also those which offend, shock or disturb the state or groups within society (*Sunday Times v UK*, 1979,

Other restrictions

ECtHR). Of the new public order offences, section 4 of the Public Order Act could probably be justified by international human rights standards, as it protects other people from violence or the threat of violence. But the other two offences do not. Section 5 does not even require that anyone actually suffer harassment, alarm or distress. As Ronald Dworkin, Professor of Jurisprudence at Oxford, has remarked: 'It is hard to imagine a scheme of regulating demonstrations in a democracy more mean-spirited to liberty, more contemptuous of the importance and value of committed protest' (Dworkin 1988: 8). Predictions that section 5 could and would be used to restrict quite harmless activities have been borne out in practice. It has been used against juveniles throwing fake snowballs, against a man who had a birthday party for his son in his back garden (he was charged even though he agreed to turn the music down), against a nudist on the beach and against another nudist in his own house (Thornton 1989: 37).

Section 5 has also been used directly to restrict freedom of expression. In 1986 it was used against two 19-year-old males for kissing in the street and in 1987 against four students who were putting up a satirical poster during the election depicting Mrs Thatcher as a sadistic dominatrix. Ultimately charges were dropped in the second case, but convictions in the first case were upheld on appeal on the basis that heterosexuals might feel insulted seeing such conduct (*Masterson v Holden*, 1986). This raises an additional breach of international standards, namely, discrimination based on sexuality (see **pp. 120–121**).

In addition to freedom of expression, both the International Covenant and the European Convention protect the right to privacy. The European Court has confirmed that sexual life forms an important part of a person's private life and the Commission has made it clear that respect for a homosexual relationship comes within the ambit of 'private life'. It seems clear that no consideration was given to international human rights standards when section 28 of the Local Government Act 1988 was enacted. As the International Centre Against Censorship (Article 19) have argued, 'any restriction on a minority group in their attempts to present an accurate image of themselves is an intolerable limitation on the right to impart ideas' (*Index on Censorship*, May 1988). This is particularly so when there is clearly a climate of growing intolerance and hostility towards lesbians and gay men (Colvin 1989: 61). Gay men are frequently the targets of physical assault and murder. Unlike sex discrimination and race relations legislation which seeks to make prejudice less respectable, section 28 gives legitimacy to greater hostility and intolerance. As Dworkin wrote, the decision 'sent a chilling message of intolerance that is explicable only on nasty political grounds' (Dworkin 1990: 6).

By contrast, other European countries have introduced legislation aimed at limiting discrimination against lesbians and gay men. For example, Norway has made it illegal to 'publicly threaten, insult, or bear hatred towards, persecute or hold in contempt a person or group on the ground of homosexual orientation or way of life' (Colvin 1989: 61). International human rights instruments do allow for restrictions on the freedom of expression and privacy for the protection of public morals; but the argument that simply giving information on homosexual life is injurious to public morals cannot be sustained.

The government originally claimed that it was responding to complaints of corruption and indecency in schools and about a particular children's book, *Jenny Lives with Eric and Martin*. But it had to concede that this claim was groundless. Conservative MP Robin Squires pointed out that:

> in our discussions on this matter and in our attempts to extract evidence, it appears that most of that evidence arises from one book in one teachers' centre, in one school under one authority. I may be wrong, but I have seen no other evidence. Indeed, as I understand it, that book was kept to help teachers who are occasionally asked to advise pupils who come from homes with gay parents.
>
> (HC Deb, 9 March 1988, c376–377)

The word 'necessary' in the phrase 'necessary in a democratic society' must be understood as implying the existence of a 'pressing social need'. Squires's information undermines any pretension to compliance with international human rights standards. Finally, equality pervades all the rights and freedoms protected in the International Covenant and European Convention. Section 28, by its own definition, violates this fundamental requirement of human rights (see **p. 119**).

Prosecutions for treason are fortunately rare, for the punishment for treason is death by hanging. It is very hard to justify such a punishment in international human rights terms for any act, however violent. The sixth protocol of the European Convention (not ratified by the UK) prohibits the death penalty, except during war or under the imminent threat of war. This is a far cry from treasonable acts like 'imagining' the death of the Queen. The last person to hang for treason was William Joyce who had broadcast as 'Lord Haw-Haw' from Germany during the Second World War (*R v Joyce*, 1946).

Sedition began its life as an anti-democratic offence and so it remains. Not only is truth not a defence, but evidence of truth is totally prohibited at trial. Given the extent of public order law (see Chapter 10), it serves no useful purpose. It may very well seem to be simply an obsolete relic, like for example the blasphemy laws. But, like them, no one can be sure that it will not be used. The High Court refused to allow the opponents of Salman Rushdie to pursue him for sedition, but its ruling that sedition requires an intention to provoke violence has added further uncertainty to the law (*R v Bow Street Magistrates' Court ex parte Choudhury*, 1991). As one commentator has noted, 'the uncertainty surrounding the scope of the offence makes it particularly objectionable as a restriction on expression, since people potentially held [in terror] may be afraid to exercise political rights guaranteed under Articles 9, 10 and 11 of the European Convention' (Feldman 1993: 680). Thus the law contravenes the Convention.

DATA

Ownership and control of the media

There is no unified press or broadcasting law in the United Kingdom. In general, the media operate under restrictions which apply to the rest of the population. Many

Control of the media

of the laws already examined in this chapter – in particular official secrets, contempt of court, open justice and defamation – are of special importance to the press, but they are not part of a discrete code applying exclusively to them.

The status, ownership and control of the media have a profound effect on democracy generally and the exercise of political rights in particular. No special rules govern the ownership of the press in the United Kingdom. In principle, anyone can set up in business as a publisher. However, anyone who takes a controlling interest in a newspaper or group of newspapers exceeding 500,000 daily copies (usually by a take-over bid) must obtain the consent of the secretary of state. This consent cannot be given without an investigation by the Monopolies and Mergers Commission unless the secretary of state considers that the newspaper in question is not economic as a going concern and the take-over is urgent (Fair Trading Act 1973). If called upon, the Commission is required to report on 'whether the transfer in question may be expected to operate against the public interest, taking into account all matters which appear in the circumstances to be relevant and, in particular, the need for accurate presentation of news and free expression of opinion'.

Newspapers are also required to register their titles and the names, occupations, places of business and places of residence of their proprietors (Newspaper Libel and Registration Act 1881). But the government has no discretion to refuse registration and it is intended as a source of information as to the newspaper's owners rather than a means of censorship.

Ownership and control of the broadcasting media (radio and television) is fairly tightly controlled. The BBC is established under Royal Charter and subject to governors appointed by the government. It operates under the terms of that charter, as well as under its licence and agreement from the Home Secretary, who also determines the rate of the annual licence fee on which the BBC largely relies for its funding. Non-BBC television and radio services (including cable and satellite stations) are regulated by the Broadcasting Act 1990 which established the Independent Television Commission (ITC) and the Radio Authority to licence and regulate such services. Members of the ITC and Radio Authority are appointed by the Home Secretary.

In extreme circumstances, the government possesses direct legal powers over radio and television, including a power to send troops in to take possession of the BBC in the name of and on behalf of the Crown (Licence Agreement, section 19). The Home Secretary has a more general power to prohibit the BBC from transmitting any item or programme at any time. There is no safeguard against this, although the BBC 'may' (not 'must') tell the public that it has received an order from the Home Secretary, thus highlighting interference in its scheduling. The Home Secretary may also order the ITC to 'refrain from broadcasting any matter or classes of matter' on commercial television (Broadcasting Act 1990, section 10).

The absence of journalistic privilege

The European Court consistently emphasises the special role of the press in a democratic society. Enhanced privileges (as well as special duties) are attached to the press to enable it to perform its dual role of 'purveyor of information and public watch-dog' (*Lingens v Austria*, 1986). No such privileges attach to the media in the UK; instead, real concerns exist.

The Contempt of Court Act 1981 provides that no court may require an author or journalist to disclose the source of published information,

> unless it is established to the satisfaction of the court that this is necessary in the interests of justice or national security or for the prevention of disorder or crime.
>
> (section 10)

Despite this presumption against disclosure, judicial faith in the importance of protecting journalists' sources has been very limited. During the large-scale steel strike in 1980, Granada TV obtained secret documents from the publicly-owned British Steel Corporation concerning its massive losses. In confirming an order that Granada had to disclose its source, one member of the House of Lords remarked that 'this case does not touch on the freedom of the press even at the periphery' and only one member stated that protecting sources was democratically important (*British Steel Corporation v Granada TV*, 1982). Although the case was decided before the 1981 Act was passed, predictions that the 'interests of justice' exception to section 10 would have led to the same result appear to have been well-founded (International Centre Against Censorship 1993b: 187).

In April 1990, William Goodwin, a trainee journalist on *The Engineer* magazine, was fined £5,000 for refusing to comply with a court order to reveal the source of confidential information he had been given about a company's financial affairs. The company, citing potential financial loss, sought disclosure to identify the source, whom they believed to be within the company. The House of Lords ruled that the administration of justice required disclosure, although the company had already won an injunction to prevent publication of the article based on the information (*Re Goodwin*, 1990). In March 1996 the European Court of Human Rights held that the disclosure ordered by the House of Lords was not 'necessary in a democratic society' (*Goodwin v UK*).

Ownership and control of the media

On the question of ownership and control, the UN Human Rights Committee has made it clear that:

> Because of the development of modern mass media, effective measures are necessary to prevent such control of the media as would interfere with the right of everyone to freedom of expression in a way that is not provided for in paragraph 3 [of Article 19].
>
> (General Comment 11(19), 1983)

Similarly, the European Commission of Human Rights has indicated that an issue might arise under Article 10 of the European Convention 'where a State fails in its

Control of the media

duty to protect against excessive press concentrations' (*Geillustreerde Pers v Netherlands*, 1976, ECmHR). The same theme is reflected in a resolution of the Parliamentary Assembly of the Council of Europe in 1978, calling for national laws restricting press monopolies and concentrations and recognising the likely need for public subsidies to ensure the financial viability of newspapers (Recommendation 834, 1978).

The operation of the Fair Trading Act 1973 and the question of ownership and control of the media in the UK has not yet been directly raised with the European human rights authorities or the UN Human Rights Committee. The requirement that newspaper mergers be referred to the Monopolies and Mergers Commission undoubtedly reflects the spirit (if not the letter) of international standards. But there is cause for concern. In particular, ministers have demonstrated a marked reluctance to examine closely claims made by prospective buyers that a newspaper is 'not a going concern'. As a consequence, many take-overs have not been referred to the Monopolies and Mergers Commission under the 1973 Act. By 1994, ownership of newspapers in the UK had become highly concentrated. Some 70 per cent of national daily newspapers, and 80 per cent of national Sundays, were published by four multinational companies. Regional newspapers were largely controlled by four commercial corporations (International Centre Against Censorship 1993b: 171). If the trend continues, there may soon come a point at which the UK fails in its duty to protect against excessive press concentrations.

Government interference in the media

There is growing evidence of direct interference by government ministers in the media. Government ministers have interfered in the BBC since its very first days, but the BBC coverage of the Falklands War in the early 1980s led to a 14-year government campaign to bring the BBC to heel (Barnett and Curry 1994). Mrs Thatcher, the then Prime Minister, was convinced that the BBC was biased against her – as previous Prime Ministers, like Harold Wilson, had been too. A government has three levers of control over the BBC: appointing the BBC Governors; fixing the annual licence fee; and renewing the BBC Charter. Mrs Thatcher packed the Board of Governors with like-minded people who soon sacked an obstinately independent BBC Director-General in 1987. For a period, the very future of the BBC as a public broadcasting service was in doubt. A regime of direct political pressures and internal censorship developed (Weir 1994). Perhaps the most notorious incident came in 1985. The Governors cancelled the broadcast of a documentary, *Real Lives*, which included an interview with an IRA sympathiser, in the face of strong criticism from Mrs Thatcher, who condemned the programme unseen. The programme was eventually shown in a modified form after BBC staff held a one-day strike. But this and other episodes called into question the BBC Board of Governors' commitment to freedom of expression (Robertson and Nicol 1992: 28).

The BBC was not alone in being subjected to intense government pressure. A major controversy erupted over an investigative Thames TV documentary, *Death on the Rock*, which effectively challenged the official version of the SAS killings of three unarmed IRA terrorists in Gibraltar in March 1988. The Foreign Secretary tried to persuade the regulating authority (then the Independent Broadcasting Authority) not to transmit the programme, but failed. The Prime Minister and Home Secretary attacked the documentary as substantially untrue. As the broadcast came four months before the official inquest into the killings, ministers also claimed that it would prejudice the inquest. Asked whether she was furious about the programme, Mrs Thatcher replied that her feelings went 'deeper than that' (Barnett and Curry 1994: 118 and 123). The programme was broadcast when the government was shaping the new structure for ITV, under which Thames ultimately lost its lucrative London weekday licence.

Yet in 1989, an independent report by Lord Windlesham found that the programme was substantially true, while criticising two lapses in its making, and concluded that it had not prejudiced the inquest (*The Windlesham Rampton Report*, 1989). The inquiry also declared that Thames TV had been right not to bow to government pressure to ban the programme. The programme asked a number of uncomfortable questions about the killings which the European Court was later to consider in coming to its judgment that the killings had breached the European Convention's protection of the 'right to life' (*McCann and Others v UK*, 1995, ECtHR).

Douglas Hurd, the then Home Secretary, used his powers to prohibit broadcasts by the BBC and IBA (see above) in October 1988 by issuing an order banning them from interviewing or broadcasting speech by individuals associated with a range of Northern Irish groups, including Sinn Fein, or from broadcasting any statement that incited support for such groups. The NUJ challenged the ban in judicial review proceedings. The details of that challenge are set out in detail in Part 2 (**p. 97**). For our purposes here it is enough to note that the House of Lords refused to accept that the Home Secretary's discretionary powers to ban broadcasts should be only exercised in a way which conformed with the European Convention (*R v Home Secretary ex parte Brind*, 1991).

The ban did not preclude journalists from reporting the words used by members of Sinn Fein or other organisations in indirect speech, and broadcasters soon realised that they could dub actors' voices onto footage of such people speaking to breach it in spirit. Yet any suggestion that this did not amount to an interference with freedom of expression cannot be sustained. In 1987, the European Commission rejected the government's argument that a judge's order prohibiting actors from reading transcripts of a trial did not amount to 'interference' with freedom of expression (*Hodgson v UK*). The way information was conveyed to the public required protection just as the content of information did. The only real question was therefore whether the broadcasting ban was justified because it pursued a legitimate aim and was 'necessary in a democratic society'. In that same democratic society, Sinn Fein was throughout the duration of the ban a legal political party which won around 35 per cent of the nationalist vote in Northern Ireland and had one elected MP and some 60 local councillors.

After the House of Lords refused to take the European Convention into account, the NUJ applied to the European Commission. The journalists' union accepted the pressing social need to combat terrorism, but argued that the broadcasting ban's terms had no rational connection with that objective. The NUJ informed the Commission that the Home Secretary, on introducing the ban, plainly stated that he had no criticism of the conduct of the broadcasters; and that there was no evidence that any programmes that might have been transmitted but for the ban had in the past caused public offence or promoted the status of terrorist organisations. However, just before the ban was revoked in 1994, the Commission rejected the NUJ's claim as 'manifestly ill-founded' – without an oral hearing (*Brind and others v UK*, 1994).

Despite the Commission's ruling, it is difficult to see how the broadcasting ban could have been justified by international human rights standards. Freedom of expression may be restricted to protect public order and prohibit crime, but states bear the burden of proving – with *specific evidence* – that measures taken on this ground are necessary (*Alba Pietroroia v Uruguay*, 1979; *Sunday Times v UK*, 1979; and *Autronic AG v Switzerland*, 1990). No such evidence was put before the Commission. For that reason, our conclusion is that the broadcasting ban fell short of international human rights standards. We are fortified in our view, by the finding of the UN Human Rights Committee a year earlier that a similar ban in the Irish Republic infringed the right to receive and impart information under Article 19 of the International Covenant (Comment on Initial Report Under Article 40 from Ireland: CCPR/C/68/Add. 3, 28 July 1993).

Conclusions

There is no guarantee of freedom of expression in the UK; it is hedged about by numerous restrictions. Of these, the law of defamation is the most troublesome. It fails to give proper weight to freedom of expression or justice. Unless it is radically reviewed to reflect the more mature attitude adopted now in the European Court of Human Rights, the gap between Britain's law of defamation and international human rights standards will become unbridgeable. Criminal libel, blasphemy and sedition laws do not conform with international human rights standards. Obscenity and indecency laws are less irksome, but they too flirt with non-compliance.

Public order legislation also requires review. Some laws – most notably sections 4A and 5 of the Public Order Act 1986 dealing with abusive and insulting behaviour – are loosely drafted and fall short of international standards. Other laws are ineffective or ineffectively applied. In particular, the huge disparity between perhaps 70,000 racially-inspired attacks and just 15 prosecutions taken out against alleged perpetrators over similar periods of time justifies far more concern than the government has shown. Nor can the failure to afford protection against religious hatred in all parts of the UK be justified.

Section 28 of the Local Government Act 1988, prohibiting the promotion of homosexuality in schools, fails international human rights standards on several grounds, including equality and non-discrimination. And although it has now been revoked, the broadcasting ban cannot be said to have complied with international human rights standards.

10   The Residual Right of Public Protest

Freedom of assembly

People exercise their freedom of assembly when they visit the cinema, hold a birth-day party, join a picket, or march in protest. The focus of this chapter is on activities which have a public or political dimension – marches, meetings, rallies, demon-strations, pickets and festivals. These activities enable citizens to organise independently of government, both for their own ends and to protest or influence national or local policies on issues of concern. In many ways, they represent a collec-tive freedom of expression.

Assemblies of all kinds are vital to a culture of freedom (**pp. 10–12**). In repres-sive societies, the willingness to join together in marches or demonstrations can represent the ultimate safeguard for democracy. The popular demonstrations in central and eastern Europe in 1989 provide a successful example of this expression of anonymous 'people power'. Even in free societies, freedom of assembly can provide a degree of pluralism which is often missing in the media, political parties and other institutions. Finally, freedom of assembly performs an important role in building an active and informed civil society able to participate in public affairs. In 1994, the UN Centre for Human Rights noted:

> The right of assembly must be respected, since public demonstrations and political rallies are an integral part of the election process and provide an effective mechanism for the public dissemination of political information.
> (United Nations 1994: 8)

The right of people to engage in activities like these has to be balanced against the rights and freedoms of other citizens. The International Covenant and the European Convention first define and provide a formal guarantee of the right of free assembly – and then allow specific exceptions. In the United Kingdom, by contrast, freedom of assembly only exists as a negative right; when people gather together, they are not necessarily breaking the law, but the law does not give them any positive *right* of assembly. The law regulates where people can meet together, what assemblies are allowed and who may participate.

For anyone wanting to organise a march or any other public event, the first ques-tion is 'Where?' This is not an easy question because no public land with unrestricted rights of access exists in Britain. All land is vested in some person or institution and subject to legal restrictions on freedom of assembly. An organiser must then ask, 'Is my march or event lawful?' For the authorities may ban or impose conditions on marches and other public gatherings. Some may be illegal, such as 'trespassory assemblies'. The final question is, 'Who can come?' Even if the place and event are lawful, some people may be banned from attending under the conditions of their bail or other restrictions. The people who do attend cannot necessarily act as they wish. The three sections of this chapter address the three questions we have posed.

Human rights index: freedom of assembly

Everyone has the right to freedom of peaceful assembly . . .
(Universal Declaration on Human Rights: Article 20)

The primary sources of international standards on freedom of assembly are Article 21 of the International Covenant and Article 11 of the European Convention, which protect freedom of assembly in almost identical terms. A citizen's right to free assembly can only be restricted in specific circumstances which are clearly set out. However, both instruments only protect public assemblies so long as they are peaceful. That does not mean that the state can sit back and allow a peaceful assembly to become violent – for example, through the activities of certain factions outside the control of the organisers, or by the intervention of counter-demonstrators. But it does mean that states may impose restrictions on assemblies and even, in extreme circumstances, ban or break them up.

The democratic importance of freedom of assembly places states under a greater duty to protect it than they are to protect rights exclusively exercised for private interests (Nowak 1993: 370–371). This duty can include taking measures to ensure that peaceful protestors are protected from violent activities of factions or opponents. In the opinion of the European Commission of Human Rights:

> The right to freedom of peaceful assembly is secured to everyone who has the intention of organising a peaceful demonstration . . . the possibility of violent counter-demonstrations, or the possibility of extremists with violent intentions, not members of the organising association, joining the demonstration cannot as such take away that right.
> (*Christians Against Racism and Fascism v UK*, 1984)

The extent to which states are obliged to go further than this – for example, by providing meeting rooms or re-routing traffic – is unclear. So far, the UN Human Rights Committee has not issued any general comments on the scope of Article 21 and has not decided any individual complaints. Similarly, the European Commission and Court of Human Rights have heard very few cases involving freedom of assembly. Therefore, while the Court has made it clear that effective freedom of assembly requires more of a state than to refrain from interfering, it has not yet developed a general theory of the positive obligations on member states. However, if facilities are made available by the state for assemblies, there should be no discrimination on political or other grounds, except where this is necessary for one of the legitimate purposes justifying restriction (Nowak 1993: 382).

Although it is firmly recognised that freedom of assembly is crucial to democracy, the purposes of any meeting or procession need not themselves be democratic. A Soviet proposal to this effect during the drafting of the International Covenant was specifically rejected (Nowak 1993: 371). Nor does the respect accorded to freedom of assembly depend on the acceptability of those purposes or the views expressed. A demonstration may annoy or offend people opposed to the ideas or claims being promoted, but the participants must be able to hold the demonstration.

Since freedom of assembly often represents collective freedom of expression, inter-national standards governing the latter are also relevant. The full index for freedom of expression and the inter-connected freedom of information is set out elsewhere **(pp. 142–146** and **165–168)**. The key features are incorporated in the indexes below.

Restricting rights

Formal recognition of civil and political rights is not enough. It is essential that any restriction of all rights recognised by both the International Covenant and the European Convention be closely scrutinised. The two instruments set out a strict three-part test:

1.   Any restriction on civil and political rights must be 'prescribed by law'
2.   The restriction must be justified by one of the aims under the International Covenant or European Convention
3.   The restriction must be shown to be 'necessary in a democratic society'.

This test is of fundamental importance. For that reason, we deal with it in detail in **Box A, pp. 21–22**. Here, broadly, the test requires that ordinary citizens can readily discover what legal restrictions to any right exist with enough clarity for them to be able to regulate their conduct. Any restrictions must then meet one of the aims recognised under either instrument as a legitimate ground for the restriction of civil and political rights. These aims are: the protection of the rights and freedoms of others; national security; public safety; public health and morals; and the prevention of public disorder or crime. This list is intended to be exhaustive. States may not introduce other restrictions or stretch the meaning of the criteria listed above to add others. Finally, states must show that the restriction fulfils a pressing social need and that it is proportionate to the aim of responding to that need. They cannot merely assert that the restriction is 'necessary in a democratic society', but must provide concrete evidence of a genuine and serious threat.

The bodies which interpret the tests – the UN Human Rights Committee and the European Court and Commission of Human Rights – have framed their notion of 'democratic society' in terms of such concepts as 'pluralism, tolerance and broadmindedness'; and have made it clear that although the term 'necessary' is not synonymous with 'indispensable', it does not simply mean 'reasonable' (*Handyside v UK*, ECtHR, 1976). The evolving human rights standards which apply to restrictions on freedom of assembly are:

■   The prohibition or break-up of a procession or meeting can only be justified when milder measures, such as imposing conditions, would be insufficient (Nowak 1993: 379).

International standards

- But where it is not practicable for a demonstration to proceed peacefully, it can be banned. A state can even impose a 'blanket' ban covering more than one demonstration (*Christians Against Racism and Fascism v UK*, 1984, ECmHR).

- However, a state must consider the effect of a blanket ban on activities which do not threaten public order before imposing the ban. Only when the disadvantage of such activities being caught is *clearly outweighed* by the security considerations justifying the ban *and* there is no possibility of narrowing the scope, can a blanket ban be regarded as 'necessary in a democratic society' (*Christians Against Racism and Fascism v UK*).

- The rights of passers-by must be taken into account, but it is the state's duty to uphold their rights *and* safeguard freedom of assembly (Nowak 1993: 382).

- An obligation on organisers of marches or meetings to give information to the police and/or seek authorisation for their activity does not necessarily infringe the right to freedom of assembly – so long as its purpose is to enable the state either to prevent non-peaceful assemblies or to take positive steps to ensure that peaceful assemblies are not disrupted (*Rassemblement Jurassien and Unité Jurassienne v Switzerland*, 1978, ECmHR).

- Freedom of assembly is so important that punishing an individual simply for participating in an assembly cannot be justified, unless he or she personally commits a reprehensible act; an individual's failure to disassociate himself or herself from such acts is not enough (*Ezelin v France*, 1991, ECtHR).

Highways

No public land with unrestricted rights of access exists in Britain. All land is vested in some person or institution and subject to legal restrictions on freedom of assembly.

The use of highways – roads, footpaths and bridleways – for marches, meetings, rallies, demonstrations, pickets and festivals is fraught with difficulties involving the civil and criminal law. Over the years the courts have made clear their view that highways were never really intended for these activities – they are essentially for people to pass along. It follows that the public have a right to pass along a highway for the purpose of legitimate travel, *not a right to be on it*. Activities which are 'incidental to passage' – for example, a motorist attempting to repair a car, a pedestrian resting, people queuing for a bus – are lawful. Using the highway for any other purpose is considered to be trespass (*Harrison v Duke of Rutland*, 1893).

Obstruction of the highway is both a criminal offence and a civil wrong. The Highways Act 1980 provides that a person who 'without lawful authority or excuse in any way wilfully obstructs the free passage of the highway' is guilty of an offence. In Northern Ireland, Public Order (NI) Order 1987 provides that someone who sits, stands, kneels, lies down or otherwise behaves in a public place so as to wilfully obstruct traffic or to hinder any lawful activity commits an offence.

Obstructing the highway also amounts to 'public nuisance' under the civil law, for which damages or an injunction, or both, can be claimed (*Hubbard v Pitt*, 1976).

A civil action may be brought by the Attorney-General, or by anyone who has suffered special loss over and above the inconvenience suffered by the public at large. Even where there is no obstruction, civil proceedings can be brought for 'private nuisance' whenever any activity on a highway interferes with someone's property rights. According to Justice Forbes in *Hubbard v Pitt*:

> A man's right to enjoy his property which abuts on the highway and to have access to that property both for himself and his invitees is a right which is fully entitled to the support of the courts if and when the courts are asked to support it.

Such legal niceties do entail larger questions. For example, during the miners' strike 1984–85 the courts held that 'unreasonable' harassment of workers who wished to use the highway to go to work was a civil wrong which might be described as 'a species of private nuisance' (*Thomas v NUM (South Wales Area)*, 1985).

The largely forgotten (but still unrepealed) Town Police Clauses Act 1847 prohibits a whole catalogue of activities on highways (30 paragraphs worth in all) which obstruct, annoy or cause danger to residents or passers-by. These include: rolling or carrying any cask, tub, hoop, wheel, ladder, plank, pole, timber or log on any footway (apart from loading and unloading goods or crossing the footway); flying a kite; hanging washing in the street; beating or shaking of carpets, rugs or mats; and using profane or obscene language. In 1983, the House of Lords, with some reservations, approved its continued use by police officers (*Wills v Bowley*, 1983).

Since 1906, there has been a measure of protection for peaceful pickets not afforded to other activities. When picketing forms part of industrial action, it is lawful for pickets to attend at their own place of work, peacefully to obtain and communicate information or persuade any person to work or abstain from working (now under the Trade Union and Labour Relations (Consolidation) Act 1992). This protects pickets and their unions from civil actions in trespass and for inducing breach of contract, but not in respect of unreasonable obstruction of access to premises and unreasonable obstruction of the highway (*Thomas v NUM (South Wales Area)*, 1985). The government's Code of Practice states that 'pickets and their organisers should ensure that in general the number of pickets does not exceed six at any entrance to a workplace; frequently a smaller number will be appropriate'.

Open spaces

It is generally believed that people have a *right* to meet in certain places such as Trafalgar Square or Hyde Park. They do not. Open spaces, parks, recreation grounds and the like are usually vested in the Crown, a local authority or some other body with special powers to make regulations or bylaws restricting public assemblies in them. For example, the Trafalgar Square Regulations 1952 prohibit assemblies, parades or processions without written permission from the secretary of state. Challenges to the legality of such regulations or bylaws have usually failed. Perhaps most significantly for this audit, no challenge on the ground that freedom of assembly has been unduly restricted seems ever to have succeeded.

The historic caselaw relating to three traditional meeting places in London – Hyde Park, Clapham Common and Trafalgar Square – still survives and provides a valuable snapshot of the law. In 1873, the validity of regulations prohibiting meetings in Hyde Park unless they took place at certain prescribed places was challenged. The basis of the challenge was that the Parks Regulation Act 1872, under which the regulations were made, specified that regulations should not authorise 'any interference with *any right* whatever to which any person or persons may be by law entitled [our emphasis]'. Freedom of assembly should therefore prevail. The High Court disagreed, holding that there was no such thing as a 'right' to hold public meetings in the park (*Bailey v Williamson*, 1873).

Seven years later the High Court upheld a bylaw which prohibited the delivery of any public speech, lecture, sermon or address of any kind, on Clapham Common, except with the written permission of the board in charge of the park and then only on those parts of the common for which such permission was given (*De Morgan v Metropolitan Board of Works*, 1880).

Finally, two cases in 1888 confirmed that there was no right of public meeting in Trafalgar Square (*R v Cunninghame Graham and Burns* and *Ex Parte Lewis*). In the second, a judge ruled that 'Trafalgar Square . . . is completely regulated by Act of Parliament and whatever rights exist must be found in the statute if at all. The right of public meeting is not among them.'

Publicly-owned premises

The public has no general right to use a public building for a meeting (apart from one or two exceptions; see below). A local authority or other public body controlling the building can decide any request to do so more or less at its discretion (so long as it does not breach sex or race relations laws). There are some signs that courts will intervene on public law principles. But the courts have not yet imposed an obligation on a public body to allow its property to be used for meetings, in the absence of a statutory requirement or contract to do so. For example, in October 1979, the Court of Appeal held that the Labour-controlled Great Yarmouth Council could not veto a booking for the annual conference of the National Front accepted by the council when the Conservatives had been in power, but only because the agreement was subject to the ordinary rules of contract (*Verrall v Great Yarmouth Borough Council*, 1981).

There are two statutory rights to hold meetings in public buildings. Under the Representation of the People Act 1983, parliamentary and local government candidates are entitled to hold meetings in schools and other publicly-maintained premises before elections. Consequently, where local councils have tried to prevent groups such as the National Front holding election meetings, their decisions have been overturned in the courts (*Webster v Southwark LBC*, 1983). University and college authorities have a positive duty to 'ensure that freedom of speech within the law is secured to members, students and employees of the establishment and for visiting speakers' (under the Education (No. 2) Act 1986). This duty was imposed after several university and college authorities banned meetings in the mid-1980s because they feared that speakers might be subject to heckling or even threats (Feldman 1993: 565). The duty is framed to ensure that the use of the premises is not denied to any individual on grounds of his or her views or beliefs.

Privately-owned premises

Activities on private land or private premises are more or less unregulated. It is up to the owner to decide what activities can take place and on what terms. Disputes are usually dealt with in the civil courts, either in contract or trespass cases. In recent years, criminal sanctions have also been introduced, all of which relate to specific events or activities and are therefore dealt with later.

How free are people to join together?

Hundreds of thousands of citizens in the UK take part in marches, meetings, rallies, demonstrations and festivals on the highway every year. Yet none has a *right* to do so. With two exceptions – non-violent marches and lawful pickets – freedom of assembly on the highway is a matter of 'good grace' – not law. In other words, up and down the country the organisers of activities on the highway and the people participating rely on the good sense of their local authorities (not to sue them for trespass), of landowners (not to sue them for nuisance) and the police (not to arrest them for obstruction). This is a very fragile basis for freedom of assembly, as the leading case of *Hubbard v Pitt* in 1976 demonstrates.

The defendants were a group of people who disliked the 'gentrification' of parts of Islington, in north London, where they lived and worked. They attributed this process in part to the assistance given by the local estate agents to higher-income house-buyers. In spring 1974 they organised a campaign to preserve the social composition of the area and to persuade leading estate agents to adopt a code of conduct in dealing with tenants and tenanted property. Every Saturday morning they stood outside Prebble & Co, a local estate agents, carrying inoffensive placards and distributing leaflets. The partners of Prebble & Co issued a writ for damages and went to court for an immediate injunction.

The defendants stood on their freedom of assembly, arguing that the campaign

> was carried out in peaceful and orderly fashion in pursuance of the lawful right enjoyed by the defendants and other participants to express their opinions about, and draw public attention towards, a matter of substantial public interest and concern.
>
> (paragraph 4 of their defence)

In the Court of Appeal, Lord Denning accepted this and commented that:

> The pickets were arranged with the full knowledge and agreement of the local police. The police station is only 300 yards away. The police inspector

has thanked them for their cooperation in making sure that nothing unlawful was done. In the photographs the police can be seen talking in a friendly manner with the pickets . . . No crowds collected. No queues were formed. No obstruction caused. No noises. No smells. No breaches of the peace.

(Hubbard v Pitt)

He was in the minority. The other two judges refused to overturn the decision of Justice Forbes in the High Court who had granted an injunction to stop the campaign from continuing. The judge accepted that the public could easily get past the group of people outside the estate agents' shop, but ruled that they nevertheless had a 'right' to go on every part of the highway. The picket was therefore a 'public nuisance' which should be stopped.

The failure of the courts to give any weight to freedom of assembly is a significant violation of international human rights standards. Justice Forbes dismissed the relevance of Article 11 of the European Convention to the case on the grounds that it 'does not give a right to assemble in public anywhere the convenors of a public meeting choose, and in particular, does not give a right to assemble on the highway'. This misses the point. International human rights standards do not set up unassailable rights. But they do require that restrictions on rights such as freedom of assembly be carefully scrutinised and only permitted if it can be shown that they pass a prescribed set of tests (see above **pp. 21–22**). The law in the UK requires no such scrutiny. Positive rights to the full enjoyment of property override negative rights such as freedom of assembly.

Broadly speaking, the criminal law relating to highways is slightly less restrictive. For example, animal rights protesters who were holding banners and handing out leaflets outside a shop selling fur in Bradford were found not guilty of obstruction under the Highways Act 1980, on the basis that their activity was 'not unreasonable use' of the highway (*Hirst and Agu v Chief Constable of West Yorkshire*, 1986). But the 'not unreasonable use' is not adopted in civil cases, where the test remains whether the highway was being used for passage or activity 'reasonably incidental' to passage.

Yet the arcane Town Police Clauses Act 1847 remains in force and, though rarely used, creates a host of trivial offences, including (it seems) carrying banners or placards in the street. Until 1983 the Act seemed to have slipped into obscurity. But now that it has been resurrected, its actual use depends on the discretion of the police – despite a plea from Lord Elwyn-Jones in the House of Lords 'for early attention' to the Act by Parliament, 'if it is still considered necessary to use it despite the many changes in the law relating to public order which have been made since 1847' (*Wills v Bowley*, 1983). By creating absolute offences without regard to any notion of freedom of assembly, the 1847 Act falls far short of international human rights standards.

A framework of law which leaves freedom of assembly on the highway to the 'good grace' of local authorities, land-owners and the police is far removed from the positive duty imposed on states by International Covenant and the European Convention to ensure that peaceful assemblies are protected. Clearly conflicts between different groups will arise. Both instruments demand that in such conflicts the rights of others – such as passers-by – should be *balanced* with those of people who wish to engage in an assembly. So far as is possible, states must uphold freedom of assembly and the rights of people involved in a march or protest on the highway. The 'good grace' approach effectively leaves freedom of assembly to the mercy of a police officer's 'blind-eye', or to the public spirit of local council officers and members or neighbouring property-owners.

Parks, commons and other open spaces are no more freely available for public assemblies than the highways. Local authorities and other bodies with power to make regulations or bylaws in relation to open spaces, parks recreation grounds and the like, can restrict or prohibit public assemblies without regard to international human rights standards. In most parks, dogs have more rights than demonstrators (Robertson 1989: 68).

In practice, local authorities and other bodies often do permit meetings in open spaces, parks and recreation grounds – but no *right* to meet publicly in them can be assumed. The use of even traditional public places for protest, like Trafalgar Square, requires the prior approval of the police. CND, the 'Save Greece from Fascism' group and the Northern Ireland Civil Rights Movement have all been denied the use of Trafalgar Square – indeed, since 1972, all meetings in Trafalgar Square concerning Ireland have been banned. Freedom of assembly in public places – for protest marches, meetings and the like – is again largely a question of 'good grace' or 'commonsense' on the part of the authorities, not a citizen's legal right.

Anyone wishing to use a public building for a meeting is in the same position as someone hiring private premises. Save where statute expressly provides for meetings – for elections and at universities and colleges (see Data above) – no one has the *right* to hold a public meeting. The legal owners have the final say, except that for publicly-owned premises, 'perverse' decisions and those which breach the sex and race discrimination laws can be challenged.

The working assumption of most judges when restricting the activity of protestors is that 'they are free at some other place, and by legitimate means, to bring their dislike . . . before the public', as Justice Forbes said in banning the peaceful picket of the estate agents, Prebble & Co (*Hubbard v Pitt*, 1976). This is simply wrong. The cumulative effect of the law in the UK on highways, open spaces and public buildings is that no one has a right of peaceful assembly anywhere. At every turn the ability to gather together to protest or discuss matters of public importance is largely a matter of discretion for some other person or body.

DATA

Banning and imposing conditions on public gatherings

There is no unqualified right to organise a public protest. The authorities may ban or impose conditions on marches and other public gatherings. Some may be illegal, such as 'trespassory assemblies'.

Banning orders

Banning

Historically, the police have always been able to ban marches and meetings under the common law, using their powers to prevent a breach of the peace (see below, **p. 199**). The Public Order Act 1936, now extended by the Public Order Act 1986, has added statutory powers. A chief constable can apply for a banning order on any 'procession' (which simply means any number of people moving together along a route) if he or she reasonably thinks that the power to impose conditions on the event will not be sufficient to prevent 'serious public disorder'. Outside London, the chief constable applies to the district council, which then considers whether or not to make the order; in London, the Commissioner of Police makes the order. In both cases, the Home Secretary must consent.

An order may cover all or part of a district and may ban all processions or just certain types. Police practice in recent years has been to seek blanket bans to cover all processions to avoid suggestions of bias. The standard formula is to ban 'all public processions other than those of a traditional or ceremonial character' (Wadham 1994: 6). Bans can last for up to three months. Failure to comply with a banning order is a criminal offence.

Banning orders have recently been extended to cover 'trespassory assemblies' in England and Wales – that is, gatherings about to take place on any land to which the public has no right of access, or only a limited right of access, *and* which do not have full permission from the occupier of the land. The powers were introduced to deal with travellers by the Criminal Justice and Public Order (CJPO) Act 1994). A chief constable can apply for a blanket order if he or she reasonably believes that a 'trespassory assembly' may result in serious disruption to the life of the community or damage to land, buildings or monuments of historical, architectural or archaeological importance. The procedures are the same as for processions (above). The bans prohibits all trespassory assemblies for up to four days within a five-mile radius. To enforce a ban, police officers have the power to stop anyone they 'reasonably' believe is on the way to a banned assembly. Anyone who defies their order is guilty of a criminal offence – whether or not they were going to the event.

In Northern Ireland, the Secretary of State has powers to ban open air processions and meetings, if he or she is satisfied that they are likely to cause serious public disorder, cause serious disruption to the life of the community, or make undue demands upon the police or military forces (under the Public Order (NI) Order 1987). Again, a banning order can last up to three months and can prohibit all processions and meetings or specified processions and meetings. A person who knowingly organises or takes part in a banned event is guilty of an offence for which the maximum penalty is two years in prison and an unlimited fine.

Finally, the police now have special powers to prevent 'raves' under the CJPO Act 1994. The act defines a 'rave' as any open air gathering of 100 or more people at which amplified music will be played during the night and which is likely to cause serious distress to local people. A police superintendent or higher-ranking officer who reasonably believes that two or more people are preparing a 'rave', or 10 or more people are waiting for or attending one, may order them to go and take with them their vehicles and belongings. Anyone who refuses or returns within seven days may be imprisoned for three months. Powers similar to those for 'trespassory assemblies' (above) enable police officers to turn back would-be 'ravers'.

Imposing conditions

The police also have powers to impose conditions on processions and assemblies. The Public Order Act 1986 underpins these powers by requiring organisers to give six clear days' advance notice of a march intended to publicise a cause or campaign, support or oppose the views or actions of any group, or mark or commemorate an event. Notice need not be given if it is not *reasonably practicable to do so* – this is intended to allow for completely spontaneous events, for example, when a meeting turns into a march. In addition, no notice is needed for funeral processions or processions which are 'commonly or customarily' held (like the Lord Mayor's Show, the Notting Hill Carnival, other local parades and religious occasions). Notice must be given in writing and state the time and date of the march and its proposed route.

Conditions can be imposed on *all* marches and assemblies (whether or not notice was given). For marches, they can be imposed in writing in advance by the chief constable, or during the event by the most senior officer present. In each case the officer concerned must reasonably think that the march might result in serious public disorder, serious damage to property or serious disruption to the life of the community – or that the organisers intend to intimidate others 'with a view to compelling them to do an act they have a right to do, or to do an act which they have a right not to do'. An officer should impose only conditions which are *necessary* to prevent disorder, damage, disruption or intimidation. Failure to comply with a condition is a criminal offence. The procedures for imposing conditions on assemblies are similar. The chief constable can impose conditions in advance (in writing) or the most senior officer can act as soon as 20 people have assembled.

AUDIT

The broad scope of banning orders

The power to ban processions under the Public Order Act 1986 broadly conforms with international human rights standards. The procedure and criteria are clear, the chief constable must fear 'serious public disorder' and must have considered lesser measures or specific conditions to be insufficient. In 1981, the European Commission of Human Rights rejected a claim that a two-month blanket ban on marches in London (under the old 1936 Act) violated Article 11 of the European Convention (*Christians against Racism and Fascism v UK*, 1984).

However, according to evolving human rights standards, a state cannot merely assert that a particular restriction on freedom of assembly is necessary for this or that purpose. To satisfy international standards and establish that the restriction is 'necessary in a democratic society', a state must provide concrete evidence of that necessity and institute some independent control against abuse (see **pp. 21–22**). The limited scope for judicial review of banning orders in England and Wales raises questions of compliance with those standards.

The case of *Kent v Metropolitan Police Commissioner* (1981) demonstrates the point. Following extensive disorder in Brixton in early 1981, Sir David McNee, then Commissioner of the Metropolitan Police, obtained an order banning all marches in London for 28 days. The ban covered 786 square miles from Radlett to Croydon and from Kenley to Heathrow. It prohibited dozens of events arranged months before the Brixton disorder, none of which had anything to do with it. One of these was a CND 'Schools against the Bomb' march. Bruce Kent, on behalf of CND, applied for a declaration that the order was too wide and should not have been made. If international human rights standards had been applied by the court, Sir David would have been called upon to justify the scope of the ban and to explain why it was 'necessary'. Instead, the Court of Appeal decided that it was for Bruce Kent to show why the order should *not* have been made. Whether the result would have been the same if the 'human rights' test had been applied is open to question – but there are strong grounds to think not. Lord Denning had said that the ban 'troubled him considerably'; to another judge, the reasons for the ban 'seemed meagre'.

Nor can it be assumed that all blanket bans in the UK comply with international law merely because the European Commission rejected the application from Christians against Racism and Fascism in 1981. That ban was imposed in the run-up to a by-election in 1978 following a series of National Front rallies. The European Commission recognised that there had been considerable violence between fascists and anti-fascists and that the aim of the ban was to ensure a peaceful period before the by-election. Further, the organisation could simply have delayed the march for a few days and avoided the ban. On this basis the Commission declared the case inadmissible.

There have been similar bans since 1981 which may not have been so easily disposed of by the European Commission. For example, a nine-day ban on marches in Manchester in 1987, imposed to stop a clash between Loyalist and Republican groups, also prevented a quite different march in support of Viraj Mendis, a Sri Lankan threatened with deportation (and subsequently deported).

Another concern is that the trigger for bans on 'trespassory assemblies' is lower than that for marches – 'serious disruption to the life of the community or damage to land, buildings or monuments of historical, architectural or archaeological importance' rather than 'serious public disorder'. It remains to be seen how these terms are interpreted by the courts, but if their approach to a challenge to any ban follows that of the Court of Appeal in the 1981 CND case (above), there is certainly room for bans which fall outside the scope of restrictions permitted by international human rights standards.

Banning powers in relation to 'trespassory assemblies' also raise special problems. As we have seen, the public only have limited rights on highways and limited rights of access to open spaces. Any standing meetings on a highway and any unauthorised meetings in an open space are theoretically 'trespassory assemblies'. Once a banning order is in place, *all* trespassory assemblies are prohibited, as Arthur Pendragon found when he tried to hold a druid ceremony on a grass verge near

Stonehenge in the summer of 1995. The police had applied for and been granted an order banning all trespassory assemblies around Stonehenge during the summer solstice because they (legitimately) feared that trouble-makers might try to reach the stones. The police accepted that Arthur Pendragon, head of the Glastonbury druids and a member of the British Council of Druids, posed no threat himself. The druids had been praised by the Chief Constable of the Wiltshire Police for their responsible behaviour at Stonehenge in the past. But King Arthur's legal challenge to the banning order failed – and since there is no *right* to hold a meeting on a grass verge, he and his supporters would constitute a 'trespassory assembly' if they met for the ceremony (*R v The Chief Constable of the Wiltshire Police and Wiltshire District Council ex parte Pendragon*, 1995). If UK law recognised a right of assembly, the police could have obtained their order (and used it to head off the trouble they feared) and Arthur Pendragon could have celebrated his ceremony.

Public order law in Northern Ireland also raises particular issues of compliance with international human rights standards. The Public Order (NI) Order 1987 provides that public processions and open-air meetings may be banned where the Secretary of State 'is of the opinion' that imposing conditions would not be enough to prevent serious public disorder, serious damage to property, serious disruption to the life of the community, or intimidation. But the Order also provides that they may be banned if he or she 'is of the opinion' that they are likely to cause serious public disorder, serious disruption to the life of the community or undue demands on the police or military forces. There is no duty on the Secretary of State to consider whether conditions would have sufficed.

Accordingly, in contrast to the powers under the Public Order Act 1986, the Secretary of State can order a ban even if certain conditions may have averted the need for it. The power to issue a ban to prevent undue demands on the police or military forces is also difficult to squeeze into one of the categories of restrictions permitted by the International Covenant or the European Convention. Since it stands as an alternative to serious public disorder and serious disruption to the life of the community, it presumably means that a protest or political event could be banned even where these problems do not arise.

Worse still, the 1987 Order states that 'the recital in [a banning order] ... by the Secretary of State as to his opinion and the information upon which that opinion was formed shall be conclusive of the matters stated therein.' This is clearly intended to rule out judicial review of any decision. The provision calls into question compliance with the general principle, enshrined in international human rights instruments, that there should be effective control against abuse of restrictions on freedom of assembly (see **pp. 21–22**).

Existing rules in England and Wales by which organisers must give the police six days' advance notice of marches (above) do not violate international human rights standards. The information required is not extensive. There is no evidence that it is used for purposes which would not be legitimate under the International Covenant or European Convention.

But the question of imposing conditions on marches and assemblies is less straightforward. Those imposed on the grounds that they are necessary to prevent serious public disorder, serious damage to property or intimidation of others broadly conform to international human rights standards. But prevention of 'serious disruption to the life of the community' is more difficult to reconcile with those standards. Imposing conditions for this purpose would not necessarily be contrary to the International Covenant or European Convention. The problem lies in clearly defining what is meant by the phrase 'serious disruption to the community'. The conditions imposed on the Campaign Against the Arms Trade (CAAT) in 1988 show how widely it can be used – in this case, to stop a peaceful gesture which could not possibly cause 'serious disruption' to anyone.

The Campaign planned to release 2,000 black balloons, bearing the slogan 'Say No to the Arms Trade', from a roundabout near an arms fair in Aldershot ('Home of the British Army'). The police intervened on the basis that release of the balloons would disrupt traffic. The campaigners suggested a nearby field. The police objected again, this time on the basis that it would disrupt residents. Next, CAAT tried to secure a London venue, but they were refused permission to use Soho Square or Victoria Tower Gardens. They could have used Hyde Park, but only if all the slogans were removed from the balloons (under existing bye-laws; see above). Talks with the police continued. The police held that a balloon launch anywhere in central London would disrupt the life of the community (on the basis that motorists might complain). Eventually CAAT was allowed to use Lincolns Inn Fields in Holborn, but only on a week-end, when it was deserted and unused – and far removed from Aldershot and the immediate object of the protest, the arms fair.

No coordinated records of the circumstances in which conditions are imposed are kept. So it is difficult to draw general conclusions from CAAT's experience. But it does not appear to have been an isolated incident. In 1992, the Anti-Nazi League were only permitted to march on condition that no banners other than 'flimsy' banners were carried. In the same year, CAAT were only allowed to demonstrate at the Aldershot arms fair if they confined themselves to the middle of a busy roundabout two and a half miles from the fair and did not 'inconvenience' people arriving at Aldershot Railway Station. In 1993, the annual Nottingham and District Trades Council march was re-routed from its usual and preferred route on grounds of 'traffic management'.

These examples demonstrate that because freedom of assembly is not a positive right recognised in law, it need not be weighed in the balance before less than compelling conditions are imposed on those wishing to protest or demonstrate. The case of the black balloons is especially worrying. In effect, the police destroyed a peaceful protest.

DATA

The individual and freedom of assembly

Even if a protest and its location are lawful, some people may be banned from attending under bail restrictions, 'bind-overs' or injunctions. And protesters do not have an unqualified right to behave as they wish. Here we examine the restrictions on people's exercise of their freedom of assembly. The use of temporary injunctions (that is, injunctions pending trial) is not considered here, as their compliance with international human rights standards has already been considered (see **pp. 162–164**).

Breaches of the peace and bind-overs

Police officers can take any reasonable action – including stopping someone attending an event such as a march, demonstration or assembly – on the grounds that they fear a breach of the peace. So, for example, a trade unionist who disagreed with a police rule only allowing two pickets at each entrance of premises where an industrial dispute was taking place and attempted to join a picket was found guilty of obstructing a police officer in the execution of his duty (*Piddington v Bates*, 1961). Similarly, during the 1984–85 miners' strike, police officers routinely turned back groups of miners five miles from collieries where they wished to join other picketers (*Moss v McLachlan*, 1984).

The power of the police in relation to breach of the peace is not confined to turning people away from an event. The police may arrest anyone for causing a breach of the peace or simply being likely to do so (*Albert v Lavin*, 1982). The police may then choose between simply detaining them until the danger of a breach of the peace has passed, and then releasing them (for example, at the end of a march); or taking them before a magistrates' court to be 'bound over' to keep the peace, or to be of 'good behaviour', or both.

Breach of the peace is centuries old, but it has never been defined by Parliament. Its precise meaning is hard to discern, even on close scrutiny of the case-law. In 1982, the Court of Appeal decided that there cannot be a breach of the peace, unless something is done or threatened which harms people, or in their presence harms their property (*R v Howell*, 1982). Yet in the same year the Court of Appeal approved a different definition. In *Chief Constable for Devon and Cornwall ex parte CEGB*, 1982, Lord Denning decided that there was a breach of the peace whenever a person who is lawfully carrying out his work is unlawfully and physically prevented by another from doing it. Since then variations on both definitions have been used.

The meaning of 'good behaviour' is similarly unclear. One senior judge has suggested that it is a question that should be left to the magistrates, on the basis that it is 'conduct which has the property of being wrong rather than right in the judgment of the vast majority of contemporary citizens' (*Hughes v Holley*, 1988). A bind-over is not a conviction or a penalty, but an undertaking as to future conduct. The order binds a person over for a specific period of time (often 12 months) for a sum of money (say, £100) which is forfeited if during the period the person bound-over strays from being of 'good behaviour'. Anyone refusing to be bound over can be sent to prison for up to six months.

Bail conditions

Under the Bail Act 1976, anyone charged with an offence may be bailed until their case is heard. The court can impose conditions to secure that the accused person returns to the court for trial, does not commit offences whilst on bail, and does not interfere with witnesses or otherwise obstruct the course of justice. These conditions are capable of being made both more flexible and more extreme than common law powers to deal with actual or anticipated breaches of the peace. For example, they can be used to restrain someone from attending protests, marches or meetings over a prolonged period of time.

It became common during the miners' strike for magistrates' courts to impose bail conditions on people awaiting trial on charges arising from the strike, the standard condition being that the defendant was 'not to visit any premises or place for the purpose of picketing or demonstrating in connection with the current trade dispute . . . otherwise than peacefully to picket or demonstrate at his current place of employment' (Feldman 1993: 836–837). Similar conditions have since been developed and deployed in other contexts. In 1992–95, as anti-roads protests increased significantly, magistrates' courts frequently imposed bail conditions on defendants restricting their freedom to protest. For example, a typical condition imposed by Redbridge magistrates in 1994 on practically everyone charged with an offence which was in any way related to the construction of the new M11 extension – however trivial – was 'not to go within 50 yards of any M11 construction site'.

Aggravated trespass

A new exclusion order was introduced by the Criminal Justice and Public Order Act 1994. The Act created an offence of 'aggravated trespass' largely to restrict the activities of hunt saboteurs. Any trespasser on land in the open air who does anything with the intention of intimidating, obstructing or disrupting the lawful activity of others commits the offence of aggravated trespass. The senior police officer at the scene of a possible aggravated trespass possesses special powers to enforce the law. The officer can order anyone who has committed or is committing, or who may be reasonably thought to intend committing the offence of aggravated trespass, to leave the land. It is an offence not to leave as soon as practicable or to return as a trespasser within three months. There is no appeal from the order to leave.

Minor criminal offences and obstructing the police

People participating in a peaceful march or meeting can easily commit one of various minor offences. The direct bearing of such offences, like obstruction of the highway, on freedom of assembly has been discussed above. The effect of another minor offence, involving the use of abusive or threatening words or behaviour, or 'disorderly' behaviour, likely to alarm or harass others, on freedom of expression has already been assessed (see **pp. 176–179** on section 5 of the Public Order Act 1986). But it also directly affects freedom of assembly.

Each of these minor offences also has an *indirect* impact on freedom of assembly, through the use of a very widely-used offence: obstructing a police officer 'in the execution of his duty'. Anyone who makes it more difficult for police officers to do their job commits this offence. It is comparatively rare for police officers supervising a march or demonstration actually to arrest protesters for minor offences, like obstructing the highway or carrying a placard (under the Town Police Clauses Act 1847). The police normally give instructions to the participants – usually on the pretext of a possible highway obstruction or other minor offence. Anyone who refuses to obey or questions the instruction is considered to be making it more difficult for the officers to do their job, and can then be arrested for obstructing a police officer. The wide powers vested in the police to deal with breach of the peace (see above) can be used in the same way to justify an arrest for obstruction if someone refuses to comply with a direction from the police.

Restrictions and compliance with international standards

Powers to ban individuals from participating in marches or public protests, or to regulate the conduct of participants, are too uncertain and widely-framed to satisfy evolving human rights standards. To take common law powers to deal with breach of the peace first, the very concept of breach of the peace is unclear. We have noted the two definitions given by the Court of Appeal in 1983 above. Less than ten years later, further difficulties and ambiguities were added by the High Court decision in the case of *R v Morpeth Ward Justices ex parte Ward* (1992). Protesters entered a field in Northumberland in an attempt to stop a pheasant shoot. There was no evidence that they physically harmed anyone or damaged property, or put anyone in fear of such acts. But when they were arrested and brought before the local magistrates, they were bound over to keep the peace for nine months. The High Court upheld this decision, holding that while the protesters' behaviour was peaceful, it was likely to have the natural consequence of *provoking others* to violence.

The standard international human rights test – that any restriction of freedom of assembly must be 'prescribed by law' – requires that citizens must have an adequate indication of the legal rules that apply to them in the circumstances, and that such rules must be framed with enough clarity to enable them to regulate their conduct. Breach of the peace fails this test: the courts have approved several different definitions of breach of the peace, and citizens are held liable not only for their own behaviour, but the likely (or even unlikely) behaviour of others.

The power to bind citizens over fails the same test. The notion of 'good behaviour' is hopelessly vague. It is almost impossible to predict what conduct 'has the property of being wrong rather than right' in the judgment of 'the vast majority of contemporary citizens'. The Law Commission was quick to point this out in its 1994 report on bind-overs: in its view, the effect of the judgment in the case of the protest against the pheasant shoot in Northumberland (above) was 'to make it difficult for those who wish to involve themselves in protests . . . to know what they may or may not do' (Law Commission Report No. 222, HMSO, 1994: 38). A law which is based on concepts as uncertain as these is contrary to elementary notions of fair process. The Law Commission warned that 'we have little doubt that if the point were tested, it would be found inconsistent with the requirements of the [European] Convention' (p. 62).

The use of bail conditions to restrict the activities of protesters also raises serious questions of compliance with international human rights standards, particularly since they can restrain an individual from participating in a variety of activities over a prolonged period of time. The issue of whether such bail conditions were lawful was tested in the High Court in 1985. As noted above, common conditions were imposed by magistrates' courts on defendants having anything to do with the miners' strike to prevent them engaging in picketing or other protests. These conditions were said to be necessary to prevent them from committing further offences while on bail. However, the defendants claimed that they had been routinely imposed without regard to the particular circumstances of each individual and without any proper inquiry about their necessity. The conditions certainly soon became known as 'the usual conditions' (Wallington 1985: 156). And the procedure adopted in the Mansfield magistrates' court provided evidence for the claim. Eight people at a time in the dock had their applications simultaneously dealt with; and the clerk merely attached stick-on slips, with the conditions already typed out, to the bail form. However, the High Court refused to intervene in the merits of a magistrates' court decision (*R v Mansfield Justices ex parte Sharkey*, 1985).

The imposition of bail conditions preventing defendants from engaging in public protests of various kinds can very easily violate the right to freedom of assembly guaranteed under both the International Covenant and European Convention. This is particularly the case since the High Court rejected the argument that, before imposing bail conditions, the magistrates should have substantial grounds for believing that offences would be committed. This falls short of the requirement, derived from international human rights standards, that states must have specific and concrete evidence before a restriction on freedom of assembly can be said to be 'necessary in a democratic society'.

The new offence of 'aggravated trespass' also fails to comply with international standards. A police officer can place an individual citizen under order to leave a place and to stay away for up to three months, with no scope for representations from the person whose liberty is to be restricted, for review by a senior officer or a court, or for a right of appeal. Both the International Covenant and European Convention require that states institute effective controls against abuse of restrictions on freedom of assembly (*Silver v UK*, 1983, ECtHR).

The major problem common to minor criminal offences and obstruction of a police officer is the low threshold for such offences. As noted above, the wide powers given to police officers under the Highways Act 1980, the Town Police Clauses Act 1847 and breach of the peace mean that virtually any disobedience to a police officer's instruction during the course of a march or assembly will amount to an offence. In a similar vein, making insulting words or disorderly behaviour which merely causes 'distress' to another person a criminal offence, potentially rules out many otherwise legitimate forms of demonstration. A great deal obviously depends on the context in which the offences are committed. But there is a clear danger that these offences violate the need recognised in international human rights standards for broad-mindedness and the specific protection of views that shock or offend.

Conclusions

The UK government's first report to the UN Human Rights Committee in 1977 stated:

> Freedom of assembly is one of the oldest common law rights and there are no restrictions on the exercise of this right, other than those prescribed by law in the interests of the community as a whole and for the protection of the rights and freedoms of others.
>
> (CCPR/C/I/Add. 17: 108)

This statement was utterly misleading then, and more so now. There is no positive right of assembly and protest in the United Kingdom. Nor does the way in which the authorities and courts hold the balance between people's rights of assembly and protest and 'the protection of the rights and freedoms of others' and 'the interests of the community as a whole' satisfy international human rights standards. Both the European Convention and International Covenant hold this balance by first establishing a formal guarantee of the right to assembly and protest – to which specific exceptions are then made. By contrast, British law simply recognises a 'negative' freedom of assembly and protest and then loads a host of major and minor restrictions upon it. The behaviour of the authorities, police and courts falls far short of the careful balancing exercise they are expected to conduct under both instruments.

In essence, both oblige states to wrestle with the difficult problems of allowing the maximum freedom of public protest – by way of marches, demonstrations, pickets, festivals, and so on – that is consistent with public order and safety, and the legitimate rights and needs of others. In the United Kingdom, freedom of assembly – and protest – is increasingly permitted only when the cost to public convenience is low and the protest does not arouse official disapproval or distaste. The refusal of the police to allow campaigners to release balloons no nearer than 60 miles from the arms fair against which the balloons were an imaginative form of protest on the flimsy pretext that motorists *might* protest demonstrates the absurd extremes to which the authorities will now go to protect public convenience at the expense of political protest.

The cumulative effect of the trespass laws, minor criminal offences, common law rules, bye-law regulations and general and specific police powers means that there is no place in which citizens can insist on meeting. They depend at all turns on the 'good grace' or 'commonsense' of the authorities. This represents too fragile a base for such an important political right.

Statutory powers to ban or apply conditions to assemblies broadly conform to international human rights standards (with one or two notable exceptions). Common-law powers, relating to breach of the peace and bind overs, are far too wide.

Overall, there exists a serious and widespread breach of international human rights standards, which has clear implications for the quality of democracy in this country. There is a clear danger that new statutory offences created under the 1994 Act, such as 'aggravated trespass', will combine with existing common-law and statutory offences and rules to create a yet thornier thicket of obstacles about the beleaguered right to freedom of assembly.

11   The Mixed Record

Freedom of association and trade unionism

Freedom of association is broad-backed. It comprises a *civil* right, a *political* right and a *social and economic* right – as international human rights law and standards recognise. In all these respects, it has two dimensions – safeguarding both the right of individuals to combine freely with others and the collective liberty of the group itself (Ewing 1994a: 240).

As a civil right, freedom of association should safeguard individuals or groups from arbitrary interference whenever they wish to associate with others. As a political right, it provides the basis of the right to form and join political parties and pressure groups (including trade unions), and to meet, discuss and publicise matters of common concern. In both respects, it is indispensable to democracy. Finally, as a social and economic right, it guarantees the freedom to form and join trade unions and to pursue common interests through trade union activity.

The links between freedom of association and democracy were forged during the struggles for the franchise, popular political parties and free trade unions in the nineteenth and early twentieth century. The need for a vigorous 'civil society', as a counterweight to the state and underpinning of democracy, was again made clear by the experience of countries subjugated by the Soviet Union during the cold war years. The basic principles were thus recently re-emphasised in the Copenhagen Document of the Conference on Security and Co-operation in Europe 1990, which declared that 'vigorous democracy depends on the existence, as an integral part of national life, of democratic values and practices as well as an extensive range of democratic institutions'. States were urged to encourage the development of free associations, public interest groups, political parties, human rights organisations, religious groups, and independent trade unions.

For the purposes of this chapter, it is convenient to deal with the overall concept of freedom of association first and then trade unionism separately. However, there is a significant overlap between the concept of freedom of association and trade unionism. While the International Labour Organisation (ILO) covenants protect trade unionism, the International Covenant and European Convention both recognise the right to form and join trade unions as a special element of the civil and political rights to free association.

This chapter first examines how far British law and practice comply with international standards on citizens' rights to associate and *not* associate with others; freedom of association clearly involves a freedom to choose and citizens have a right not to be compelled to join organisations against their will. (This has raised particular problems with membership of trade unions.) We then examine the special question of restrictions on the free association of state employees, who can be denied full protection under the international instruments (see below).

The right to freedom of association

Everyone has the right to freedom of ... association. No one may be compelled to belong to an association.
>   (Article 20, Universal Declaration of Human Rights)

Everyone has the right to form and to join trade unions for the protection of his interests.
>   (Article 23(4), Universal Declaration of Human Rights)

Freedom of association is essential to effective participation in civil and political society and to social and economic activity. Therefore, it occupies a prominent role in a wide variety of international instruments. Broadly speaking, the International Covenant and the European Convention protect the civil and political aspects of the right to freedom of association, while the International Labour Organisation covenants, the International Covenant on Economic, Social and Cultural Rights and the European Social Charter protect the social and economic aspects, including trade union activity.

The basic right of freedom of association is set out in Article 22 of the International Covenant and Article 11 of the European Convention. In almost identical terms, they guarantee to all 'freedom of association with others, including the right to form and to join trade unions'. The meaning of the word 'association' in this context has caused difficulties. It now seems agreed that it refers to voluntary groups with a common goal or purpose (Sieghart 1983: 345). Consequently, a medical organisation created by the state, whose purposes were to ensure the observance of medical ethics and maintain the honour, discretion, probity and dignity of its members was held not to be an 'association' within the terms of the European Convention (*Le Compte, Van Leuven and de Meyere v Belgium*, 1981, ECtHR). But freedom of association very clearly protects political parties, pressure groups, trade unions and religious societies.

The two instruments guarantee freedom of association on a 'vertical' and 'horizontal' plane. States must not only refrain from prohibiting or otherwise interfering with associations and their activities (the *vertical* plane), but must also protect them from interference by private bodies (the *horizontal*). So, for example, the European Commission on Human Rights observed that if an action taken by the state as employer violates Article 11 of the Convention, the state may be held responsible for the same violation perpetrated by a private employer if the state has failed to secure, by legislation or otherwise, that private employers also comply with the Convention's terms (*Schmidt and Dahlström v Sweden*, 1972).

International standards

Restricting rights

Formal recognition of civil and political rights is not enough. It is essential that any restriction of all rights recognised by both the International Covenant and the European Convention be closely scrutinised. The two instruments set out a strict three-part test:

1. Any restriction on civil and political rights must be 'prescribed by law'
2. The restriction must be justified by one of the aims under the International Covenant or European Convention
3. The restriction must be shown to be 'necessary in a democratic society'.

This test is of fundamental importance. For that reason, we deal with the test in detail in **Box A, pp. 21–22**. Here, broadly, the test requires that ordinary citizens can readily discover what legal restrictions to any right exist with enough clarity for them to be able to regulate their conduct. Any restrictions must then meet one of the aims recognised under either instrument as a legitimate ground for the restriction of civil and political rights. These aims are:

- the protection of the rights and freedoms of others
- national security
- public safety
- public health and morals
- and the prevention of public disorder or crime.

In addition, in the case of freedom of association, certain categories of people are exempted from full protection, in particular, members of the armed forces, the police and, more controversially, public employees. Finally, citizens are as free *not* to associate with others as they are to associate with them.

This list is intended to be exhaustive. States may not introduce other restrictions or stretch the meaning of the criteria listed above to add others. Finally, states must show both that the restriction fulfils a pressing social need and that it is proportionate to the aim of responding to that need. They cannot merely assert that a particular restriction is 'necessary in a democratic society', but must provide concrete evidence of a genuine and serious threat.

The bodies which interpret the tests – the UN Human Rights Committee and the European Court and Commission of Human Rights – have framed their notion of 'democratic society' in terms of such concepts as 'pluralism, tolerance and broad-mindedness'; and have made it clear that although the term 'necessary' is not synonymous with 'indispensable', it does not simply mean 'reasonable' (Handyside v UK, ECtHR, 1976).

Restrictions on the right to form and join trade unions under the ILO conventions, the International Covenant on Economic Social and Cultural Right and European Social Charter (see below) are tighter than the general right to freedom of association. This is obviously of significance in cases where the two rights overlap.

Evolving human rights standards

The evolving human rights standards which apply to restrictions on freedom of association are as follows:

- The prohibition or dissolution of an association is only justified when a milder measure, restricting the association's sphere of activities, would be insufficient (Nowak 1993: 394). Accordingly, prohibition should be reserved for 'state-threatening' organisations (*M.A. v Italy*, 1981, HRC).

- Although contracting states enjoy a certain 'margin of appreciation' in assessing the need for interference with the right to freedom of association, that need must be convincingly established and the margin of appreciation strictly supervised (*Sunday Times v UK*, 1979; *Autronic AG v Switzerland*, 1990).

- Under the UN International Convention on the Elimination of all Forms of Racial Discrimination (1966), states must condemn all organisations based on ideas or theories of racial superiority or which justify or promote racial hatred and discrimination in any form and also declare illegal and prohibit such organisations (Article 4).

The 'residual right' to free association

Law in the UK does not positively protect a general right to freedom of association. People are free to associate for any purpose, provided that it is not otherwise forbidden. Unlawful discrimination and trade union exclusion apart, there is therefore very little scope for legal redress if a person is excluded from a group or prevented from joining one.

The law of conspiracy

The law of conspiracy applies to people who join together for an unlawful purpose. In the criminal sphere, this prohibits agreements to commit crime or fraud, to corrupt public morals or to outrage public decency (Criminal Law Act 1977). As a civil wrong or tort, conspiracy can be committed in one of three ways: by two or more people agreeing to act unlawfully; or to carry out a lawful act by unlawful means; or to inflict damage on someone else where no legitimate interest is being pursued by them. The civil law is therefore wider in scope than the criminal law (but anyone suing must prove that he or she has suffered loss).

Autonomy and the rule-book

Voluntary associations set up for lawful purposes may determine their own membership and rules. When, for example, APEX expelled a member to comply with a ruling of the TUC Disputes Committee that he had been wrongly recruited and should transfer to ACTSS (his original trade union) the Court of Appeal held the

Restrictions

expulsion to be invalid (*Cheall v APEX*, 1983). Lord Denning relied on Article 11 of the European Convention to construct a fundamental principle of common law that anyone has the right to join a trade union of his or her choice and cannot be expelled by a rule which is unreasonable. However, the House of Lords reversed his decision and restored the autonomy of the association (in this case, APEX) to control its own membership, and, while special statutory provisions have now been introduced for trade unions (see below), this remains the common law position for all other voluntary groups.

The degree of autonomy recognised by the common law has its price. Voluntary associations may determine their own membership and rules, but they must also observe them. Hence, for example, the League Against Cruel Sports was restrained from making donations to the Labour Party on the basis that there was no provision for such payments in its rule-book (*Simmonds v Heffer*, 1983).

Concerns about the conspiracy law

The 'hands-off' approach of UK law to freedom of association complies in almost every respect with international human rights standards. However, the civil law of conspiracy raises two question-marks which preclude full compliance. First, the law is now so ambiguous that it is extremely difficult to know when the line between lawful and unlawful association and activity is crossed. For example, people protesting peacefully against the construction of a motorway through the countryside at Twyford Down were lumped together by the High Court with other protesters who had caused significant damage to contractors' vehicles (*Department of Transport v Williams and others*, 1993). The peaceful protesters were restrained by injunction from further protest and were obliged to pay a proportion of the costs when the Department of Transport discontinued the case.

Secondly, the extension of the law of civil conspiracy to prohibit acts which are performed purely to inflict damage on a third party, but which are not otherwise unlawful (see above), appears to go beyond the restrictions permitted by either the International Covenant or the European Convention which do not recognise this broad-based protection for third parties.

Legislation and proscribed organisations

The banning of organisations takes two forms in UK law. First, participation in the running of organisations may be prohibited by reference to the general purpose of the organisation. For example, the Public Order Act 1936 does not ban any specific organisation, but it does make it an offence to take part in the control, management, organisation or training of a body which is 'organised and trained', or 'organised and equipped', so that it can usurp the functions of the police or the armed forces; or can use or display force in promoting any political object. The offence is punishable with up to two years' imprisonment and an unlimited fine (prosecution requires the Attorney-General's consent).

Secondly, certain organisations are specifically 'proscribed' by law and individuals are prohibited from joining them or from participating in their activities. The Prevention of Terrorism (Temporary Provisions) Act 1989 (PTA) and the Northern Ireland (Emergency Provisions) Act 1991 (EPA) both provide for specific proscription. The PTA makes it an offence to belong or to profess to belong to a proscribed organisation in England, Wales and Northern Ireland. The only organisations currently banned are the Irish Republican Army (IRA) and INLA. However, the Northern Ireland Secretary of State may add organisations to the proscribed list by statutory instrument if he or she believes they are involved in terrorism in the UK and in Northern Irish affairs. In addition, it is an offence to arrange or address a meeting of three of more people knowing that the meeting is in support of a proscribed organisation (PTA s.2(c)). It is also an offence for anyone in a public place to dress or wear, carry or display any article, which arouses reasonable concern that he or she is a member of a proscribed organisation (s.3).

The EPA applies only to Northern Ireland, is in similar terms, and lists more proscribed organisations, including Loyalist organisations such as the Ulster Defence Association (UDA) and the Ulster Volunteer Force (UVF).

Legal challenges to proscription

Few prosecutions have been taken under the Public Order Act 1936, the PTA 1989 or the EPA 1991. This makes an evaluation of their provisions difficult for the purposes of this audit. But international standards specifically allow for restrictions to protect the rights of others, and it is therefore hard to maintain that existing laws infringe them. But there are two areas of concern.

First, prohibition can only be justified when 'prescribed by law' and when milder measures are insufficient (see **pp. 21–22**). So there is a strong argument that there ought to be either parliamentary or judicial supervision of proscription. But under both the PTA and EPA any group can simply be added to the list of proscribed organisations by statutory instrument – a procedure which generally avoids parliamentary scrutiny. If an organisation is proscribed on insufficient grounds, there is little possibility of legal challenge to the order. There is no right of appeal against proscription and judicial review, whilst theoretically available, is likely to be extremely limited (Fenwick 1994: 231).

A government order banning Republican clubs or any like organisation was challenged in a landmark case in 1976, on the grounds that it potentially outlawed all Nationalist political parties (*McEldowney v Forde*, 1971). However, the House of Lords was very reluctant to intervene.

There is also evidence to suggest that the motive for proscription (in both the PTA and EPA) falls outside one of the 'legitimate aims' of restriction recognised in both instruments. Lord Jellicoe, reviewing their provisions for the government, said:

> Proscribing an organisation is unlikely either to impair substantially its capacity for carrying out terrorist acts or to deter those most deeply involved

Proscribed organisations

in its activities. But the terms of the legislation suggest a wider range of purposes than the merely symbolic. At the least practical level, it enshrines in legislation public aversion to organisations which use, and espouse, violence as a means to political ends ... It is at the more presentational level that proscription under this Act (i.e. in Great Britain) seems to have been most successful, in that there have been few demonstrations or open displays of support by or on behalf of either the IRA or INLA.

(Jellicoe Report 1983)

The UN Human Rights Committee and the European Court and Commission are unlikely to find that the present law and practice infringes international standards. But in view of the two points above, and the current international trend away from any form of prior restraint (see, for example, the Copenhagen Document of the Conference for Security and Cooperation in Europe, 1990), the time may now be ripe for a re-examination of the three statutes dealing with proscription.

Freedom of association and trade unions

The right to join and form trade unions enjoys special status in international human rights law. It is explicitly recognised by the International Covenant (A.22.1) and European Convention (A.11.1) within the general context of freedom of association. Article 22 gives specific protection to the International Labour Organisation Convention of 1948 on the right to organise and free association, stating that nothing in its general provisions authorised states that have signed the ILO Convention 'to take legislative measures which would prejudice, or apply the law in such a manner as to prejudice, the guarantees provided for in that Convention'.

The European Court has also consistently held that the scope and meaning of Article 11 should be interpreted with regard to the contents and interpretation of the principal ILO conventions to ensure that they remain in harmony with international labour law and practice (*National Union of Belgian Police v Belgium*, 1975; *Svenska Lokmannaforbundet v Sweden*, 1976).

Two ILO conventions are of particular relevance here – No. 87, The Freedom of Association and Protection of the Right to Organise Convention, and No. 98, The Right to Organise and Collective Bargaining Convention. The first guarantees to workers and employers 'the right to establish and join organisations without previous authorisation' (A.2) and the right of those organisations to draw up their own constitutions and rules, including rules freely to elect their representatives (A.3). The second guarantees the protection of workers' and employers' organisations against acts of interference, not only from the state but also from each other (A.2). The obligations they set out are more specific than those in the International Covenant and European Convention. Further, states which ratify the ILO conventions are obliged to follow a special procedure for regular international supervision and control.

In particular, the ILO has set up special machinery to deal with issues of freedom of association. A Fact-Finding and Conciliation Commission, composed of independent experts, examines complaints of infringements of trade union rights. And a Freedom of Association Committee carries out preliminary assessments on behalf of the ILO Governing Body.

The International Covenant on Economic, Social and Cultural Rights and the Council of Europe Social Charter (ESC; adopted in 1961) reflect the ILO approach. They do not refer to the general right to freedom of association, but specifically guarantee the right to form and join trade unions as a right in itself. They make detailed provisions for trade union activity pursuant to that right; for example, the right to strike.

Like freedom of association generally, the right to form and join trade unions can be restricted, but only if any such restriction is 'prescribed by law' and 'necessary in a democratic society' for one of the purposes specifically listed (see **p. 206**). As for those purposes, both International Covenants (the ICCPR and ICESCR), the European Convention and European Social Charter include the interests of national security and the protection of the rights and freedoms of others; all but the ICESCR, the protection of health or morals; the ICCPR and the European Convention, the interests of public safety; the ICCPR alone, the interests of public order; the European Convention alone, the prevention of disorder or crime; and the European Social Charter alone, the public interest.

Evolving human rights standards

The evolving human rights standards which apply to the right to form and join trade unions are as follows:

- Freedom to form and join trade unions imposes two obligations on states: one negative, the other positive. The first requires the absence of any legislation, regulation or administrative practice, which impairs the freedom of employers or workers to form or join their respective organisations. The second obliges states to take adequate legislative or other measures to guarantee the exercise of the right of association and, in particular, to protect workers' organisations from any interference on the part of employers (European Committee of Experts interpretation of Article II/5 of the European Social Charter; see also Sieghart 1983: 354).

- Consequently, states should take steps to curtail any action by employers which violates the right to freedom of association and should also provide the necessary remedies for employees (Legal Affairs Committee (1978) Council of Europe Parliamentary Assembly, Council of Europe Document 4213; *National Union of Belgium Police v Belgium*, ECtHR, 1976; *Schmidt and Dahlström v Sweden*, ECtHR, 1976).

- Hence, for example, workers should enjoy adequate protection against acts of anti-union discrimination in respect of their employment (ILO Convention No. 98, Article 1(1)); employment should not be conditional on joining or leaving a trade union and workers should not be dismissed or prejudiced for union membership or activities (ILO Convention No. 98, Article 1(2)).

International standards

- Workers' and employers' organisations should have the right to draw up their constitutions and rules, to elect their representatives in full freedom, to organise their administration and activities and to formulate their programmes (ILO Convention 87, Article 3(1)).

- Trade unions should be free to determine their own practices without control by the state except on the basis of the restrictions laid down in the relevant articles (*Cheall v UK*, 1985, ECmHR).

- Exceptions are permitted to promote 'democratic principles within trade union organisations', including ballots prior to industrial action, members' rights to see their union's accounts and access to the courts for union members who have a grievance against their union (ILO (1985) Committee of Experts 71st session; ILO (1989) Committee of Experts 76th session; European Committee of Experts on Article II/6 of the European Social Charter).

- Restrictions on the freedom of trade unions to discipline members who refuse to participate in lawful strikes and other industrial action, or who seek to persuade fellow members to refuse to take such action, are in breach of ILO Convention No. 87, Article 3 (ILO (1989) Committee of Experts 76th session; ILO (1991) Committee of Experts 78th session; ILO (1992) Committee of Experts 79th Session).

- States should promote joint consultation between workers and employers and, where necessary and appropriate, states should also promote the establishment and use of appropriate machinery for conciliation and voluntary arbitration for settling disputes (Article II/6 European Social Charter; ILO Convention No. 98).

- While 'great importance' is attached to the principle that employers should recognise workers' organisations for the purposes of collective bargaining, employers are not 'obliged to negotiate with such organisations' (ILO (1992) Case 1518 Committee of Experts 79th session).

- Both workers and employers have the right to collective action, including (for workers) the right to strike (ICESCR, Article 8(1)(d); European Social Charter Article II/6; ILO Committee of Experts Digest of Decisions (3rd edn) para. 360–362).

- The right to strike is vested in workers not trade unions: any law which prohibits strikes unless they are called by a recognised trade union violates this right (European Committee of Experts on European Social Charter Article II/6).

- But the right to strike is not absolute; general restrictions can be applied to restrict the right to strike for certain categories of people (for example, the armed forces, the police, judges and senior civil servants; European Social Charter Article 31); the right to strike can only be exercised in conformity with domestic law (ICESCR, Article 8(1)(d)); and it may be restricted by collective agreement (European Social Charter Article II/6(4)).

- However, a rule according to which a strike terminates contracts of employment is in principle not compatible with Article II/6 of the European Social Charter (European Committee of Experts). It is therefore inconsistent with the right to strike for an employer to be able to refuse to reinstate striking employees at the conclusion of industrial action, without those employees having the right to challenge the fairness of the dismissal before an independent court or tribunal (ILO (1989) Committee of Experts 76th session; ILO (1991) Committee of Experts 78th session; ILO (1992) Committee of Experts 79th session).

- Likewise, workers and trade unions should have a measure of protection against civil liability for strikes (ILO (1989) Committee of Experts 76th session; (1992) Committee of Experts 79th session).

Finally, trade unions are affected by the general principle, set out in the Universal Declaration, that 'no-one may be compelled to belong to any association' (Article 20(2)). Broadly speaking, this is reflected in the standards that have evolved since it was adopted in 1948. The issue of freedom not to associate was specifically considered by the European Court of Human Rights in the trade union case, *Young, James and Webster v UK*, 1982. The applicants had refused to join a trade union and because their employer, British Rail, operated a closed shop, they were dismissed. The European Court did not express a final opinion on whether every closed shop in itself violated Article II of the Convention. But it made clear that workers should not be required to join a particular trade union; they should have a choice of union; and no workers should be compelled to join any union where membership would conflict with other freedoms protected by the Convention, such as freedom of conscience and religion and freedom of expression. In its view, if every kind of compulsion to join an association were permitted this 'would strike at the very substance of the freedom it is designed to guarantee'.

The right to form and join trade unions

The legal status of trade unions in the UK has greatly improved since early nineteenth century laws proscribing them as criminal organisations. Membership of trade unions is lawful and guaranteed as a positive right against employers by a combination of statutory employment protection rights and the law of unfair dismissal. Under the Trade Union and Labour Relations (Consolidation) Act 1992 (TULCRA), it is automatically unfair to dismiss an employee for joining, belonging to or taking part in trade union activities outside working hours (or during working hours with the employer's consent). The Act also prohibits less favourable action short of dismissal on the same grounds (section 146).

Protection at the point of recruitment is a more recent addition to UK legislation. Drawing on the EU Community Charter (Article 14), the Employment Act 1990 makes it unlawful to refuse to employ someone because he or she is a member of a trade union (now section 137, TULCRA). However, this clause applies only to trade union membership. It is still lawful to turn down a candidate on grounds

Collective rights

of trade union activities. Further, the government has recently approved the introduction of incentive schemes designed to discourage trade union membership. In 1993, the Court of Appeal struck down an arrangement at the *Daily Mail*, which restricted pay rises to employees who renounced their right to union representation. The government immediately intervened with a late amendment to the Trade Union Reform and Employment Rights Bill 1993 to reverse the court's decision. As it happens, a year later, the House of Lords overturned the Court of Appeal's decision anyway (*Wilson v Associated Newspapers*, 1995).

Trade union autonomy

Common law respect for the autonomy of voluntary associations has been transformed by recent statutes affecting trade unions. In 1984, three new rules were introduced (all of which are consolidated in the Trade Union and Labour Relations (Consolidation) Act 1992). Trade unions are required to hold elections by secret ballot every five years for trade union executive committee members. They must also hold secret ballots before industrial action, as a condition of immunity from any liability for losses to the employer. They must also ballot members every ten years for authority to continue to promote political objects and maintain a political fund. All ballots must now be fully postal and trade union members and employers can sue in respect of any failure to hold a ballot. Finally, the Employment Act 1988 made it unlawful for trade unions to discipline members who refused to take part in lawful strikes or who tried to persuade fellow members to refuse.

Collective action

Domestic law treats strikes as a fundamental breach of contract which allows an employer to dismiss striking employees on the spot without notice or warning. Provided that everyone taking part in the strike is dismissed, no one can claim unfair dismissal. Only if some strikers are dismissed, but others are not, can such a claim be brought. Even this limited right has recently been curtailed for anyone involved in *unofficial* strike action. Since 1990, employees taking part in unofficial strikes are prohibited from claiming unfair dismissal in any circumstances (now TULCRA section 237).

Further legal control over strikes is exercised by making the organisers of strikes, in particular trade unions, liable in damages for the consequences of industrial action in certain circumstances. This area of the law is complex and a comprehensive analysis is not possible here. However, the reduction of the immunity granted to trade unions for liability in respect of strikes has been at the centre of much of the trade union legislation introduced in the last 15 years.

Gaps in the protection for trade unionists

Statutory employment protection rights and the law of unfair dismissal, set out above, combine to guarantee a positive right to membership of a trade union which broadly complies with international human rights standards. However, those standards are not being met in two areas of concern.

The Employment Act 1990 (since consolidated in the 1992 Act) allows employers to turn down a candidate for employment on grounds of trade union activity. The ILO Committee of Experts were quick to spot a gap. In their review of UK law in 1991, they asked the government to indicate 'whether section 1 [of the 1990 Act] provides protection against denial of employment on grounds of past trade union membership or on grounds of trade union activity' (ILO, Committee of Experts, 78th Session). The ILO Freedom of Association Committee raised the same issue in 1992, following a complaint by the TUC. The TUC emphasised the significance of the loophole in UK law by highlighting the activities of organisations, like the now defunct Economic League, which circulated 'blacklists' of active trade unionists. The Committee concluded that the ILO convention on collective action (No. 98), which prohibits acts of anti-trade union discrimination, had been breached on the basis that

> all practices involving the blacklisting of trade union officials or members constitute a serious threat to the free exercise of trade union rights and . . . in general, government should take stringent measures to combat such practices.
> (287th Report of Freedom of Association Committee, para. 267)

The late amendment to the Trade Union Reform and Employment Rights Act 1993, allowing employers to award pay rises selectively in order to encourage employees to give up union membership, is likely to be enormously influential in deterring employees from joining trade unions. It has yet to be considered by any of the international bodies, but it would appear to breach two ILO requirements: first, that states ought generally to take adequate measures to protect workers' organisations from interference by employers; and more specifically, that workers should not be prejudiced for trade union membership or activities (ILO Convention No. 98 Article 1(2)).

Trade union autonomy

The extent to which the inroads into trade union autonomy since 1984 infringe international standards has recently been considered by the ILO Committee of Experts. In keeping with its view that exceptions to the rule that trade unions should be free to determine their own rules and practices and are permitted to promote 'democratic principles within trade union organisations', it found that secret executive committee ballots do not violate ILO Convention No. 87 (ILO 71st Session, Report III, p.197). Nor does the obligation to ballot before industrial action; the Committee commented: 'it does not appear . . . that the procedures prescribed are so cumbersome as to render lawful strikes impossible' (ILO 71st Session, Report III: 198). Finally, while ballots on the promotion of political objects and political funds 'undoubtedly constrained the use of union funds' in the Committee's view, it concluded that 'there was no breach on the basis that none of the provisions removed the freedom to support political parties or to undertake measures of political action' (ILO 71st Session, Report III: 198).

All international instruments recognise a general right for trade unions to determine their own practices. But since the government's changes do not breach even the most elaborate of these (ILO Convention No. 87), it cannot be argued that the changes brought about in 1984 breach international human rights standards.

However, there is one respect in which the law may have gone too far. As noted above, the Employment Act 1988 makes it unlawful for trade unions to discipline members who refuse to take part in lawful strikes or who seek to persuade fellow members to refuse. This provision was criticised by the ILO Committee of Experts in 1989 as inconsistent with the guarantee of trade union freedom to devise and implement their own rules (ILO Convention No. 87 Article 3). The government defended itself on the ground that the ILO guarantees were, on the admission of the Committee of Experts itself, subject to respect for fundamental human rights and that the 'right of every trade union member to refuse to take industrial action' (regardless of the procedures followed by the trade union before calling such action) was one such 'fundamental human right' (Brown and McColgan 1992: 273). As one commentator has pointed out, 'it is not clear whence this human right is derived; it certainly does not appear, expressly or by implication, in any international treaties to which Britain is a party' (Ewing 1994b: 41).

The absence of a right to strike

There is no right to strike in the UK. There is simply a degree of immunity from the legal consequences of a strike – provided strict rules are observed. But striking employees have little protection from instant dismissal. This state of affairs causes considerable concern to international bodies.

Taking the question of dismissal first: even before the law was changed to remove all protection from participants in unofficial strike action, the Council of Europe and the ILO Committee of Experts had condemned the absence of protection for individuals who participate in strikes as inconsistent with the right to strike (Ewing 1994b: 35). The view of the Committee of Experts was later endorsed by the ILO Freedom of Association Committee report on a case brought by the National Union of Seamen. In 1988, more than 2,000 striking seafarers were dismissed by P&O European Ferries after taking industrial action in response to new terms of employment being imposed by the company to reduce labour costs. Some accepted the offer of re-engagement on new terms, but the majority remained on strike and were not taken back. The Freedom of Association Committee found that ILO Convention No. 87 Article 3 had been breached and called on the government to amend the law, both in respect of official and unofficial strike action (ILO case no. 1540; see Ewing 1994b: 35–36). In addition, according to the European Committee of Experts, dismissals of this kind represent a clear violation of international standards (interpretation of Article II/6 of the European Social Charter). The labour law expert, Lord Wedderburn, has noted that continental colleagues find it astonishing that we profess the values of freedom of association in international instruments to which we have put our name yet leave our law in the archaic condition that causes every strike to be breach of employees' contracts of employment no matter how legitimate the dispute.

(1993 Law Quarterly Review, vol. 19: 241)

The reductions of trade union immunity for the consequences of strike action are severely criticised. The ILO Committee of Experts observed that although some restrictions on industrial action were permitted, the 'restrictions relating to the objectives of a strike and the methods used should be sufficiently reasonable as not to result in practice in an excessive limitation of the exercise of the right to strike' (ILO, Committee of Experts 76th Session, Report Part III, 238). Applying these principles to restrictions on immunities introduced since 1979, the Committee concluded that the restrictions had gone too far, the overall effect of the legislation being to withdraw protection from industrial action in circumstances where it ought to be permitted (Ewing 1994b: 34).

The findings of the ILO Committee of Experts are given considerable weight in this audit. It should be remembered that the UN International Covenant provides that nothing should be taken to authorise measures which would prejudice ILO Convention No. 87 (Article 22(3)). The European Court of Human Rights has made it clear that it will have regard to the contents and interpretation of ILO Convention No. 87 and Convention No. 98 in its consideration of Article 11 of the European Convention (*National Union of Belgian Police v Belgium,* 1976). However, the government refuses to endorse this approach. The 1992 report of the ILO Committee of Experts criticised the government on seven issues, all of which had already been drawn to its attention. But the government was unmoved by the ILO's repeated decisions that its trade union policies were in breach of its international obligations:

> Rather than accepting the competence of the ILO to adjudicate on the interpretation and application of the Convention, however, the Government has chosen to apply its own interpretations to declare in most instances that, contrary to the decisions of the relevant Committees, it considers its actions to be compatible with international law.
>
> (Brown and McColgan 1992: 271)

The government's interpretation of its international obligations is rejected in this audit. The views of the expert bodies are all one way: the law and practice in the UK on collective action by trade unions, and particularly on strikes, falls short of the international human rights standards set out in the index above and there is no indication that matters are about to improve.

Refusals to join

The right not to join a trade union

Whether or not the right not to join a trade union is violated depends largely on the degree of compulsion involved. Dismissal for failure to join a trade union under the Labour government's Trade Union and Labour Relations Act 1974 was held to violate the European Convention (*Young, James and Webster v UK*, 1981, ECtHR; see Index above). The European Court's approach is likely to be reflected in any interpretation of Article 22 of the International Covenant, given the similarity between the content and historical background of the two articles (Nowak 1993: 390). In response to the European Court's ruling, the law in the UK was changed. Dismissal for refusing to join a trade union is now unlawful if the person dismissed objected to joining on the grounds of a deeply-held conviction to being a member of a trade union. This appears to correspond with the principles espoused by the Court (Index above).

Restrictions on state employees

Certain categories of people may not enjoy full rights of freedom of association. However, the precise categories excluded from full protection and the extent to which their freedom of association can be restricted are not altogether clear.

The International Covenant permits the imposition of restrictions on the rights to free association of members of the armed forces and the police, so long as they are 'lawful' (Article 22(2)). The European Convention adds a further group of state employees to those who do not have full protection – members of the administration of the state (Article 11(2)). This difference cannot be resolved solely by reference to the terms of the social and economic instruments. The key ILO conventions permit member states some flexibility in the extent to which they are applied to the armed forces and the police (Convention No. 87 Article 9(1); Convention No. 98 Article 5(1)). Nevertheless, the ILO Committee of Experts has specifically noted that public servants come within the protection guaranteed by ILO Convention No. 87 (ILO (1989) case 1261, Committee of Experts 76th session). The European Committee of Experts to the European Social Charter also states that public servants also possess the freedom to organise under Article 5 of the Charter (but excludes the armed forces and police). Moreover, the Committee has stipulated that any restriction on civil servants' choice of trade unions could not be regarded as compatible with the Charter (Sieghart 1983: 354).

However, the International Covenant on Economic Social and Cultural Rights specifically permits the imposition of restrictions on members of the administration of the state, in similar terms to the European Convention.

In the circumstances, establishing the evolving human rights standards in respect of restrictions on state employees is a difficult exercise. The following features can be included with a degree of certainty:

- Restrictions on the right to form and join both associations in general and trade unions in particular are permitted in respect of the armed forces and police (all instruments).

- Whereas restrictions on political rights are usually only permitted if they can be shown to be 'necessary in a democratic society' (see **Box A**, **pp. 21–22**), restrictions on the armed forces and police only need to be 'lawful', which simply means 'in accordance with national law' (*Council of Civil Service Unions v UK*, 1985, ECmHR).

- The key point is that these restrictions apply only to the *exercise* of the right to freedom of association. The preparatory texts of the International Covenant show that a total prohibition on the right of free association for excluded categories of citizens was not intended; but only restrictions on the right to join particular associations or the exercise of certain activities, such as the right to strike (E/CN.4/SR.121,10,12,SR.171).

- Only the European Convention permits a comprehensive ban on trade union membership for civil servants (*Council of Civil Service Unions v UK*, above).

- By contrast, ILO Convention No. 87 permits public employees, like workers in the private sector, to establish organisations of their own choosing to further and defend their interests (ILO Freedom of Association Committee, Digest of Decisions and Recommendations, ILO (1985) para. 214).

- The right to freedom of association in the case of public employees does not necessarily imply the right to strike (ILO (1985) Case 1261, CoE 71st session): 'Workers whose functions relate to security matters would fall into the category of those in respect of whom it is possible to curtail the right to strike' (ILO (1991) Case 1261, CoE 78th session).

DATA

Restrictions on free association of state employees

In the UK, the armed forces and the police are barred from trade union membership (Army Act 1955; Police Act 1964). In addition, the Police Regulations 1987 provide that a police officer 'shall at all times abstain from any activity which is likely to interfere with the impartial discharge of his duties or which is likely to give rise to the impression amongst members of the public that it may so interfere; and in particular shall not take any part in politics'. This appears to preclude police officers from participating in the affairs of political parties and high-profile pressure groups (Ewing 1994b: 247).

In the UK, civil servants can conveniently be divided into three main groups. The first are the 'politically restricted'. These are senior members of the service who are debarred from national political activities (including the public expression of views on matters of national political policy). They are, however, entitled to take part in local political activities, with the consent of their department, provided they act with 'moderation and discretion' (Civil Service Pay and Conditions of Service Code). The second category of civil servants is a large intermediate group, consisting of clerical officers, typists and employees charged with technical and specialised responsibilities not involving questions of political policy. Members of this group may take part in both national and local political activities, but they must obtain their department's

State workers' rights

consent first. Other civil servants are politically unrestricted, except insofar as they have to observe the Official Secrets Acts; may not engage in political activity while on duty, in uniform or on official premises; and must observe a due measure of restraint so as to avoid embarrassing their ministers and departments.

Civil servants are not generally barred from trade union membership, but are subject to lesser restrictions (see below). However, one group of civil servants was singled out for special attention in January 1984, when Mrs Thatcher, then Minister for the Civil Service by virtue of being Prime Minister, issued an Order in Council to vary the contracts of employment of the staff at the Government Communications Headquarters in Cheltenham (GCHQ). The effect was to ban the staff from joining national trade unions. Six union members applied for judicial review on the ground that she had been under a duty to act fairly by consulting the civil servants affected before issuing the Order. The House of Lords found that the decision-making process was unfair, but as she had been acting on grounds of national security the courts would not intervene (*CCSU v Minister for the Civil Service*, 1985). The unions complained both to the ILO and to the European Commission. The ILO decided in 1984 that there was a violation of ILO Convention No. 87 (see below) and urged the government to reach agreement with the unions. The government took no steps to do so and in 1988 dismissed the remaining trade union members at GCHQ.

The government also recently imposed an important, largely-unknown restriction on the right of non-industrial civil servants freely to choose trade union membership. As a matter of policy, the government prohibited these civil servants from belonging to any trade union affiliated to the Labour Party. In April 1992, in furtherance of this policy, it informed Ministry of Defence security guards that it would no longer recognise the TGWU and GMB as their representatives due to the political affiliations of those unions.

Recently, the political activities of local government employees have also been restricted. The Local Government and Housing Act 1989 created 'politically restricted posts' (which, broadly speaking, include all posts where the rate of remuneration exceeds £19,500) and effectively excluded their holders from representative political activity. Holders of politically restricted posts are not only disqualified from becoming elected members of local authorities and the House of Commons (see Chapter 14) but also prohibited from acting as elections agents, as an officer of a political party (or any branch of such a party), from canvassing on behalf of such a party or candidate for election, and from speaking to the public with the apparent intention of affecting public support for a political party (Local Government Officers (Political Restrictions) Regulations 1990).

State employees and trade union membership

The legal position of the army and police conforms with international human rights standards. The police are forbidden to join a trade union of their choice or to strike. But their representative body, the Police Federation, is powerful and able to speak out and negotiate effectively on their behalf.

However, the position at GCHQ has caused considerable controversy. As noted above, the unions complained both to the ILO and to the European Commission. The ILO Committee on Freedom of Association found that the restrictions imposed by Mrs Thatcher violated ILO Convention No. 87 which requires that 'workers and employers, without distinction whatsoever, shall have the right to establish and, subject only to rules of the organisations concerned, to join organisations of their choosing without previous authority' (Article 2: ILO (1984) Case No. 1261).

The government argued that the civil servants were covered by the ILO Convention on the Right to Organise in the Public Sector, which exempts public employees engaged in work of a highly confidential nature from its general guarantee of freedom of association. The ILO Committee rejected this argument, pointing out that this particular Convention did not override 'more favourable provisions' in other ILO Conventions, including the broadly-based right to freedom of association established in ILO Convention No. 87. The government clung to its view, informing the House of Commons that the ILO Committee on Freedom of Association had been mistaken in its decision (Brown and McColgan 1992: 273–274). The government was again condemned in 1989 and 1991 by the ILO Committee for its actions and for its continuing failure to negotiate with the unions.

In the proceedings before the European Commission, the government defended itself on two grounds. First, that a restriction imposed to protect national security came within Article 11(2) of the European Convention and Britain's discretion, or 'margin of appreciation' (see **pp. 20–22**), in this respect should be wider than for other permitted exceptions. Second, Article 11(2) specifically allowed restrictions to be imposed on 'members of the administration of the State'.

From the outset, the Commission accepted that the ban amounted to a breach of Article 11. The question was therefore whether it could be justified: i.e., was it lawful? The Commission interpreted the word 'lawful' to mean 'in accordance with national law' and so found that the ban did not violate the Convention. More surprisingly, the Commission found that although the ban was absolute, it was not disproportionate to the aim pursued – national security. Finally, the Commission went on to find that the applicants were 'members of the administration of the State' and accordingly that the restriction was permitted.

The conflict between the views of the ILO and European Commission presents obvious difficulties for this audit. However, on balance, we prefer the view of the ILO. First, there are good grounds to believe that if the trade unions had been able to complain to the UN Human Rights Committee, that authority would have found a breach of Article 22 of the International Covenant. Article 22 permits restrictions on freedom of association only for the armed forces and the police, not public servants generally. And, as noted above, the International Covenant specifically provides that nothing in that article authorises any state which, like the UK, has signed ILO Convention No. 87 to apply the law in such a manner as to prejudice the guarantees provided for in that convention.

Strictly speaking, the GCHQ ban may not have breached Article 11 of the European Convention. But it does not necessarily follow that the UK conforms to the evolving human rights standards set out above. The drafters of the European

State workers' rights

Convention anticipated that in certain circumstances European Convention rights may fall short of protections guaranteed by other agreements. Article 60 therefore provides that:

> Nothing in this Convention shall be construed as limiting or derogating from any of the human rights and fundamental freedoms which may be ensured under the laws of any High Contracting Party or under any other agreement to which it is a Party.

Finally, it was not simply the ILO's specialist Committee on Freedom of Association which upheld the unions' complaint. A whole range of ILO supervisory agencies – including the Committee of Experts (on several occasions) and the Conference Committee on the Application of Standards – reviewed and upheld the complaint. An academic lawyer noted that:

> at every turn and in every forum, the government has been criticised, not only for its breach of Convention 87 but also for its obstinate and calculated refusal to accept that it acted unlawfully and to take steps to remedy the position in accordance with the requirement of the Convention.
>
> (Ewing 1994b: 24–25)

The unease of the Conference Committee is significant because it reflects a general 'world-view' of the UK's position. The workers' members from Sweden and Germany expressed particular concern and urged that the case be sent for a final decision to the International Court of Justice. Such a course is the most severe sanction that can be taken against a recalcitrant state and has never been employed against a leading member. Britain came perilously close to 'the edge of international disgrace', with the vote being 56,845 in favour of taking the case to the International Court, 60,398 against and 9,555 abstentions (Ewing 1994b: 28).

On balance, therefore, the conclusion of this audit is that while the 1984 GCHQ ban was not considered by the European Commission to violate the European Convention, it does amount to a breach of the evolving international human rights standards on freedom of association. Further, whilst the government's restrictions on non-industrial civil servants do not amount to an absolute ban on trade unions, they are clearly in breach of the requirement that everyone be entitled to join a trade union 'of his choice' (UN International Covenant, Article 8(1)(a)).

Moreover, the restrictions on civil servants and local government employees mentioned above have to be justified according to the stricter test set out in the 'General Restrictions' index above, rather than the *Council of Civil Service Unions v UK* test (which does not require such restrictions to be 'necessary in a democratic society'). By this test, it is difficult to see how the restrictions on local government employees 'fulfil a pressing social need' and are not disproportionate to the aim of responding to that need.

Conclusions

British citizens' rights to freedom of association are generally unrestricted. Law and practice broadly comply with international human rights standards. In some respects the law needs clarifying – for example, the civil law of conspiracy – but otherwise it is relatively clear. Very few associations are specifically proscribed and the bans can almost certainly be justified as measures to protect the rights of others. However, there ought to be either parliamentary or judicial supervision of proscription and the need for specific bans should be regularly scrutinised.

The UK record on trade union rights is mixed. Trade union membership is guaranteed. The right not to belong to a trade union is protected in accordance with international human rights standards. But UK law and practice on active trade unionism and collective action falls short of those standards. Individual workers who engage in trade union activities and collective actions, and their trade unions, are not sufficiently protected. Restrictions on freedom of association for the army and police conform with international human rights standards; but not restrictions on state employees, such as the staff at GCHQ.

12   The Chilling Effect of State Surveillance

State surveillance

State surveillance of citizens not only invades their privacy, but also has a 'chilling effect' on their exercise of other rights and liberties. This effect has long been recognised by the US Supreme Court and was recently articulated by the West German Constitutional Court in its 1983 decision holding a new Census Act unconstitutional:

> If [someone] reckons that participation in an assembly or a citizens' initiative will be registered officially and that personal risks might result from it, he may possibly renounce the exercise of his respective rights.
>
> (*Human Rights Journal*, vol. 5, no. 1: 100)

In the UK, surveillance is carried out on behalf of the state by the security service (MI5), which operates mainly in the UK; by the secret intelligence service (MI6), which operates mainly abroad; by the Government Communications Headquarters (GCHQ), which intercepts and analyses signals intelligence (including the communications of other countries, companies and private individuals); and finally by the police and Special Branch. The first section of this chapter assesses how far their functions and powers comply with international standards.

Surveillance takes many forms, ranging from simple observation with the naked eye to highly sophisticated electronic listening and visual devices. Broadly speaking, most forms of surveillance by the state in the UK are lawful and unregulated – save for the interception of mail or telephone calls, which is now covered by the Interception of Communications Act 1985. The second half of the chapter examines the Act in detail since it was intended to bring UK law into conformity with the requirements of the European Convention, as well as other forms of surveillance (in particular, the use of secret listening devices and telephone 'metering').

Rules for state surveillance

> No one shall be subjected to arbitrary interference with his privacy, family, home or correspondence ... Everyone has the right to the protection of the law against such interferences or attacks.
>
> (Article 12, Universal Declaration of Human Rights)

The right to privacy is recognised and protected by a number of international instruments. Article 17 of the International Covenant draws directly from Article 12 of the Universal Declaration, but is more emphatic in prohibiting 'arbitrary *or unlawful*' interference. There were proposals at the drafting stage to include a limitation clause describing the acceptable limits to the right of privacy, but these were rejected.

Article 8 of the European Convention adopts the more traditional approach to individual rights: first declaring the right to respect for private and family life, home and correspondence; then setting out qualifications which permit interferences with privacy only if they are 'in accordance with law', justified by one of the prescribed aims (which are listed) and 'necessary in a democratic society' (see **pp. 21–22**).

Restricting rights

Formal recognition of civil and political rights is not enough. It is essential that any restriction of all rights recognised by both the International Covenant and the European Convention be closely scrutinised. The two instruments set out a strict three-part test:

1.   Any restriction on civil and political rights must be 'prescribed by law'
2.   The restriction must be justified by one of the aims under the International Covenant or European Convention
3.   The restriction must be shown to be 'necessary in a democratic society'.

This test is of fundamental importance. For that reason, we deal with the test in detail in **Box A, pp. 21–22**. Here, broadly, the test requires that ordinary citizens can readily discover what legal restrictions to any right exist with enough clarity for them to be able to regulate their conduct. Any restrictions must then meet one of the aims recognised under either instrument as a legitimate ground for the restriction of civil and political rights. These aims are:

●   the protection of the rights and freedoms of others
●   national security
●   public safety
●   public health and morals
●   the prevention of public disorder or crime
●   and the economic well-being of the country.

This list is intended to be exhaustive. States may not introduce other restrictions or stretch the meaning of the criteria listed above to add others. Finally, states must show both that the restriction fulfils a pressing social need and that it is proportionate to the aim of responding to that need. They cannot merely assert that a particular restriction is 'necessary in a democratic society', but must provide concrete evidence of a genuine and serious threat.

The bodies which interpret the tests – the UN Human Rights Committee and the European Court and Commission of Human Rights – have framed their notion of 'democratic society' in terms of such concepts as 'pluralism, tolerance and broadmindedness'; and have made it clear that although the term 'necessary' is not synony-mous with 'indispensable', it does not simply mean 'reasonable' (*Handyside v UK*, ECtHR, 1976).

However, the reference to 'the economic well-being of the country' is unusual. Its inclusion reflects the fact that, when the European Convention was drafted, a number of countries still had exchange control mechanisms and wished to reserve the right to open mail as a means of enforcing them (Robertson and Merrills 1993: 128).

Since there has been little material interpreting the right to privacy under the International Covenant, the extent to which the prohibition on 'arbitrary and unlawful' interference with privacy overlaps with the specific qualifications allowed by the European Convention is unclear. However, one commentator has suggested that it has two implications. One is that 'arbitrariness' may include invasions of privacy which are committed within the law, particularly when an abuse of administrative discretion is involved. The other is that 'unlawful' includes invasions of privacy by entities other than government, and imposes an obligation on states to provide laws to protect their inhabitants against such invasions (Michael 1994: 20).

Under both the Covenant and the Convention, the right to privacy is a derogable right which states may set aside in times of war or public emergency which 'threatens the life of the nation' (ICCPR, A4 and ECHR, A15).

The evolving international human rights standards governing restrictions imposed by the right to privacy on surveillance are as follows:

- The right to privacy is infringed if state authorities keep individuals under surveillance, maintain records of their activities, tap telephones or interfere with correspondence (*Klass v Germany*, 1978, ECtHR; *Malone v UK*, 1984, ECtHR).

- Powers of secret surveillance of citizens characterise a police state and are tolerable only insofar as strictly necessary for safeguarding democratic insti-tutions (*Klass v Germany*, 1978, ECtHR).

- However, secret surveillance can in principle be justified for the purpose of effective counter-measures against sophisticated forms of espionage and terrorism (*Klass v Germany*).

- States enjoy a degree of discretion in deciding how to operate systems of surveillance, but their discretion is not unlimited. Since secret surveillance can undermine or even destroy democracy on the ground of defending it, there must be adequate and effective safeguards against abuse (*Klass v Germany*).

- Whilst it is desirable in principle that supervisory control should be in the hands of a judge, supervisory bodies are capable of providing an adequate and effective safeguard against abuse so long as they enjoy sufficient independence to give an objective ruling (*Klass v Germany*).

- The requirement that any interference with the right to privacy be 'in accord-ance with law' has a special meaning when applied to secret state surveillance or interceptions of communications. Citizens are not entitled to be able to foresee when the authorities are likely to observe them or intercept their communications (and thereby enable them to adapt their conduct). But the law must give an adequate indication of the circumstances in which, and the conditions under which, authorities are empowered to resort to this 'secret and potentially dangerous interference with the right to respect for private life and correspondence' (*Malone v UK*, 1984, ECtHR).

■ It is therefore essential to have clear rules on the interception of communications, including details of the categories of citizens liable to have their telephones tapped, the offences which might give rise to such an order, the duration of tapping and the circumstances in which recordings have to be destroyed (*Kruslin and Huvig v France*, 1990, ECtHR).

■ The protection afforded to 'correspondence' covers all forms of communication over distance (letters, telephone, telegram, telex, telefax, and other mechanical or electrical means (Nowak 1993: 304).

■ The release to the police of information gained by telephone metering – whereby numbers dialled by a telephone user are secretly recorded – without the subscriber's consent amounts to interference with the right to privacy, and must be justified according to the requirements and safeguards listed above (*Malone v UK*, 1984, ECtHR).

The activities of state surveillance agencies

State surveillance is as old as the state itself. Britain's security service agencies were established (in 1909) and operated under royal prerogative powers until rocked by a series of scandals (see for example Wright 1987; Leigh 1988). MI5 was then put on a statutory footing by the Security Service Act 1989 and MI6 and GCHQ by the Intelligence Services Act 1994. The scheme of both Acts is very similar: the existence of the various security service bodies is acknowledged and their functions set out. Power is given to the secretary of state to issue warrants, justifying activities carried out by them, which would otherwise be unlawful. Under each Act, a commissioner and tribunal are established to review some of the working of the relevant secret services and deal with complaints. Finally, the 1994 Act established for the first time a system of parliamentary accountability for all three services.

Under the 1989 Act, the function of MI5 is 'the protection of national security and, in particular, its protection against threats from espionage, terrorism and sabotage, from the activities of agents of foreign powers and from actions intended to overthrow or undermine parliamentary democracy by political, industrial or violent means'. (In 1995, the government announced proposals to give MI5 a role in combating serious crime.) The 1994 Act empowers MI6 'to obtain and provide information relating to the actions or intentions of persons outside the British Isles . . . in the interests of national security, with particular reference to the defence and foreign policies of Her Majesty's Government in the United Kingdom . . . [or] of

Statutory arrangements

the economic well-being of the United Kingdom . . . [or] in support of the prevention or the detection of serious crime'. The 1994 Act gives GCHQ similar powers and objectives, save that its operations involve the monitoring or interference with transmissions, decoding, encoding and translation.

Under both Acts, the secretary of state may issue warrants to any of the three services (MI5, MI6 or GCHQ) to interfere with property, trespass on land or interfere with wireless transmissions. For a warrant to be issued, the action proposed must be 'likely to be of substantial value in assisting' the functions set out above and the aim of that activity must not be capable of being achieved by other means. Warrants can be granted for a period of up to six months and are renewable.

The Security Service Commissioner and the Intelligence Service Commissioner can review the issue of warrants and authorisations of acts by the security services. They have a duty to report to the Prime Minister each year on the exercise of those functions. Their annual reports are laid before each House of Parliament, although matters which 'would be prejudicial to the continued discharge of the functions' of the secret services can be excluded. Finally, the two Acts establish tribunals with similar powers and functions to investigate complaints from citizens 'aggrieved' by anything they believe the security agencies have done relating to them.

Surveillance by the police is necessarily very wide-ranging since it encompasses many forms of criminal investigation. A comprehensive review is not possible here. However, the unique role played by police Special Branches throughout the UK does warrant particular attention because of their close relationship with the security services. Each police force has its own Special Branch, primarily 'to acquire intelligence, to assess its potential operational value and to contribute more generally to its interpretation' (Home Office Guidelines on Special Branch Work in Great Britain 1994). This function is carried out both to meet local policing needs and to assist the security services.

There is a special emphasis on counter-terrorism. In partnership with the security service, Special Branches acquire intelligence on those who may be responsible for acts and threats of terrorism, their sponsors and supporters. According to the Home Office Guidelines: 'When necessary, they take action to prevent or disrupt any developing terrorist activity'. The Metropolitan Police Special Branch exercises a special role 'to ensure that intelligence is exploited to the maximum to counter terrorist activity' (1994 Home Office Guidelines).

However, Special Branches have more general duties. They gather intelligence on 'animal rights extremists' activity' and contribute to an Animal Rights National Index. They collect and analyse intelligence for chief officers about threats to public order – a key responsibility. In many forces, they act as the focal point for immigration and nationality work when the police are asked to provide assistance to the Home Office.

Limited surveillance of the security forces

Widespread public concern about the unregulated nature of the activities of the security services existed prior to the enactment of the Security Services Act 1989 and the Intelligence Services Act 1994. The absence of either legal recognition of the services or protection of individual liberties against their activities had been criticised since the early 1960s. They seemed to be beyond the law. In 1985, Cathy Massiter, a former security service officer, revealed in a Channel 4 television programme that individuals engaged in lawful campaigning and pressure groups were routinely put under surveillance by MI5. The telephones of trade unionists involved in strike action were tapped; in one case, officers broke into the house of Ken Gill, general secretary of TASS, to plant a bugging device. Leading CND members were placed under surveillance. Files were kept on the legal officer and general secretary of the National Council for Civil Liberties (now renamed Liberty) – Harriet Harman and Patricia Hewitt. Two years later, Peter Wright, a retired senior officer in MI5, claimed in his memoirs that he and others 'bugged and burgled our way across London at the State's behest, whilst pompous bowler-hatted civil servants in Whitehall pretended to look the other way'. He maintained that there had been an MI5 plot to destabilise the Wilson government (Wright 1987: 54 and 362–372).

The allegations led Harman and Hewitt, now prominent Labour Party modernisers, to apply to the European Commission of Human Rights complaining of violations of their right to respect for private life and the absence of an effective domestic remedy (under Articles 8 and 13 of the Convention). The Commission decided that their rights had been breached because information had been kept on their private lives. The breach (of Article 8) could not be justified because the UK had no legal rules regulating the security services and no adequate remedy for the victims of such surveillance as required by Article 13 (*Harman and Hewitt v UK*, 1986). The UK government concluded a friendly settlement with the applicants which led to the Security Service Act 1989 and (ultimately) to the 1994 Act.

The secretive nature of the regulatory measures put in place by the two Acts has caused considerable disquiet and leaves their effectiveness in doubt. The investigations of the two tribunals established under the Acts are undertaken in secret. Those citizens who complain cannot know what information is being considered and cannot make further representations. The tribunals decide only whether the secret services had 'reasonable grounds' for their actions. And a tribunal cannot question whether the decision to take any particular action or surveillance was justified in the first place. Nor can a tribunal question the grounds for an agency's actions in cases where the person complaining belongs to a group or category of people regarded by the security services as requiring investigation. Most significantly, a tribunal's final decision does not provide any indication of what was ascertained; only that a determination was made for or against the complainant. Although a tribunal can direct that activities should cease where it has found that they are unjustified, it is under no obligation to do so. Finally, no reasons are given by the tribunals and their decisions cannot be challenged in the courts.

These arrangements fall short of the standards derived from international human rights instruments; namely, that there should be clear rules on surveillance; and that the bodies supervising surveillance provide adequate and effective safeguards against abuse. But when Harman and Hewitt returned to the European Commission in

Regulating state agencies

1993 to raise such issues, the Commission dismissed their case as manifestly ill-founded. A series of further cases before the European Commission have been equally unsuccessful. In particular, on the question of how adequately the tribunal and Commissioner set up under the 1989 Act provide a safeguard against abuse, the Commission decided,

> in the absence of any evidence or indication that the system is not functioning as required by domestic law ... the framework ... achieves a compromise between the requirements of defending democratic society and the rights of the individual which is compatible with the provisions of the Convention.
>
> (*Esbester v UK*, 1993)

In our view the European Commission has retreated too far from the guiding principles set out by the European Court (which is superior to the Commission) in *Klass* and *Malone* – states do enjoy a discretion within which they can carry out secret surveillance, but since such surveillance can undermine or even destroy democracy, there must be adequate and effective safeguards against abuse (see **p. 226**). In the UK, where there is no right to privacy (see above), it is imperative that the tribunals set up to investigate surveillance by the secret services have power to question whether the surveillance complained about was justified; and to report their findings either way. Otherwise, whether they provide an adequate and effective safeguard is unknowable. Equally, the fact that a tribunal cannot 'go behind' a decision of the secret services to target an individual because he or she belonged to a group or category of people regarded by them as requiring investigation presents the tribunal with a circular obstacle (it may be popularly described as a 'Catch-22' situation). It hardly fulfils the requirement that citizens be entitled to foresee when the authorities are likely to observe them or intercept their communications. The two Acts clearly improve upon the previously unregulated system, but even within new legal structures, members of organisations tend to carry on as before and even to infuse new structures with their traditions. Given the evidence of failed attempts to reform the agencies in the 1980s, it is vital that their operations under the new Acts are effectively scrutinised. As matters stand, the regulation of these agencies still fails to conform fully with international human rights standards.

The failure to control Special Branch activity

The functions and powers of police Special Branches give further cause for concern and have not yet been tested by the European authorities. Their functions are not set out in law, but in 'quasi-legislation' – non-legally binding Home Office Guidelines. Even more significantly, although they carry out intelligence-gathering, Special Branches do not come within the terms of either the 1989 or the 1994 Acts. Whereas a citizen who is aggrieved by *anything* which he or she thinks the security or intelligence services have done may at least complain to either the Security Services Tribunal or the Intelligence Services Tribunal, a citizen aggrieved by possible actions of the Special Branch has recourse only to the Police Complaints Authority. This has significant consequences.

Both the Security Services Tribunal and the Intelligence Services Tribunal have powers to investigate whether a person complaining has been the subject of inquiries by the security services (even if no warrant was necessary). In other words, the tribunal can investigate surveillance by the security services even where such surveillance is clearly not illegal (for example, bugging). The Police Complaints Authority has different and more limited powers of investigation as Mr Govell found out in 1993 when he discovered a secret listening device in the wall behind the settee in his flat in Leeds. He complained to the Police Complaints Authority (PCA) which began to investigate. The authority accepted that the device had been installed by police officers, but ran into a major problem, as they explained to Mr Govell:

> Your . . . complaint – that your privacy was invaded without justification – has provided a technical problem in that invasion of privacy . . . is not a criminal offence in this country, neither does the allegation fit easily into the police disciplinary code.
>
> (*R v Chief Constable of West Yorkshire, ex parte Govell*, 1994)

Since the PCA's powers are confined to the consideration of criminal or disciplinary charges, it declined to take any action. Subsequently judicial review proceedings – unable to consider the merits of the Authority's decision (see **pp. 95–99**) – failed to provide Mr Govell with a remedy.

Given the wide scope of Special Branch functions and the close relationship with the security services, this is a matter of considerable concern. As mentioned above, Special Branches gather intelligence on animal rights activists, general threats to the public, immigration and nationality cases as well as suspected terrorist activities. There is evidence to suggest that they exceed these functions. When John Alderson took over as Chief Constable of the Devon and Cornwall Police, he discovered that almost half of the files held by Special Branch should never have been created, 'either because they were a waste of time and clogging up the machine, or they were records of activities which should not be in the banks of information' (BBC Radio Four, File on Four, August 1982). Alderson ordered the wholesale destruction of files on anti-nuclear protestors, ten-year-old files on 'Stop the (South African) Rugby Tour' organisers and one on someone noted for having had lunch with Tony Benn MP.

As the *Govell* case established, the powers of the Police Complaints Authority to control this type of secret surveillance are very limited. Much of the surveillance work by the police and special branch can effectively be carried out in the unregulated manner of the secret services before 1989. The only guidelines are non-binding and not published. In the circumstances, this represents a significant loophole in the protection against abuse required by international human rights standards.

Safeguards against unlawful interceptions

The law in the UK does not recognise a free-standing right to privacy (*Kaye v Robertson*, 1991). Privacy is protected only so far as it overlaps with other recognised rights (in particular property or quasi-property rights). Hence, for example, damages for trespass have been awarded against a defendant who secretly installed a microphone above the plaintiff's bed (*Sheen v Clegg*, 1967). The interceptions of communications by telephone or mail are an exception to the rule, since they are afforded a degree of protection by the Interception of Communications Act 1985.

The 1985 Act makes telephone tapping and mail interception an offence unless it is carried out under a warrant issued by a secretary of state. In the first instance applications for warrants are initiated by the police, Customs and Excise, or the security services. These applications are channelled through the Home Office, Foreign Office, Scottish Office or the Northern Ireland Office, as the case may be. Warrants may only be issued in the interests of national security; to prevent or detect serious crime; or to safeguard the economic well-being of the UK. Table 12.1 shows how many warrants are issued annually for both telephone and mail intercepts, and how many remain in force at the end of each year. Publication of Foreign Office and Northern Ireland Office warrants are deemed to be a risk to national security and are published in a confidential annex to the report. In 1993, over 1,000 warrants were issued in Great Britain, of which over 400 remained in force at the end of the year.

Individuals who suspect that their mail or telephone calls have been interfered with may appeal to a special tribunal set up under the Act. The tribunal investigates whether a warrant has been issued to authorise interception and, if so, whether it was issued on proper grounds applying the standards which would be applicable in judicial review proceedings. If the tribunal finds that the statutory requirements have been breached, it reports its conclusions (but not its *reasons*) to the person who has complained and reports its findings in full to the Prime Minister. It can order (but need not) that the interception stop, that records be destroyed and compensation be paid to the applicant. If the tribunal finds an interception has not been authorised by a warrant, the sanction is a criminal prosecution (but only with the consent of the Director of Public Prosecutions).

A Commissioner – a senior judge or former judge – works alongside the tribunal and assists in its work. This official keeps under review the performance of the Home Secretary's functions under the 1985 Act and the adequacy of arrangements to ensure that intercepted material is not improperly disclosed.

The 1985 Act applies only to the interception of communications in the public postal or telecommunications systems. All other forms of surveillance, such as the use of secret listening devices and telephone 'metering', remain lawful (whether carried out by the security services, the police or anyone else). Therefore, so long as they do not incidentally involve the interception of telephonic transmissions or the mail – or trespass or damage to property – no warrant is needed and no remedy is available to the victim of such surveillance.

While there may be internal guidelines for the secret services before secret listening devices are employed, the only guidelines known to this audit are the Guidelines on

Table 12.1 Interception of communications, 1985–1993

Type	Home Secretary warrants		Scottish Secretary warrants	
	Issued during year	Still in force on 31 December each year	Issued during year	Still in force on 31 December each year
1985 Telecommunications	403	212	59	22
Letters	40	74	9	2
TOTAL	443	286	68	24
1986[1] Telecommunications	573	202	84	33
Letters	95	76	4	2
TOTAL	668	282	88	35
1987 Telecommunications	438	223	54	29
Letters	34	71	3	1
TOTAL	472	294	57	30
1988 Telecommunications	412	225	54	27
Letters	48	75	5	3
TOTAL	460	300	59	30
1989 Telecommunications	427	232	63	24
Letters	31	59	1	0
TOTAL	458	291	64	24
1990 Telecommunications	473	225	66	20
Letters	42	52	2	1
TOTAL	515	277	68	21
1991 Telecommunications	670	239	81	23
Letters	62	50	1	0
TOTAL	732	289	82	23
1992 Telecommunications	756	265	87	26
Letters	188	72	5	1
TOTAL	874	337	92	27
1993 Telecommunications	893	317	112	30
Letters	105	55	10	7
TOTAL	998	372	122	37

Source: Annexes to the Interception of Communications Commissioner's Annual Reports for 1988 and 1993

Note:
1 The figures for 1986 reflect the need to replace all outstanding non-statutory warrants when the Act came into force in April 1986

Interceptions

the Use of Equipment in Police Surveillance Operations, issued by the Home Office in 1984. These are not made public and do not have the force of law.

Telephone 'metering' is a process whereby the numbers dialled on a particular telephone and the time and duration of each call are recorded. The police do not have any power (in the absence of a court order) to compel the production of the records of 'metered' telephones from British Telecom. But in practice records are occasionally made available to them if they are considered essential to police inquiries.

Concerns about the regulation of interceptions

The Interception of Communications Act 1985 was introduced in response to the European Court's ruling that the absence of legal regulation of state interceptions of communications and protection against arbitrary interception in the UK infringed the privacy of British citizens (*Malone v UK*, 1984). To be justifiable, the power to intercept telephone calls had to be laid down with a sufficient degree of precision. Since telephone tapping was unregulated by law, the Court decided against the government.

The 1985 Act dealt with the some of the Court's concerns by putting the arrangements for intercepting telephone calls and mail on a statutory footing. However, there are still pockets of concern. Warrants to intercept communications can be issued on grounds of national security or the economic well-being of the state – yet neither is defined in the Act. Since the investigative tribunal does not give reasons for its findings, there is little prospect of the public finding out how these terms are actually being applied in practice. This is related to a wider limitation. While the *Klass* judgment in the European Court contemplates the possibility that supervision against abuse of powers of interception might be left in the hands of special bodies capable of providing an adequate and effective protection, it clearly suggests that judicial supervision is desirable. Yet this course was not adopted when the 1985 Act was introduced.

In addition, the judgment of the House of Lords in the case of two men convicted of offences related to a conspiracy to supply drugs has opened up a huge loophole in the protection offered by the 1985 Act (*R v Effick*, 1994). Evidence arising from the interception of telephone communications, carried out by the police without a warrant, was central to the prosecution case. The trial judge admitted the evidence and the Court of Appeal upheld his ruling on the basis that while unauthorised interception was a criminal offence, no rule held that evidence obtained illegally was inadmissible. This demonstrated an important shortcoming in the protection afforded by the Act.

On appeal, the House of Lords neatly evaded the dilemma by deciding that as the telephone intercepted was cordless, it did not form part of a 'public telecommunications system' and therefore fell outside the scope of the 1985 Act. One judge went so far as to state that the Act was not designed to protect people from eavesdropping, but simply to preserve the integrity of the public system. Thus the tapping of the growing category of mobile telephones – five million people now use them – is once again totally unregulated. Neither the International Covenant nor the European Convention confine their protection only to publicly-administered communications. Thus by excluding cordless phones from protection under the Act, the UK's highest court has ensured that this country violates international human rights standards.

The use of secret listening devices

The protection afforded under Article 17 of the International Covenant and Article 8 of the European Convention covers all forms of communication over distance. The European Court and Commission have clearly established that the right to privacy is infringed if state authorities keep individuals under surveillance and/or maintain records of their activities. Therefore in principle, there is no reason why the approach taken by the European Court to telephone tapping should not be applied equally to other forms of surveillance, including the use of secret listening devices and telephone metering.

No warrant is required for the use of secret listening devices by state agencies and such guidelines as exist are neither made public nor legally binding. International human rights standards cannot therefore possibly be honoured. These were the key features identified by the European Court in *Malone* which led to the finding that UK law on telephone tapping was unclear and uncertain (see above). However, the European Commission recently issued a very restrictive decision on one aspect of these issues (*Redgrave v UK*, 1993).

The actress Vanessa Redgrave was a member of the Workers' Revolutionary Party and since 1985, when the WRP split, had been a member of the Marxist Party. In February 1991 she discovered an electronic listening device in a house which she owned and used for meetings with political colleagues. A former member of the WRP claimed to have installed the device, but Ms Redgrave believed that he may have been involved, willingly or otherwise, by the security services. She therefore complained to the Security Services Tribunal. The tribunal investigated the complaint and in accordance with its functions simply advised her that no determination was made in her favour. She then complained to the European Commission that the government had violated Article 8 of the Convention by installing and monitoring the electronic listening device in her house. The Commission found it unnecessary to decide whether the security services were responsible for planting the device. It considered that, given the nature of Redgrave's continuing political commitments, it was reasonably likely that she had been subject to surveillance by the security services. The Commission went on to decide that such surveillance was both 'in accordance with law' and 'necessary in a democratic society'.

The Commission relied heavily on its previous decision in the *Esbester* case (**p. 230**) which approved the combination of the security services commissioner and tribunal as adequate safeguards against abuse of privacy by the security services. This is important because, as already mentioned, other bodies such as the police, and in particular Special Branch, are not subject to the same regime. The use of secret listening devices by them is unregulated by law and therefore out of step with international human rights standards.

Telephone metering

The issue of telephone metering

Telephone metering involves no interception of communication, but it clearly is an invasion of privacy. Equally clearly, it is useful to the security services and the police. Metering records assist them to build up a picture of an individual's friends, acquaintances and contacts. If several individuals' calls are monitored, telephone trees can be extrapolated and connections made. A chart compiled from the records of calls made from a single Edinburgh telephone in a two-week period in 1990 was among documents stolen in a burglary at a major police station that year. Over 150 calls were logged and the names, addresses and telephone numbers of 78 people and organisations were listed.

Whether telephone metering in the UK complies with international standards was directly raised by Malone in his case before the European Court. He was unable to provide evidence that his telephone use had been metered, but the Court considered that it was likely that it had been. The Court rejected the government's argument that since the content of calls is not recorded, metering falls outside the scope of civil liberties concerns and requires no oversight. The Court noted rather that UK law does not prohibit the release of such information to the police without the subscriber's knowledge or consent and that there are no legal rules concerning the scope and manner of metering. Accordingly, it considered that metering, as with telephone tapping, was not 'in accordance with law'.

Despite the ruling, the government has persisted with its argument that metering requires no oversight. Metering is not regulated under the Interception of Communications Act 1985. In a letter to the Scottish Council for Civil Liberties in September 1992, a Scottish Office minister wrote that 'the question of metering was very carefully considered when the legislation was being prepared and was very fully debated in Parliament during the passage of the Act'. In fact, Hansard records only one exchange on the subject of metering late at night on 3 April 1985 when the Home Office minister, David Waddington, responded to a proposed amendment to the bill put forward by the Liberal Democrat MP, Robert Maclennan. Waddington repeated the government argument that metering was fundamentally different from interception and was dealt with differently in the bill (Hilton 1993). It was not dealt with in the bill at all and the UK remains in clear breach of international human rights standards as recognised by the European Court in the *Malone* case.

Conclusions

Once any form of state surveillance is recognised as legitimate, a tension is set up between the liberty of the state to gather information and the privacy of its citizens. Since surveillance can have a profound effect on the exercise of political rights, it is paramount that the balance between legitimate surveillance and privacy be properly maintained. Before 1985 law and practice in the UK was heavily weighted in favour of the state and unregulated secret surveillance. The intervention of Strasbourg, prompted by two cases, inspired three statutes which have introduced a degree of privacy against state interference and an unknowable measure of regulation. But the citizen's right of privacy seems to be heavily compromised. If there was a general right to privacy in the UK, issues relating to secret surveillance could be determined by the courts. As it is, citizens have to rely totally on the investigative tribunals set up under the three Acts. It is therefore important that those bodies have full investigative powers and can report their findings fully. None have such powers. Therefore the UK still fails to conform fully with international human rights standards on secret surveillance.

The surveillance activities of the police and Special Branch have still not even been put on a statutory footing. The use of secret listening devices by the security agencies, the police and Special Branch is unregulated by law. Users of cordless, or mobile, telephones are not protected by the Interception of Communications Act 1985 – as a result of an opportunistic judicial decision. These defects all point to a systemic failure. They are the product of a system for protecting human rights which does not recognise a right of privacy – against which *all* law and practice can be reviewed. The piecemeal approach inevitably leaves gaps between UK law and practice and international human rights standards.

13   The Use of Force, Arrest and Detention

Life and personal liberty

Freedom from fear and intimidation are essential prerequisites of a participatory democracy. The circumstances in which the state can deprive citizens of their life or liberty determine the extent to which citizens are able to enjoy, if at all, their political and civil rights. If people live in fear of being killed or subjected to torture or ill-treatment by the police, army or security services, randomly stopped and searched or detained without charge or a fair trial, they are unlikely to feel free to speak their mind, engage in protest activity or join the political organisations of their choice.

At a more general level, violations of the rights to life and liberty for certain individuals or groups in society have a direct impact on the degree of political equality possible in that society and affect the culture of democracy and freedom on which everyone's rights ultimately hang.

Life and liberty in the United Kingdom are said to be guaranteed by the general rule in the United Kingdom that all people are free from arbitrary arrest and detention. The circumstances in which a power of arrest can arise – and legal rules on the degree of force which may lawfully be employed – therefore assume great importance. Much of the chapter is concerned with an extensive examination of these circumstances and rules. Limitations of space dictate a narrow approach and the emphasis is on criminal arrest and ill-treatment in detention.

The right to life and liberty

Everyone has the right to life, liberty and security of person.
(Article 3, Universal Declaration of Human Rights)

The United Nations Human Rights Committee has consistently held the right to life to be the 'supreme right'. A general overview of all the issues this principle raises is not possible here. Our focus is on the arbitrary taking of life by the state – particularly, 'extra-judicial killings', by which we mean the taking of life outside the judicial process by or with the consent of public officials, other than as necessary measures of law enforcement. Invariably such killings are controversial and have a serious impact on the relationship between those responsible for maintaining law and order and the communities in which they take place.

International standards are relatively clear. Article 6 of the UN International Covenant provides that, 'Every human being has the inherent right to life' which 'shall be protected

International standards

by law' and further that, 'No one shall be arbitrarily deprived of his life'. Similarly, Article 2(1) of the European Convention provides that, 'Everyone's right to life shall be protected by law'. The right to life is non-derogable – it may not be suspended, even in the event of an emergency threatening the life of the nation. A simple legal prohibition on extra-judicial killings is not enough under either instrument. States are obliged to engage in full investigation of the circumstances of any such death and faithfully to seek to bring the perpetrators of any unlawful killings to justice.

Whereas the International Covenant prohibits the 'arbitrary' deprivation of life, the European Convention prohibits the 'intentional' deprivation of liberty. The Convention goes on to set out the circumstances in which it is deemed that there is no violation of the right to life when a citizen is killed: namely,

- when the death results from the use of force which is no more than is absolutely necessary in defence of any person from unlawful violence
- to effect a lawful arrest or to prevent the escape of a person lawfully detained
- and in action lawfully taken for the purpose of quelling a riot or insurrection.

Arrest

International law broadly deems that arrest begins the process of detention and should only occur when authorised by law. To give full effect to this basic principle, the various international bodies have all adopted a broad concept of arrest. It covers activities which in domestic law might be considered as falling short of actual arrest – like police powers to stop and search citizens in the street, breach of the peace and special powers of detention under the Prevention of Terrorism Act 1989. All have been included in this audit.

Upon arrest, the International Covenant and the European Convention require the authorities to give an arrested person reasons for the arrest to enable that person to prepare a defence and petition for release. Both instruments also require that anyone arrested or detained on a criminal charge be brought *promptly* before a judge or other officer authorised by law to exercise judicial power and that he or she subsequently be brought to trial within a reasonable period.

In the meantime, the International Covenant, but not the European Convention, creates a presumption that bail will be granted and, consequently, the UN Human Rights Committee has taken the view that detention pending trial is only acceptable in the strictest of circumstances. By way of an additional safeguard, both instruments require that anyone detained be entitled to take proceedings by which the lawfulness of that detention can be determined by a court (commonly known as *habeas corpus* proceedings).

The treatment of people under any sort of detention or restraint has huge implications for democracy. The basic provisions in international law prohibiting torture, degrading and inhuman treatment apply and, in this context, have been strengthened by further specific instruments such as the UN Standard Minimum Rules for prisons. In this audit, special attention is paid to treatment in police custody, prison, forced deportation and the removal of allegedly illegal immigrants.

International standards

Standards for life and liberty

The evolving human rights standards which apply to the right to life are as follows:

- States should tightly limit the circumstances in which deprivation of life is permissible and control these strictly (UN Human Rights Committee, General Comment 6/16).

- States must take measures not only to prevent deprivation of life by criminal acts, but also arbitrary killings by their own security forces (UN Human Rights Committee, General Comment 6/16).

- The use of force permitted to enable law enforcement officials to carry out their duties is only such as is strictly necessary (United Nations Basic Principles on the Use of Force and Firearms by Law Enforcement Officials, 1990).

- The right to life is not a purely negative right: states should take positive measures to safeguard it (UN Human Rights Committee, General Comment 6/16; Nowak 1993: 105).

- States are bound to provide bodyguards indefinitely to protect the lives of people who fear that they are likely to be attacked (*X v Ireland*, 1973, ECmHR).

- The duty on a state under international law to protect the right to life includes a duty to investigate cases of death and to bring to justice those responsible – irrespective of whether it is alleged that the government is responsible (*December Murders in Surinam Case*, HRC, 1983; McGoldrick 1991: 332).

- The duty to investigate is particularly strict in suspected cases of extrajudicial killing (United Nations Principles on the Effective Prevention and Investigation of Extra-Legal, Arbitrary and Summary Executions (UNPPE, 1989).

- Investigation of extra-judicial killing should be thorough, prompt and impartial and the purpose should be to determine the cause, manner and time of death, the person responsible and any pattern or practice which may have brought about that death (UNPPE, Principle 9).

- The investigating authority should have the power to obtain all necessary evidence, including the power to oblige officials allegedly involved in the killing to appear and testify (UNPPE, Principle 10).

- Families of the deceased and their legal representatives should be informed of, and have access to, the investigation hearing as well as to all information relevant to the investigation, and shall be entitled to present other evidence (UNPPE, Principle 11).

- A written report should be made public within a reasonable period on the methods and findings of such investigations. The report should include the scope of the inquiry, procedures and methods used to evaluate evidence as well as conclusions and recommendations based on findings of fact and on applicable law. A government should reply to the report within a reasonable period or indicate the steps to be taken in response to it (UNPPE, Principle 12).

DATA

The 'reasonable' use of force

In the United Kingdom, the deliberate taking of life is a criminal offence for which the mandatory penalty is imprisonment for life. Of the recognised defences, this audit considers the use of force in self-defence, to carry out an arrest or to prevent crime, since it is obviously central to the right to life.

The use of such force as is both reasonable and necessary in self-defence is a defence to murder. Moreover, UK law also accepts that pre-emptive force may be used in self-defence in the face of an immediate threat of violence, so long as it is not disproportionate to the harm feared. In addition, the Criminal Law Act 1967 (and its Northern Ireland counterpart) permits the use of lethal force to prevent crime, or to effect or assist in the arrest of offenders, suspected offenders or 'of persons unlawfully at large'. The force used must be 'reasonable in the circumstances'. Police officers and soldiers have no special dispensation in relation to the use of lethal force.

If death occurs through the lethal use of force, there may be a criminal investigation with a view to arresting and charging suspects, or an internal police or army inquiry, or both. There is no general requirement for a public inquiry by an independent body, apart from the limited inquiries carried out by coroners' inquests in all cases of sudden or unexpected death.

AUDIT

The need for 'absolute necessity'

The formal law outlawing the use of lethal force in this country conforms with international human rights standards. However, the use of lethal force by security forces in Northern Ireland over the last two decades demands special examination, focusing on the meaning of 'reasonableness' when firearms are used by security forces; and the adequacy of investigations into incidents where lethal force is used.

In its third report to the UN Human Rights Committee, the UK government boldly asserted that 'a serviceman may employ lethal force only if he believes there is imminent danger to life (his own or the life of others) and there is no other way of averting that danger' (1989, para.70). This does not accurately reflect the wording of the Criminal Law (Northern Ireland) Act 1967, still less the case law which has followed. The courts take an indulgent view of the Act's requirements whenever the security forces are involved.

For example, a British soldier on patrol in Northern Ireland shot and killed an unarmed man, who had run away when challenged. The soldier had an honest but mistaken belief that the man was a terrorist. A judge sitting without a jury acquitted him of murder, holding that the killing was justified within the meaning of the Criminal Law (Northern Ireland) Act 1967. On appeal, the House of Lords agreed, finding that the proper test of 'reasonableness' under the Act was whether a reasonable person might think that the use of lethal force was justified to protect others from harm if the deceased were allowed to escape (*AG for Northern Ireland's Reference (No. 1 of 1975)*, 1977). Thus the courts took a very broad view of the prevention of harm to others; in particular, that there was no need for an immediate threat to life from the suspect to be established.

This broad approach is far removed from the European Convention's requirement that lethal force to prevent escape can only be justified where *absolutely necessary*; and equally far removed from rules under the UN Basic Principles on the Use of Force, requiring law enforcement officials to limit their use of lethal force to that which is *strictly necessary* to carry out their duties. This difficulty has not escaped the statutory Standing Commission on Human Rights in Northern Ireland (see **pp. 71–73**) which noted in 1993 that:

> There is substantial divergence between the legal standard for the use of lethal force in the United Kingdom . . . and the prevailing international standards.
>
> (SACHR Annual Report 1992–93: 12)

The Commission recommended that the 1967 Act be amended to embody a test of 'absolute necessity' as in the European Convention. The act has not been amended in England, Wales or Northern Ireland. There are therefore good grounds to determine that the UK fails to meet international standards. Faced with a challenge under the European Convention in 1983, the government at once paid substantial damages to the man's widow, by way of a friendly settlement (*Farrell v UK*, 1983).

There is also hard evidence that the British government has failed in its international obligation to take positive measures to prevent arbitrary killings by their own security forces. Between 1969 and November 1993, about 350 people were killed by members of the security forces (SACHR Annual Report 1992–3). The government has consistently denied that the security forces in Northern Ireland have on occasions adopted a 'shoot-to-kill' policy (i.e., deliberately killing suspects as an alternative to arresting them). But well-respected human rights bodies and academics have categorically rejected these denials.

Amnesty International carried out detailed investigations over a period of ten years into killings in disputed circumstances by members of the security forces in Northern Ireland. In 1994 it reported that it remained unconvinced by government statements that no shoot-to-kill policy existed. Amnesty pointed out that such statements were not substantiated by evidence of an official will to investigate fully and impartially each incident, to make the facts publicly known, to bring the perpetrators to justice or to bring relevant legislation into line with international standards (Amnesty International 1994: 1). Amnesty's investigation began with three incidents in late 1982 when six unarmed people were killed by members of a covert anti-terrorist squad within the Royal Ulster Constabulary (RUC). Prosecutions were brought concerning two of the deaths, but no police officer was convicted.

It soon emerged that senior police officers had concocted a false version of events and instructed policemen, under the Official Secrets Act, to give false testimony. In response to public protest, John Stalker, a senior British police officer, was appointed by the RUC Chief Constable in May 1984 to examine the cover-ups. He carried out his own re-examination of the evidence in all the cases and believed that he had uncovered crucial new evidence. He alleged that he was obstructed from carrying out a full investigation and, before it was completed, he was removed from duty in suspicious circumstances. The inquiry was completed in April 1987 by Colin Sampson, a British chief constable. The findings of the Stalker/Sampson inquiry have never been published. In January 1988, the Attorney General announced that the inquiry revealed evidence that RUC officers had attempted or conspired to pervert the course of justice. But no officers were prosecuted because the authorities wished to safeguard 'national security' and the 'public interest'. Internal disciplinary hearings resulted in 18 officers being reprimanded and one cautioned (Amnesty International 1994: 3).

The implications of these cases are far-reaching. In many other fatal incidents where the security forces allegedly killed rather than arrested people, the authorities have advanced exactly the same justifications as those given in the 'shoot-to-kill' cases investigated by Stalker and Sampson: either that a suspect appeared to reach for a gun and was shot in self-defence, or that the driver of a car drove through a road block and the car was fired on subsequently (Amnesty International 1994: 4).

The government announced that there was no evidence of a 'shoot-to-kill' policy when the results of the Stalker/Sampson inquiry were presented to Parliament (HC Deb, 25 January 1988, c21–35). Stalker's own verdict was different; while there was 'no written instruction, nothing pinned upon a notice-board', he concluded, 'there was a clear understanding on the part of the men whose job it was to pull the trigger that was what was expected of them' (*The Times*, 9 February 1988).

In 1995, the government's policy for handling incidents involving terrorists, or terrorist suspects, was dealt a severe blow by the European Court of Human Rights. By the margin of a single vote, the Court held that the killings of three terrorists in Gibraltar in March 1988 by members of the SAS violated the right to life under Article 2 of the European Convention. The Court pointed out that use of force was permissible under the Convention only where it was 'absolutely necessary' in self-defence or to carry out an arrest. The Court accepted that, in practice, the difference between 'absolute necessity" and 'reasonableness' in the law in Gibraltar (which reflects UK law) may not have great significance. The Court therefore exonerated the three SAS soldiers, but criticised the UK authorities' overall lack of appropriate care in control and organisation of the arrest operation. In its view, the use of force in killing the three terrorists was more than absolutely necessary (*McCann and others v UK*, 1995).

Defects in the investigations into killings

The investigation of suspected cases of extra-judicial killing in Northern Ireland also raises serious questions of compliance with international human rights standards.

Investigating deaths

Of the 350 killings by security forces in the period 1974 to 1993, only 18 cases came to full trial and of those, only two resulted in convictions, one for murder and one for manslaughter (SACHR Annual Report 1992–93: 153 and 173). Internal police or army inquiries are neither public nor independent. Only coroners' inquests take place in public, but a special inquiry by Professor Tom Hadden, an academic lawyer, in 1992, revealed serious deficiencies in their operation in Northern Ireland.

The Standing Advisory Commission on Human Rights invited Hadden, a former member, to inquire into the law on inquests in Northern Ireland and to make proposals for reform in response to considerable public concern. Hadden's report (published as an annex to SACHR's 1993–94 report) sets out a catalogue of defects, many of which appear to stand in stark contrast to the requirements of international human rights standards. The most serious are considered below.

Delays in holding inquests into fatal incidents involving the security forces became notorious in Northern Ireland. The delays often ran to several years. The inquest into the deaths of three unarmed men, Burns, McKerr and Toman, who were killed in November 1982 has yet to be concluded (at December 1995). People naturally suspected that some delays were deliberate and reflected the reluctance of the security authorities to submit their actions to public scrutiny. Nothing was done to dispel that suspicion when in June 1993, the then Lord Chancellor, Lord Hailsham, admitted that there were 'legitimate policy reasons', as well as administrative reasons, for the delays in inquests (SACHR Annual Report 1993–94: 252). This clearly contradicts both the letter and the spirit of international human rights standards which require prompt and impartial investigation of all suspected cases of extra-judicial killing.

Coroners are forbidden to compel people who are suspects, or who have been or are likely to be charged with an offence arising from a death, to give evidence (Coroners (Practice and Procedure) Rules 1963). So soldiers and police officers who are responsible for a disputed killing cannot be called to give evidence. Instead, coroners adopted the practice of admitting signed statements from them. What is contained in the statements cannot be challenged by cross-examination or otherwise. This falls far short of the requirement, embodied in international human rights standards, that those charged with investigating suspected extra-judicial killings should have the authority to oblige officials allegedly involved to appear and testify. These difficulties were compounded by the frequent issue of 'public immunity certificates' by the Northern Ireland Secretary to prevent the hearing or production of particular evidence at inquests. The use of these certificates is considered in some detail in the chapter on freedom of information (**pp. 160–162**). But clearly their frequent use in Northern Ireland falls short of the requirement that all available evidence should be given to the investigators.

Relatives of the deceased are not entitled to advanced information on any statements or other evidence or to call their own witnesses at coroners' inquests. This contradicts, almost word for word, the UNPPE Principle 11 (see above) which requires that they and their lawyers should have access to all information relevant to the investigation and should also be entitled to present other evidence.

Finally, the authorities prohibited verdicts in coroners' courts in Northern Ireland, replacing them by findings which do not attribute blame. They are therefore unable to satisfy the expectation under international human rights standards that investigations shall determine the cause, manner and time of a death, the person responsible and any pattern or practice which may have brought about that death. In the circumstances, the Standing Advisory Commission on Human Rights was driven to conclude that: 'it is doubtful whether an inquest serves any useful purpose in the investigation of [controversial killings]' (SACHR Annual Report 1992: 18). Given the total absence of any other public investigation, and the doubtful circumstances surrounding the only vigorous internal inquiry, the inevitable conclusion for this audit is that the law and practice relating to the investigation of suspected extra-judicial deaths in Northern Ireland falls far short of the evolving human rights standards described in the index above.

INDEX

The international rules governing arrest

> Everyone has the right to ... liberty and security of person.
>   (Article 3, Universal Declaration of Human Rights)

> No one shall be subjected to arbitrary arrest ...
>   (Article 9, Universal Declaration of Human Rights)

Freedom from arbitrary arrest and detention are guaranteed by Article 9 of the International Covenant and Article 5 of the European Convention. Both prohibit any arrest or detention save 'in accordance with law'. Article 5 of the European Convention goes on to set out the limited categories of situations in which such deprivation of liberty is permitted, including arrest or detention to bring a person before a 'competent legal authority' provided there is 'reasonable suspicion' that he or she has committed an offence.

The attempt to draw up a similar list under Article 9 of the International Covenant was aborted at the drafting stage. Instead the proposal prohibiting *arbitrary* arrest or detention was adopted. In practice, the UN Human Rights Committee has interpreted the word 'arbitrary' broadly. It is not to be equated with 'against the law', but to include elements such as inappropriateness, injustice and lack of predictability (*Hugo van Alphen v Netherlands*, 1988).

The evolving human rights standards which establish the right to be protected from arbitrary arrest and detention include the following:

- The deprivation of liberty is a broad concept and can include house arrest, banishment and compulsion to reside in a given area pending trial (*Monja Jaona v Madagascar*, 1982, HRC; *Members of Parliament in Zaire*, 1983; *Guzzardi v Italy*, 1980, ECtHR).

- However, an infringement of the right to liberty and security of person must involve actions over and above a mere restriction on liberty of movement (*Guzzardi v Italy*, 1980, ECtHR).

International standards

■ The purpose of arrest and detention on 'reasonable suspicion' is to bring the person concerned before a competent legal authority with a view to trial on a specific criminal offence or offences. Detention for the purpose of general interrogation is not permitted (*Lawless v Ireland*, 1960); *Guzzardi v Italy*, 1980, ECtHR).

■ A level of suspicion below 'reasonable suspicion' will not be sufficient. 'Reasonable suspicion' presupposes the existence of facts or information which would satisfy an objective observer that the person concerned might have committed the offence; hence, honest belief alone is not enough (*Fox, Campbell and Hartley v UK*, 1990, ECtHR).

■ A person's detention must end as soon as there are no longer grounds for suspicion (*Stogmuller v Austria* (1969) ECtHR).

■ A person who is arrested must be informed of the reasons for his or her arrest (International Covenant, Article 9; European Convention, Article 5).

■ Those reasons must be given 'at the time of arrest' (UN Body of Principles for the Protection of All Persons under Any Form of Detention or Imprisonment (*UN Principles of Detention, Principle 10, 1988*).

■ The reasons for arrest need only be given in general terms, but must indicate the substance of the allegation against the person arrested (*Drescher Caldas v Uruguay*, 1979, HRC).

■ The authorities are under a duty to record: the time of a person's arrest; the reasons for that arrest; the time at which an arrested person was first taken to a place of custody; the identity of the law enforcement official involved (*UN Principles of Detention*, Principle 12, 1988).

DATA

Police and emergency rules of arrest in the UK

The rules governing the exercise of police powers of arrest and detention in England and Wales are largely contained in the scheme created under the Police and Criminal Evidence Act 1984 (PACE). Broadly, the police may arrest anyone without a magistrate's warrant on reasonable suspicion of an 'arrestable offence' (i.e., one that carries a penalty of five years' or more imprisonment) or on reasonable suspicion of any lesser offence if certain specified conditions are met, which make the service of a summons inappropriate or impracticable (PACE sections 24 and 25). These conditions apply, for instance, where arrest is necessary to prevent the person from causing physical harm to himself or herself or others, or from damaging property or from causing an unlawful obstruction of the highway. Anyone arrested by a police officer must be told both the fact of and the reasons for the arrest, either at the time of arrest or as soon as reasonably practicable afterwards (PACE section 28).

Under the Prevention of Terrorism (Temporary Provisions) Act 1989 (PTA), which covers the whole of the UK, police officers may also arrest anyone without a warrant where they have reasonable grounds for suspecting that a person has been concerned in the 'commission, preparation or instigation of acts of terrorism' connected with Northern Ireland or any foreign country (PTA section 14) (see **Table 13.1**).

In Northern Ireland, the Police and Criminal Evidence (Northern Ireland) Order 1989 (known as the 'PACE Order') mirrors the PACE rules. Additionally, the Northern Ireland (Emergency Provisions) Act 1991 (EPA) authorises arrest on reasonable suspicion of a 'scheduled offence' (i.e., those commonly committed by terrorists, including murder, manslaughter, riot, kidnapping and false imprisonments; see EPA, schedule 1). The 1991 Act also authorises soldiers to arrest a person on reasonable suspicion of 'any offence' and to detain him or her for up to four hours (EPA section 18). The only information that need be given on such an arrest is that it is being effected by 'a member of Her Majesty's forces' (EPA section 18(2)).

Other powers of detention

As observed above, the word 'arrest' in international law has a broad meaning. Anything over and above a temporary interference with freedom of movement is likely to trigger the international standards set out in the Index above. Powers vested in the police, other than those of arrest, must therefore be scrutinised to check whether they comply with international human rights standards. In particular: the power to stop and search citizens in the street; the power to detain citizens whenever a 'breach of the peace' is feared; and the special power of detention at ports of entry under the 1989 PTA.

(a) Stop and search powers

The Police and Criminal Evidence Act 1984 gives police officers a general power to stop and search individuals in the street if they have a reasonable suspicion that stolen goods, offensive weapons or other prohibited articles might be found on them. The scope of 'reasonable suspicion' is similar to that applicable to arrest (see above). Before carrying out a search, a police officer should take reasonable steps to tell the person stopped his or her name and police station, the objects and grounds of the proposed search and that a record of the search will be made and will be available for inspection. The Criminal Justice and Public Order Act 1994 introduced additional powers of stop and search. It empowers a police superintendent (or in an emergency an inspector) to authorise officers to carry out stop and searches for up to 24 hours without the requirement of *reasonable suspicion* in an area where senior people think there may be incidents of serious violence. In addition, failure to stop in a defined area when asked by the police to do so was made punishable by one month in prison or a £1,000 fine.

In Northern Ireland, soldiers on duty have the power to stop people at any time, whether on foot or in a vehicle, and question them to find out their identity, their movements and what they know concerning any recent explosion or incident endangering life (EPA 1991). Any person who fails to stop when required to do so, or refuses or fails to answer questions to the best of his or her ability, commits an offence.

Powers of arrest

(b) Breach of the peace

Whenever there is a breach of the peace, or it looks likely, a police officer can arrest any person and take him or her to a magistrates' court to be 'bound over'. (See also **pp. 199, 201–202**). Alternatively, the officer may take other steps, short of arrest, to defuse the situation. In particular, he or she may detain anyone for as long as that officer considers necessary, even if the person detained is not actually causing the breach of the peace.

(c) Detention at ports of entry

The Prevention of Terrorism (Temporary Provisions) Act 1989 authorises examining officers (i.e., the police, immigration officers, customs officials and soldiers) to examine anyone on arrival or departure from Great Britain or Northern Ireland by ship or aircraft, or travelling by land between Northern Ireland and the Republic, to determine whether they have been concerned in the commission of acts of terrorism; are subject to an order excluding them from Great Britain; or are carrying a prohibited article. There is no need for 'reasonable suspicion', yet an officer may 'examine' someone on this basis for up to 12 hours. Examining officers also have the power to require the production of information and have extensive search powers.

Misuse of powers of arrest and detention

The rules for arrest by the police require that the arresting officers have reasonable grounds for suspecting that anyone arrested is about to commit, is committing, or has committed a criminal offence. And those grounds must be objectively made out – in other words, facts or information must actually be in existence which would satisfy an objective observer that the person concerned might have committed the offence. This fully conforms with international human rights standards. The position under the PTA and EPA is not so straightforward.

A police officer need only have reasonable grounds for suspecting that a person is concerned in the preparation or instigation of 'acts of terrorism' under PTA legislation (section 14). The officer does not have to have a reasonable suspicion that a *particular* offence is about to be, is being or has been committed. Moreover, once arrested under the PTA, a person may be detained for up to seven days for questioning. There is considerable evidence to suggest that the combined effect of these two features has enabled the authorities to use their powers of arrest under the PTA simply to gather information, rather than as a *bona fide* exercise to bring suspects to justice.

The great majority of people arrested under the PTA are later released without charge. From 1983 to 1993, some 1,782 people were arrested, and the proportion released ranged from 74 per cent in 1992 to 83 per cent in 1987 and 1989 (see **Table 13.1**). These are disturbing figures which indicate substantial misuse of the PTA powers. Sir Leon Brittan, then the Home Secretary, confirmed that such misuse was a matter of policy when, in 1985, he was asked to comment on the figures:

I think that is a very misleading figure because that suggests that the purpose of detention is simply to bring a charge. If that were so, there might almost be no need for the legislation. What the figures do not tell you is how much information was obtained, not only about the people concerned but about others, and how many threats were averted as a result of obtaining information from those who were detained. *The object of the exercise is not just to secure convictions but to secure information* [our emphasis].

(Radio Telefis Eireann, 'This Week', June 1985)

The proportion of charges to arrest remained roughly consistent from 1985 up to 1993. Therefore, it is reasonable to suppose that the government's policy remained broadly the same and would be resumed in similar circumstances. The wording of the Home Office circular to chief constables on the exercise of arrest powers under the PTA seems to confirm our supposition:

The prime objective of the exceptional powers in section 14 is to enable sufficient usable and admissible evidence to be obtained as a result of the *additional investigations they make possible* so that proceedings can be instituted against persons involved in the kinds of terrorism covered by the section [our emphasis].

(Home Office Circular 27/1989, para. 4.5)

Table 13.1 People detained, excluded and charged under PTA emergency laws (Great Britain, 1983–93)

	Total people detained	Exclusion orders made[1]	Charged with offence Under PTA	Other offence	Released	Percentage
1983	191	13	16	15	147	77
1984	159[2]	1	14	9	135	85
1985	193	2	15	23	153	79
1986	147	7	13	18	109	75
1987	184	15	9	8	152	83
1988	170	16	10	8	136	80
1989	163	10	8	10	135	83
1990	169	14	6	19	130	77
1991	121	10	4	3	104	86
1992	140	1	9	27	103	74
1993	145	4	5	25	111	77

Source: Home Office Statistical Bulletin, 'Statistics on the Operation of the Prevention of Terrorism Legislation', February 1994, Government Statistics Service

Notes:
1 Persons charged and subsequently excluded are shown under 'exclusion orders made' only
2 The 1984 figures include one person detained under the 1976 Act and subsequently excluded under the 1984 Act

Powers of arrest

The Index (above) shows quite clearly that detention for the purposes of general interrogation is not permissible under international human rights instruments. The arrests and detention of up to nearly 200 British citizens annually under the PTA, largely for intelligence purposes, therefore violates international human rights standards.

Finally, it is clear that the rules in PACE and the PACE Order conform with international requirements for reasons to be given 'at the time of arrest'. But the Emergency Provisions Act 1991, which allows soldiers to arrest citizens in Northern Ireland and explain merely that they are being arrested by a 'member of Her Majesty's armed forces', clearly fails to comply with international standards.

The arbitrary use of stop and search powers

The extent to which police powers to stop and search individuals are covered in international law is unclear. The European Court of Human Rights has decided that there must be something over and above a mere restriction on liberty of movement to constitute an infringement of the right to liberty and security of person (*Guzzardi v Italy*, 1980). A power simply to stop a citizen, therefore, may well not trigger international rules.

But where, as in the UK, the police have additional powers to search someone, and to detain them for as long as is necessary in order to carry out a search, the safeguards set out in the International Covenant and the European Convention may well apply. This is particularly likely where someone is stopped in the street and then taken to a police station to be searched (a power which is not infrequently used by some police forces for drugs-related searches).

This has an important consequence since Article 5 of the European Convention does not provide for a power to interfere with a person's liberty for the purpose of a search. The nearest it comes to doing so is in paragraph (1)(c) which authorises:

> the lawful arrest or detention of a person effected for the purpose of bringing him before the competent legal authority on reasonable suspicion of having committed an offence or when it is reasonably considered necessary to prevent his committing an offence or fleeing after having done so.

This could justify a search in circumstances which simultaneously gave rise to an arrest – but not otherwise. The PACE Code of Conduct clearly contemplates a situation which would appear to fall the wrong side of the line:

> where a police officer has reasonable grounds to suspect that a person is in innocent possession of a stolen or prohibited article, the power to stop and search exists notwithstanding that there would be no power of arrest.
>
> (Code A, para. 1.5)

In our view, such cases may constitute a breach of international human rights standards.

The latest figures (1993–94) for police use of 'stop and search' powers under the Police and Criminal Evidence Act 1984 indicate very considerable abuse of these powers. In the period 1986 to 1993, the police stopped and searched some two million people and vehicles; of them, only between 13 and 17 per cent were arrested in any one year (see **Table 13.2**). Concern about this arbitrary practice is compounded by very serious questions of discrimination. A majority of studies show that Afro-Caribbeans are far more likely to be pulled in for stop-searches than any other groups (Fitzgerald 1993). Practices of this sort have a major impact on the degree of political equality in a democracy (see Chapter 7).

The nature of the powers under the Criminal Justice and Public Order Act 1994 and the Emergency Provisions Act 1991 are even more worrying. Police officers are not required to have a 'reasonable suspicion' that the person they stop has committed an offence or is carrying a prohibited article. These powers can properly be described as arbitrary in the international law sense. To compound the violation of international standards, the police need give the person no reasons for the stop or search and need keep no records (despite the clear wording of Article 9(2) of the International Covenant, Article 5(2) of the European Convention and Principles 10 and 12 of the UN Principles on Detention).

Breach of the peace is a notoriously vague concept. Despite its long history, it has yet to be clearly and fully defined – in itself a violation of international human rights standards, which insist that any deprivation of liberty must always be 'prescribed by law' (see Chapter 10 on its effect on freedom of assembly). Further, as breach of the peace is not of itself a criminal offence, any arrest or detentions under its terms cannot be justified under Article 5 of the European Convention on

Table 13.2 The use of police 'stop and search' powers

	Searches	Arrests	Arrests as percentage of searches
1986	109,800	18,900	17
1987	188,300	19,600	17
1988	149,600	23,700	16
1989	202,800	32,800	16
1990	256,900	39,200	15
1991	303,800	46,200	15
1992	351,700	48,700	14
1993	442,800	55,900	13

Source: 'Table A: Searches of persons or vehicles under Section 1 of the Police and Criminal Evidence Act 1984 and other legislation, and resultant arrests, by reason for search and reason for arrest'. Home Office Statistical Bulletin, 'Operation of Certain Police Powers under Pace', June 1994

Powers of arrest

Human Rights (which requires at least suspicion that a criminal offence has been committed before anyone may be arrested or detained). Even if it were an offence, Article 5 would still not be satisfied since the *purpose* of arrest and detention must be to bring a person before a competent legal authority. However, a police officer can detain anyone for an indefinite period to deal with a feared breach of the peace and then release the person. Usually the person detained is not taken to a police station, still less before a magistrates' court. Thus, breach of the peace provisions for arrest and detention violate the Convention in several ways.

The 1989 PTA powers to detain people for up to 12 hours at ports, airports, etc., without any need for 'reasonable suspicion' that they have committed an offence or are carrying a prohibited article, violate Article 9 of the International Covenant, Article 5 of the European Convention, and Principles 10 and 12 of the UN Principles on Detention (for the same reasons as above). These powers affect a huge number of citizens. Lord Colville's official review in 1987 of the then existing 1984 PTA found that some one million people were stopped at ports of entry each year, to be questioned by an officer or made to fill out an embarkation card detailing their name, address, occupation, nationality, purpose of travelling and details of where they will be staying.

Powers of internment in the UK

The detention of people without trial has, on occasion, been employed in Northern Ireland (for example, it was used extensively between 1972 and 1975). In 1978, the European Court of Human Rights registered its disapproval of this practice (*Ireland v UK*, 1978). Internment powers have not been used since. But the power to detain people without trial remains on the statute book and could be invoked at any point. In theory, if not practice, this represents a serious violation of international human rights standards.

International standards on detention

The general rules prohibiting arbitrary arrest and detention referred to above in the Index section on arrest continue to apply throughout any period of detention. In addition, further specific rules apply. Article 9(3) of the International Covenant and Article 5(3) of the European Convention require that anyone arrested or detained on a criminal charge shall be brought promptly before a judge (or other officer authorised by law to exercise judicial power) and shall be entitled to trial within a reasonable time or to release. Article 9(3) of the International Covenant goes on to specify that

> It shall not be the general rule that persons awaiting trial shall be detained in custody, but release may be subject to guarantees to appear for trial.

On the question of testing the legality of detention, otherwise known as *habeas corpus*, Article 9(4) of the International Covenant and Article 5(4) of the European Convention require that anyone who is deprived of his or her liberty by arrest or detention should be entitled to take proceedings before a court to test the lawfulness of that detention and released if the detention is not lawful.

The evolving human rights standards which apply to detention pending trial include the following:

- To comply with the requirement that detained persons be brought 'promptly' before a judge or a suitably authorised official, delays must not exceed a few days (HRC General Comment 8/9).

- Four days and 6 hours was too long for someone to be held without being brought before a judge, even in a case involving the special difficulties attached to investigating terrorist offences (*Brogan v United Kingdom*, 1988, ECtHR).

- Pre-trial detention should be an exception and as short as possible (HRC, General Comment 8/9). It should only be necessary in limited circumstances, such as preventing interference with witnesses or repetition of the offence and absconding (HRC, General Comment 8/16).

- The presumption of bail has recently been strengthened by the UN Standard Minimum Rules for Non-Custodial Measures (1990), commonly referred to as the Tokyo Rules, which emphasise that pre-trial detention should be a last resort; and then only if there are reasonable grounds to believe that the persons concerned have been involved in the commission of the alleged offences *and* there is a danger of their absconding or committing further *serious* offences, or a danger that the course of justice will be *seriously* interfered with if they are left free.

- Account should be taken of the circumstances of the individual case, in particular the nature and seriousness of the alleged offence, the strength of the evidence, the penalty likely to be incurred, and the conduct and personal and social circumstances of the person concerned, including his or her community ties (Tokyo Rules, paragraph 2(c)).

- Pre-trial detention should not be ordered if the deprivation of liberty is out of proportion with the alleged offence and the expected sentence (Tokyo Rules, paragraph 2(d)).

- Although *habeas corpus* proceedings are not subject to all the requirements of a fair trial, the principle that each side have equal facilities does apply. Consequently, a detained person must have access to all relevant papers (*Sanchez-Reisse v Switzerland*, 1986, ECtHR; *Lamy v Belgium*, 1989, ECtHR).

Initial detention

Initial detention in criminal proceedings

In England and Wales, once a person has been arrested, detention at a police station is governed by Part IV of the Police and Criminal Evidence Act 1984. The custody officer (usually a sergeant on duty at the police station who has not been involved in the arrest) plays a central role. The custody officer must first ensure that a suspect has been properly arrested. If there is sufficient evidence to charge the person arrested at that stage, the suspect must be charged and then released on police bail or detained to be brought before a court. If there is insufficient evidence for a charge, the custody officer can authorise detention at a police station to secure or preserve evidence relating to the offence for which the person was arrested.

PACE sets an overall limit of 24 hours on detention at a police station without charge, unless the suspect is held in connection with a 'serious arrestable offence'. These are of two types: those which are always serious by their very nature (for example, murder, manslaughter, rape, etc.); others which in a particular case pose a particularly serious threat (for example, to security, to the administration of justice, of death, etc.). In such cases, suspects may be held for 36 hours, on the authority of a superintendent. Beyond that, a warrant of further detention may be applied for from a magistrates' court. The period of such further detention can vary but must not exceed 36 hours, after which further warrants must be sought. The overall maximum period for detention without charge in respect of serious arrestable offences is 96 hours (i.e., four days).

The detention of a person in a police station must be regularly reviewed to ensure that the criteria for detention are still met. The first review should be within six hours of the initial authorisation; subsequent reviews every nine hours thereafter. For the whole time that a suspect is being held at a police station, the custody officer must ensure that the provisions of PACE and the Codes of Practice made under it are complied with.

The position under the 1989 PTA is different. The PACE rules for detention do not apply to someone arrested under section 14 of the 1989 act (see above, **pp. 246–247**). The person arrested may be detained for up to 48 hours following arrest and prior to charge. This period can be extended by the secretary of state for up to seven days. In contrast to the rules under PACE, the extension of detention is not a matter for the courts.

Detention pending trial

In England and Wales, a suspect who has been charged must either be released (on bail or without bail) or brought before a magistrates' court, where he or she will either be released on bail or remanded in custody. Most cases of bail are decided under the Bail Act 1976 which creates a so-called 'right to bail'. The circumstances in which this right can be removed are stricter in cases where the offence charged does not itself carry a prison sentence. Significant changes to the Bail Act were introduced by Part II of the Criminal Justice and Public Order Act 1994. Bail will not be granted in any circumstances to a person arrested for murder, attempted murder, manslaughter, rape or attempted rape, if he or she has previously been convicted of the same offence. In addition, the presumption of bail has been reversed in respect of persons accused or convicted of committing an offence on bail.

Habeas corpus

Habeas corpus is a procedure whereby a detained person may make an urgent application for release from custody. This is usually done by issuing a writ for *habeas corpus*. The court hearing the application does not sit as a court of appeal to consider the merits of the detention: it confines itself to a review of the lawfulness of the detention. Convicted prisoners can apply for *habeas corpus,* but may not use this as a means of appealing against the conviction or sentence itself. If a detention has been ordered by an administrative official, for example, under the Immigration Act 1971, *habeas corpus* provides an opportunity for a review of the detention by the courts.

Derogation from international standards on detention

The extensive rules set out in PACE are sufficient to satisfy international requirements that detention should not be arbitrary and that a person arrested should be brought before a judge or other officer authorised by law to exercise judicial power. But there is evidence that the strict requirements of PACE are not always observed. For example, research in 1990 revealed that it is almost unknown for a custody officer to refuse to authorise detention of an arrested person at a police station where the arresting officer requests it (McKenzie *et al.*, 1990; Dixon *et al.* 1990). The routine use of rubber-stamps by several police forces when filling in custody records indicating that PACE has been complied with hardly reflects the careful consideration by custody officers envisaged when the Act was passed. There is insufficient evidence of the practice under PACE to establish whether international standards are being breached. However, there is clearly some cause for concern.

No such ambiguities arise when the position under the Prevention of Terrorism (Temporary Provisions) Act 1989 is considered. The UK is in clear breach of international standards. In 1989, the European Court gave a ruling on the question of detention under the identical provisions of the earlier Prevention of Terrorism (Temporary Provisions) Act 1984 (*Brogan v UK*, 1988). Four men had been arrested on suspicion of having been involved in committing, preparing or instigating terrorist acts. The initial periods of 48 hours detention were extended by the Northern Ireland Secretary to periods of five days 11 hours, six days 16.5 hours, four days and four hours and four days and 11 hours respectively. None of them were charged. Among other matters, they complained that they had not been brought 'promptly' before a court, a breach of Article 5(3). The European Court rejected the government's argument that special features ought to be taken into account in the context of terrorism in Northern Ireland and declared each case to be a violation of Article 5(3).

Rather than change the law in accordance with the European Court's decision, the government chose formally to derogate from its obligations to its citizens under

PTA derogation

Article 5(3) on the basis that a 'public emergency threatening the life of the nation' existed in Northern Ireland (for derogation from international human rights treaties, see Chapter 2). This derogation was itself challenged in the subsequent case of *Brannigan and McBride v UK* (1993), but the European Court accepted the validity of the derogation.

Strictly speaking, there is no breach of international law in cases where derogation is held valid. But the government's decision to derogate has been the subject of sustained criticism by human rights groups such as Amnesty International and Liberty. There is some force in their criticism. The UK derogated as long ago as 1957 in respect of Northern Ireland, but this derogation was withdrawn in 1984. Since British troops have been deployed in Northern Ireland since 1972 and there was no significant rise in violence from 1984 to 1989, it is difficult to discern an objective basis for the derogation. The Standing Advisory Commission on Human Rights has on several occasions also informed the government that derogation is not necessary. Before the *Brogan* case was heard by the European Court, the Commission had drawn the government's attention to the arbitrary nature of seven-day detention under the PTA (SACHR, Annual Report 1986–87: 73). The Commission's view, as conveyed to the Northern Ireland Secretary in September 1987, is that a suitable judicial safeguard could readily be introduced into the PTA procedure without interfering with the purpose of the legislation (SACHR, Annual Report 1990–91: 80).

Finally, it should be noted that the UNESCO Commission on Human Rights is considering a draft optional protocol concerning the right to a fair trial. This seeks to limit detention without charge to 24 hours and also to remove the power of states to derogation in respect of fair trial guarantees (UNESCO, June 1993).

Concern about new restrictions on bail

The 'right to bail' enshrined in the Bail Act 1976 reflects the presumption of bail required by Article 9(3) of the International Covenant. International standards have moved on since Article 9(3) was drafted and the UN Tokyo Rules now insist that pre-trial detention should be used as a means of last resort. Resolution 17 on Pre-trial Detention adopted by the Eighth UN Congress on the Prevention of Crime and the Treatment of Offenders (1990) only authorises such detention where there are reasonable grounds to believe that the people charged are guilty and are seriously likely to abscond or commit further serious offences, or to interfere in the course of justice (e.g., by threatening witnesses) if they are left free (see **p. 253** for precise terms). The Bail Act rules are not as strict and are now out of line with the evolving human rights standards. In addition, pre-trial detention where the alleged offences do not carry a prison sentence is seriously questionable in light of resolution 17 which states that it should not be ordered if it is out of proportion with the alleged offence and the expected sentence (paragraph 2(d)).

The 1994 Act's absolute removal of the 'right to bail' for certain offences infringes the older, more basic human rights standards enshrined in the International Covenant. Since the UK government refuses to sign the Optional Protocol to the

International Covenant which enables individuals to petition the Human Rights Committee directly, it is not possible to test this claim in practice. When this new rule was discussed in Parliament, the government could not give a single example of a person arrested for murder, attempted murder, manslaughter, rape or attempted rape who had previous convictions for the same or similar offences wrongly being given bail. In the House of Lords, Lord Ackner was quick to point out that 'The risk has been in existence for years and years and years, yet he [the minister] can give no example of the risk being wrongly taken' (HL Deb, 17 May 1994, c182). And again: 'Where the Executive seeks to interfere with the established discretion of the judiciary, it has a very heavy burden to discharge and the government have not got within miles of doing so on this occasion' (HL Deb, 15 July 1994, c1234).

The failing power of *habeas corpus*

Habeas corpus is the traditional bastion of British civil liberties, with its roots in the common law. Dicey declared that the Habeas Corpus Acts were for practical purposes 'worth a hundred constitutional articles guaranteeing individual liberty', but the constitutional lawyers, Wade and Bradley, have cast doubt on such proud claims and identified difficulties and uncertainties which are reflected even in the European Court (Wade, Bradley and Ewing 1993: 102, 727–730). The question has more than once arisen under the European Convention whether *habeas corpus* in fact meets its requirements; this is because *habeas corpus* does not deal with the merits of the detention in question, but only tests whether the court or official had the power to order detention.

In the case of mentally ill people, for example, it has been held that their detention has to be reviewed at regular intervals by the courts to comply with the European Convention. In 1981, the European Court ruled that the UK law of *habeas corpus* did not meet the requirements of the Convention because it did not permit sufficient enquiries about whether the continued detention of mentally ill patients was justified (*X v UK*, 1981). As a result, the government had to give patients the right to a hearing before a mental health tribunal for a review of the lawfulness of their detention (Mental Health Act 1983).

The detention of 180 Middle Eastern nationals during the 1990–91 Gulf crisis revealed the total inability of *habeas corpus* to provide an effective remedy in certain circumstances. The courts ruled that they had no authority to review the legality of the detention and proposed deportation of these people, since the justification put forward by the government was 'national security'. Instead the Court of Appeal expressed its confidence in the ability of the government's advisers to perform their functions fairly and efficiently (*R v Secretary of State for the Home Department ex parte Cheblak*, 1991).

International standards

The prohibition on torture and ill-treatment in detention

No one shall be subjected to torture or to cruel, inhuman or degrading treatment ...

(Article 5, Universal Declaration of Human Rights)

The prohibition on torture, inhuman and degrading treatment set out in the Universal Declaration is reflected in Article 7 of the International Covenant on Civil and Political Rights and Article 3 of the European Convention on Human Rights. In each case, the prohibition is absolute and without exception (there can be no derogation). In respect of detainees, it is supplemented by Article 10(1) of the International Covenant, which further requires that states ensure that all persons deprived of their liberty are treated with humanity and with respect for the inherent dignity of the human person. In addition, Article 14(3)(g) of the International Covenant protects the right of accused people not to be compelled to testify against themselves or confess guilt.

Both the UN and the Council of Europe have drawn up specific Conventions to strengthen these general provisions on torture, inhuman and degrading treatment: Convention Against Torture and Other Cruel, Inhuman or Degrading Treatment or Punishment (UNCA 1984); European Convention for the Prevention of Torture and Inhuman or Degrading Treatment or Punishment (ECPT 1987). Each instrument established a special committee to gather and consider information with power to carry out investigations in member states.

The evolving human rights standards which apply to ill-treatment in detention are as follows:

- Torture comprises deliberate inhuman treatment causing very serious and cruel suffering. Inhuman treatment comprises the infliction of intense physical and mental suffering. Degrading treatment comprises ill-treatment designed to arouse in the victim feelings of fear, anguish and inferiority capable of humiliating and debasing them and possibly breaking their physical or moral resistance (*Ireland v United Kingdom*, 1978, ECtHR).

- It is not sufficient for compliance with Article 7 of the International Covenant to make torture and inhuman treatment or punishment a crime: effective protection through some machinery of control must exist; complaints about ill-treatment must be investigated effectively by competent authorities and those found guilty must be held responsible; the alleged victims must themselves have effective remedies at their disposal, including the right to obtain compensation; education and information regarding the prohibition against torture should be included in the training of law enforcement personnel and any other persons who may be involved in the custody, interrogation or treatment of any individual subjected to any form of arrest, detention or imprisonment (UNCAT Article 10(1)).

- Competent authorities should proceed to a prompt and impartial investigation, wherever there are reasonable grounds to believe that an act of torture has been committed (UNCAT A.12).

- The right of suspects not to be compelled to testify against themselves or confess guilt refers to various forms of direct or indirect physical or psychological pressure, ranging from torture and inhuman treatment to various methods of extortion or duress and the imposition of judicial sanctions in order to compel the accused to testify (*Kelly v Jamaica*, 1987, HRC Application No. 253).

- No detained person while being interrogated shall be subject to violence, threats or methods of interrogation which impair his or her capacity of decision or judgement (UN Principles on Detention, principle 21(2)).

- Interrogation rules, instructions and methods should be kept under systematic review with a view to preventing any cases of torture (UNCAT A.11).

- The law must prohibit the admissibility in judicial proceedings of statements or confessions obtained through torture or other prohibited treatment (HRC General Comment 20/7; UNCAT A.15).

DATA

Statutory framework

Broadly, under UK law the use of force against a person is both a criminal offence and a civil wrong and torture is a specific criminal offence (Criminal Justice Act 1988 s.134). But the police and other law-enforcement officials may use reasonable force in the exercise of their powers in limited circumstances (for example, to carry out an arrest, to prevent an escape from prison and so on). Force is never permitted for interrogation purposes.

Yet there has been widespread concern at the use of physical force at police stations, and in 1984 the Police and Criminal Justice Act (PACE) introduced important safeguards, giving suspects the right, subject to certain limited exceptions, to legal advice; requiring that all interviews be tape-recorded; ruling inadmissible confessions obtained by oppressive means or which are otherwise unreliable; and outlawing any other evidence which was obtained in circumstances which would mean that it would adversely affect the fairness of the trial. PACE Code C lays out the procedures to be followed during police detention and interviewing of suspects, but failure to follow those procedures does not automatically mean that the evidence so obtained is inadmissible.

AUDIT

Formal compliance

At a formal level, UK law on the use of force complies with international standards. However, as Article 10 of UNCAT makes clear, it is not enough simply to criminalise ill-treatment: states must ensure effective protection through some machinery of control. Therefore, the question for audit is whether UK law is *effective* in eliminating torture, inhuman or degrading treatment. A comprehensive assessment is impossible. We concentrate on three areas of particular concern: treatment in police custody in England and Wales (in particular, during interrogation); detention in Northern Ireland; and the forced deportation and removal of allegedly unlawful immigrants.

Ill-treatment

One initial point of importance is the scope of section 134 of the Criminal Justice Act 1988. This was introduced to comply with international obligations arising from UNCAT, but it falls short of full compliance in two significant respects:

- The provision of a defence to torture on grounds of lawful authority, justification or excuse (under section 134(4)) is clearly inconsistent with the strict provisions of Article 7 of the International Covenant and Article 3 of the European Convention. Both require the absolute prohibition of torture, without exception

- There is no *specific* criminal liability in the UK in respect of inhuman or degrading treatment and consequently no duty on the police or any other public official to investigate and prosecute such conduct. Only when inhuman or degrading treatment involves the commission of an independent criminal offence or civil wrong could proceedings be commenced.

Police ill-treatment of suspects in custody

The treatment of people in police custody has always been a controversial issue. It is generally accepted that people in custody were ill-treated before the Police and Criminal Evidence Act (PACE) 1984 was introduced. On BBC-TV in 1993 three chief constables admitted that forces in which they had served had used physical intimidation, planted evidence and fabricated notes to secure convictions. The Commissioner of the Metropolitan Police, Sir Paul Condon, said: 'Quite often truth was the first casualty . . . I think that there was a time when a minority of officers were prepared to bend the rules' ('Panorama', 5 April 1993). Charles Pollard, Chief Constable of Thames Valley, went further: 'Everyone knew it happened like that – judges, magistrates, the whole criminal justice system had a sort of conspiracy that . . . if you didn't do it that way, you couldn't actually convict guilty people.'

Views diverge on whether the PACE safeguards have rendered ill-treatment of people in police custody a relic of the past. Evidence of ill-treatment is often difficult to collate and there is no fool-proof mechanism to isolate legitimate claims of ill-treatment from fabricated claims. We consider first those cases in which the courts have accepted that some form of ill-treatment was established; then, we widen the perspective with evidence from respected non-governmental organisations; and finally draw some general conclusions. In this way we can assess general patterns of behaviour without the need to pass judgement on the veracity of any particular claim. By necessity, the approach is illustrative, not exhaustive.

The starting point is criminal prosecutions of individual police officers. Since it is impossible to list and consider all such cases, the following snapshot is offered of the 12-month period from 1987–88 (see, generally, Thornton 1989: 54).

- Two Lancashire police officers were gaoled for life for the 'cowardly and brutal' murder of a drunken man at Morecambe police station.

- Five Metropolitan Police officers were convicted for their involvement in a 'fun' attack on five schoolboys in the Holloway Road, north London.

- On the same day but in another case an 'outstanding' policeman was sentenced for beating up a defenceless prisoner in a police van.

- In Newcastle upon Tyne two police officers were convicted of wounding when they beat up football fans in a police van (with a third officer, they were also convicted of perjury and attempting to pervert the course of justice).

- In Sheffield an officer was gaoled for attacking a man who taunted him.

- In Derbyshire an award-winning constable was convicted of striking a 16-year-old boy to 'teach him a lesson'.

Individual cases can be explained away on the 'bad apple' theory. But the findings of the independent inquiry into the working practices of the West Midlands Serious Crime Squad in 1991 suggest that there are also patterns of ill-treatment in the force (Kaye 1991). In 1988–89, the activities of the squad caused considerable public concern. It was repeatedly alleged that some officers consistently flouted the legal framework for police investigations provided by PACE. In July 1989, Sir Cecil Clothier, then the retiring chair of the Police Complaints Authority, described the squad as 'an abberation', adding:

> I don't know any other place where anything on this scale has happened. Obviously there is a nucleus of officers there willing to misbehave in order to secure convictions which they probably think are justified.
>
> (*Guardian*, 28 July 1989)

The independent inquiry, set up in 1990, investigated 67 cases. In every case the inquiry recorded an allegation of fabricated confessions and frequent allegations of physical or threatened abuse of suspects. In every case which proceeded to trial, an alleged confession formed the cornerstone of the prosecution case. In many, an uncorroborated and disputed confession was the sum total of the Crown's evidence. In every case, except one, a suspect's request for legal advice was delayed. Yet when legal advice was eventually given, none of the suspects made incriminating statements. The inquiry expressed deep concern and the courts shared that concern. Between 1989 and 1992, 13 people were released either by the trial judge or by the Court of Appeal in cases investigated by the serious crime squad.

There is no reason to believe that non-compliance with PACE is a feature exclusive to the West Midlands Serious Crime Squad. Many appeal cases have highlighted repeated breaches of the rules relating to interrogation (see notably, *Samuel* 1988; *Keenan* 1990; and *Canale* 1990). In the case of three men convicted of murder in Cardiff (*Miller, Paris and Abdullahi*), the Court of Appeal was 'horrified' after listening to tapes of Miller's interview and said:

> The officers . . . were not questioning him so much as shouting at him what they wanted him to say. Short of physical violence, it is hard to conceive of a more hostile and intimidating approach by the officers to a suspect.
>
> (16 December 1992)

Police ill-treatment

Yet, more generally, both the inquiry into the West Midlands Serious Crime Squad and a more recent study by Justice establish that allegations of physical abuse appear to have fallen since PACE was introduced (Kaye 1991: 73; Justice 1993: 5).

Allegations of torture are extremely rare (section 134 of the Criminal Justice Act 1988 has never been invoked). But there is continued cause for concern over ill-treatment. PACE appears to have improved matters, but cannot yet be described as an 'effective machinery of control' as required by the evolving human rights standards.

Evidence of ill-treatment in Northern Ireland

Ill-treatment of detainees in Northern Ireland has been a matter of concern for some time. In 1972, the Irish Government complained formally to the European Commission about the interrogation techniques then being used by the security forces in Northern Ireland. These included noise abuse, hooding suspects, standing them against a wall for many hours balancing on toes and finger-tips, deprivation of sleep and limited diet. The Commission found that such interrogations violated Article 3 of the European Convention, on the basis that the five techniques amounted to torture and inhuman treatment. The European Court agreed that the five techniques constituted inhuman treatment, but not torture, since they did not occasion suffering of the degree of intensity and cruelty implied by the word 'torture' (*Ireland v United Kingdom*, 1978). The five interrogatory techniques had already been abandoned, but concerns about ill-treatment persisted.

In 1991, Amnesty International pulled together many allegations of ill-treatment during interrogation, concluding that the records showed that 'existing procedures and safeguards are inadequate to prevent the ill-treatment of detainees' (Amnesty International 1991). For the first time, Amnesty issued an 'urgent action' notice in relation to Northern Ireland – that is, a request for Amnesty members to contact the authorities on behalf of a particular victim. In this case, Damien Austin (then aged 17) alleged that the RUC ill-treated him at Castlereagh interrogation centre. Austin claimed that he was verbally abused, punched, slapped and spat upon. In the Northern Ireland High Court, Austin's doctor swore an affidavit stating that he

> examined him in detail and found evidence of severe assaults to his body. In addition to the physical injuries, he appeared dazed and apprehensive . . . I can confirm that Damien Austin is being subjected to severe ill-treatment and the police doctor agreed with me on this.

In October 1991, Amnesty referred Austin's case to the UN Committee on Torture. In the same year, the civil liberties group, the Committee on the Administration of Justice in Northern Ireland, which monitored more than 20 cases, noted that there were still numerous allegations of assaults committed by police officers during interviews. A year later, an analysis of the instructions taken from 268 prisoners by Madden & Finucane, a Belfast firm of solicitors, given in evidence to the Northern

Ireland Human Rights Assembly in London, revealed that more than a third alleged physical assault (34 per cent) and another third (37 per cent) death threats (Hodgson 1993). In 1993, Helsinki Watch, the global human rights body, reported that its mission to Northern Ireland in April 1992 found that children were frequently stopped on the street, kicked, hit, insulted and abused by security forces and that 'ill-treatment of detainees during interrogation continued in 1992' (Helsinki Human Rights Watch Report, 1993).

In July 1992, the Northern Ireland Court of Appeal quashed the convictions of three soldiers from the Ulster Defence Regiment on the basis that interview notes had been fabricated. The three had been convicted solely on the basis of confessions allegedly obtained through ill-treatment and coercion while they were being detained incommunicado.

The European Committee for the Prevention of Torture and Inhuman or Degrading Treatment or Punishment has received a number of reports of ill-treatment of terrorist suspects by the security forces in Northern Ireland since it was set up in 1990. The Committee became so concerned that it visited Northern Ireland in July 1993 and its report specifically advised that conditions of detention at Castlereagh Holding Centre be improved without delay (CPT 1994: 45). In July 1995, the UN Human Rights Committee recommended the closure of the centre 'as a matter of urgency' (CCPR/C/79/Add. 55, para. 22).

Overall, therefore, there is evidence of ill-treatment in Northern Ireland, but no certainty as to the degree and extent of it. The ill-treatment probably does not constitute 'torture' within the meaning laid down by the European Court (in *Ireland v UK*), but in some instances it does constitute 'inhuman treatment'. To that extent it can be said that there is no effective machinery of control in Northern Ireland to safeguard people in detention against violation of their rights under Article 7 of the International Covenant and Article 3 of the European Convention.

Forced deportation and removal of immigrants

Home Office orders for the deportation and removal of immigrants are enforced by immigration officials with the assistance of the police or private security officers. There is evidence that the degree and manner of force used to effect these orders has amounted to inhuman and degrading treatment and possibly torture. In 1994, Amnesty International gave this example of the deportation of a Ghanaian man:

> Although his appeal against the deportation order had not been decided, this man was removed from a detention centre on 9 June 1993 by members of the S01(3) Deportation Squad. He was driven directly to the rear of an aircraft, forced up the stairs and then buckled into a seat even though he was still restrained in the body belt. When he became distressed and began to shout, he was held down by one officer and gagged with adhesive tape by the other in-flight escort.
>
> (Amnesty International 1994)

Unknown to the Deportation Squad, the deportation order had in fact been cancelled. The Immigration Service later apologised and claimed that 'despite efforts to the contrary', it was not possible for the removal to be halted.

The use of the mouth gag was finally suspended by the Commissioner for the Metropolitan Police in August 1993 after the death of Joy Gardner. On 28 July 1993, this 40-year-old Jamaican woman was arrested by immigration and police officers from the Deportation Squad for removal from the UK. Having been bound and gagged, Joy Gardner collapsed, fell into a coma and died in hospital four days later without regaining consciousness. After an investigation by Essex Police for the Police Complaints Authority, three police officers were prosecuted and acquitted of any criminal offence. The report will not be made public.

Conclusions

Historically, the physical integrity of most British citizens has been well protected in law and practice (but see stop and search). In cases not involving the security forces that remains the case. The laws governing the use of lethal force, arrest and detention in non-terrorist cases tend to comply with international human rights standards. However, the disparity between UK law and practice and those standards whenever the security forces are involved is alarming. The government has failed to assuage fears that there was a 'shoot to kill' policy in Northern Ireland; and it is certainly the case that entirely innocent people were shot down by the security forces in the incidents which gave rise to these fears. The judgment of the European Court of Human Rights that the lack of appropriate care in control and organisation of the arrest operation when three terrorists were killed in Gibraltar in 1988 violated the right to life was perhaps predictable.

The failure effectively and publicly to investigate killings involving the security forces compounds the dangers of bad practice on the part of the security forces. Coroners' inquests are a poor enough vehicle for such inquiries in any event, but the catalogue of problems facing coroners in Northern Ireland, long delays in hearings, and restrictions on their verdicts rule out any realistic possibility that the investigation of killings at the hands of the security forces conforms to international human rights standards. The sabotage of the one investigation known to be a serious attempt to get at the truth fuels suspicions that the authorities are more concerned to prevent their operational methods from being made known than to ensure that justice is done even in the trying circumstances of Northern Ireland.

The law and practice in relation to arrest and detention follow a similar pattern. Arrests which are carried out in compliance with the requirements of the Police and Criminal Evidence Act 1984 fully conform with international human rights standards. There is evidence of failings in practice, but it is not substantial enough to warrant an adverse finding. However, the powers of arbitrary arrest and frequent detentions for information-gathering purposes under the Prevention of Terrorism (Emergency Provisions) Act 1989 and the Emergency Provisions Act 1991 clearly violate international standards.

The accumulation of greater police powers to stop and search people without officers being required first to establish a 'reasonable suspicion' that people being stopped have committed an offence or are carrying a prohibited article can properly be described as arbitrary and contrary to international human rights standards. The fact that no reasons for the stop and search need be given in certain circumstances, and that people may be detained for up to 12 hours in others, compounds the violation of international standards. The fact that black people are disproportionately liable to be stopped and searched by police raises serious questions about claims to political equality in the United Kingdom.

Formally UK law adequately prohibits ill-treatment during detention. However, the allegations of ill-treatment set out above are a stark reminder of the potential for serious violations of human rights where no effective statutory scheme exists to regulate arrest and detention.

14   Britain's Missing Voters

The right to vote and stand for election

Free, fair and regular elections stand at the very heart of representative democracy. They embody the Audit's basic principles of popular control and political equality. Ultimately, it is on the ability of citizens to dismiss their elected representatives, and the parties for which they stand, that the principle of popular control over government is founded. The ideas of an equal value for each vote, and an equal right to stand for election, are central to the principle of political equality. Both principles thus require that the right to vote and to stand for election are legally guaranteed as individual rights if they are to be effectively realised.

Yet the essence of human rights law is the idea that these 'representative' rights cannot be fully realised without the protection of other civil and political rights – which, in turn, flourish only in a democracy. The Preamble to the European Convention, for example, identifies 'an effective political democracy' as the best protection of fundamental freedoms. Throughout the Convention and International Covenant, only those limitations on rights which are 'necessary in a democratic society' are permissible.

The United Nations has held that any law which restricts the ordinary enjoyment of the civil and political rights which are constitutive of democratic society is incompatible with the conduct of free and fair elections (United Nations 1994). This followed a statement by the Secretary General of the UN in 1991 that,

> democracy implies far more than the mere act of periodically casting a vote, but covers the entire process of participation by citizens in the political life of their country.
>
> (Report of the Secretary-General of the UN, A/46/609 and Corr.1, para. 76)

Thus the analysis of the rights to vote and stand for election, audited in this chapter, cannot be viewed in isolation from the other rights being examined in this book. They stand together.

International human rights instruments do not require states to introduce particular electoral systems, as the method of voting is not regarded as a human rights issue. Therefore this chapter – which tests UK electoral arrangements against international standards – does not address the question of the existing plurality (or 'first-past-the-post') voting used in most UK elections. However, the Democratic Audit's principle of political equality demands that citizens should possess votes of 'equal value'.

Plurality, or as it is better known, 'first-past-the post', voting in most elections in the United Kingdom does not give electors votes of equal value. The voting question is addressed in the companion Democratic Audit volume on political institutions. Other important issues, such as the under-representation of women and ethnic minorities in Parliament, the influence of the media on elections, and the unequal and secret funding of political parties are also dealt with in that volume. These factors have an important bearing on the aims of free and impartial elections and of equality between political parties.

INDEX

Rights to vote and stand in elections

> *Everyone has the right to take part in the government of his country, directly or through freely chosen representatives. Everyone has the right to equal access to public service in his country. The will of the people shall be the basis of the authority of government; this will shall be expressed in periodic and genuine elections which shall be by universal and equal suffrage and shall be held by secret vote or by equivalent free voting procedures.*
> (Universal Declaration of Human Rights, Article 21)

The right to vote is recognised in the European Convention (ECHR, Protocol 1, A.3), the International Covenant on Civil and Political Rights (ICCPR, A.25) and the CSCE Copenhagen Document (A.6). The former two instruments also guarantee a right to stand for election and to seek public office. The UN Conventions on the Political Rights of Women (As 1–3), the Elimination of All Forms of Discrimination Against Women (As 1–3) and the Elimination of All Forms of Racial Discrimination (A.5.c) confer the rights to vote, to be elected, to hold public office and to participate in public life without discrimination. The last two instruments specifically charge states with the responsibility for ensuring that equality of access is upheld.

None of the above articles explicitly mention the term 'democracy'. However, the notion of democratic elections may be said to be rooted in the concept of self-determination recognised in the UN Charter (A1.2) and Article 1 of the UN International Covenant states that, by virtue of their right to self-determination, all peoples have a right freely to determine their political status.

In 1962 the UN Sub-Commission on the Prevention of Discrimination and Protection of Minorities adopted the Draft General Principles on Freedom and Non-Discrimination on the Matter of Political Rights ('the UN Principles'). These elaborate on the standards in the Universal Declaration (A.21). In 1989, the Framework for Future Efforts at Enhancing the Effectiveness of the Principle of Periodic and Genuine Elections was adopted by the UN Commission on Human Rights ('the UN Framework').

The right to vote is expressed in different terms in the European Convention than every other article in that instrument. Instead of the usual phrase, 'Everyone has the right to . . .' or 'No one shall . . .' Protocol 1 (A.3) pledges, 'The high contracting parties undertake to hold free elections at reasonable intervals by secret ballot, under conditions which will ensure the free expression of the opinion of the people in the choice of the legislature.'

International standards

At first, the European Commission took the view that this means that states are obliged to guarantee elections, but individual citizens cannot invoke the right. In 1975, however, the Commission held that Protocol 1 (A.3) does imply 'the recognition of universal suffrage' and a right to stand for election (*W,X,Y & Z v Belgium*, 1975, ECmHR). This approach was confirmed by the European Court in 1987. The Court held that the phrasing does not reflect any difference in substance from other Convention rights. Rather it stems from 'the desire to give greater solemnity to the commitment under-taken' and to emphasise that the prime responsibility on the state is not so much non-interference, but positive measures to hold free and fair elections (*Mathieu-Mohin and Clefayt v Belgium*, 1987, ECtHR).

The International Covenant places far more emphasis on broader participation in public life. Its Article 25 confers the right to vote and to be elected in periodic elections 'by universal and equal suffrage' and guarantees 'the free expression of the will of the electors'. But it also gives citizens a right to take part 'in the conduct of public affairs', not just through elected representatives but also 'directly' and guarantees access 'on general terms of equality' to public service. (Broader issues concerning participation in public and political life are covered in detail in the companion Audit volume.)

Constitutional protection of elections

The rights to vote and stand for elections are expressed in very general terms in human rights instruments. The jurisprudence on these rights is limited; by the end of 1993, the European Court had heard just one case. The UN Human Rights Committee has yet to draw up a General Comment on the relevant ICCPR Article 25, but over the past three decades UN principles and guidelines have sought to establish accept-able democratic practices and procedures, culminating in a 1994 training handbook, *Human Rights and Elections*. On the basis of these developments it is possible to iden-tify the emergence of an 'evolving human rights standard' on the need for some degree of constitutional protection of elections.

■ 'Since it enshrines a characteristic principle of democracy ... [the right to vote] is accordingly of prime importance in the Convention system' (*Mathieu-Mohin and Clefayt v Belgium*, 1987, ECtHR).

■ Even a 'public emergency threatening the life of the nation' would not justify the suspension of parliamentary life (*The Greek Case*, 1969, ECmHR). If the right to vote were suspended for a long period, a state's membership of the Council of Europe could be called into question.

■ Those principles which ensure freedom and non-discrimination in the exer-cise of political rights can best be guaranteed in a constitution or other funda-mental law which should not be subject to repeal or alteration by ordinary legislative procedure (UN Draft General Principles on Freedom and Non-Discrimination in the Matter of Political Rights, 1962).

- Laws which might have the effect of discouraging political participation should be repealed or suspended (*UN Human Rights and Elections* 1994, para. 32).

Protecting the right to vote

Rights to vote and stand for election in the United Kingdom are governed by statute, in particular the Representation of the People Act 1983 (RPA). There are no special procedures to protect these rights. In theory, they could be repealed by a single statute passed by a simple parliamentary majority. In virtually every other liberal democracy, the right to vote is enshrined in a written constitution which can only be amended by special parliamentary majorities or a national referendum.

Some commentators maintain, however, that the acts which govern the franchise are protected by convention and form part of the unwritten British constitution. Given this conventional status and the weight of public opinion, it is unthinkable that Parliament would suspend elections or ignore their results (see, for example, Wade and Bradley, 1992: 21).

The absence of constitutional protections

Conventions by their very nature are elastic and capable of change. In moments of political panic and passion, British parliaments have shown themselves capable of passing controversial Acts of Parliament very fast; in the case of the Official Secrets Act 1911, in a single day (see **p. 76**). During the second world war elections were suspended. It is difficult to conceive of the circumstances in which national elections would be abolished in peacetime. The measures mentioned above had the consent of the public. While clearly the principal defence against any major attempt to suspend, delay or abolish elections would rest with that public, they lack the additional protection of constitutional rules to prevent them from being cancelled by a simple parliamentary majority. To this extent it is hard to argue that the right to vote and stand for election in the UK is given the special standing or 'solemnity' envisaged by international standards.

This has had particular significance for local democracy. With no written constitution, the respective powers of central and local government are determined by the government of the day. Over the past 15 years, central government has substantially reduced the status and powers of local authorities, even though convention had it that local government should be protected as a counterweight to the centre. The recent transfers of responsibility for many local services to non-elected local boards serve in effect to by-pass local democratic and electoral processes (Weir and Hall 1994: 36–40). In this context local elections are particularly vulnerable to interference.

This weakness was graphically illustrated in 1984 when the government cancelled elections for the Greater London Council by a 'paving bill' in advance of the abolition of this elected local authority two years later. As a result, responsibility for governing the capital city passed from an elected Labour authority to Conservative central government and various quangos.

Government interference

The poll tax – indirect interference in elections

The absence of constitutional protection for elections also means there are no formal safeguards to prevent the government of the day from indirectly interfering with the electoral process in a way that favours its interests, intended or otherwise. There is evidence to suggest that this was one of the consequences of the Community Charge, or 'poll tax', which was introduced in 1989 in Scotland and extended to England and Wales the following year. To facilitate the enforcement of this flat-rate per capita charge, local authorities were obliged to compile a register of residents in their areas. The register was drawn up and kept separately from the electoral register. But local authorities were allowed to check names and addresses in the electoral register.

Tens of thousands of electors faced large poll tax bills and many sought to evade payment; at the height of the popular discontent, a Gallup poll in 1990 found that 25 per cent claimed not to have paid their poll tax, of whom half said they had no intention of doing so (Smith and McLean 1994). It has been estimated that as many as 350,000 people in England and Wales deliberately took themselves off the electoral register in order to avoid paying the poll tax – with an additional number doing likewise in Scotland (Hodgson 1993).

The impact of the poll tax on voter registration was not uniform. For example, Labour-controlled Haringey and Lambeth, which set high poll taxes, experienced falls of 4.5 and 3.5 per cent respectively in their electoral registers between 1990–91, with a further 1.5 per cent fall in Haringey in 1992. In contrast, the electoral rolls actually rose in the Conservative boroughs of Wandsworth and Westminster, which received direct government assistance in achieving the lowest poll taxes in the country. Thus not only did the right to vote become indirectly linked to people's ability (and willingness) to pay the tax, but the impact on electoral rolls varied unevenly across constituencies. It was influenced by the government's distribution of local subsidies with a knock-on effect on support for political parties.

On one expert estimate, the poll tax may have cost the Labour Party up to seven seats, and the Liberal Democrats three, at the 1992 general election (Smith and McLean 1994). While such estimates have to be treated with caution, given the difficulty of separating out the factors which affect registration and voting preference, the former Prime Minister, Margaret Thatcher, herself gave credence to such estimates when she claimed that the poll tax won the 1992 election for the Tory party (*Sunday Telegraph*, 12 April 1992).

There were many warnings of the potential effect of the poll tax on the electoral register. But in the absence of constitutional protection of the electoral process, there was no mechanism for independent scrutiny and judgement. Instead, this important democratic issue became simply part of partisan debate, to be determined by the Conservatives' parliamentary majority. The poll tax was abolished when John Major replaced Mrs Thatcher. But the effect of the poll tax on the electoral register persists in many areas. And, crucially, the constitutional framework within which the poll tax was introduced remains. The impact the tax had on the right to vote suggests that, at least while the tax was still in force, Britain failed to provide the level of protection required by evolving international standards; in particular by those of the

UN Guidelines which require that laws which have the effect of discouraging political participation be repealed.

There is an interesting parallel with a recent case in the United States. In 1964, the American Bill of Rights was amended to prevent voting rights from being 'denied or abridged' for failing to pay 'any poll tax or other tax' (Amendment xxiv). As a result, the Supreme Court declared unconstitutional the practice in several southern US states of barring electors who had not paid the poll tax from voting – a measure which disproportionately affected black citizens.

INDEX

Restrictions on voting and standing for election

Most international and regional human rights instruments are universal in their application. They apply to all individuals who come within the jurisdiction of a state which has ratified them, and not just citizens of the state. Restrictions on rights generally apply only to the circumstances in which they operate: for example, protection of national security and public order are legitimate grounds for constraining many of the rights in the European Convention and International Covenant.

Rights to vote and stand for election are an exception to these general rules. They may be confined to citizens and certain categories of people can legitimately be excluded; then, however, evolving human rights standards allow for virtually no circumstances in which it is justified to curtail them. There is no explicit exclusion of 'election' rights from the articles which can be suspended in times of war or other public emergency (ECHR A.13 or ICCPR A.4). But as we have seen, the European Commission has suggested that even a state of emergency is not sufficient justification for suspending elections.

- Article 25 of the International Covenant is the only provision in the ICCPR that does not guarantee a universal human right. Only citizens have the right to vote, be elected and participate in public life. The term is not defined, but it may be assumed that citizenship is determined by nationality (Nowak 1993: 45). The CSCE Copenhagen Document also restricts 'election' rights to citizens.

- However, Article 25 states that the 'election' rights it confers must apply 'without any of the distinctions mentioned in Article 2' (race, colour, sex, language, religion, political or other opinion, national or social origin, property, birth or other status). They must also apply 'without unreasonable restrictions'. Reasonable restrictions are allowed, provided that they can be individually justified, do not breach the principle of proportionality and do not destroy the essence of the rights enshrined in A.25 (*Pietraroia v Uruguay*, 1979, HRC).

- The European Convention does not specify who is entitled to vote, beyond an undefined reference to 'the will of the people' (Protocol 1.A3). Restrictions on 'the political activity of aliens' are allowed (under A.16), but this is not explicitly linked to the right to vote as it is to other rights in the Convention.

International standards

Restricting the vote to nationals who reside in the country of which they are citizens is not a breach (*X v UK*, 1979, ECmHR).

■ More recently, the Council of Europe declared that resident foreigners are now a permanent feature of European societies, and they should all be granted the right to vote and stand for election in local authority elections. They must fulfil the same legal requirements as apply to nationals and have been lawful and habitual residents in the state concerned for five years (Council of Europe Convention on the Participation of Foreigners in Public Life at Local Level, 1992, Preamble and Chapter C, A.6).

■ Although states are given a 'margin of appreciation', or discretion, to attach conditions to the rights to vote and stand for election (see Chapter 2), these conditions must have a legitimate aim, the means employed must be proportionate to the aim, and they must not impair the very essence of the rights conferred (*X v Federal Republic of Germany*, 1960, ECmHR; *X and others v Belgium*, 1961, ECmHR; *Mathieu-Mohin and Clefayt v Belgium*, 1987, ECtHR). (See also, in general, **Box A, pp. 21–22**.)

■ All the major instruments accept that legitimate restrictions on voting rights include age and mental incapacity. The CSCE Copenhagen Document explicitly guarantees suffrage only to 'adults'. The only permissible exclusions mentioned in the preparatory meetings in which ICCPR A.25 was drafted were minors and people whose capacity is affected because they are mentally ill (Nowak 1993: 446).

■ There is less unanimity about the voting rights of prisoners. The European Commission has indicated that the suspension of the franchise for convicted prisoners is an acceptable limitation on voting rights (*H v Netherlands*, 1983, ECmHR). However a resolution adopted by the Council of Ministers as early as 1962 on the Electoral, Civil and Social Rights of Prisoners states that 'the mere fact of imprisonment shall not impede a prisoner from exercising his civil rights in person or through a representative acting on his behalf'. The electoral rights of prisoners can only be denied 'by law or by court order' (Resolution 62.2). Under the ICCPR, 'excessive limitations' on the voting rights of convicted criminals are unacceptable (HRC, ICCPR/C/SR.711 [1987]).

■ A similar set of limitations apply to the right to stand for election. Unreasonable restrictions on candidature would not only be a breach of the right to seek election under the ICCPR (A.25) but would interfere with the right of the people freely to express their will in elections. But given the higher level of responsibility involved in standing for election, additional exclusions may be acceptable, at least as far as the ICCPR is concerned. For example, certain groups like civil servants or military personnel might legitimately be excluded (Nowak 1993: 446–447).

■ Restrictions on the right to political participation on the grounds of political opinion are specifically prohibited. But limitations on political activities are permissible when they fall within the terms of other articles: specifically, ICCPR A.20 which prohibits incitement to race hatred or propaganda for war; and ECHR A.17 and ICCPR A.5 which prohibit states or individuals from destroying the rights of others. Under Article 17, the European Commission upheld a Dutch law which deprived people convicted of 'uncitizen-like conduct' during the second world war of the right to vote for life (*X v Netherlands*, 1974, ECmHR).

Who may vote or stand for election

The key criteria for eligibility to vote in British national and local elections are age, citizenship and residence (see **Box B** for disqualifications). Under the Representation of the People Act 1983 (RPA), all British, Commonwealth and Irish citizens of 18 years and above who are resident in the UK have a right to vote. In 1985, the RPA was amended to extend the franchise to the two and a half million British citizens living abroad. They are now entitled to register, as though they were still resident at their last address, for 20 years after leaving Britain and to vote in general elections. The minimum age at which citizens resident in the UK may stand for election to the House of Commons and their local councils (but not the second chamber of Parliament, the House of Lords) is 21.

Candidates for national elections have to be residents of the UK, but not of the constituency they are standing for (see **Box C**). Local government candidates must be on the electoral register for the council area (but not necessarily the ward) in which they are standing for election, or have lived, worked or occupied land or premises in that area throughout the previous year (see **Box D**).

BOX B   PEOPLE DISQUALIFIED FROM VOTING IN THE UK

- Individuals who are neither British citizens nor Commonwealth or Irish citizens who live in the UK (in Euro-elections, electors must be citizens of the EU)
- Minors (under the age of 18)
- People who because of mental illness, or another infirmity (including drunkenness), lack the capacity at the moment of voting to understand what they are doing
- Peers and peeresses (in national elections only) and the monarch. (With the creation of European Citizenship under the Maastricht Treaty 1992, it is widely believed that the Queen, along with peers, is entitled to vote in Euro-elections)
- Convicted prisoners following sentence and while they are in prison (unless they were imprisoned for contempt of court or failing to pay a fine)
- Anyone compulsorily detained under the Mental Health Act 1983 (unless they had registered to vote before being admitted into hospital)
- Anyone convicted of corrupt or illegal practices under the RPA 1983 (the period of disqualification varies with the offence)

BOX C   PEOPLE DISQUALIFIED FROM BEING MPs

- Individuals who are not British, Commonwealth or Irish citizens and do not live in the UK
- Anyone under 21 years of age
- Peers and peeresses and the monarch
- Church of England or Ireland clergy, ministers of the Church of Scotland and Roman Catholic priests
- Bankrupts for five years from the declaration of bankruptcy
- Anyone convicted of corrupt or illegal practices under the RPA 1983 may be disqualified for between five and ten years (disqualification may be confined to a particular constituency)
- Anyone convicted and imprisoned for a year or more (to last during the period of detention)
- Sitting members detained under the Mental Health Act 1983 for more than six months
- Employees in the civil service
- Any holder of a 'politically restricted post' in a local authority (Local Government and Housing Act 1989)
- Members of the regular armed forces and police force
- Any holder of a full-time judicial office (not a lay magistrate)
- Members of a range of commissions, boards, tribunals and other public authorities (the disqualification may apply only to particular constituencies)

BOX D   PEOPLE DISQUALIFIED FROM BEING LOCAL COUNCILLORS

- Individuals who are not British, Commonwealth or Irish citizens
- Anyone under 21 years of age
- Anyone who has not lived, worked or occupied land or premises in the local authority area for the previous year
- The monarch
- Bankrupts
- Anyone convicted of corrupt or illegal practices at previous elections
- Anyone convicted of a criminal offence and sentenced to imprisonment (suspended or otherwise) of three months or more without option of a fine is disqualified for five years
- Any local councillor surcharged by the district auditor for unlawfully incurring over £2,000 expenditure is disqualified for five years
- Any council employee who works in the area of the local authority or who holds a 'politically restricted post' in any other local authority

BOX E   PEOPLE DISQUALIFIED FROM BEING EURO-MPs

- Anyone who is not a citizen of the European Union and does not live in the territory of the EU
- Anyone under 21 years of age
- Anyone disqualified from membership of the House of Commons (excluding peers and peeresses and ministers or deacons of any religious denomination)
- Any member of the government (but not parliament) of any EU state
- Anyone who holds a 'politically restricted post' in any local authority
- Any member of the European Commission, European Court of Justice or Court of Auditors
- Any EU official or other official of a specialised body attached to an EU institution
- Any member of a range of committees or other bodies attached to the European Coal and Steel Community or the European Atomic Energy Community

All citizens of the European Union are also entitled to participate in elections to the European Parliament. A recent EU Directive gives all EU citizens the right to vote and stand for elections for the European Parliament in whichever EU state they live in, provided that they satisfy the same conditions as apply to the nationals of that state (see **Box E**). If, at their request, Community voters are entered on the electoral roll of their country of residence, their right to vote in their home state is waived (Directive 93/109/EC).

AUDIT

People who are denied the right to vote

With three exceptions, the restrictions in the UK on both voting and candidacy broadly conform to international standards. The three categories of people who are denied the franchise to a degree which does not reflect evolving human rights standards are: most prisoners, mental health detainees and 'aliens' under British immigration law (that is, residents who are neither British, Irish or Commonwealth citizens).

A resolution on the rights of prisoners, adopted by the Committee of Ministers of the Council of Europe in 1962, suggests the way that standards are developing in this sphere (although its force has been somewhat muted by the Commission ruling in the *H v Netherlands* case; see above). The resolution emphasises that where prisoners cannot exercise their civil rights in person they should be allowed to be represented. It also specifically states that where the law permits electors to vote without personally visiting the polling-booth, a detainee should be allowed this prerogative 'unless he has been deprived of the right to vote by law or by court order'.

Loss of the vote

Under common law, a prisoner likewise remains vested with all civil rights which are not taken away expressly or 'by necessary implication' (*Raymond v Honey*, 1983). Although it is the case that the right to vote has been 'expressly' removed from most convicted prisoners by statute, it is difficult to conceive of a reasonable justification for this additional, and somewhat arbitrary, punishment which goes against the drift of evolving international standards.

The denial of the franchise to nearly all convicted prisoners seems especially arbitrary, given that the same blanket ban does not apply to all election candidates. Until 1981, convicted prisoners were not disqualified at all from standing for parliament, even if their incarceration meant that a winning candidate could not attend parliament in person. In 1981, the law was amended, but largely to prevent prisoners convicted of terrorist offences in Northern Ireland from being elected to the Commons. Prisoners sentenced for a year or more are now barred from standing for election, or keeping their seat if already elected, for the duration of their detention (RPA 1981). Those sentenced for less than a year are still free to stand.

In a country which operates proxy voting for those who cannot attend a polling station as a result of disability or sickness (see below), it is difficult to argue that the denial of the right to vote to prisoners is a 'reasonable' restriction which can be justified because it meets a pressing social need, like enhancing the security of the public. Yet all limitations on human rights, unless they are explicitly allowed, should meet this test under international standards.

'Excessive limitations' on the voting rights of convicted criminals have, as we have seen, been deemed unacceptable by the UN Human Rights Committee. Committee members expressed concern about the denial of the franchise to prisoners when questioning British representatives about the government's record in 1990 (UN Doc. 1047, para. 59). As a consequence, the government's latest report to the committee states that it is reviewing its policy on this issue (Fourth Periodic Report by the UK to the HRC, 1994).

An even more extraordinary anomaly exists with regard to the voting rights of people detained under the Mental Health Act 1983. Mental illness is not in itself a bar to voting. Anyone who is deemed incapable of understanding what they are doing when they exercise their vote can be turned away by the presiding officer at the poll. But such incapacity is clearly not an inevitable consequence of mental illness.

However, under the RPA (s.1), people compulsorily detained under the Mental Health Act are prevented from using the hospital in which they are forced to live as their address for registration purposes. The act does not prevent detained patients from using another address, such as their home, but Home Office guidance prevents mental health detainees from being regarded as residents outside the hospital where they are detained (Electoral Registration of Mentally Ill or Learning Disabled People, Code of Practice, Note No. 5).

Voluntary patients, on the other hand, can use their previous residence as their registration address. Indeed mental health detainees who have already registered their vote prior to admission into hospital can exercise their right to vote, either through a postal vote or under escort to a polling station.

Loss of the vote

Bureaucratic procedures concerning registration therefore determine whether mental health patients can vote. Lord Rix challenged the government to amend the legislation in the Lords, but the Home Office Minister, Lord McKay, argued that it could distort local election results if psychiatric hospitals were to become recognised addresses for the purposes of registration. Whatever validity such an argument might once have had in the era of very large mental institutions, it carries little conviction in the era of community care. The minister also expressed doubt about whether electoral registration officers are qualified to assess the mental capacity of detained patients. But they already take such decisions in respect of patients in the community (HL Deb, 20 July 1995, c434–440).

This anomalous and arbitrary denial of the franchise to mental health detainees who have not already registered their vote does not seem to conform to international human rights standards. Mental incapacity is clearly a legitimate ground for restricting the franchise, but the same cannot be said for the mere fact of living in a particular institution at the time that the electoral register is compiled. No obvious pressing social need is met by this restriction. On the contrary, given that residents in other homes and hospitals can register to vote, and that mental health detainees who have registered prior to their detention are not barred from voting, it could be argued that this restriction breaches the equality provisions of both the Convention and Covenant (mental health detainees being potentially covered by the category 'other status') as well as the general equality provisions of the International Covenant (see **pp. 114**).

The position of aliens who live in Britain

Long-term residents of the United Kingdom, who are not British citizens by birth, registration or naturalisation, are disqualified from voting or standing in elections. These non-citizens are disenfranchised, regardless of how long they have lived or worked in the UK and whether or not they pay taxes here.

Two groups of people escape this restriction: first, the 1.5 million citizens from other parts of the Commonwealth (who are technically British subjects); and 400,000 Irish citizens resident in Britain who are eligible both to vote and stand for election (Report of the House of Commons Home Affairs Select Committee on the Representation of the People Acts, 1982–83, vol. 2: 1).

The second exception applies only in elections to the European Parliament. Since 31 December 1993, European Union citizens living in the UK, as in any other member state, can vote or be a candidate in Euro-elections on the same conditions as nationals of that state. Although the UK has formally complied with this requirement, British voting procedures and publicity have not been adjusted to assist EU citizens from elsewhere to participate in Euro-elections (see below).

From 31 December 1994, all European Union citizens have also been entitled to vote and stand for election in municipal elections in any part of the EU in which they reside, again on the same terms as citizens of the country. The government has not yet (September 1995) made any formal arrangements to meet this requirement. Assuming the EU continues with its drive towards integration, it is likely that the rights of EU citizens to vote and stand for election will in fact be extended to the national level.

The European Commission has also come out in favour of extending voting rights for local elections to all long-term residents in any member state, regardless of nationality (*Voting Rights in Local Elections*, House of Lords Select Committee on the European Communities, 6th Report, 1989/90). In 1992 the Council of Europe issued a Convention on participation in public life which likewise grants foreign residents of five years standing the right to vote and stand for elections. Norway, Sweden and Italy are the only countries to have ratified it to date (Italy with a reservation against the voting provision) whilst the UK and Denmark have signed it. Denmark, Norway, Sweden, Holland and Ireland already permit residents to vote in local elections, regardless of citizenship; the UK does not.

The granting of full civic rights to Commonwealth and Irish citizens is often said to illustrate the inclusive nature of Britain's democracy. On the other hand, the treatment of other long-term residents, who are denied any democratic rights, suggests that it is more of a historical accident of empire. Everyone born in the British Empire was deemed to be a British subject under the common law. If they lived in Britain, they were entitled to vote and put themselves forward as election candidates (though at least until the last phases in a colony's history, they had no vote at all in their home countries).

The contrast with the recent enfranchisement of non-resident British nationals speaks for itself. Yet developing democratic standards are, as we have seen, increasingly placing as much, if not more, emphasis on place of residence rather than inherited nationality in determining who should be eligible to vote – and stand for election – in a given state.

State obligations to ensure free and fair elections

International human rights standards require contracting states to take specific measures to ensure that the rights to vote and stand for election apply equally to all eligible citizens. Indeed, as we have seen, the European Convention sets out these rights as obligations on states rather than as individual rights (Protocol 1.A2). The evolving human rights standards for states in this sphere include the following features:

- Governments must take positive measures to guarantee that all eligible citizens have an equal opportunity to exercise their right to democratic participation. Proxy and absentee voting provisions should be designed to encourage the broadest possible participation (*Human Rights and Elections*, UN 1994: para. 110). It is not enough to extend the franchise to all citizens, including the elderly, disabled, pre-trial detainees, residents who are abroad, etc., if measures are not taken to ensure they have the opportunity to exercise it (Nowak 1993: 441).

- States must provide independent supervision of elections, appropriate voter registration and reliable balloting procedures and methods for preventing electoral fraud and resolving disputes (*UN Framework for Elections*, 1989).

- While elections must be 'free, at reasonable intervals' and by 'secret ballot', states are not required under the ECHR or ICCPR to introduce a specific voting system, such as proportional representation or majority voting. States possess wide discretion in their choice of electoral model, provided that the essence of the protected right is not impaired (*X v UK*, ECmHR, 1977; *Lindsay v UK*, ECmHR, 1979; *Liberal Party et al. v UK*, ECmHR, 1979; *Mathieu-Mohin and Clefayt v Belgium*, ECtHR, 1987; *Human Rights and Elections*, UN, 1994: para. 77).

- For the will of the electors to be freely expressed (ECHR, Protocol 1, A.2; ICCPR A.25.b), the principle of equality of treatment of all citizens in the exercise of their right to vote and stand for election must apply. Electors should not be put under any pressure or given inducements to vote for particular candidates. But this principle does not extend to requiring that all votes must have equal weight in determining the outcome of the election, or that all candidates must have an equal chance of victory. Any electoral system must be assessed in the light of the political evolution of the country concerned (*Mathieu-Mohin and Clefayt v Belgium*, ECtHR, 1987; see also *X v UK*, ECmHR 1977).

DATA

Rules for elections in the UK

Elections are regulated by the Representation of the People Act 1983. Most of the rules apply to the elections at constituency level and the main thrust is the prevention of corrupt and illegal practices. Responsibility for the official conduct of an election in each constituency lies with the returning officer, who is a senior local government officer (usually the local authority's chief executive). All voting is by secret ballot. The 1983 act seeks to achieve equality between candidates at local level by applying strict spending limits on candidates' local campaigns (which are nevertheless frequently evaded). The act also prohibits certain forms of expenses (for example, payments to an elector to display posters). There are no corresponding expenditure limits on national campaigns.

The United Kingdom has no formal Electoral Commission, as in Australia, India and New Zealand, to oversee the conduct of elections at a national and local level and to provide independent scrutiny. The Hansard Society Commission on Electoral Campaigns specifically recommended establishing an Electoral Commission in the United Kingdom (Hansard Society 1991: 68). The commission was especially impressed by the evidence of the Association of Electoral Administrators (AEA), which argued that bringing the responsibilities for the conduct of elections under a single body would provide continuity, ensure good practice and regulate the activities of EROs and returning officers. The removal of responsibility for registering voters from local authorities enables EROs to be seen 'to perform their duties independently and free of any perceived restrictions' (Hansard Society 1991: 69).

Northern Ireland has a Chief Electoral Officer who already, to all intents and purposes, performs the functions of an independent electoral commissioner. The AEA considers that this official has 'proved a success', while arrangements in Great Britain are 'less than satisfactory'.

The only formal means for reviewing electoral law and practice, outside the courts, is by way of a Speaker's Conference – a private meeting of party leaders, impartially chaired by the Speaker. In 1948, Winston Churchill described this as a 'well-established custom', which allowed issues affecting the interests of rival parties to be decided by agreement rather than 'be settled by the imposition of the will of one side over the other' (HC Deb, 16 February, c859).

It is possible to challenge an election result after it is declared by election petition to the Electoral Court consisting of two High Court judges (Representation of the People Act 1983). These are private actions between the petitioner and either the winning candidate or returning officer. Grounds for petition broadly fall into three categories – corrupt or illegal practices, administrative irregularities, or the ineligibility of the winning candidate. The Court has an inquisitorial role to seek out corrupt or illegal practices. The Court decides whether the winning candidate was properly elected or declares the election void. The Court then reports to the Speaker (Parliament has the final say) and the High Court. Election Courts to hear local election petitions are presided over by barristers.

There are no fixed parliamentary terms in British law. Parliament must be dissolved, and elections held, by the end of a five-year period. The terms for local authorities are fixed and more varied provisions exist. Elections to the European Parliament are held every five years.

There is a national system for voter registration which is updated annually. It is an offence not to be registered on the electoral roll (but there is no requirement to vote as such). Electoral registration officers (EROs) are required to prepare an annual register of electors in each constituency. Anyone who deliberately fails to be entered on the register may be prosecuted. In Great Britain, 10 October serves each year as the qualifying date for inclusion on the electoral register for the constituency in which potential electors are living. After a period during which a draft register is published, the register comes into force the following February. Since 1981, any eligible voter who was resident in an area on the qualifying date can add their name to the register if they have been left off (but not someone who has moved into the area since).

In Great Britain, no qualifying period is required to establish residency; people need only be in place on the actual day. In Northern Ireland, electors must have been resident in their constituency for three months before the qualifying date (15 September). This rule is apparently intended to prevent Irish citizens from crossing the border shortly before the qualifying date in order to gain the right to vote in Northern Ireland elections.

Since 1948, a number of categories of electors have been able to exercise proxy or postal votes when circumstances prevent them from attending a polling station in person. These include people who are unwell, or elderly, people with disabilities and people on holiday. The 1983 act also allows people who have to be absent from their home for up to six months in the course of their work to register in their 'home' constituency. This applies even if they have let their home in this period, provided they intend to return to their address at the end of that period. There are also special arrangements for members of the armed forces, merchant seamen or civil servants working overseas.

Absence of independent supervision

The conduct of elections in the United Kingdom falls well within international guidelines. There is no evidence of conspicuous abuses, such as intimidation, 'booth capture' and rigged registrations. The independent Election Court has, however, recently exposed one significant faultline in the system for supervising elections. British electoral law is almost totally blind to the existence of political parties; it regulates elections in terms of individual candidates and it was only in 1970 that political party descriptions could be entered on voting papers. Under existing law, the party descriptions are optional, and it is not necessary to include such a description to qualify as a candidate. Nor are political parties required to register. The informality of the regime under which political candidates and parties in the UK operate, means that the safeguards against candidates standing under misleading or confusing political labels are weak (*Sanders v Chichester*, 1994).

In other European states and even Commonwealth countries, like Australia and New Zealand, with 'Westminster-model' constitutions, parties are required to register. Their candidates are protected against opponents usurping their party label or standing under a deliberately confusing label. Electoral Commissions can decide doubtful cases at once, rather than retrospectively, as in the UK.

The dangers of this informality became clear in the 1994 Euro-elections. The Liberal Democrat candidate in the Devon and East Plymouth constituency lost to the Conservatives by 700 votes, while a previously unknown candidate standing as a 'Literal Democrat' polled over 10,000 votes. The official Liberal Democrat candidate had applied for judicial review of the ERO's decision that the 'Literal Democrat' nomination paper was valid. Complaints from voters poured in and the Liberal Democrats pursued the first election petition of any kind since 1962. The Divisional Court found that there is no requirement that the party description 'be true, fair or not confusing'. Mr Justice Dyson said, 'It is . . . clear that the Rules do not prohibit candidates (whether out of spite or a wicked sense of fun) from describing themselves in a confusing way or indulging in spoiling tactics' (HL Deb, 25 May 1994, c1101). The judge suggested that parliament might wish to re-consider whether the UK should not adopt a more formal regime for the conduct of elections.

The absence of an Electoral Commission compounds the problems highlighted by the 'Literal Democrat' case. Churchill's praise for the Speaker's Conference on electoral law could not disguise its inherent weaknesses. In that very year, he complained bitterly that Labour had broken undertakings given at the 1944 Speaker's Conference – not to introduce controversial electoral changes – in the Representation of the People's Act 1948. For their part, Labour ministers argued that the Conference's recommendations were not binding after the end of the wartime Parliament. In 1944, of course, the Conservatives had a clear majority in the

Conduct of elections

Commons and at the Conference; in 1948, Labour were in the majority (see Butler 1963: 109–122).

So much for consensus. But the Speaker's conference is simply not a suitable device for resolving matters of controversy between rival parties. The conferences are held in private, the reasons for their recommendations are not usually published, and the recommendations are clearly not binding on government (Wade, Bradley and Ewing 1993: 183). Moreover, electoral issues are too important for the democratic well-being of society and political equality to be left to partisan bargaining between the parties represented in parliament, or a mutually beneficial deal between the two major parties. UN Guidelines require states to provide *independent* supervision of elections.

The implications of the 'Literal Democrat' case are receiving 'close attention' by the government, but they are not being considered independently and openly. Rather Home Office officials have met representatives of the 'main political parties' to discuss ways round the problem, and are (as we write) preparing an options paper for a second meeting (HL Deb, 25 May 1994, c1114). The immediate problem may be dealt with, but it reveals a systemic weakness in the control of elections in Britain which will remain unresolved.

Britain's falling electoral rolls

A more widespread concern is the recent decline in voter registration, which is exacerbated by the obsolete system for registering voters. In Britain, between 5 and 9 per cent of the eligible population – that is, between two and 3.5 million people – are unable to exercise their right to vote.

The registration system was last fully revised in 1918. The register is compiled in October and is out of date when it comes into force (the following February); by the time it ceases to be operational, it is 16 months out of date. The system remains posited on the model of a stable family and a stable population. People now move home more frequently; as the Office of Population Censuses and Surveys (OPCS) study of the 1991 census found, nearly one in ten people move every year. In some areas there is more movement than in others. The population is now less homogenous, too: there is a wider spread of ethnic origin. Family life has broken down. Both old and young people often live apart from their families and there are far fewer recognised 'heads of household', willing and able to take responsibility for registering everyone living in a house.

The failure of the system to respond is reflected in the rising level of non-registration. The official figures for registered voters show a serial decline since the mid-1980s, from a peak of 97.7 of eligible voters in 1983–84, to 96.1 in 1989 and 95 in 1993–94 (HL Deb, 25 May 1995, c1113). 'The figures suggest . . . that a decline set in after 1984 and became more marked after 1987' (Population Trends, no. 64, HMSO 1991). But the official statistics over-estimate the proportion of eligible electors who are on the register for their qualifying address. An OPCS study, based on a sample check, shows that the official estimate in the Electoral Statistics of 95.3 per cent in Great Britain in 1991 actually represented just 92.9 per cent of eligible voters registered at their qualifying address (Heady *et al.* 1995: 2).

Other specific studies of unregistered voters, based on census returns, reveal a serial decline deeper than that the official 'broad-brush' statistics indicate. After the census of 1966, the OPCS estimated that 4 per cent of eligible electors were unregistered; in 1981, that figure had risen to 6.5 per cent, and then rose again to 9 per cent by the time the register came into force, leaving over three million citizens disenfranchised. The 1991 census revealed that over 7 per cent were not on the initial register. A special study, carried out by the OPCS social survey division for the same year, put the figure at between 7.4 and 9 per cent of eligible people in private households in England and Wales. More recently, Harry Barnes MP has analysed the official statistics for 1994 and found again that official estimates (which suggest that about two million potential voters are missing from the register) under-estimate the problem. Barnes's figures suggest that more than three million eligible people are not on the register in England and Wales. Barnes says that an internal memorandum from Dennis Roberts, OPCS Director of Statistics, states, 'surely the estimate produced by Mr Barnes is broadly correct' (press release from Harry Barnes's office, 16 August 1995; *Independent*, 17 August). Such figures are significantly higher than the 3–4 per cent margin of error which is officially deemed to be 'acceptable', given the inevitable shift of population each year (Report of the House of Commons Home Affairs Select Committee on the Representation of the People Acts, 1982–83, vol. 2: 203).

The government has been urged to modernise Britain's out-of-date registration system. In his Representation of the People (Amendment) Bill 1994, Barnes proposed the introduction of a computerised rolling register. In 1995, Lord Monkswell sponsored a debate on registration in the Lords and drew attention to the practice in some US states of allowing electors to go to the polling station on polling day to register and vote (HL Deb, 25 May, c1098). But a report by a Home Office Working Group in February 1994 dismissed the reform, largely on the grounds of the estimated cost (between £4 and £12 million). Ministers are said to be still considering the report and no conclusions are expected before the next election.

Inequalities in the process of disenfranchisement

This process of disenfranchisement is unequal. Further OPCS research for the 1991 Census Validation Survey found that non-registration was highest among ethnic minorities, young people, people living in private rented accommodation, and people who had recently moved. Lower levels of registration are also directly associated with Britain's poorer inner-city areas (see **Table 14.1**). The non-registration rate in inner London in 1991 was 20.4 per cent – in other words, more than one elector in five in these generally poorer areas is not registered to vote. Comparable figures for the rest of England, Scotland and Wales were 7.3, 6.6 and 4.8 per cent respectively (Smith and McLean 1994).

People in the specific groups who tend to be disproportionately excluded due to 'structural' factors, such as ethnic origin, disability, age, private renting and homelessness, also tend to live in urban areas. **Table 14.1** sets out striking contrasts, for example, between people born in the UK, Ireland and the 'Old Commonwealth'

Unequal disenfranchisement

Table 14.1 Who are missing from the electoral register?

	Not registered (%)
People living in	
Inner London	20.4
Outer London	10.3
Other metropolitan areas	6.0
Suburbs and country areas	6.3
People aged	
17	21.9
18–19	12.1
20	19.5
21–24	20.6
25–29	14.9
30–49	5.8
50 and over	2.1
Mobility	
Moved in the year preceding the census	27.6
Did not move	5.2
People's origins	
Born in UK, Ireland or Old Commonwealth	6.4
New Commonwealth citizen	36.6
Ethnicity	
White	6.5
Black	24.0
Indian, Pakistani, Bangladeshi	15.1
Other groups	23.5
People's housing	
Owner occupied (with mortgage)	6.0
Owned outright	2.6
Rented with job or business	18.3
Council houses or flats	6.4
Housing association homes	10.1
Privately rented (furnished)	38.2
Privately rented (unfurnished)	19.4

Source: Patrick Heady, Sharon Bruce, Stephanie Freeth and Stephen Smith, 'Coverage of the Electoral Register', OPCS, 1995

and 'New Commonwealth citizens' – just 6.4 per cent of eligible voters in the former group were not registered, as against 36.6 per cent of the latter. Taking ethnic origin, just 6.5 per cent of eligible 'white' citizens are not registered, as opposed to 24 per cent of 'black' citizens, 15 per cent of Asian citizens, and 23.5 per cent of 'other groups'. Established people who own their homes outright show a high level of registration (97.4 per cent); whereas less than two-thirds of people in the least secure homes – rented furnished from private landlords – are on the register (61.8 per cent).

Young people are also under-represented. A report in 1993 estimated that young people aged 18–25 comprised 18 per cent of the total electorate – but one in five fail to register to vote (British Youth Council 1993). The 1991 figures show that one in five 17-year-olds, who would qualify to vote in the following year, failed to register; and that after a small boost at the qualifying age for voting (18–19), only about one in five of 20–24-year-olds registered. So a high proportion of young people were likely to be disenfranchised at the 1992 general election. The absence of many of them from the register, however, represents disaffection from the political process more than structural disadvantage or discrimination; a recent Demos survey found that more than half of people aged under 25 were 'profoundly disconnected' from politics (Demos 1995: 17).

Homeless people – young and not so young – do suffer from unnecessary discrimination. To be classified as resident for the purposes of registration depends not on the nature of a person's accommodation, but on the permanence of their address. People living on the street will normally not be able to register because they do not pass the established legal test of 'a substantial degree of permanence'; in practical terms, permanence normally requires six months in the same place. But prejudice rules alongside the law in such cases. Certain local authorities, like Manchester, Camden and Haringey, will register homeless people at particular benches or doorways, and in 1985 the Court of Appeal found the women living in tents outside Greenham Common air base had properly been registered as eligible residents by the local registration officer.

People living in hostels, night shelters and bed-and-breakfast hotels are frequently not registered because electoral registration officers (EROs) do not consider that their accommodation has the required degree of permanence. Hostel dwellers tend to move from hostel to hostel; bed-and-breakfast occupants are by definition in 'temporary' accommodation. No guidance has been issued to officials on registering homeless people. They use their own discretion in interpreting the term 'permanent'.

It is very hard to estimate the size of the problem. The Campaign for the Homeless and Rootless (CHAR) estimates that nearly 63,000 people were living in temporary accommodation in 1992. Barrie Lane, registration officer in the north London borough of Camden, said that in 1994 about 2,500 people presented themselves as homeless to the borough. The 1991 census found 2,700 people sleeping rough in England and Wales; the housing charity Shelter estimated that the figure was nearer 8,000. Asked by the Labour MP Harry Barnes what records are kept by the Home Office of unregistered homeless people, the minister Charles Wardle replied: 'None.

Unequal disenfranchisement

Homeless people are not identified in the electoral register and no research has been undertaken on behalf of the Home Office into the number registered' (HC Deb WA, 21 April 1994, c643).

People with disabilities frequently suffer from a form of institutional discrimination which affects the general principle of the equal right to vote – the neglect of access for them to polling booths. SCOPE (formerly the Spastics Society) estimates, for example, that nearly nine out of ten polling stations (88 per cent) are inaccessible to people with physical disabilities. The government gives grants for the provision of temporary ramps, but only £70,000 was spent on this programme in 1994.

People with disabilities, and old and sick people, can use proxy or postal votes, but some at least of them have been deterred from using these methods for fear that their vote will go astray or be misused. Applications for a postal or proxy vote are made on the same form, and after the last election, a number of such electors found that they had been deprived of their postal vote and instead a proxy vote had been cast for a party other than their chosen party, in most cases for the Conservative Party (see 'Granny Farmers', *Guardian*, 2 November 1994). There are complaints that postal and proxy votes are poorly advertised and forms are not readily available.

People who have applied for a postal or proxy vote are kept on a permanent list. People can also apply for such a vote in a particular election up to 13 days before polling day (or six days in the case of sudden illness or incapacity). Disability groups have argued that postal and proxy votes should be better publicised and that the 'cut-off' dates for applying are too restrictive. Postal and proxy votes, available on demand and with later deadlines, would enable many people who are old, or disabled, or otherwise disadvantaged, to exercise their most basic democratic right of all – the right to vote.

Since there is a tendency among the most affected groups to vote Labour or Liberal Democrat, the combined impact of this unequal access to the register has the potential to alter the outcome of a general election. In many constituencies, the loss of eligible voters is greater than the parliamentary majority. This is of particular concern given the requirement under international standards that elections be fair and that all citizens be treated equally in the exercise of their vote.

The duty to promote voting

The British government is under a duty actively to promote registration. The UN Human Rights and Elections guidelines emphasise that governments are obliged to take positive steps to ensure that the citizens have the right to vote. But the government in general displays a remarkable complacency, to which Wardle's reply above is partial testimony. In 1994, the government spent just £700,000 on the Home Office's national campaign to publicise the need to register, and local authorities spent some £40 million between them. It has been calculated that the government spends in total only 1.2p for each eligible elector on promoting voter registration nationally (Blackburn 1993: 79). For the past two years, the government has begun

Table 14.2 Estimated local spending on registration of electors, 1994–1995

Approximate spending per head (mid-1993)	No. of authorities spending at this level
Over £2.00 per head	3 (City of London, Kensington & Chelsea and Westminster)
£1.50 to £2.00	13
£1.00 to £1.49	70
50p to 99p	241
1p to 49p	37
Total	364

Source: HC Deb WA, 25 April 1955, c477

Note: This table is compiled from figures for each local authority which may vary by up to 2p from the actual level. This means that the number of local authorities in the categories above may vary from 5 to 16 against those shown. The true level for the City of London lies within the range £18.99–£19.24

to use television advertising, some of it targeted, via satellite and cable TV, on young people, inner-city residents and members of ethnic minorities. This publicity has raised awareness of the opportunity to register from 27 per cent of the population to 57 per cent, and among 16–24-year-olds from 22 to 41 per cent (Baroness Blatch, HL Deb, 25 May 1995, c1104–1105).

The Home Office refuses to provide MPs with figures for spending at local level on the ground that the information is 'not available centrally', let alone to give the relevant figures on a per capita basis. (In fact, there is an annual survey of EROs; the information is available, but is kept confidential.) The Democratic Audit asked Tony Wright MP to seek local figures for registration expenditure in 1994–95 from the Department of the Environment itself (HC Deb WA, 25 April 1995, c472) and then combined the figures with population estimates from 1993 to produce approximate per capita totals for every local authority. The figures for *per capita* expenditure on registration of voters (see **Table 14.2**) reveal remarkably wide disparities of spending among local authorities.

In all, 278 authorities – three quarters of the total – spent less than £1 a head on registration. Even among the same types of authorities wide variations in spending are apparent. For example, among London's inner boroughs expenditure varied between £2.61 a head in Kensington & Chelsea and £2.06 in Westminster to 87p in Lambeth and 72p in Lewisham. The OPCS annual survey of registration officers in 1993 found that just over half (52 per cent) of 334 authorities responding spent less than £1, with another 45 per cent spending between £1 and £2 (Freeth 1994: 12).

The 1983 act sets a minimum standard for registration processes locally. The act requires EROs 'to take reasonable steps to obtain the information required'

Promoting the vote

Table 14.3 Canvassing for the 1993 electoral register

	Initial canvass	First reminder	Second reminder	Third reminder
Post	27	31	16	11
Post and hand delivery	22	14	4	0
Hand delivery	37	24	8	1
Personal contact attempted	14	30	69	64
No reminder	—	—	3	25
Base: 390 local authorities				

Source: 'Compiling the Electoral Register', 1993, HMSO

(section 9), which include 'house to house or other sufficient inquiry' (section 10). The judge in the Milton Keynes case (see below) emphasised that EROs were obliged to 'make sufficient house to house inquiries', but overall the act's requirements leave EROs with a high degree of discretion in carrying out their duties. The Home Office states that EROs 'need to operate a simultaneous local publicity campaign' (posters, local newspaper and radio publicity) to supplement its own national effort. It also encourages best practice through its annual surveys, recommending the use of personal canvassers and of specially designed forms (the pre-printed Form A which differs from the standard HMSO design). Using both methods would, according to OPCS estimates, raise response by 3.1 per cent. However, in inner London and other inner-city areas, the 'difficult environment' outweighs the benefits of their use (Freeth 1994: viii).

Personal canvassers, as recommended by the Home Office, are the most prominent method at second and third reminder stages (see **Table 14.3**). A steady growth in the use of hand and postal delivery, at the expense of using personal canvassers, between 1987 and 1992, did not continue at these stages into 1993. Only 7 per cent of EROs did not use personal contact at all; over 70 per cent attempted personal canvassers at some stage. The use of pre-printed Form As doubled between 1987 and 1993 from 20 to 39 per cent of authorities, with London boroughs (62 per cent) and metropolitan councils (67 per cent) in the van.

In 1993, about 80 per cent of local authorities organised a local publicity campaign. London boroughs were most likely to have a campaign (95 per cent), while non-metropolitan districts were least likely (75 per cent). Most local publicity relied on Home Office posters (81 per cent) and local newspapers (79 per cent).

There has been considerable criticism of local efforts to register electors, but largely at the anecdotal level. Individual EROs state that many local authorities 'just don't bother'. A series of interviews with EROs for the Home Office found that 'a high proportion' of them were almost unaware of the Home Office's Code of Practice, issued in 1984, and that they rarely followed official advice to collect information on their performance. Response levels remain the most critical information necessary for choosing canvass methods and targeting areas of poor response. Yet, in 1993, only half the EROs, for example, knew the initial or final response rates for individual poll districts. 'While still low, this has improved since 1990 when only a third could supply response figures,' the OPCS annual survey notes (Freeth 1994: 9). The 1987 study was also very critical of the variable quality of canvassing in local authority areas (Pinto-Duschinsky 1987). Since then, however, the Home Office has taken measures to raise standards and some 97 per cent of EROs participate in the annual OPCS surveys.

EROs themselves are servants of the Crown, and thus formally independent of local authorities. But they are funded and resourced by their authorities which can therefore influence their conduct. On occasion, it is alleged that authorities have taken political decisions not to pursue their responsibilities towards electors as actively as they should. In Brent, in north London, the level of registered voters fell by 15 per cent between November 1991 and 1992 (*Independent*, 11 December 1992). The minority Labour group on Brent council initiated judicial review proceedings against the alleged failure of the ERO to establish the real number of eligible electors. The council, which had initially claimed that the register was reasonably accurate, employed a private company to canvass residents. Some 15,000 electors were restored to the register.

The Labour Party did take a case to court in 1993 against Milton Keynes council and the ERO who had failed to conduct a house-to-house canvass. The council instructed the ERO to reduce his budget and stated that its target figure of registering 80 per cent of eligible voters was sufficient to discharge his statutory duties. The High Court ruled that the council could not restrict registration (*Independent*, 4 October 1993). Most local authorities are not so foolish as to specify targets of this kind.

With regard to European elections, the government has done no more to promote registration of EU citizens resident here than to send information sheets to embassies and specialist agencies. In February 1994, Peter Lloyd, the Home Office Minister, stated that EU citizens would have to apply themselves to register to vote; 'We shall not be placing on electoral registration officers a duty to seek out non-British or non-Irish citizens for registration' (HC Deb, 15 February 1994, c817). It is hardly surprising, therefore, that the UK achieved only 0.72 per cent take-up, the lowest of all EU countries, in the 1994 Euro-elections (HL Deb, 25 May 1995, c1107).

However, spending on electoral registration is generally low, at national and local level, and the need to update and improve the system is evidently being blocked largely for reasons of cost. Local campaigns in general are also poorly resourced. Efforts in a sizeable minority of authorities seem often to be confined to the duty of EROs to 'take reasonable steps' to ensure that the register is accurate, rather than pro-active measures to add to it. While any judgement has to be on the basis of inadequate official information, the figures add weight to the suggestion that the government is not adequately fulfilling its obligation under UN guidelines to take positive action to encourage citizens to register in order to participate in elections.

Conclusions

National elections in the UK broadly meet evolving human rights standards, being held at regular intervals by secret ballot and being free of intimidation, bribery and other abuses. Nevertheless, the informality of the rules and practices governing elections means that damaging defects can prejudice fully free and impartial elections. Our analysis establishes that the reputation this country still holds as a leading exponent of fair elections, whilst substantially merited, is not fully reflected in the conduct of British elections. The 1918 registration system is obsolete and needs to be adapted to the needs of a more mobile and pluralist society. Between 2 and 3.5 million eligible voters are disenfranchised at any one time. The main reason for government inaction seems to be a desire to save between £4 and £12 million annually, which is scarcely a large sum to secure what Baroness Blatch, a government spokesperson, accurately described as 'one of the most fundamental elements of our democracy' (HL Deb, 25 May 1995, c1109). Not only are progressively fewer eligible people registered. The under-registration of disadvantaged groups points to structural inequalities in the operation of registration procedures.

The denial of voting rights to most convicted prisoners and homeless people, and the arbitrary bureaucratic refusal to give classes of mental health detainees the vote – not on the grounds of competence, but on secondary grounds – comes close to violating evolving human rights standards and certainly falls short of best international practice. Long-term residents who are non-citizens are also denied civic and political rights – a situation which also goes against the grain of best practice. Defects in arrangements for postal and proxy votes go unremedied, thus denying elderly and sick people, people with disabilities and others a full opportunity to exercise their votes.

The informality of the voting system is vulnerable to abuse. The most serious problem is the absence of strict rules governing the descriptions of candidates and parties on ballot papers. As the 'Literal Democrat' case shows, this absence can deprive a serious candidate of a winning majority because another candidate – for political advantage, 'spite' or 'a wicked sense of fun' – elects to enter a misleading description on the ballot paper. The courts are powerless to give an aggrieved candidate – and the local electors – any remedy and reform lies not in the hands of an independent and impartial body, but with the government of the day and informal talks with other political parties. This is another illustration of the weakness of Britain's informal approach to questions of democratic practice.

Certain specific defects, then, require to be amended before the rights to vote and stand for election in the UK can be said wholly to meet evolving human rights standards. Not least, UK elections require constitutional protection, which goes beyond reliance on statute law and convention, to buttress their popular defence if it should ever become necessary.

PART 4

The Balance Sheet

15 Findings

The system and individual freedoms

In this section, we extract a series of findings from Parts 2 and 3 auditing first the system for protecting political rights and freedoms in the United Kingdom, and then each individual right itself. These findings are not necessarily all negative. In all, 25 main findings emerge from the chapters examining the system for protecting political freedom and 76 findings relate to individual rights and freedoms. This section is followed by the overall conclusions of the audit.

PART 2 THE UK FRAMEWORK FOR PROTECTING RIGHTS

Parliament

- Parliament is traditionally regarded as the forum in which the civil liberties of UK citizens are protected both against the state and private encroachment. However, by virtue of its disciplined majority in the House of Commons, the government of the day dominates the chamber, determines the legislative programme and normally delivers its legislation without hindrance. Parliament is not equipped and organised to bring strong and informed scrutiny to bear on intended legislation and normally votes, even at committee stage where bills are supposed to be closely assessed, wholly on party political lines (**pp. 46–57 and 61–66**).

- The doctrine of ministerial responsibility is supposed to render ministers and public officials accountable in Parliament, but it is a fiction of convention which tends to block any real measure of accountability of either ministers or public servants or bodies to members (**pp. 64–65 and 70**).

- Delegated and quasi-legislation can give rise to serious violations of rights, but Parliament has scarcely any effective oversight of the mass of secondary instruments which pour through the chamber annually. Such instruments cannot be amended and even those safeguards which exist are commonly by-passed (**pp. 66–67**).

- The House of Lords performs the role of a revising chamber. The House possesses delaying powers, but its lack of democratic legitimacy makes peers reluctant ever to press amendments; thus the Lords normally advises, and consents to the rejection of its advice (**p. 89**).

Public opinion

- Any free and democratic nation ultimately depends for its protection against oppression on the culture of democracy and liberty of individual citizens. The UK has a strong civil society, in which a great diversity of national and local organisations are active, many of them devoted to protecting rights of all kinds. But public opinion is not constant and has occasioned and been used to justify notorious violations of human rights over the past century. The current trend in public opinion is towards attitudes which are less tolerant of political protest and other political rights and more tolerant of restrictions on the rights of accused persons or suspects (Chapter 4 and **pp. 134–135**).

The courts

- By interpreting statutes in conformity with general notions of fairness and justice, judges can and do strengthen democracy in the UK; but their ability to protect internationally recognised human rights by this means is severely restricted (**p. 92**).

- The courts lack the means to restrain Parliament when it passes legislation which violates internationally recognised human rights or 'basic interests' under the common law. The principle of parliamentary sovereignty requires the courts to apply any legislation properly passed by Parliament, regardless of its effect on human rights (**p. 93**).

- Judges may resolve ambiguities in the law to minimise the infringement of fundamental rights, but the very same rights must be overridden if the meaning of legislation or its 'necessary implication' is clear (**p. 93**).

- International human rights treaties, such as the International Covenant on Civil and Political Rights and European Convention on Human Rights, are shown by the available evidence to have little or no effective influence in the domestic courts (**pp. 105–107**).

- Even where ambiguities in the law give judges the opportunity to take international human rights instruments, such as the European Convention, into account, the extent to which they do so varies widely from judge to judge (**p. 93**).

- In theory the International Covenant has the same status in UK law as the European Convention. In practice, it is infrequently cited in argument and even more rarely relied upon in judgments (**p. 106**).

- The ability of the courts to ensure, through judicial review, that public bodies and officials do not exceed the authority given to them by Parliament can and sometimes does act as an effective brake on the erosion of civil liberties in the UK. But there are significant limitations to their powers of restraint:

  — the judiciary are still very reluctant to intervene in certain key areas of government activity (for example, national security, official secrecy, etc.)

- — the merits of a decision cannot be questioned, even where it conflicts with internationally recognised human rights
  - — compliance with international human rights obligations is not considered to be a requirement of fair decision-making
  - — the courts have resisted all attempts to re-fashion the irrationality principle in judicial review proceedings to reflect the approach taken by the European Court of Human Rights to the curtailment of civil and political rights (**pp. 95–99**).

- Insofar as the political rights and freedoms, recognised and protected in international human rights instruments, coincide with the 'basic interests' recognised by the common law, they receive full and effective protection in the UK. Where they diverge, aggrieved citizens receive less effective protection of their civil and political rights – or none at all (**p. 100**).

- Privacy, freedom of information and even equality, are not recognised as 'basic interests' by the common law – and so these fundamental rights and freedoms are poorly protected, if at all (**pp. 100–103**).

- Equality before the law does not mean equal access to the law. Legal aid remains unavailable in many cases which affect ordinary citizens – inquests, libel, unfair dismissal and discrimination – and sharp financial reductions in other cases have seriously damaged the reality of the principle (**pp. 100–101**).

- The flexibility of law in the UK, with no written constitution, can advance and protect fundamental rights through statute and the common law. Equally, both areas of the law can act against them – even on occasions infringing the basic international rule that all restrictions on civil and political rights be 'prescribed by law' (**pp. 104–105**).

- European Union law does recognise fundamental rights derived from international human rights instruments, such as the European Convention, and such rights can infiltrate into UK law. But EU law is limited to areas of economic activity and its influence in the UK has so far been confined to certain aspects of equality at work and freedom of movement for workers throughout Europe (**pp. 108–109**).

Equality

- The absence both of a constitutional and judicial principle of equal protection of the law contravenes the International Covenant on Civil and Political Rights and means that significant inequalities in areas of life not covered by anti-discrimination laws remain unchecked in the UK (**pp. 117–120**).

- There is no comprehensive code which prohibits discrimination in the UK. What statutory protection there is outlaws particular types of discrimination in specific and carefully defined circumstances. Statute and common law therefore fall short of international human rights standards (**p. 118**).

- The nature and scale of exemptions to the anti-discrimination legislation, especially those for public officials dealing with the public, are too wide to comply with those standards (**pp. 125–128**).

- There is no evidence to suggest that the UK government has reviewed its national and local policies and amended, rescinded or nullified any laws and regulations which have the effect of creating or perpetuating racial discrimination, as it agreed to do when it signed the UN Covenant on the Elimination of All Forms of Racial Discrimination (**p. 127**).

- Long delays and other practical defects in procedure in some cases under the anti-discrimination legislation call into question UK compliance with international requirements of effective remedies for aggrieved citizens (**p. 128**).

- The Disabled Persons (Employment) Act 1944 has proven to be wholly ineffective in protecting disabled people from discrimination. It is yet to be seen how effective the Disabilities Discrimination Act 1995 proves to be in practice, but it is too limited to give disabled people the full equal protection of the law required under evolving human rights standards (**pp. 128–129**).

- The absence of legislation prohibiting religious discrimination in England and Wales, and racial discrimination in Northern Ireland, clearly violates international standards (**pp. 129–130**).

- None of the limited measures in UK law permitting a degree of positive discrimination exceed the scope allowed for such measures by international instruments (**pp. 131–132**).

PART 3   POLITICAL RIGHTS AND FREEDOMS – THE AUDIT

Freedom of information

- Contrary to the trend in international human rights standards, the United Kingdom remains opposed to any general freedom of information legislation (**p. 149**).

- While states may withhold information for specific purposes, the *routine* non-disclosure of most public records under the 30-year rule cannot be justified as 'necessary in a democratic society' (**pp. 149–152**).

- The Official Secrets Act 1989 broadly complies with international standards, but three features of the Act create doubt:
  — the absence of any form of 'public interest' defence for those charged with disclosing official information
  — the failure to allow those charged with disclosure to plead that the material disclosed is already in the public domain
  — making *all* information on 'international relations' controlled information which cannot be disclosed (**pp. 153–155**).

Freedom of expression

- The imposition of strict liability under the Contempt of Court Act 1981, once *substantial risk* to the course of justice is shown, may fail to allow the maximum possible freedom of speech consistent with the proper administration of justice, as envisaged by evolving human rights standards. This is particularly so since the British courts have tended to interpret the 1981 act widely (**pp. 158–159**).

- The laws governing the restriction of public access to the courts and of the reporting of court cases are not ideal, but largely comply with international standards. The practice of *routinely* hearing bail applications in private in the Crown Court is a violation (**p. 160**).

- The use of public interest immunity certificates in criminal proceedings raises serious questions of compliance, particularly since ministers signing the certificates do not *always* scrutinise the contents carefully and do not undertake the careful balancing exercise between the public interest in non-disclosure and the administration of justice. The government's law officers and legal advisers generally tell ministers that they have no discretion to refuse to sign them. Practice in individual cases has violated defendants' rights to fair trial (**pp. 160–162**).

- The imposition of temporary injunctions to restrain freedom of speech is an undesirable example of prior restraint which raises fundamental problems of compliance. There is a marked disparity between the courts' 'balance of convenience' test in the UK and the stricter three-part 'restrictions' test required by international human rights instruments (see **pp. 163–164**).

- The law of defamation in the UK is unduly rigid, damages are excessive and legal aid is unavailable, even for the poorest litigants. Unless it is radically overhauled, it will soon constitute a violation of evolving human rights standards (**pp. 170–171**).

- The law of criminal libel violates international human rights standards (**p. 171**).

- The law of blasphemy fails the test of non-discrimination under the International Covenant and cannot be justified as 'necessary in a democratic society'. A violation (**pp. 173–174**).

- The failure of the UK courts clearly to define what is meant by the phrase 'deprave and corrupt' in relation to public morals makes the law of obscenity vulnerable to challenge for non-compliance (**p. 174**).

- It is likely that British indecency laws constitute a violation (**pp. 174–175**).

- There is a conflict in international human rights instruments between protecting freedom of expression and prohibiting discrimination. However, the law on racial hatred has not been an effective weapon against racial harassment (**pp. 175–176**).

- The Public Order Act 1986 creates offences when a person's threatening or abusive or insulting words or behaviour is intended or likely to harass or distress someone else (sections 4A and 5). The breadth of these offences could lead to violations of human rights standards in individual cases (**pp. 177–178**).

- The statutory ban on the dissemination of information on homosexual life by local authorities (under section 28 of the Local Government Act 1988) violates the International Covenant's rules against discrimination and cannot be justified as 'necessary in a democratic society'. The argument that providing such information is injurious to public morals cannot be sustained by international human rights standards (**pp. 178–179**).

- The law of sedition fails to meet international human rights standards (**p. 179**).

- The Fair Trading Act 1973 rules on the take-over of newspapers reflect international standards. But if ownership of the national press becomes yet more concentrated than it is already, there may soon come a point at which the UK fails in its duty to protect the public against excessive concentration (**pp. 181–182**).

- The 'broadcasting voice ban' on television and radio interviews with representatives of Sinn Fein and other Northern Irish organisations, and on statements in their favour, revoked in 1994, did not comply (**pp. 182–184**).

Freedom of assembly

- There is no positive right of public assembly and protest in the United Kingdom. The European Convention and International Covenant require states to maintain the maximum freedom of public assembly and protest that is consistent with public order and safety, and the legitimate rights and needs of others. The United Kingdom does not apply the careful balancing exercise between conflicting rights and interests required and increasingly permits public assembly and protest only when the cost to public convenience is low (**pp. 191–193**).

- The failure of British laws to give any weight to freedom of assembly on the highway constitutes a violation (**pp. 192–193**).

- The Town Police Clauses Act 1847 creates a wide variety of minor highway offences which are nevertheless 'absolute' and have no regard for the principle of freedom of assembly. The Act falls far short of international human rights standards (**p. 192**).

- Local authorities and other bodies with power to make regulations and bye-laws in relation to open spaces, parks, recreation grounds and the like, can restrict or prohibit public assemblies without taking international human rights standards into account. Another violation (**p. 193**).

- Public Order Act 1986 powers to ban marches, rallies, etc., broadly conform. But the limited scope for judicial review of banning orders in England and Wales raises questions of compliance with those standards (**pp. 195–196**).

- In Northern Ireland, the power to ban public processions and meetings fails to meet international standards on two counts:

— the Secretary of State may order a ban when the simple imposition of conditions may have averted the need for it (**p. 197**)

— the exclusion of scrutiny by the courts of such orders fails to comply with the principle that there should be effective control against abuse of restrictions on freedom of assembly (**p. 197**).

- The statutory rules requiring organisers of marches to give the police six days' advance notice and police powers to impose conditions to prevent serious public disorder, serious damage to property, or intimidation, do not violate international standards (**p. 197**).

- Common law powers to deal with breach of the peace and impose 'bind-overs' are not clear and accessible enough in law and practice to satisfy international standards (**p. 201**).

- Bail conditions are widely used by magistrates to prevent people awaiting trial from attending meetings and demonstrations without clear evidence of any risk to other people or property. Such conditions are not adequately subject to judicial review. As international human rights instruments demand concrete evidence for any curtailment of freedom of assembly and controls against abuse of restrictions, this practice is in violation (**pp. 201–202**).

- Police powers to serve exclusion orders on individuals suspected of 'aggravated trespass' with no scope for representations by those individuals and no right of appeal fail to satisfy requirements under the International Covenant and European Convention for effective control against abuse of restrictions on freedom of assembly (**p. 202**).

- There is a clear danger that the low thresholds at which people may be guilty of minor criminal offences and of obstructing a police officer at public assemblies fail to take into account the need for 'broadmindedness' and the protection of views that may shock or offend, recognised in international human rights standards (**p. 202**).

Freedom of association

- The 'hands-off' approach of UK law to freedom of association complies in almost every respect with international human rights standards (**p. 208**).

- The civil law of conspiracy raises two concerns:

— The law is now so ambiguous that it is extremely difficult for people to know where the line between lawful and unlawful association and activity is crossed (**p. 208**)

— The extension of the law of civil conspiracy to prohibit acts which are performed purely to inflict damage on a third party, but which are not otherwise unlawful, appears to go beyond the restrictions permitted by international human rights standards (**p. 208**).

Part 3

- Since restrictions on freedom of association can be justified to protect the rights of others, the present law and practice in the UK proscribing certain organisations linked to political violence does not infringe international standards. But there should be either parliamentary or judicial supervision of proscription and the need for proscription should be regularly scrutinised (**pp. 209–210**).

- The combination of statutory employment protection rights and the law of unfair dismissal, which together guarantee a positive right to membership of a trade union, comply with the broad principles underpinning the international human rights standards on the right to freedom of association (**pp. 214–215**).

- The gap in employment law which permits employers to turn down a candidate for work on grounds of trade union activity (rather than trade union membership) violates international standards on collective action, which prohibit acts of anti-trade union discrimination (**p. 215**).

- Inroads into trade union autonomy – in particular, balloting requirements for executive members and industrial action – do not breach international standards on freedom of association (**pp. 215–216**).

- The law and practice in the UK on collective action by trade unions, in particular strikes, falls short of the international human rights standards. In particular, the ability of employers to dismiss anyone taking part in strike action violates recognised standards of freedom of association (**pp. 216–217**).

- Legislation in the UK limiting trade union 'closed shops' complies with international standards (**p. 218**).

- Current restrictions on the freedom of association of members of the army and police force also conform (**p. 220**).

- The present restrictions on freedom of association imposed on state employees, in particular staff at GCHQ, amount to a breach of evolving international human rights standards (**pp. 221–222**).

Surveillance

- The 1989 and 1994 Acts putting the secret services on a statutory footing and creating a complaints mechanism vastly improve on the previously unregulated position, but still fail fully to comply. The secret nature of the controlling mechanisms put in place by the two Acts leaves their effectiveness in doubt (**pp. 228–230**).

- Surveillance by the police and Special Branch and, more specifically, their use of secret listening devices are unregulated by law. Both practices represent significant loopholes in the protection against abuse required by international human rights standards (**pp. 230–231**).

- The exclusion of cordless phones from the protection of the Interception of Communications Act 1985 against secret surveillance is a violation (**pp. 234–235**).

- The Interception of Communications Act 1985 was enacted to comply with the European Court judgment in the 1984 case, *Malone v UK*. But the government deliberately excluded regulation of telephone metering from the Act's terms, even though the European Court had identified unregulated telephone metering as an abuse. This is therefore a clear breach (**p. 236**).

Life and personal liberty

- The law in the UK outlawing the use of lethal force conforms with international human rights standards. But its indulgent interpretation in fatal incidents involving the use of firearms by the security forces in Northern Ireland reveals a substantial divergence between the standard actually in practice for the use of lethal force and prevailing international human rights standards (**pp. 241–243**).

- Delays in holding inquests in Northern Ireland in cases involving killings by the security forces contradict both the letter and the spirit of international human rights standards which require prompt and impartial investigation of all suspected cases of extra-judicial killing (**pp. 243–245**).

- The refusal to allow coroners to compel people who are suspected of causing death to give evidence at an inquest violates international standards. Officers or courts charged with investigating suspected extra-judicial killing are required to have the authority to oblige officials allegedly involved in any such deaths to appear and testify (**p. 244**).

- Failure to provide the relatives of those who have died with advance disclosure of information, statements and other evidence to be given at inquests constitutes another violation (**pp. 244–245**).

- Arrests which are carried out in strict compliance with the requirements of the Police and Criminal Evidence Act 1984 fully conform with international standards (**p. 249**).

- There is overwhelming evidence that numerous arrests have been made under the Prevention of Terrorism (Temporary Provisions) Act 1989 merely to gather information – another infringement (**pp. 249–250**).

- The Emergency Provisions Act 1991, which authorises soldiers to arrest citizens in Northern Ireland, simply stating that they are being arrested by a 'member of Her Majesty's armed forces', is yet another infringement (**p. 250**).

- Police powers to stop and search individuals in the street may sometimes violate international human rights standards, particularly where citizens are searched in circumstances which do not simultaneously give rise to a power of arrest (**pp. 250–251**).

- Everyday discrimination against members of the ethnic minorities in police use of 'stop and search powers' violates the principle of equality which pervades international human rights standards (**p. 251**).

- Arbitrary police 'stop and search' powers under the Criminal Justice and Public Order Act 1994 and the Emergency Provisions Act 1991, are a violation. Officers can stop and search citizens without first establishing a 'reasonable suspicion' that the person stopped has committed an offence or is carrying a prohibited article (**p. 251**).

- The detention of citizens to prevent or abate a breach of the peace is not justified by any of the provisions permitting arrest and detention under Article 5 of the European Convention on Human Rights (**p. 252**).

- The rules under the Prevention of Terrorism (Temporary Provisions) Act 1989, which permit the detention of people for up to 12 hours at ports or airports without the requirement of 'reasonable suspicion' that they have committed an offence or are carrying a prohibited article, violate Article 9 of the International Covenant, Article 5 of the European Convention, and principles 10 and 12 of the UN Principles on Detention (**p. 252**).

- The extensive rules set out in the Police and Criminal Evidence Act 1984 relating to the detention of people in police custody are sufficient to satisfy international requirements (**p. 255**).

- The rules allowing for extended detention for up to seven days in police custody under the Prevention of Terrorism (Temporary Provisions) Act 1989 clearly breach international human rights standards (the government has derogated from the requirement that detained people should be brought promptly to court) (**pp. 255–256**).

- The 'right to bail' enshrined in the Bail Act 1976 reflects the presumption of bail required by Article 9(3) of the International Covenant on Civil and Political Rights, but the trend away from detention in custody which is being established by evolving human rights standards is not being followed in the UK (**p. 256**).

- The Criminal Justice and Public Order Act 1994 removes the 'right to bail' completely for certain offences and constitutes an infringement of the International Covenant (**pp. 256–257**).

- *Habeas corpus* has been found wanting under the standards set by the European Convention because the courts are unable to review the merits of the detention (**p. 257**).

- UK law prohibiting torture broadly complies with international human rights standards. Allegations of torture are extremely rare and section 134 of the Criminal Justice Act 1988 (which creates a statutory offence of torture) has never been invoked (**pp. 259–260**).

- Protection against inhuman or degrading treatment raises difficult questions of compliance. Allegations of inhuman or degrading treatment are rare. However, unlike torture there is no *specific* criminal offence of inhuman or degrading treatment. Only when such treatment involves the commission of an independent criminal offence or civil wrong could proceedings be commenced (**p. 260**).

- The Police and Criminal Evidence Act 1984 rules governing the detention of accused persons have led to fewer allegations of ill-treatment. But too many examples of abuse occur in practice for the Act to be regarded as the 'effective machinery of control' required by international standards (**pp. 260–262**).

- The treatment of suspects in Northern Ireland has improved, but the nature and extent of ongoing allegations of ill-treatment indicate that no effective machinery of control in Northern Ireland exists to safeguard suspects against violation of their rights (**p. 263**).

- The forced deportations of allegedly illegal immigrants raise very serious concerns about compliance with basic human rights standards and have a heavy adverse impact on political equality in the UK (**pp. 263–264**).

The right to vote

- National elections in the United Kingdom broadly meet evolving international standards, being held at regular intervals by secret ballot, being free of intimidation and abuse, and giving full opportunities for free choice (**p. 281**).

- The law and practice governing the right to stand for election meet international standards (but structural and cultural factors severely restrict the opportunities for women and members of ethnic minorities to stand as candidates) (**p. 275**).

- Free and regular elections are provided for by statute and form a central part of political expectations. However, there is a need for constitutional guarantees of the right to free elections to give them the standing required under international standards (**p. 269**).

- Up to 3.5 million eligible voters may be missing from the electoral rolls at any one time. People from the ethnic minorities and from disadvantaged inner-city areas, and young people are disproportionately disenfranchised (**pp. 282–286**).

- Laws and practice which deny the vote to most convicted prisoners and homeless people, and arbitrary rules which deprive classes of mental health detainees of the vote for reasons other than their competence, may be violations (**pp. 275–277**).

- The absence of precise rules governing the descriptions of candidates and parties on ballot papers allows candidates to mislead voters and distort the results in individual constituencies. Disadvantaged candidates have no remedy in the courts. This is a clear breach of the right to fair elections (**pp. 281–282**).

- The system for proxy or postal votes is too restrictive and complex and effectively denies many elderly or sick people, people with disabilities, and others a full opportunity to vote (**p. 280**).

Conclusions: Political Freedom in the UK

The democratic audit

We have carried out a rigorous and specific audit of political rights in the United Kingdom and a close scrutiny of the arrangements for protecting and securing those rights. We did not expect that this audit would find that British law and practice on political rights and freedoms complied fully with international human rights standards. It would be unrealistic to expect any country to do so.

In fact, as may be expected, we found no examples of widespread or gross violations of human rights, other than the disturbing responses to terrorism in Northern Ireland that we discuss later. Government in this country does not kidnap, or torture, or kill its opponents. Citizens in this country are free openly to criticise the government and can combine at free and regular elections to turn it out of office, if they are so minded. Citizens generally have ready access to their elected representatives and civil liberties groups may raise matters of concern with politicians, public servants and the public with no fear of reprisals. In other words, British citizens live in a democracy.

But the audit found that the United Kingdom offers far less formal legal protection of fundamental political rights and freedoms than international standards require and ordinary citizens are entitled to expect. Our findings disclose a series of breaches of those standards, right across the spectrum of such rights. They raises a number of very serious issues for UK citizens and their governments. For what emerges from our audit are not fairly random pockets of non-compliance – the odd statute too narrowly drawn, this or that protection ineffective in practice – but a pattern of systemic weakness. It is, as we shall go on to demonstrate, a weakness at the very heart of Britain's political and constitutional system and calls into question the adequacy of the UK's arrangements for protecting its citizens' democratic rights on the verge of the twenty-first century.

We started this audit from the assumption that any democratic political system is capable of protecting human rights. There is no special magic in the incorporation of key human rights treaties into domestic law or the adoption of a Bill of Rights which reflects the terms of such treaties. As the UN Human Rights Committee has repeatedly acknowledged, that is not the only course. There is a diversity of arrangements for protecting human rights around the world. It would, for example, be an acceptable alternative for the UK to conduct a thorough review of its law and practice to ensure compliance with its international obligations under the human rights treaties it has ratified. Thereafter, of course, the government would have to put in place mechanisms for regular and effective scrutiny, especially of new legislation, to ensure continuing compliance; and to establish a means for giving its citizens a readily available and effective domestic remedy when their rights are violated (which they do not now possess).

The United Kingdom has followed neither course. Key human rights treaties, such as the International Covenant on Civil and Political Rights and the European Convention, have not been incorporated into our law. The courts have resolutely refused to accept that such instruments could provide the basis for individual rights in the UK. They are scarcely ever referred to in argument in the higher courts; since the early 1970s, the International Covenant has only been cited in ten cases (0.01 per cent of the total) and the European Convention in 173 (0.2 per cent). They are allowed a marginal role in resolving ambiguities in statute or the common law. But they cannot assist in the interpretation of statute when it is clearly framed, even if it is equally clearly a violation of international human rights standards; nor does the judiciary use them to bolster, say, the introduction into the common law of protection from invasions of privacy, or other fundamental rights which go unprotected. Even when developing broad principles for judicial review, the courts have resisted almost every attempt to introduce international human rights standards into the process.

Aggrieved citizens, therefore, must turn to the European Commission and Court in Strasbourg for remedies which will be costly and long-delayed – on occasion, too late for the aggrieved individual. But even when individual citizens succeed in demonstrating a deficiency in UK law or practice, successive governments have shown a real reluctance to deal with the issue which lies at the heart of the complaint to the European Court. They prefer to deal with the narrow point raised by the individual applicant, rather than undertake a broad overview of the adequacy of domestic arrangements to protect the right or freedom in question. This grudging and unsystematic attitude means that the protection of political rights and freedoms in the UK generally moves forward in a slow, crab-like progression, by small increments, directed by the haphazard nature of individual applications and driven by the stick of Strasbourg. On occasions the beast moves so slowly or reluctantly that adverse European Court judgments pile up around its unsteady advance (as, for example, in a series of prisoners' rights cases in the 1980s).

This forced march is no substitute for the comprehensive and ongoing review of law, regulation and practice which all British governments, despite their protestations, have failed to undertake for 50 years. Instead, they consistently insist that arrangements in this country satisfy international standards and claim to have carried out periodic reviews. But there is simply no evidence that such reviews have ever taken place and no sign of any effective mechanism within government to carry them out. In fact, the very absence of any such review is in itself a breach of the UK's most immediate and elementary obligations under the human rights treaties it has ratified. The European Convention obliges signatory states to 'secure the rights and freedoms' it contains. The International Covenant clearly requires all states ratifying the treaty 'to adopt such legislative or other measures as may be necessary to give effect to the rights recognised' in the Covenant.

Failure to adopt internationally recognised civil and political rights, or constantly to review law and practice for compliance, has further significance in the long run.

Conclusions

Like democracy, human rights are not an all or nothing construct; both are living processes of change and adaptation. International human rights standards have evolved considerably since the adoption of the Universal Declaration of Human Rights in 1948. Distinct trends can clearly be traced; yet the UK has no built-in mechanism for harnessing itself to these changes. As a consequence, laws which once may have complied with international human rights standards are now perilously close to violating them. For example, unless the law of defamation is radically over-hauled in the near future, the gap between it and international human rights standards will soon become unbridgeable. Likewise, contrary to the trend in inter-national human rights standards, the UK remains opposed to any general freedom of information legislation. And on the question of bail, UK law and international standards are fast moving in opposite directions.

The necessarily haphazard case-by-case audit undertaken at Strasbourg by the European Court has so far been the only measure of the UK's failure adequately to protect and secure the political rights of its citizens. The Court's adverse judg-ments are often said to show that the United Kingdom has violated the Convention more than any other European nation. In fact, they do no such thing – they merely show that our arrangements for protecting rights fail fairly frequently. But for a variety of reasons – often political – they are an incomplete record even of cases which go to Strasbourg. For example, the Commonwealth Immigrants Act 1968, one of the worst UK violations, did not go to the Court; it was quietly settled by the European Commission to avoid too much embarrassment for the UK govern-ment. Other important cases – like that of Harriet Harman and Patricia Hewitt's complaint about government surveillance in 1986 – were also dealt with at Commission level. In 1990, the Commission ruled a case brought by a prisoner at Wormwood Scrubs (the *Raphaie case*) out-of-time, not counting Raphaie's use of the prison complaints process as complying with his obligation to exhaust domestic remedies first. The Commission's tact undoubtedly saved the UK from further embarrassment. The European Committee for the Prevention of Torture had just found that prison conditions in the UK were so bad that they were in breach of Article 3 of the European Convention. The government would undoubtedly have lost the case had it been allowed to proceed.

Other cases are resolved by 'friendly settlements'. The most significant example of this is the case of an unarmed man shot dead by a soldier in Northern Ireland. When his widow took the case to Strasbourg in 1983, the government paid her substantial damages and so avoided any review at Strasbourg of the UK's rules for the use of lethal force (*Farrell v UK*). Several cases involving deportees have also been settled in the same way, thus ensuring that no cases testing UK procedures against Article 8 of the Convention have been resolved in the Court (*Lamguindaz v UK*, 1993; *Fadele v UK*, 1987).

British infringements of international standards

The UN Human Rights Committee delivered a substantial verdict on the UK system in July 1995, making use of a new procedure which allowed the Committee to

BOX F

Concerns about political freedom: the UN Human Rights Committee, July 1995

1. Government powers under statutory provisions allowing infringements of civil liberties – 'such as extended periods of detention without charge or access to legal advisers, entry into private property without judicial warrant, imposition of exclusion orders within the UK' – are excessive.
2. 'Note is taken of the government's own admission that conditions at the Castlereagh detention centre . . . are unacceptable.'
3. While prison conditions have improved, the Committee is concerned 'by the high number of suicides of prisoners, especially among juveniles'.
4. The Committee is disturbed by reports of the continuing practice of 'strip-searching male and female prisoners' in the light of the low-security risks and the existence of sound alternative search techniques.
5. External investigations by the police of incidents involving the police or military, 'especially incidents that result in death or wounding', lack sufficient credibility.
6. 'Members of some ethnic minorities, including Africans and Afro-Caribbeans, are often disproportionately subjected to "stop and search" practices.'
7. The extension under the Criminal Justice and Public Order Act 1994 of the legislation in Northern Ireland, 'whereby inferences may be drawn from the silence of persons accused of crimes, violates various provisions in Article 14 of the Covenant, despite the range of safeguards built into the legislation'.
8. 'Many persons belonging to minorities frequently feel that acts of racial harassment are not pursued by the competent authorities with sufficient rigour and efficiency.'
9. 'The incarceration of persons ordered to be deported and particularly the length of their detention may not be necessary in every case . . . [the Committee] is gravely concerned at incidents of the use of excessive force in the execution of detention orders.'
10. The privatisation of core state activities 'which involve the use of force and the detention of persons' weakens the protection of Covenant rights. The Committee stresses that the UK government remains 'responsible in all circumstances for the observance of those rights.'

deliver comments as a whole. The Committee agreed that 'the legal system of the United Kingdom does not ensure fully that an effective remedy is provided for all violations of the rights contained in the Covenant'. It noted that protection of political and civil rights was impeded by 'the combined effects' of the non-incorporation of the Covenant into domestic law, the absence of a domestic Bill of Rights, and the refusal to allow individual citizens to petition the Committee.

The UN Committee also undertook a thorough review of political freedoms in the United Kingdom and the measures that the government was taking to resolve matters of concern. Its list of concerns is summarised in **Box F**. The Committee also urged the UK government to undertake a major campaign to tackle 'remaining problems of racial and ethnic discrimination and of social exclusion'; and to ensure that women played an equal role in British society, stressing the need for education of the police, judiciary and legal profession. They also queried the continuing need for derogation over state powers and practice in Northern Ireland (UN HRC, CCPR/C/79/Add. 55, July 1995; see also Klug, Starmer and Weir 1995).

This study provides a more detailed audit still. In the previous section, we set out a series of 97 findings drawn from the chapters in Parts 2 and 3. Overall, these findings provide powerful support for the UN Human Rights Committee's conclusion. We found positive aspects in the record, as did the Human Rights Committee. But we also found 42 examples of law or practice which we considered, after careful discussion and consultation, to be infringements of the international human rights standards for political and civil rights set out in the Human Rights Index. We also found 22 examples of law and practice which come close to violating these standards or which give cause for concern. In five cases, we found that while the broad intent of legislation or provisions may not infringe those standards, nevertheless, the rights of individuals have been, or could be, violated under current practice. It is, for example, debatable whether the rules for the use of lethal force satisfy international standards. But these vital rules are interpreted, both in practice and in the courts in the UK, with a degree of discretion which means that in practice they have been violated in individual cases; that of Farrell, the unarmed man shot dead in Northern Ireland (see above), is a case in point. Similarly, while the provision for public interest immunity certificates may not breach international standards as they are formally set out, actual government practice has prevented accused people from obtaining a fair trial, and has led to some of them being wrongly convicted (see the Scott Report, vol. 4, Chapter 6).

These findings affect community life and the lives of all citizens in the United Kingdom. For example, the absence of a constitutional and judicial principle of equal protection of the law does not only contravene the International Covenant. It means that discrimination which is not prohibited by the patchy and inadequate coverage of anti-discrimination laws continues unchecked in British society. Even government legislation shamefully promotes intolerance of homosexuals.

Freedom of information is suffocated by the demands of official secrecy, national security and political convenience. As the Scott report demonstrated, ministers are prepared 'deliberately' and 'designedly' to mislead Parliament to avoid public challenge to their policies, thus prejudicing the principle of ministerial accountability to Parliament which stands at the heart of parliamentary democracy in this country (the Scott report, paras K8.1–16). Government has recently prosecuted public servants for revealing information that they believe that Parliament and the public should know and then removed the right to a 'public interest' defence when a jury decided it should exist. The careless reform of state surveillance leaves the police free to 'bug' individual citizens, without resort to any outside authority; the security forces and police may tap mobile telephones; and telephone metering has not been made subject to formal rules. A family in Northern Ireland may lose a father, or son, shot dead though they were unarmed and uninvolved in terrorist activities, and be denied a full and thorough investigation into the circumstances of his death. The statute book contains Acts which interfere with people's lives and are known to violate international human rights standards – archaic laws of criminal libel, blasphemy, sedition, even the use of the roads, as well as new public order and police legislation.

Other findings are more diffuse, but no less serious. Hundreds of thousands of British citizens in the UK take part in marches, meetings, rallies, demonstrations and festivals on the roads every year. Yet none has a *right* to do so. The cumulative effect of the trespass laws, minor criminal offences, common law rules, bye-laws, regulations and general and specific police powers means that citizens are virtually unable to insist on meeting, marching or demonstrating in common on any land or road in the country. Every public protest depends ultimately on the 'good grace' or 'common sense' of the authorities. This represents too fragile a base for such an important political right. Public protests have been banned, curbed, or re-routed, not to protect the public from major disruption or to prevent violence or serious disorder, but simply to prevent inconvenience.

Of course, any democratic government must balance the political and other rights of individual citizens against those of other citizens, and must balance the interests and demands of different sections of the community. They must pass laws and devise policies in the interests of the public as a whole as well as of groups who have special needs. In doing so, they will inevitably restrain the freedoms of some citizens to enhance those of others, or simply to protect their lives and property. But political rights and freedoms are singled out for special protection in international human rights treaties because they ought to be exempt, in principle, from the everyday commerce of politics. Democracy depends on people being able to say, or read, or see and hear, or write what they wish without government being able to interfere as it wishes. Democracy depends on people being able to protest publicly, or even to offend and anger others, or to go on strike and to seek to persuade workers not to work, so long as they are doing so peacefully.

The 'troubles' in Northern Ireland put this country's system under severe strain. The democratic process and fundamental political and civil rights were seriously restricted in Northern Ireland for half a century. No-one should question the need for stringent security measures against terrorism and brutal intimidation. However, the test of the strength of a country's attitude towards human rights also lies in its record in such circumstances. It seems that the authorities here have taken a wide range of powers as much for expressive reasons (to reassure the public, for example) as for purely security purposes. Very often they seemed to be concerned not only to protect the security of the population against terrorism, but also their own policies and practices against criticism and judicial scrutiny. We have reviewed arrest and detention powers under the PTA; restrictions on assemblies; delays and restrictions on coroners' hearing in Northern Ireland; the failure to investigate allegations about a 'shoot to kill' policy; concerns about the ill-treatment of suspects in detention. In Northern Ireland, the government is advised by a special body – the Standing Advisory Commission on Human Rights – which has gained an international reputation for the care and seriousness of its response to government policies and terrorist activities. Repeatedly, the Commission has advised government that it was unnecessarily infringing international human rights standards: repeatedly, it has been ignored. But the government's greatest failure lay in its refusal to discipline its own forces in Northern Ireland and to investigate fully deaths at the hands of those forces promptly as they occurred. The government was obliged ultimately to commission an inquiry into allegations of a shoot-to-kill policy. But its serious prosecution by a highly respected senior police officer was aborted in suspicious circumstances; vital evidence in official hands went missing; no report was published; and none of the officers involved in a known cover-up were disciplined, supposedly for reasons of national security.

Britain's record of systemic failure

International human rights instruments recognise that governments must, in certain circumstances or on certain occasions, be able to restrain citizens from participating in activities which may endanger national security or other citizens, or put society's best interests at risk. They have therefore carefully framed allowable restrictions on people's rights to take part in such activities and established precise tests for assessing exactly how these restrictions work in practice. Their standards and tests put the onus on governments, authorities and officials to demonstrate that any interference with these rights is absolutely necessary for the protection of other people's rights or property.

This brings us to the heart of our concern about the systemic failure of existing arrangements to protect political and civil rights. The British system precisely does not put the onus on government to justify interference with fundamental political rights. Parliamentary sovereignty in practice raises the executive above any systematic legal or political restraint. The doctrine is quite as much an enemy as a friend of such rights, for it places Parliament at the disposal not of independent-minded representatives of the people, but of the very state against which they look for protection. It is also, of course, the state to which they look for protection as well. But despite the claims made for parliamentary sovereignty as the prime source of the protection of fundamental rights, governments and Members of Parliament have – as the European Court, the UN Human Rights Committee, this audit and numerous other witnesses and organisations have shown – entirely failed to provide citizens with a systematic set of independent and enforceable civil and political rights over the past half century.

Because it is the creature of government, Parliament fails to protect individual rights against encroachment by the state, either by way of legislation or administrative action. True, some members are devoted to civil liberties, but they are in a minority. For the most part, members of both Houses generally are too overworked and under-equipped. Besides which, the actions of government, ministers and departments, and public bodies generally, are far removed from effective parliamentary oversight. Ministers possess wide discretionary powers – which are in effect at the service of the whole bureaucracy – to drive the machinery of government. Parliament lacks the will, and as currently constituted, the means too, adequately to check the mass of statutory instruments which passes through it annually and confers yet more powers on the executive. Through a variety of such instruments, 'quasi-legislation' and statutory and non-statutory codes and guidance, violations of the European Convention occur and are identified by the European Court (**Table 3.1**). Other violations go unchecked, and yet have real impact on the lives of people whose rights are most vulnerable to administrative decision – prisoners, state beneficiaries, police suspects, and others. As the European Union takes on wider functions, through democratically unaccountable organisations such as Europol, European directives and agreements are likely further to demonstrate Parliament's inability to check new sources of violation.

All government activity is supposed to be answerable to Parliament through the doctrine of ministerial accountability. It is a commonplace that this doctrine, if anything, limits genuine accountability to Parliament (Chapter 3). Further, Lord Justice Scott found 'example after example' of an apparent failure by ministers to discharge the obligation to give Parliament (and the public) as full information as possible about their policies and actions which lies 'at the heart of ministerial accountability' (the Scott report, paras K8.1 and 2). As the pivot of democratic accountability to the people's representatives in Parliament for the universes of decision-making of a complex extended state, it is a fiction. Parliament is an unreliable pillar for the protection of political rights and freedoms. There are obvious reforms which would strengthen Parliament against the executive, many of which have been advanced by Commons committees. The simple fact is that government has no interest in making a rod for its own back and has blocked the great majority of reforms.

Halsbury's Laws of England states that public opinion is a mainstay of the 'liberties of the subject'. A culture of liberty is indeed the ultimate safeguard of popular rights – and in the absence of public support for democracy and freedom, constitutional guarantees, however firmly entrenched in law, can save neither. But public opinion can also sanction, or even encourage, violations of basic political rights and freedoms, or politicians will enact (in Lord Scarman's electrifying phrase) 'instant legislation, conceived in fear and prejudice' which infringes people's liberties. Witness the Asylum and Immigration Bill, introduced into Parliament in 1995 – the second such measure in less than three years. As the election drew near, the government seemed to be conjuring up the spectre of an uncontrollable surge in illegal immigrants and bogus asylum seekers. The bill not only severely curtailed rights of appeal for asylum-seekers, but further provided that employers would become guilty of a new offence if they employed certain categories of immigrants – these to be defined by an order issued by the Secretary of State and pushed through Parliament as secondary legislation. Leaked cabinet papers revealed that at least one minister – the Education and Employment Secretary – recognised that these provisions would deter employers from employing workers from the ethnic minorities in case they turned out to be 'illegal' – and so encourage yet more racial discrimination in employment. (See also Glidewell, 1996.)

The evidence of opinion surveys suggests that public opinion as a whole is moving in less tolerant and 'anti-reformist' directions which do not indicate that it will readily champion minority rights or traditional protections, such as a suspect's right to silence. The public are poorly educated in such matters, anyway, and are prepared to admit it. Proper constitutional and legal safeguards are vital precautions, not only to reinforce popular support for liberties, but also to safeguard political rights and freedoms when public opinion is inflamed or neglectful (Chapter 4).

The courts jealously preserve their independence from the executive, but in many respects they are subordinate to it and vulnerable to executive inroads into the judicial sphere. Britain's informal arrangements provide limited protection for such constitutional principles as the separation of powers, except by the increasingly hollow currency of convention. But their major weakness from a human rights viewpoint stems from the practical effects of the overriding rule of parliamentary sovereignty. They are thus bound to apply any legislation which has passed properly through Parliament, even if it clearly violates political rights and freedoms, as measured either by domestic values or by this country's international obligations. Yet the courts perform three vital functions which bear on the protection of such rights. They interpret and apply legislation; they have the power to review executive actions; and they protect 'basic interests' through the common law (Chapter 6).

However, their actual powers to protect fundamental human rights and to control the executive are constrained by legal and procedural limits. They cannot review the contents of legislation nor consider the merits of executive actions. The vast expansion of judicial review is still channelled into three conduits, *illegality*, *irrationality*, and *procedural impropriety*, which confine it almost wholly to questions of process, not substance. *Irrationality*, for example, is not sufficiently robust (to the dismay of some judges) to outlaw the blatant discriminatory practice of the military authorities in dismissing homosexuals serving in the armed forces, entirely irrespective of their conduct. Since the International Covenant and European Convention have not been incorporated into domestic law, judges cannot apply their provisions and prohibit violations. Thus, they are also unable to apply the strict three-part test and standards of 'proportionality' developed under such instruments in judicial review of executive action. Moreover, the judiciary imposes further restrictions on itself, most notably in cases involving national security.

The common law protects 'basic interests' rather than 'positive rights'. These interests are a poor fit with modern political rights and freedoms, as defined by international human rights standards. Thus, while the right to life and liberty is protected as a basic interest under the common law, other rights – such as free speech and assembly – are protected only in the negative sense, that people are entitled to do as they wish, so long as they do not break the law or infringe the rights of others. The law in the UK fails to provide the rigorous protection inherent in international requirements that restrictions on such rights should be strictly limited and clearly laid down in law; and that people should have remedies in law where they are denied (Chapter 6).

Even where the common law has historically been capable of protecting fundamental rights, it is impotent in the face of legislation which is continually eating away at the 'residue of liberty' its guardians deploy. New laws and rules restricting liberty are now becoming frequent: old ones are rarely repealed. The Criminal

Justice and Public Order Act 1994 and the Emergency Provisions Act 1991 empower police officers to stop and search citizens without first establishing a 'reasonable suspicion' that they may be carrying a prohibited article of some sort. These arbitrary powers offend international human rights standards. Yet no claim for assault or false imprisonment could possibly succeed in the domestic courts on either basis. Similarly, *habeas corpus*, the traditional common-law bastion of British civil liberties, can be partly breached by ministers by the simple removal of bail for certain offences by statute (the Criminal Justice and Public Order Act 1994). Judicial authority is also partially reduced.

We have demonstrated the narrow remit of the race, sex and disability anti-discrimination laws, concentrating as they do on employment and the supply of goods and services; the significant statutory and judicial limits on that remit; and the restricted nature of the remedies they offer (Chapter 7). These laws do not even apply uniformly throughout the United Kingdom: religious, but not racial, discrimination is prohibited in Northern Ireland; racial, but not religious, discrimination in the rest of the UK. Even in relation to race, sex and disability, there is no protection against discrimination in the UK on many of the grounds covered by the European Convention (such as in the right to privacy, free association or free assembly). The United Kingdom provides no protection against discrimination in other significant areas, including age, health (where HIV-positive people are especially at risk) and sexual orientation. Incidents of direct discrimination abound in these spheres.

At the root of this arbitrary, variably effective patchwork of legislation lies the absence of a general right to the equal protection of the law (Chapter 7). This right to equality is explicitly required by Article 26 of the International Covenant. In its absence, major categories of people in need receive no protection against discrimination at all from the law, and even those who do receive only partial protection.

Equality before the law is one of the proudest canons of the law in the United Kingdom. All laws, it has been claimed from Dicey onwards, are applied equally, regardless of status or creed. But public bodies, officials and ministers are specifically allowed to take discriminatory actions which would be against the law if performed by private individuals. Restrictions on the types of cases and legal forums in which legal aid is available, and the low qualifying financial criteria for eligibility, devalue equality before the law for most people in most circumstances. Thus, the proposition that citizens are free to do as they wish, unless expressly prohibited by the law, is of dubious worth.

At the centre of this systemic failure is the supremacy of the government-in-Parliament. Separately as well as in combination, the three pillars of liberty cannot adequately protect political rights and freedoms under a near absolute executive. The truth is that the historic doctrine of parliamentary sovereignty makes the protection of basic rights impossible. It insists that Parliament must have absolute power to do anything it wishes and to make, or un-make, any law. The idea of strictly-defined rules binding Parliament's powers is utterly incompatible with this fundamental principle of the UK constitution. Since, in fact, 'Parliament' rarely exists in its own right as a collective entity of independent MPs, but is almost invariably under the command of government by virtue of its disciplined majority in the House of Commons, international human rights instruments pose a direct challenge to the 'British way of doing things'. For the central point of these instruments, their standards and their judicial and expert activity is to bind, or at least restrain, government.

There is another aspect of the UK dilemma – the attitudes and culture of government have prejudiced the UK's relationship with international human rights instruments, but by their very nature are not amenable to audit. We have shown how reluctant the Attlee government was to participate in either the International Covenant or European Convention. Ministers shared the absolute conviction that the British system of law was far superior to the alternatives offered. This reluctance to take internationally recognised human rights seriously is still evident today in the absence of rigorous review of UK standards; the neglect of government reporting and educational duties; and the complacency with which Baroness Blatch, the government's spokesperson, rejected the UN Human Rights Committee's findings. Official complacency is compounded by the extraordinary degree of informality in the 'unwritten' constitutional and political system in Britain. The flexibility which is said to be the great virtue of this system often allows for arbitrary and even careless conduct at all levels of government. As we have seen, governments will pass and operate legislation, primary and secondary, which they know is in breach, or likely to be, of their international obligations; and Parliament is at once too ill-informed and weak to check them.

This flexibility is integral to the central tradition of government in the United Kingdom – the idea of 'strong government' (which is examined in greater detail in the companion Democratic Audit volume on democratic institutions). Constitutional and legal flexibility gives an executive the discretionary leeway which is believed to be necessary to strong and effective government and explains the distaste which governments of all colours express for the inflexibility of 'the legalistic approach' which may, through for example freedom of information laws, bind their conduct (see the President of the Board of Trade's speech in the Scott debate for a recent example; HC Deb, 26 February 1996, c595). In warning the postwar Labour cabinet of the dangers posed to colonial rule by the European Court (**p. 58**), Jim Griffiths restated the tradition of strong government thus: 'the essence of good government . . . is respect for one single undivided authority'. This tradition puts the maintenance of public order and respect for authority above the claims of political rights and freedoms. The latitude generally given to the authorities becomes especially serious in crisis conditions, from the control of riots and even unruly football crowds to combating terrorism.

Our conclusion is that each of the three pillars of the 'British system' for protecting rights – Parliament, public opinion and the courts – requires the additional support of a consistent set of positive rights which act as a 'higher law', to which all legislation and policy must conform. (There are a variety of mechanisms which could achieve this; see **p. 304**.) Such a resource would strengthen Parliament against the executive; would provide additional support to public opinion; and would give the courts constitutional legitimacy and established standards and tests for the interpretation of statute, judicial review and the development of common law. A set of rights, secured in law or parliamentary practice, could for the first time introduce the democratic principle of equality into United Kingdom law and practice; and provide aggrieved citizens with remedies in the domestic courts, instead of at the end of the long and costly process of appeal to the European Commission and Court. Above all, a set of positive legal rights would provide a constitutional 'fail-safe' mechanism which is now missing. There is an urgent need for restraint of government-in-Parliament and its much-vaunted flexibility which too often degenerates into a licence for misrule. The trouble with flexibility, political, administrative or legal, is that it is not always a flexible friend of liberty, but can be its worst enemy.

Just as the problems are at heart systemic, they ought not to be seen as party-specific. Postwar Labour governments have passed immigration laws which violate international standards, refused to legislate for freedom of information, deported inconvenient American journalists at the request of the US government, and even prosecuted their own investigative journalists. But the past 16 years have thrown the significance of the systemic nature of the problem into sharp relief. The challenge is to change the system for governing the country, not this or that government for another. It is important to see this systemic failure in a wider perspective. For any government in the United Kingdom finds itself entrenched at the heart of a highly-centralised and unified executive system, which is not only largely unconstrained by Parliament, but by any other checks and balances, such as national assemblies in Scotland and Wales, or regional English authorities, or even by an independent system of local government. There are scarcely any countervailing institutions in this country between the weight of the executive and its coercive powers and the lives of ordinary citizens. It is in this perspective, set out in more detail in the companion Audit volume, that we must contemplate the absence of secure protection for political rights and freedoms.

The horrors of a war which inspired the United Nations to promote human rights after 1945 began under defective constitutional arrangements in another west European democracy. The British do not simply believe that they live in one of the freest countries in the world. They believe their democratic freedoms are among the longest-lived in the world. It is a dangerous belief for representative democracy is in truth a comparatively recent phenomenon which belongs throughout the world to the early part of this century. In Britain, it dates from the years immediately following the first world war, not to the period of Anglo-Saxon resistance to Norman invasion or a Norman barons' revolt. What lies at the heart of the complacency about political freedom in this country is the unjustified assumption that government will never fall into undemocratic hands.

Appendix I   The Democratic Audit of the United Kingdom

The Democratic Audit of the United Kingdom was founded in 1992 to inquire into the quality of democracy and political freedom in this country. Its main task is to research and publish major 'landmark' studies, against which both democracy and political freedom in the United Kingdom can be measured over time; and thus to enable the public to judge whether the country is becoming more or less democratic and free. The current intention is to publish a companion Audit volume on political institutions in 1997, and then to publish the first two follow-up volumes for the year 2000.

The Audit also publishes specific reports on particular issues. The first Audit publication was David Beetham's paper, *Auditing Democracy in Britain* (1993), which set out the principles and methodology on which the Audit would proceed. The Audit's first major research activity was in the field of quangos. Two reports have been published: the first, *EGO TRIP* (1994), investigated the expansion of executive agencies at national and local level and for the first time quantified that expansion and arrangements for making executive quangos open and accountable; the second, *Behind Closed Doors* (1995), reported on the openness and accountability of advisory quangos. The significance of such bodies is often under-estimated; but they in effect rule on and regulate the safety of processed foods, medicines, nuclear waste, pesticides, and so on. The Audit's work inspired a Channel 4 documentary of the same name in the 'Dispatches' series.

In 1995, the Audit was commissioned to supply a working brief on national quangos for the Nolan Inquiry into Standards in Public Life. David Beetham and Kevin Boyle were asked to prepare a book, *Introducing Democracy: 80 questions and answers*, for UNESCO. It has been published in six different languages (the English version is published by Polity Press, Cambridge).

Also in 1995, the Audit published *In Place of Fear*, by Stephen Livingstone and John Morison – a study of the nature of political institutions in Northern Ireland as a base for discussion in peace talks. The study was also circulated with *Fortnight* magazine throughout Northern Ireland and a special conference was held at The Queen's University, Belfast.

In 1996, the Democratic Audit published *The Other National Lottery*, a report on electoral arrangements in the UK. It is also hoped that the *Human Rights Index,* employed as the auditing tool in this book, will be used by *Justice* to monitor new legislation in the UK and its compliance with international human rights standards.

The Democratic Audit

The work of the Democratic Audit has a strong international dimension. The Human Rights Centre at the University of Essex is a multi-disciplinary research and teaching centre with an international reputation. In 1993, the Centre hosted jointly with the Council of Europe a major European conference on disillusionment with democracy.

The Democratic Audit is currently developing an international training programme on sustaining democracy. A first international seminar, sponsored by the British Council, took place at the University of Essex in January 1996. In 1994–95, Stuart Weir acted as Senior International Facilitator on Democracy and Good Government for the Government of Namibia on a programme funded by the European Union. In 1995, Weir co-produced a report, *Consolidating Parliamentary Democracy in Namibia*, which has been adopted by the two Houses of the Namibian Parliament. In 1995, the Audit organised an Indo-British conference on democracy and human rights in New Delhi, jointly with the Rajiv Gandhi Foundation. Among the UK delegates were Lord Howe, Helena Kennedy QC, Lord Lester QC, and Baroness Williams.

The Democratic Audit is a collaborative enterprise, which involves scholars from universities other than Essex, as well as journalists, lawyers, civil servants and others. Some 28 political scientists and academic lawyers from 15 other universities have contributed to its work. The Audit has working relationships with the Doughty Street Chambers in London, the Public Policy Group of the London School of Economics, and the Charter 88 Trust – the charitable educational and publishing arm of Charter 88.

The Audit is sponsored by the Joseph Rowntree Charitable Trust. It has also received grants from the British Council, the Foreign and Commonwealth Office, the Arthur McDougall Trust, and Unison. The academic editor of the Audit is Professor Kevin Boyle, director of the Human Rights Centre. Professor David Beetham of the Politics Department, University of Leeds, acts as consultant on the 'benchmark' volumes.

The Democratic Audit was assisted greatly in its initial phases by an ad hoc advisory group, consisting of Anthony Barker, Reader in Government, Essex; Anthony Barnett, former coordinator of Charter 88; David Beetham; Ivor Crewe, now Vice-Chancellor of the University of Essex; Patrick Dunleavy, Professor of Politics, LSE; Françoise Hampson, Senior Law Lecturer, Essex; Paul Hirst, Professor of Politics, Birkbeck College, London; David Marquand, of the Political Economy Research Centre, University of Sheffield; Elizabeth Meehan, Professor of Politics, The Queen's University, Belfast; Ken Newton, Professor of Government, Essex; Dawn Oliver, Professor of Constitutional Law, University of London; Jim Ross, former civil servant and author of *The Scottish Claim of Right*; Maurice Sunkin, Senior Lecturer in Public Law, Essex; and Bryan Turner, Professor of Sociology, Deakin University, Victoria, Australia.

You are invited to send comments on this volume to Professor Kevin Boyle, academic editor, Human Rights Centre, University of Essex, Wivenhoe Park, Colchester, Essex CO4 3SQ.

THE DEMOCRATIC CRITERIA

The Democratic Audit has derived a checklist of 30 questions – or 'democratic criteria' – which form the basis of the Audit.

Elections

The regular election of public officials in a competitive process constitutes the key instrument of popular control in a representative democracy. Elections demonstrate that political power derives from the people, and is held in trust from them; but it also requires the prospect of losing office to ensure that those elected fulfil that trust, that they keep in systematic touch with their electorate, and that they maintain the standards of public office. For elections to be an effective mechanism of political control and accountability, however, they must extend to the main legislative and executive offices of state, and be free from control and manipulation by those supposedly subject to them. These issues of the reach and independence of the electoral system are covered by questions 1 and 2.

1   How far is appointment to legislative and government office determined by popular election, on the basis of open competition, universal suffrage and secret ballot?

2   How independent of government and party control are the election and procedures of voter registration, and how free from intimidation or bribery is the process of election itself?

Besides providing an effective controlling mechanism, elections must fulfil a further democratic requirement: that they produce governments and legislatures that are representative of the electorate. How far they do so depends in part on the range of choice which the party and electoral system allows the voters. It depends on the extent to which the principle of political equality is realised, so that all votes carry equal weight, and there is effective equal opportunity for people from all social groups to stand for public office and to influence the electoral process. Finally, given the important role that the media now play in elections, it also depends on equal access to the press and television and the treatment of the parties by the media. These issues of representativeness and political equality are covered by questions 3–5.

3   How effective a range of choice and information does the electoral and party system allow the voters, and is there fair and equal access for all parties and candidates to the media and other means of communication with them, and an overall balance in the treatment of the various parties and candidates by the media?

4   To what extent do the votes of all electors carry equal weight, and how far is there equal effective opportunity to stand for public office, regardless of which social group a person belongs to?

5   What proportion of the electorate actually votes, and how closely does the composition of parliament (or legislature) and the programme of government reflect the choices actually made by the electorate?

Government institutions

Although elections are fundamental in determining the relationship between governors and governed, they occur only infrequently. For popular control to be ongoing requires that those elected be responsive and accountable to the electorate on a continuing basis. Responsiveness demands that there be systematic procedures for government consultation of public opinion and of relevant interests in the conduct of its policy, and effective institutions for the formation and expression of public opinion. It also depends upon ready access by citizens to their representatives, and assured means of redress in the event of maladministration (questions 6 and 7).

The accountability of government occurs at a number of different levels, and depends upon the relationship between different institutions of state. In the first place there are the procedures which ensure that all non-elected members of the executive (civil servants, police, armed forces, security officials) are accountable to elected politicians. Then there are the arrangements which ensure that the government or executive as a whole is accountable to parliament, that parliament has the necessary powers to fulfil its scrutinising function on behalf of the electorate, and that parliamentarians are not beholden to any special interests in doing so. There are also the key judicial institutions and procedures guaranteeing the independence of the judiciary, so that the accountability of government to the laws enacted by parliament can be enforced. Finally, underpinning all the above, is the requirement that the public should have access to information about what the government is doing, and about the effects of its policies, through sources that are independent of the government's own public relations machine. These issues of accountability are covered by questions 8–14.

Equality of citizenship will be treated more generally below, but it has a particular relevance to government institutions in respect of their recruitment and promotions policies, and their conditions of service, in view of the exemplary significance of government employment for society as a whole.

6   How systematic and open to public scrutiny are the procedures for government consultation of public opinion and of relevant interests in the formation and implementation of policy and legislation?

7   How accessible are elected politicians to approach by those who elected them, and how effective are procedures for citizen redress in the event of maladminisration?

8   How effective and open to scrutiny is the control exercised by elected politicians over the non-elected personnel and organs of state?

9   How extensive are the powers of Parliament to oversee legislation and public expenditure, and to scrutinise the elected and non-elected components of the government, or executive; and how effectively are they exercised in practice?

10   How accessible to the public is information about what the government does, and about the effects of its policies, and how independent is it of the government's own information machine?

11   How publicly accountable are elected representatives for their private interests and sources of income that are relevant to the performance of their public office, and the process of election to it?

12   How effective are the procedures for ensuring that all state institutions and personnel are subject to the rule of law in the performance of their functions; and how far are the courts able to ensure that the executive obeys the rule of law?

13   How independent is the judiciary from the executive, and from all forms of interference?

14   How far is the administration of law subject to effective public scrutiny?

15   How far are appointments and promotions within state institutions subject to equal opportunities procedures, and do conditions of service infringe employees' civil rights?

The territorial dimension

The audit questions so far apply to all levels of government, from national through to local, with the exception of two that refer to central institutions alone. Questions 16–18 cover the more specific issues to do with the territorial organisation of government. Question 16 concerns the degree of popular consent to the organisation of government, whether in respect of immediate locality or the definition of nationhood. Question 17 considers how far the powers of local or regional government are sufficient for them to formulate and carry out policies in a manner that is responsive to their electorates. Question 18 addresses the supra-national level, and asks how democratic its decision-making processes are.

16   How far do the arrangements for government below the level of the central state satisfy popular requirements of accessibility and responsiveness?

17   To what extent does sub-central government have the powers to carry out its responsibilities in accordance with the wishes of its own electorate, and without interference from the centre?

18   How far does any supra-national level of government meet the criteria of popular control and political equality, whether through national parliaments or through representative institutions of its own?

Citizenship rights

In discussing the question of rights – be they internationally defined human rights or those established in a particular country – a distinction is usually drawn between civil and political rights, and social or economic rights. One difference that is frequently urged between them is that the former depend primarily on the removal of interferences (such as restrictions on the freedoms of speech, of movement or of association), and that they can therefore be legally guaranteed, whatever the level of economic development of a given country. Economic and social rights, on the other hand, depend upon the active provision of resources and opportunities by society, through the agency of government; and the necessary resources are not always and everywhere available. Civil and political rights, it is argued, must therefore have a universality which social and economic rights do not possess.

However, the distinction between these different types of right is much more blurred in practice. The right to join a trade union and withdraw one's labour, for example, can be seen as an important application of a general freedom of association, yet it is also a key economic right. On the other side, many of the core civil and political rights, such as access to the law, to trial by jury, and the guarantee of physical security, depend upon the provision of extensive resources by society if they are to be effectively secured. And there is surely something odd about prioritising civil and political rights or liberties, when a condition of exercising them at all is that people first have access to the basic means of livelihood. In a developed economy such as our own, there is a good argument for saying that the exclusion of a section of society from those features of life which the majority takes for granted, such as access to paid employment, affordable housing and dependable transport, constitutes an exclusion from citizenship in the broadest sense, and has significant consequences for the exercise of civil and political rights. In general, political equality becomes the more difficult to realise, the greater the socio-economic inequalities within a society.

If, in formulating the criteria for democratic audit, we concentrate in the first instance on civil and political rights, this does not mean that we ignore the social and economic considerations relevant to their exercise. The main thrust of questions in this section is directed to the issue of equality, between individuals and different groups of citizens, in respect of civil and political rights, and to the effectiveness of the system for their protection. We also ask about the role of voluntary, or non-governmental, organisations active in the field of citizen's rights, since their validity is itself an important index of democracy. And since the most basic condition for exercising rights is to know what they are, we emphasise the need to inform people of their rights and to provide for education in civic rights and responsibilities at school.

Question 23 confronts the contentious issue of who should be included in the category of citizen. In one respect, the democratic idea of popular rule is a universal goal, in that it rests on the assertion of common human capacities. But it has a narrower, more particular role, too, in that it defines the distinctiveness of a nation and 'a people' and the validity of its claim to self-government. Among other things, this claim involves the right to determine who from abroad shall live in the territory, and what criteria they must satisfy for citizenship. Although there is no simple way of resolving the tension between the twin aspects of democracy at this point, a minimum requirement consistent with democratic principle should be that the criteria for admission to refugees, immigrants and others to live in the territory should not allow for arbitrary discrimination (for example, on grounds of gender, race or religion), and that living within the country for a reasonable period of time should entitle a person to the rights of citizenship, if they so choose.

19   How clearly does the law define civil and political rights and liberties of the citizen and how effectively are they defended?

20   How secure are citizens in the exercise of their civil and political rights and liberties; and how far is their equal enjoyment of them constrained by social, economic or other factors?

21   How well developed are voluntary associations for the advancement and monitoring of citizens' rights, and how free from harassment are they?

22   How effective are procedures for informing citizens of their rights, and for educating future citizens in the exercise of them?

23   How free from arbitrary discrimination are the criteria for admission of refugees or immigrants to live within the country, and how readily can those so admitted obtain equal rights of citizenship?

A democratic society

It has been an accepted principle of theorising about democracy, at least since the time of De Tocqueville and J.S. Mill, that the vitality of democracy is not just a matter of the arrangement of political institutions, or of the relationship between governors and governed, but also of the character of 'civil society', or society at large. This is for two reasons. The first is that the institutions and voluntary associations of civil society – whether sports clubs, women's groups and organisations, trades unions, professional associations, or whatever – constitute an important arena in their own right for the practice of democracy, and one that involves far more people on a regular basis than the formal political sphere can ever do. The other reason is that this practice will enhance the quality and robustness of democratic institutions in the political sphere, by virtue of the kind of citizen body that it will encourage. To put the point most sharply: if people are brought up to authoritarian relations in the family, the school, the workplace and the church, they are unlikely to see public issues as any responsibility of theirs, or to defend democratic institutions when they are under threat.

For a democratic audit there are a number of different kinds of question about civil society to address. To begin with, civil society comprises many powerful organisations whose activities can crucially affect the lives and well-being of citizens. Although the independence of such organisations forms part of the pluralism necessary to democracy, it is also important that they be subject to democratic legal regulation in the public interest, and that citizens have a similar right of redress against them as against the state, if their well-being is seriously damaged by their activities.

A second consideration concerns the internally democratic character of such organisations: to whom and how effectively are they accountable? This question is simpler for membership organisations, such as campaigning groups, trade unions or political parties, but it needs also to be addressed to business companies as well, even though we may disagree about the proper balance of their accountability to shareholders, employees and customers respectively.

Third, we need to know the extent of political activity by citizens, giving 'political activity' both its widest sense of involvement in collective self-organisation at any level, and its narrower sense of activity that concerns itself with government decision making, and is addressed to holders of public office: through membership of campaigning groups and political parties, contacting elected representatives, taking part in demonstrations or protest meetings, and so on.

Fourth, given that the role of the media is so vital to the formation and transmission of public opinion in a democracy, we need to ask specific questions about their representativeness and their effectiveness as a vehicle for informed public debate.

Finally an assessment of the traditions and culture of a society – its ceremonials, beliefs, attitudes and expectations – needs to be undertaken, even though this may prove among the most difficult aspects to assess. Two different types of question suggest themselves. One concerns the extent to which the basic principles of democracy find support in popular beliefs and attitudes. The other concerns the degree of confidence that people have in the ability of the political system to address their concerns, and in their own ability to influence it.

24　How effectively are the major institutions of civil society (whether social, economic or political) subject to external regulation in the public interest?

25　How easy is it for the citizen to gain redress if his or her vital interests are damaged by the activities of such institutions?

26　To what extent are the major institutions of civil society subject to control internally by their own members, employees or beneficiaries?

27　How widespread is political participation in all its forms; how representative of different sections of society is it; and how far is it limited by social, economic or other factors?

28   How open are the media to access from all sections of opinion and social groups and how effectively do they operate as a balanced forum for informed political debate?

29   How far do the traditions and culture of the society support the basic democratic principles of popular control and political equality?

30   To what extent do people have confidence in the ability of the political system to solve the main problems confronting society, and in their own ability to influence it?

Appendix 2   The International Covenant on Civil and Political Rights and the Optional Protocol

PART I

Article 1

1. All peoples have the right of self-determination. By virtue of that right they freely determine their political status and freely pursue their economic, social and cultural development.

2. All peoples may, for their own ends, freely dispose of their natural wealth and resources without prejudice to any obligations arising out of international economic co-operation, based upon the principle of mutual benefit, and international law. In no case may a people be deprived of its own means of subsistence.

3. The States Parties to the present Covenant, including those having responsibility for the administration of Non-Self-Governing and Trust Territories, shall promote the realisation of the right of self-determination, and shall respect that right, in conformity with the provisions of the Charter of the United Nations.

PART II

Article 2

1. Each State Party to the present Covenant undertakes to respect and to ensure to all individuals within its territory and subject to its jurisdiction the rights recognised in the present Covenant, without distinction of any kind, such as race, colour, sex, language, religion, political or other opinion, national or social origin, property, birth or other status.

2. Where not already provided for by existing legislative or other measures, each State Party to the present Covenant undertakes to take the necessary steps, in accordance with its constitutional processes and with the provisions of the present Covenant, to adopt such legislative or other measures as may be necessary to give effect to the rights recognised in the present Covenant.

3. Each State Party to the present Covenant undertakes:
   a. To ensure that any person whose rights or freedoms as herein recognised are violated shall have an effective remedy, notwithstanding that the violation has been committed by persons acting in an official capacity;

b. To ensure that any person claiming such a remedy shall have his right thereto determined by competent judicial, administrative or legislative authorities, or by any other competent authority provided for by the legal system of the State, and to develop the possibilities of judicial remedy;

c. To ensure that the competent authorities shall enforce such remedies when granted.

Article 3

The States Parties to the present Covenant undertake to ensure the equal right of men and women to the enjoyment of all civil and political rights set forth in the present Covenant.

Article 4

1. In time of public emergency which threatens the life of the nation and the existence of which is officially proclaimed, the States Parties to the present Covenant may take measures derogating from their obligations under the present Covenant to the extent strictly required by the exigencies of the situation, provided that such measures are not inconsistent with their other obligations under international law and do not involve discrimination solely on the ground of race, colour, sex, language, religion or social origin.

2. No derogation from articles 6, 7, 8 (paragraphs 1 and 2), 11, 15, 16 and 18 may be made under this provision.

3. Any State Party to the present Covenant availing itself of the right of derogation shall immediately inform the other States Parties to the present Covenant, through the intermediary of the Secretary-General of the United Nations, of the provisions from which it has derogated and of the reasons by which it was actuated. A further communication shall be made, through the same intermediary, on the date on which it terminates such derogation.

Article 5

1. Nothing in the present Covenant may be interpreted as implying for any State, group or person any right to engage in any activity or perform any act aimed at the destruction of any of the rights and freedoms recognised herein or at their limitation to a greater extent than is provided for in the present Covenant.

2. There shall be no restriction upon or derogation from any of the fundamental human rights recognised or existing in any State Party to the present Covenant pursuant to law, conventions, regulations or custom on the pretext that the present Covenant does not recognise such rights or that it recognises them to a lesser extent.

PART III

Article 6

1. Every human being has the inherent right to life. This right shall be protected by law. No one shall be arbitrarily deprived of his life.

2. In countries which have not abolished the death penalty, sentence of death may be imposed only for the most serious crimes in accordance with the law in force at the time of the commission of the crime and not contrary to the provisions of the present Covenant and to the Convention on the Prevention and Punishment of the Crime of Genocide. This penalty can only be carried out pursuant to a final judgment rendered by a competent court.

3. When deprivation of life constitutes the crime of genocide, it is understood that nothing in this article shall authorise any State Party to the present Covenant to derogate in any way from any obligation assumed under the provisions of the Convention on the Prevention and Punishment of the Crime of Genocide.

4. Anyone sentenced to death shall have the right to seek pardon or commutation of the sentence. Amnesty, pardon or commutation of the sentence of death may be granted in all cases.

5. Sentence of death shall not be imposed for crimes committed by persons below eighteen years of age and shall not be carried out on pregnant women.

6. Nothing in this article shall be invoked to delay or to prevent the abolition of capital punishment by any State Party to the present Covenant.

Article 7

No one shall be subjected to torture or to cruel, inhuman or degrading treatment or punishment. In particular, no one shall be subjected without his free consent to medical or scientific experimentation.

Article 8

1. No one shall be held in slavery; slavery and the slave-trade in all their forms shall be prohibited.

2. No one shall be held in servitude.

3. a. No one shall be required to perform forced or compulsory labour;

   b. Paragraph 3 (a) shall not be held to preclude, in countries where imprisonment with hard labour may be imposed as a punishment for a crime, the performance of hard labour in pursuance of a sentence to such punishment by a competent court;

   c. For the purpose of this paragraph the term 'forced or compulsory labour' shall not include:

      (i) Any work or service, not referred to in subparagraph (b), normally required of a person who is under detention in consequence of a lawful order of a court, or of a person during conditional release from such detention;

(ii) Any service of a military character and, in countries where conscientious objection is recognised, any national service required by law of conscientious objectors;

(iii) Any service exacted in cases of emergency or calamity threatening the life or well-being of the community;

(iv) Any work or service which forms part of normal civil obligations.

Article 9

1. Everyone has the right to liberty and security of person. No one shall be subjected to arbitrary arrest or detention. No one shall be deprived of his liberty except on such grounds and in accordance with such procedure as are established by law.

2. Anyone who is arrested shall be informed, at the time of arrest, of the reasons for his arrest and shall be promptly informed of any charges against him.

3. Anyone arrested or detained on a criminal charge shall be brought promptly before a judge or other officer authorised by law to exercise judicial power and shall be entitled to trial within a reasonable time or to release. It shall not be the general rule that persons awaiting trial shall be detained in custody, but release may be subject to guarantees to appear for trial, at any other stage of the judicial proceedings, and, should occasion arise, for execution of the judgment.

4. Anyone who is deprived of his liberty by arrest or detention shall be entitled to take proceedings before a court, in order that that court may decide without delay on the lawfulness of his detention and order his release if the detention is not lawful.

5. Anyone who has been victim of unlawful arrest or detention shall have an enforceable right to compensation.

Article 10

1. All persons deprived of their liberty shall be treated with humanity and with respect for the inherent dignity of the human person.

2. a. Accused persons shall, save in exceptional circumstances, be segregated from convicted persons and shall be subject to separate treatment appropriate to their status as unconvicted persons;

   b. Accused juvenile persons shall be separated from adults and brought as speedily as possible for adjudication.

3. The penitentiary system shall comprise treatment of prisoners the essential aim of which shall be their reformation and social rehabilitation. Juvenile offenders shall be segregated from adults and be accorded treatment appropriate to their age and legal status.

Human rights standards

Article 11

No one shall be imprisoned merely on the ground of inability to fulfil a contractual obligation.

Article 12

1. Everyone lawfully within the territory of a State shall, within that territory, have the right to liberty of movement and freedom to choose his residence.
2. Everyone shall be free to leave any country, including his own.
3. The above-mentioned rights shall not be subject to any restrictions except those which are provided by law, are necessary to protect national security, public order (*ordre public*), public health or morals or the rights and freedoms of others, and are consistent with the other rights recognised in the present Covenant.
4. No one shall be arbitrarily deprived of the right to enter his own country.

Article 13

An alien lawfully in the territory of a State Party to the present Covenant may be expelled therefrom only in pursuance of a decision reached in accordance with law and shall, except where compelling reasons of national security otherwise require, be allowed to submit the reasons against his expulsion and to have his case reviewed by, and be represented for the purpose before, the competent authority or a person or persons especially designated by the competent authority.

Article 14

1. All persons shall be equal before the courts and tribunals. In the determination of any criminal charge against him, or of his rights and obligations in a suit at law, everyone shall be entitled to a fair and public hearing by a competent, independent and impartial tribunal established by law. The Press and the public may be excluded from all or part of a trial for reasons of morals, public order (*ordre public*) or national security in a democratic society, or when the interest of the private lives of the Parties so requires, or to the extent strictly necessary in the opinion of the court in special circumstances where publicity would prejudice the interests of justice; but any judgment rendered in a criminal case or in a suit at law shall be made public except where the interest of juvenile persons otherwise requires or the proceedings concern matrimonial disputes or the guardianship of children.
2. Everyone charged with a criminal offence shall have the right to be presumed innocent until proved guilty according to law.
3. In the determination of any criminal charge against him, everyone shall be entitled to the following minimum guarantees, in full equality:

a. To be informed promptly and in detail in a language which he understands of the nature and cause of the charge against him;

b. To have adequate time and facilities for the preparation of his defence and to communicate with counsel of his own choosing;

c. To be tried without undue delay;

d. To be tried in his presence, and to defend himself in person or through legal assistance of his own choosing; to be informed, if he does not have legal assistance, of this right; and to have legal assistance assigned to him, in any case where the interests of justice so require, and without payment by him in any such case if he does not have sufficient means to pay for it;

e. To examine, or have examined, the witnesses against him and to obtain the attendance and examination of witnesses on his behalf under the same conditions as witnesses against him;

f. To have the free assistance of an interpreter if he cannot understand or speak the language used in court;

g. Not to be compelled to testify against himself or to confess guilt.

4. In the case of juvenile persons, the procedure shall be such as will take account of their age and the desirability of promoting their rehabilitation.

5. Everyone convicted of a crime shall have the right to his conviction and sentence being reviewed by a higher tribunal according to law.

6. When a person has by a final decision been convicted of a criminal offence and when subsequently his conviction has been reversed or he has been pardoned on the ground that a new or newly discovered fact shows conclusively that there has been a miscarriage of justice, the person who has suffered punishment as a result of such conviction shall be compensated according to law, unless it is proved that the non-disclosure of the unknown fact in time is wholly or partly attributable to him.

7. No one shall be liable to be tried or punished again for an offence for which he has already been finally convicted or acquitted in accordance with the law and penal procedure of each country.

Article 15

1. No one shall be held guilty of any criminal offence on account of any act or omission which did not constitute a criminal offence, under national or international law, at the time when it was committed. Nor shall a heavier penalty be imposed than the one that was applicable at the time when the criminal offence was committed. If, subsequent to the commission of the offence, provision is made by law for the imposition of the lighter penalty, the offender shall benefit thereby.

2. Nothing in this article shall prejudice the trial and punishment of any person for any act or omission which, at the time when it was committed, was criminal according to the general principles of law recognised by the community of nations.

Human rights standards

Article 16

Everyone shall have the right to recognition everywhere as a person before the law.

Article 17

1.   No one shall be subjected to arbitrary or unlawful interference with his privacy, family, home or correspondence, nor to unlawful attacks on his honour and reputation.
2.   Everyone has the right to the protection of the law against such interference or attacks.

Article 18

1.   Everyone shall have the right to freedom of thought, conscience and religion. This right shall include freedom to have or to adopt a religion or belief of his choice, and freedom, either individually or in community with others and in public or private, to manifest his religion or belief in worship, observance, practice and teaching.
2.   No one shall be subject to coercion which would impair his freedom to have or to adopt a religion or belief of his choice.
3.   Freedom to manifest one's religion or beliefs may be subject only to such limitations as are prescribed by law and are necessary to protect public safety, order, health, or morals or the fundamental rights and freedoms of others.
4.   The States Parties to the present Covenant undertake to have respect for the liberty of parents and, when applicable, legal guardians to ensure the religious and moral education of their children in conformity with their own convictions.

Article 19

1.   Everyone shall have the right to hold opinions without interference.
2.   Everyone shall have the right to freedom of expression; this right shall include freedom to seek, receive and impart information and ideas of all kinds, regardless of frontiers, either orally, in writing or in print, in the form of art, or through any other media of his choice.
3.   The exercise of the rights provided for in paragraph 2 of this article carries with it special duties and responsibilities. It may therefore be subject to certain restrictions, but these shall only be such as are provided by law and are necessary:
     a.   For respect of the rights or reputations of others;
     b.   For the protection of national security or of public order (*ordre public*), or of public health or morals.

Article 20

1.   Any propaganda for war shall be prohibited by law.
2.   Any advocacy of national, racial or religious hatred that constitutes incitement to discrimination, hostility or violence shall be prohibited by law.

Article 21

The right of peaceful assembly shall be recognised. No restrictions may be placed on the exercise of this right other than those imposed in conformity with the law and which are necessary in a democratic society in the interests of national security or public safety, public order (*ordre public*), the protection of public health or morals or the protection of the rights and freedoms of others.

Article 22

1.   Everyone shall have the right to freedom of association with others, including the right to form and join trade unions for the protection of his interests.
2.   No restrictions may be placed on the exercise of this right other than those which are prescribed by law and which are necessary in a democratic society in the interests of national security or public safety, public order (*ordre public*), the protection of public health or morals or the protection of the rights and freedoms of others. This article shall not prevent the imposition of lawful restrictions on members of the armed forces and of the police in their exercise of this right.
3.   Nothing in this article shall authorise States Parties to the International Labour Organisation Convention of 1948 concerning Freedom of Association and Protection of the Right to Organise to take legislative measures which would prejudice, or to apply the law in such a manner as to prejudice the guarantees provided for in that Convention.

Article 23

1.   The family is the natural and fundamental group unit of society and is entitled to protection by society and the State.
2.   The right of men and women of marriageable age to marry and to found a family shall be recognised.
3.   No marriage shall be entered into without the free and full consent of the intending spouses.
4.   States Parties to the present Covenant shall take appropriate steps to ensure equality of rights and responsibilities of spouses as to marriage, during marriage and at its dissolution. In the case of dissolution, provision shall be made for the necessary protection of any children.

Article 24

1. Every child shall have, without any discrimination as to race, colour, sex, language, religion, national or social origin, property or birth, the right to such measures of protection as are required by his status as a minor, on the part of his family, society and the State.
2. Every child shall be registered immediately after birth and shall have a name.
3. Every child has the right to acquire a nationality.

Article 25

Every citizen shall have the right and the opportunity, without any of the distinctions mentioned in article 2 and without unreasonable restrictions:

a. To take part in the conduct of public affairs, directly or through freely chosen representatives;
b. To vote and to be elected at genuine periodic elections which shall be by universal and equal suffrage and shall be held by secret ballot, guaranteeing the free expression of the will of the electors;
c. To have access, on general terms of equality, to public service in his country.

Article 26

All persons are equal before the law and are entitled without any discrimination to the equal protection of the law. In this respect, the law shall prohibit any discrimination and guarantee to all persons equal and effective protection against discrimination on any ground such as race, colour, sex, language, religion, political or other opinion, national or social origin, property, birth or other status.

Article 27

In those States in which ethnic, religious or linguistic minorities exist, persons belonging to such minorities shall not be denied the right, in community with the other members of their group, to enjoy their own culture, to profess and practice their own religion, or to use their own language.

OPTIONAL PROTOCOL TO THE INTERNATIONAL COVENANT ON CIVIL AND POLITICAL RIGHTS

The States Parties to the present Protocol,

Considering that in order further to achieve the purposes of the Covenant on Civil and Political Rights (hereinafter referred to as the Covenant) and the implementation of its provisions it would be appropriate to enable the Human Rights Committee set up in part IV of the Covenant (hereinafter referred to as the Committee) to receive and consider, as provided in the present Protocol, communications from individuals claiming to be victims of violations of any of the rights set forth in the Covenant,

Have agreed as follows:

Article 1

A State Party to the Covenant that becomes a Party to the present Protocol recognises the competence of the Committee to receive and consider communications from individuals subject to its jurisdiction who claim to be victims of a violation by that State Party of any of the rights set forth in the Covenant. No communication shall be received by the Committee if it concerns a State Party to the Covenant which is not a Party to the present Protocol.

Article 2

Subject to the provisions of article 1, individuals who claim that any of their rights enumerated in the Covenant have been violated and who have exhausted all available domestic remedies may submit a written communication to the Committee for consideration.

Appendix 3   The European Convention on Human Rights; and the First, Fourth, Sixth and Seventh Protocols

THE EUROPEAN CONVENTION FOR THE PROTECTION OF HUMAN RIGHTS AND FUNDAMENTAL FREEDOMS

Opened for signature by the Council of Europe on 4 November 1959. Entered into force on 3 September 1953.

The Governments signatory hereto, being Members of the Council of Europe,

Considering the Universal Declaration of Human Rights proclaimed by the General Assembly of the United Nations on 10 December 1948;

Considering that this Declaration aims at securing the universal and effective recognition and observance of the Rights therein declared;

Considering that the aim of the Council of Europe is the achievement of greater unity between its Members and that one of the methods by which that aim is to be pursued is the maintenance and further realisation of Human Rights and Fundamental Freedoms;

Reaffirming their profound belief in those Fundamental Freedoms which are the foundation of justice and peace in the world and are best maintained on the one hand by an effective political democracy and on the other by a common understanding and observance of the Human Rights upon which they depend;

Being resolved, as the Governments of European countries which are like minded and have a common heritage of political traditions, ideals, freedom and the rule of law to take the first steps for the collective enforcement of certain of the Rights stated in the Universal Declaration,

Have agreed as follows:

Article I

The High Contracting Parties shall secure to everyone within their jurisdiction the rights and freedoms defined in Section 1 of this Convention.

Section I

Article 2

1. Everyone's right to life shall be protected by law. No one shall be deprived of his life intentionally save in the execution of a sentence of a court following his conviction of a crime for which this penalty is provided by law.
2. Deprivation of life shall not be regarded as inflicted in contravention of this Article when it results from the use of force which is no more than absolutely necessary:
    a.   In defence of any person from unlawful violence;
    b.   In order to effect a lawful arrest or to prevent the escape of a person lawfully detained;
    c.   In action lawfully taken for the purpose of quelling a riot or insurrection.

Article 3

No one shall be subjected to torture or to inhuman or degrading treatment or punishment.

Article 4

1. No one shall be held in slavery or servitude.
2. No one shall be required to perform forced or compulsory labour.
3. For the purpose of this Article the term 'forced or compulsory labour' shall not include:
    a.   Any work required to be done in the ordinary course of detention imposed according to the provisions of Article 5 of this Convention or during conditional release from such detention;
    b.   Any service of a military character or, in case of conscientious objectors in countries where they are recognised, service exacted instead of compulsory military service;
    c.   Any service exacted in case of an emergency or calamity threatening the life or well-being of the community;
    d.   Any work or service which forms part of normal civic obligations.

Article 5

1. Everyone has the right to liberty and security of person. No one shall be deprived of his liberty save in the following cases and in accordance with a procedure prescribed by law:
    a.   The lawful detention of a person after conviction by a competent court;
    b.   The lawful arrest or detention of a person effected for non-compliance with the lawful order of a court or in order to secure the fulfilment of any obligation prescribed by law;

    c.   The lawful arrest or detention of a person effected for the purpose of bringing him before the competent legal authority on reasonable suspicion of having committed an offence or when it is reasonably considered necessary to prevent his committing an offence or fleeing after having done so;

    d.   The detention of a minor by lawful order for the purpose of educational supervision or his lawful detention for the purpose of bringing him before the competent legal authority;

    e.   The lawful detention of persons for the prevention of the spreading of infectious diseases, of persons of unsound mind, alcoholics or drug addicts or vagrants;

    f.   The unlawful arrest or detention of a person to prevent his effecting an unauthorised entry into the country or of a person against whom action is being taken with a view to deportation or extradition.

2.   Everyone who is arrested shall be informed promptly, in a language which he understands, of the reasons for his arrest and of any charge against him.

3.   Everyone arrested or detained in accordance with the provisions of paragraph 1(c) of this Article shall be brought promptly before a judge or other officer authorised by law to exercise judicial power and shall be entitled to trial within a reasonable time or to release pending trial. Release may be conditioned by guarantees to appear for trial.

4.   Everyone who is deprived of his liberty by arrest or detention shall be entitled to take proceedings by which the lawfulness of his detention shall be decided speedily by a court and his release ordered if the detention is not lawful.

5.   Everyone who has been the victim of arrest or detention in contravention of the provisions of this Article shall have an enforceable right to compensation.

Article 6

1.   In the determination of his civil rights and obligations or of any criminal charge against him, everyone is entitled to a fair and public hearing within a reasonable time by an independent and impartial tribunal established by law. Judgment shall be pronounced publicly but the press and public may be excluded from all or part of the trial in the interests of morals, public order or national security in a democratic society, where the interests of juveniles or the protection of the private life of the parties so require, or to the extent strictly necessary in the opinion of the court in special circumstances where publicity would prejudice the interests of justice.

2.   Everyone charged with a criminal offence shall be presumed innocent until proved guilty according to law.

3.   Everyone charged with a criminal offence has the following minimum rights:

    a.   To be informed promptly, in a language which he understands and in detail, of the nature and cause of the accusation against him;

    b.   To have adequate time and facilities for the preparation of his defence;

c.   To defend himself in person or through legal assistance of his own choosing or, if he has not sufficient means to pay for legal assistance, to be given it free when the interests of justice so require;

d.   To examine or have examined witnesses against him and to obtain the attendance and examination of witnesses on his behalf under the same conditions as witnesses against him;

e.   To have the free assistance of an interpreter if he cannot understand or speak the language used in court.

Article 7

1.   No one shall be held guilty of any criminal offence on account of any act or omission which did not constitute a criminal offence under national or international law at the time when it was committed. Nor shall a heavier penalty be imposed than the one that was applicable at the time the criminal offence was committed.

2.   This Article shall not prejudice the trial and punishment of any person for any act or omission which, at the time when it was committed, was criminal according to the general principles of law recognised by civilised nations.

Article 8

1.   Everyone has the right to respect for his private and family life, his home and his correspondence.

2.   There shall be no interference by a public authority with the exercise of this right except such as is in accordance with the law and is necessary in a democratic society in the interests of national security, public safety or the economic well-being of the country, for the prevention of disorder or crime, for the protection of health or morals, or for the protection of the rights and freedoms of others.

Article 9

1.   Everyone has the right to freedom of thought, conscience and religion; this right includes freedom to change his religion or belief and freedom, either alone or in community with others and in public or private, to manifest his religion or belief, in worship, teaching, practice and observance.

2.   Freedom to manifest one's religion or beliefs shall be subject only to such limitations as are prescribed by law and are necessary in a democratic society in the interests of public safety, for the protection of public order, health or morals, or for the protection of the rights and freedoms of others.

Human rights standards

Article 10

1.   Everyone has the right to freedom of expression. This right shall include freedom to hold opinions and to receive and impart information and ideas without interference by public authority and regardless of frontiers. This Article shall not prevent States from requiring the licensing of broadcasting, television or cinema enterprises.

2.   The exercise of these freedoms, since it carries with it duties and responsibilities, may be subject to such formalities, conditions, restrictions or penalties as are prescribed by law and are necessary in a democratic society, in the interests of national security, territorial integrity of public safety, for the prevention of disorder or crime, for the protection of health or morals, for the protection of the reputation or rights of others, for preventing the disclosure of information received in confidence, or for maintaining the authority and impartiality of the judiciary.

Article 11

1.   Everyone has the right to freedom of peaceful assembly and to freedom of association with others, including the right to form and to join trade unions for the protection of his interests.

2.   No restrictions shall be placed on the exercise of these rights other than such as are prescribed by law and are necessary in a democratic society in the interests of national security or public safety, for the prevention of disorder or crime, for the protection of health or morals or for the protection of the rights and freedoms of others. This Article shall not prevent the imposition of lawful restrictions on the exercise of these rights by members of the armed forces, of the police or of the administration of the State.

Article 12

Men and women of marriageable age have the right to marry and to found a family, according to the national laws governing the exercise of this right.

Article 13

Everyone whose rights and freedoms as set forth in this Convention are violated shall have an effective remedy before a national authority notwithstanding that the violation has been committed by persons acting in an official capacity.

Article 14

The enjoyment of the rights and freedoms set forth in this Convention shall be secured without discrimination on any ground such as sex, race, colour, language, religion, political or other opinion, national or social origin, association with a national minority, property, birth or other status.

Article 15

1. In time of war or other public emergency threatening the life of the nation any High Contracting Party may take measures derogating from its obligations under this Convention to the extent strictly required by the exigencies of the situation, provided that such measures are not inconsistent with its other obligations under international law.
2. No derogation from Article 2, except in respect of deaths resulting from lawful acts of war, or from Articles 3, 4 (paragraph 1) and 7 shall be made under this provision.
3. Any High Contracting Party availing itself of this right of derogation shall keep the Secretary-General of the Council of Europe fully informed of the measures which it has taken and the reasons therefor. It shall also inform the Secretary-General of the Council of Europe when such measures have ceased to operate and the provisions of the Convention are again being fully executed.

Article 16

Nothing in Articles 10, 11 and 14 shall be regarded as preventing the High Contracting Parties from imposing restrictions on the political activity of aliens.

Article 17

Nothing in this Convention may be interpreted as implying for any State, group or person any right to engage in any activity or perform any act aimed at the destruction of any of the rights and freedoms set forth herein or at their limitation to a greater extent than is provided for in the Convention.

Article 18

The restrictions permitted under this Convention to·the said rights and freedoms shall not be applied for any purpose other than those for which they have been prescribed.

FIRST PROTOCOL TO THE CONVENTION FOR THE PROTECTION OF HUMAN RIGHTS AND FUNDAMENTAL FREEDOMS

The Governments signatory hereto, being Members of the Council of Europe, being resolved to take steps to ensure the collective enforcement of certain rights and freedoms other than those already included in Section 1 of the Convention for the Protection of Human Rights and Fundamental Freedoms signed at Rome on 4 November 1950 (hereinafter referred to as 'the Convention'),

Have agreed as follows:

Human rights standards

Article 1

Every natural or legal person is entitled to the peaceful enjoyment of his possessions. No one shall be deprived of his possessions except in the public interest and subject to the conditions provided for by law and by the general principles of international law.

The preceding provisions shall not, however, in any way impair the right of a State to enforce such laws as it deems necessary to control the use of property in accordance with the general interest or to secure the payment of taxes or other contributions or penalties.

Article 2

No person shall be denied the right to education. In the exercise of any functions which it assumes in relation to education and to teaching, the State shall respect the right of parents to ensure such education and teaching in conformity with their own religious and philosophical convictions.

Article 3

The High Contracting Parties undertake to hold free elections at reasonable intervals by secret ballot, under conditions which will ensure the free expression of the opinion of the people in the choice of the legislature.

Article 4

Any High Contracting Party may at the time of signature or ratification or at any time thereafter communicate to the Secretary-General of the Council of Europe a declaration stating the extent to which it undertakes that the provisions of the present Protocol shall apply to such of the territories for the international relations of which it is responsible as are named therein.

Any High Contracting Party which has communicated a declaration in virtue of the preceding paragraph may from time to time communicate a further declaration modifying the terms of any former declaration or terminating the application of the provisions of this Protocol in respect of any territory.

A declaration made in accordance with this Article shall be deemed to have been made in accordance with Paragraph 1 of Article 63 of the Convention.

Article 5

As between the High Contracting Parties the provisions of Articles 1, 2, 3 and 4 of this Protocol shall be regarded as additional Articles to the Convention and all the provisions of the Convention shall apply accordingly.

Article 6

This Protocol shall be open for signature by the Members of the Council of Europe, who are the signatories of the Convention; it shall be ratified at the same time as or after the ratification of the Convention. It shall enter into force after the deposit of ten instruments of ratification. As regards any signatory ratifying subsequently, the Protocol shall enter into force at the date of the deposit of ten instruments of ratification.

The instruments of ratification shall be deposited with the Secretary-General of the Council of Europe, who will notify all Members of the names of those who have ratified.

DONE at Paris on the 20th day of March 1952, in English and French, both texts being equally authentic, in a single copy which shall remain deposited in the archives of the Council of Europe. The Secretary-General shall transmit certified copies to each of the signatory governments.

FOURTH PROTOCOL, SECURING CERTAIN RIGHTS AND FREEDOMS OTHER THAN THOSE ALREADY INCLUDED IN THE CONVENTION AND IN THE PROTOCOL THERETO

The Governments signatory hereto, being Members of the Council of Europe,

Being resolved to take steps to ensure the collective enforcement of certain rights and freedoms other than those already included in Section I of the Convention for the Protection of Human Rights and Fundamental Freedoms signed at Rome on 4 November 1950 (hereinafter referred to as 'the Convention') and in Articles 1 to 3 of the First Protocol to the Convention, signed at Paris on 20 March 1952,

Have agreed as follows:

Article 1

No one shall be deprived of his liberty merely on the ground of inability to fulfil a contractual obligation.

Article 2

1. Everyone lawfully within the territory of a State shall, within that territory, have the right to liberty of movement and freedom to choose his residence.
2. Everyone shall be free to leave any country, including his own.
3. No restrictions shall be placed on the exercise of these rights other than such as are in accordance with law and are necessary in a democratic society in the interests of national security or public safety, for the maintenance of public order (*ordre publique*), for the prevention of crime, for the protection of health or morals, or for the protection of the rights and freedoms of others.
4. The rights set forth in paragraph 1 may also be subject, in particular areas, to restrictions imposed in accordance with law and justified by the public interest in a democratic society.

Article 3

1. No one shall be expelled, by means either of an individual or of a collective measure, from the territory of the State of which he is a national.
2. No one shall be deprived of the right to enter the territory of the State of which he is a national.

Article 4

Collective expulsion of aliens is prohibited.

Article 5

1. Any High Contracting Party may, at the time of signature or ratification of this Protocol, or at any time thereafter, communicate to the Secretary-General of the Council of Europe a declaration stating the extent to which it undertakes that the provisions of this Protocol shall apply to such of the territories for the international relations of which it is responsible as are named therein.
2. Any High Contracting Party which has communicated a declaration in virtue of the preceding paragraph may, from time to time, communicate a further declaration modifying the terms of any former declaration or terminating the application of the provisions of this Protocol in respect of any territory.
3. A declaration made in accordance with this Article shall be deemed to have been made in accordance with paragraph 1 of Article 63 of the Convention.
4. The territory of any State to which this Protocol applies by virtue of ratification or acceptance by that State, and each territory to which this Protocol is applied by virtue of a declaration by that State under this Article, shall be treated as separate territories for the purpose of the references in Articles 2 and 3 to the territory of a State.

Article 6

1. As between the High Contracting Parties the provisions of Articles 1 to 5 of this Protocol shall be regarded as additional Articles to the Convention, and all the provisions of the Convention shall apply accordingly.
2. Nevertheless, the right of individual recourse recognised by a declaration made under Article 25 of the Convention, or the acceptance of the compulsory jurisdiction of the Court by a declaration made under Article 46 of the Convention, shall not be effective in relation to this Protocol unless the High Contracting Party concerned has made a statement recognising such right, or accepting such jurisdiction, in respect of all or any of Articles 1 to 4 of the Protocol.

SIXTH PROTOCOL, CONCERNING THE ABOLITION OF THE DEATH PENALTY

The member States of the Council of Europe, signatory to this Protocol to the Convention for the Protection of Human Rights and Fundamental Freedoms, signed at Rome on 4 November 1950 (hereinafter referred to as 'the Convention'),

Considering that the evolution that has occurred in several member States of the Council of Europe expresses a general tendency in favour of abolition of the death penalty,

Have agreed as follows:

Article 1

The death penalty shall be abolished. No one shall be condemned to such penalty or executed.

Article 2

A State may make provision in its law for the death penalty in respect of acts committed in time of war or of imminent threat of war; such penalty shall be applied only in the instances laid down in the law and in accordance with its provisions. The State shall communicate to the Secretary-General of the Council of Europe the relevant provisions of that law.

Article 3

No derogation from the provisions of this Protocol shall be made under Article 15 of the Convention.

Article 4

No reservation may be made under Article 64 of the Convention in respect of the provisions of this Protocol.

SEVENTH PROTOCOL TO THE CONVENTION FOR THE PROTECTION OF HUMAN RIGHTS AND FUNDAMENTAL FREEDOMS

The member States of the Council of Europe signatory hereto,

Being resolved to take further steps to ensure the collective enforcement of certain rights and freedoms by means of the Convention for the Protection of Human Rights and Fundamental Freedoms signed at Rome on 4 November 1950 (hereinafter referred to as 'the Convention'),

Have agreed as follows:

Article I

1. An alien lawfully resident in the territory of a State shall not be expelled therefrom except in pursuance of a decision reached in accordance with law and shall be allowed:
   a. To submit reasons against his expulsion,
   b. To have his case reviewed, and
   c. To be represented for these purposes before the competent authority or a person or persons designated by that authority.
2. An alien may be expelled before the exercise of his rights under paragraph 1(a), (b) and (c) of this Article, when such expulsion is necessary in the interests of public order or is grounded on reasons of national security.

Article 2

1. Everyone convicted of a criminal offence by a tribunal shall have the right to have his conviction or sentence reviewed by a higher tribunal. The exercise of this right, including the grounds on which it may be exercised, shall be governed by law.
2. This right may be subject to exceptions in regard to offences of a minor character, as prescribed by law, or in cases in which the person concerned was tried in the first instance by the highest tribunal or was convicted following an appeal against acquittal.

Article 3

When a person has by a final decision been convicted of a criminal offence and when subsequently his conviction has been reversed, or he has been pardoned, on the ground that a new or newly discovered fact shows conclusively that there has been a miscarriage of justice, the person who has suffered punishment as a result of such conviction shall be compensated according to the law or the practice of the State concerned, unless it is proved that the non-disclosure of the unknown fact in time is wholly or partly attributable to him.

Article 4

1. No one shall be liable to be tried or punished again in criminal proceedings under the jurisdiction of the same State for an offence for which he has already been finally acquitted or convicted in accordance with the law and penal procedure of that State.
2. The provisions of the preceding paragraph shall not prevent the re-opening of the case in accordance with the law and penal procedure of the State concerned, if there is evidence of new or newly discovered facts, or if there has been a fundamental defect in the previous proceedings, which could affect the outcome of the case.

3.   No derogation from this Article shall be made under Article 15 of the Convention.

Article 5

1.   Spouses shall enjoy equality of rights and responsibilities of a private law character between them, and in their relations with their children, as to marriage, during marriage and in the event of its dissolution. This Article shall not prevent States from taking such measures as are necessary in the interests of the children.

Article 6

1.   Any State may at the time of signature or when depositing its instrument of ratification, acceptance or approval, specify the territory or territories to which this Protocol shall apply and state the extent to which it undertakes that the provisions of this Protocol shall apply to this or these territories.

2.   Any State may at any later date, by a declaration addressed to the Secretary-General of the Council of Europe, extend the application of this Protocol to any other territory specified in the declaration. In respect of such territory the Protocol shall enter into force on the first day of the month following the expiration of a period of two months after the date of receipt by the Secretary-General of such declaration.

3.   Any declaration made under the two preceding paragraphs may, in respect of any territory specified in such declaration, be withdrawn or modified by a notification addressed to the Secretary-General. The withdrawal or modification shall become effective on the first day of the month following the expiration of a period of two months after the date of receipt of such notification by the Secretary-General.

4.   A declaration made in accordance with this Article shall be deemed to have been made in accordance with paragraph 1 of Article 63 of the Convention.

5.   The territory of any State to which this Protocol applies by virtue of ratification, acceptance or approval by that State, and each territory to which this Protocol is applied by virtue of a declaration by that State under this Article, may be treated as separate territories for the purpose of the reference in Article 1 to the territory of a State.

Article 7

1.   As between the States Parties, the provisions of Articles 1 to 6 of this Protocol shall be regarded as additional Articles to the Convention, and all the provisions of the Convention shall apply accordingly.

2.   Nevertheless, the right of individual recourse recognised by a declaration made under Article 25 of the Convention, or the acceptance of the compulsory jurisdiction of the Court by a declaration made under Article 46 of the Convention, shall not be effective in relation to this Protocol unless the State concerned

has made a statement recognising such right, or accepting such jurisdiction in respect of Articles 1 to 5 of this Protocol.

Article 8

This Protocol shall be open for signature by member States of the Council of Europe which have signed the Convention. It is subject to ratification, acceptance or approval. A member State of the Council of Europe may not ratify, accept or approve this Protocol without previously or simultaneously ratifying the Convention. Instruments of ratification, acceptance or approval shall be deposited with the Secretary-General of the Council of Europe.

Article 9

1. This Protocol shall enter into force on the first day of the month following the expiration of a period of two months after the date on which seven member States of the Council of Europe have expressed their consent to be bound by the Protocol in accordance with the provisions of Article 8.
2. In respect of any member State which subsequently expresses its consent to be bound by it, the Protocol shall enter into force on the first day of the month following the expiration of a period of two months after the date of the deposit of the instrument of ratification, acceptance or approval.

Appendix 4   International Human Rights Instruments Used to Compile the Index

1. Universal Declaration of Human Rights.

    Adopted and proclaimed by UN General Assembly resolution 217 A (III) of 10 December 1948.

2. International Covenant on Civil and Political Rights (UN 1966).

    Adopted and opened for signature, ratification and accession by UN General Assembly resolution 2200 A(XXI) of 16 December 1966.

3. European Convention for the Protection of Human Rights and Fundamental Freedoms (1951).

    Adopted by the Council of Europe in 1950 and entered into force in 1953.

4. Convention on the Elimination of All Forms of Racial Discrimination (UN 1969).

    Adopted and opened for signature, ratification and accession by UN General Assembly resolution 2106 A(XX) of 21 December 1965.

5. Convention on the Elimination of All Forms of Discrimination Against Women (UN 1979).

    Adopted and opened for signature, ratification and accession by UN General Assembly resolution 34/180 of 18 December 1979.

6. ILO Convention (No. 87) Concerning Freedom of Association and Protection of the Right to Organise (1950).

    Adopted on 9 July 1948 by the General Conference of the International Labour Organisation at its thirty-first session.

7. ILO Convention (No. 98) Concerning the Application of the Principles of the Right to Organise and to Bargain Collectively (1951).

    Adopted on 1 July 1949 by the General Conference of the International Labour Organisation at its thirty-second session.

8.	Convention Against Torture and Other Cruel, Inhuman or Degrading Treatment (UN 1984).	Adopted and opened for signature, ratification and accession by UN General Assembly resolution 39/46 of 10 December 1984.
9.	European Convention for the Prevention of Torture and Inhuman Degrading Treatment or Punishment (1987).	Adopted by the Council of Europe in 1987. Entered force in 1989.
10.	Convention on the Rights of the Child (UN 1989).	Adopted and opened for signature, ratification and accession by UN General Assembly resolution 44/25 of 20 November 1989.
11.	International Covenant on Economic, Social and Cultural Rights (UN 1966).	Adopted and opened for signature, ratification and accession by UN General Assembly resolution 2200 A(XXI) of 16 December 1966.
12.	European Social Charter (1961).	Adopted by the Council of Europe in 1961. Entered force 1965.
13.	Document on the Copenhagen Meeting of the Conference on the Human Dimension of the CSCE (1990).	
14.	Standard Minimum Rules for Treatment of Prisoners (UN 1955).	Adopted by the First UN Congress on the Prevention of Crime and the Treatment of Offenders, held in Geneva in 1955, and approved by the Economic and Social Council by its resolutions 663 C(XXIV) of 31 July 1957 and 2076 (LXII) of May 1977.
15	European Prison Rules.	(Council of Europe: Recommendation No. R(87) (1987)).
16.	United Nations Basic Principles on the Use of Force and Firearms Law Enforcement Officials (1990).	Adopted by the Eighth UN Congress on the Prevention of Crime and the Treatment of Offenders, Havanva, Cuba, 27 August to 7 September 1990.

17.   United Nations Principles   Recommended by UN Economic and Social
      on the Effective   Council resolution 1989/65 of 24 May 1989.
      Prevention and
      Investigation of Extra-
      Legal, Arbitrary and
      Summary Executions
      (1989).

18.   United Nations Body of   Adopted by UN General Assembly resolution
      Principles for the   43/173 of 9 December 1988.
      Protection of All Persons
      under Any Form of
      Detention or Imprison-
      ment (1988).

19.   UN Standard Minimum   Adopted by UN General Assembly resolution
      Rules for Non-Custodial   45/110 of 14 December 1990.
      Measures (*Tokyo Rules*)
      (1990).

20.   European Committee of   (1981): Rec. No. R(81)19).
      Ministers: Recommenda-
      tion on the Access to
      Information Held by
      Public Authorities.

21.   Council of Europe:
      Declaration on the
      Freedom of Expression
      and Information
      (29 April 1982).

22.   Council of Europe:
      Convention on
      Transfrontier Television
      (adopted 5 May 1989).

Table of Cases

Bold numbers refer to page references in the text. ***Bold italics*** refers to references in tables or boxes.

R v Cambridge Health Authority ex parte B
   1995 **99**
R v Canale [1990] 91 Cr.App.R 1 **261**
R v Chief Constable of West Yorkshire, ex parte
   Govell (1994) High Court, May 1994,
   unreported **231**
R v Crisp and Homewood [1919] 82 J 121 **148**
R v Cunninghame Graham and Burns (1888) 16
   Cox CC 420 **190**
R v Denbigh Justices ex parte Williams and
   Evans [1974] 2 All ER 1052 **157**
R v Deputy Governor of Parkhurst Prison ex
   parte Hague 1992 [1991] 3 All ER 733 **101**
R v Effick [1994] 3 WLR 583 **234**
R v Entry Clearance Officer ex parte Amin
   [1983] WCR 255 **127**
R v Home Secretary ex parte Brind [1991] AC
   969 **97, 183**
R v Howell [1982] QB 416 **199**
R v Immigration Appeal Tribunal ex parte
   Begum Manshoora (1986) Imm AR 385 **121**
R v Joyce [1946] AC 347 **179**
R v Keenan [1990] 203 54 **261**
R v Kirk [1984] ECR 2689 **108**
R v Mansfield Justices ex parte Sharkey [1985]
   QB 613 **202**
R v Martin Secker & Warburg Ltd [1954] 2 All
   ER 683 **172**
R v Miller TLR 24 Dec. 1992
R v Ministry of Defence ex parte Smith and
   others [1995] 4 All ER 427 **98, 121**
R v Ministry of Defence ex parte Smith and
   others [1996] 1 All ER 527
R v Morpeth Ward Justices ex parte Ward
   [1992] 95 Cr.App.R 215 **201**
R v Salisbury District Council ex parte
   Pendragon (1995) High Court, June 1995,
   unreported **96**
R v Samuel [1988] Q3615 **261**
R v Secretary of State for Home Affairs ex parte
   Bahjan Singh [1978] 2 All ER 1081
R v Secretary of State for Home Affairs ex parte
   Bahjan Singh [1975] 2 All ER 1081 **93**
R v Secretary of State for the Home Department
   ex parte Bugdaycay [1987] AC 514 **95**
R v Secretary of State for the Home Department ex
   parte Cheblak [1991] 2 All ER 319 **96, 257**
R v Secretary of State for the Home Department
   ex parte Hosenball [1977] 1 WCR 766 **96**
R v Secretary of State for Transport ex parte
   Factortame (No. 2) 1991 [1990] 2 AC 85 **108**
R v The Chief Constable of the Wiltshire Police
   and Wiltshire District Council ex parte
   Pendragon (1995) High Court, June 1995,
   unreported **196–7**
Raphaie Case (1993) UCHR Dec. 1993 **306**
Rassemblement Jurassien and Unité Jurassienne v
   Switzerland (1978) ECmHR, 17 DR 93 **188**
Raymond v Honey 1983 (1983) 1 AC 1 **276**
Re Goodwin [1990] 1 All ER 608 **81**

Redgrave v UK (1993) ECmHR **235**
Ridge v Baldwin [1964] AC 40 **95**
Roberts v Hopwood 1925 [1925] AC 578 **121**
Salomon v The Commissioners of Customs and
   Excise [1967] 2 QB 116 **92**
Sanchez-Reisse v Switzerland (1986) 9 EHRR 71
   253
Sanders v Chichester (1994) L.S.Caz.R. 37 **281**
Saunders v UK (1994) No. 19187/91 **87**
Schmidt and Dahlström v Sweden (1976) 1
   EHRR 367 **211**
Schwabe v Austria (1992) ECtHR Series A No.
   242-B **168**
Scott v Scott [1913] AC 417 **157**
Shaw v DPP [1962] AC 220 **173**
Sheen v Clegg (1967), *Daily Telegraph,* 22 June
   1967 **232**
Silver v UK [1983] 3 EHRR 475 *49*, **202**
Sim v Stretch [1936] 52 TLR 669 **169**
Simmonds v Heffer [1983] BCLC 298 **208**
Soering v UK (1989) 11 EHRR 439 **52**
Stauder v Ulm [1969] ECR 291 **107**
Steel v Union of Post Office Workers [1978]
   IRLR 978 **127–8**
Stogmuller v Austria (1969) 1 EHRR 245 **246**
Sunday Times v UK (1979) 2 EHRR 245
   21–2B, *48*, **145, 152, 158–9, 163, 167, 177,
   184, 207**
Sunday Times v UK (1991) 14 EHRR 229 **53**
Svenska Lokmannaforbundet v Sweden (1976) 1
   EHRR 617 **210**
Taylor v Co-op Retail Services [1982] ICR 600 **93**
Thomas v NUM (South Wales Area) [1985] 2 All
   ER 1 **104, 189**
Thorgeirson v Iceland (1992) 14 EHRR 239 **142,
   168**
Thynne, Wilson and Gunnell v UK (1990) 13
   EHRR 666 **53, 57**
Tolstoy Miloslavsky v UK 1995 TLR 423 *54*,
   170–1
Toonen v Australia Human Rights Committee
   1992 **114**
Tyrer v UK [1980] 2 EHRR 1 *48*, 65
Vagrancy cases (1971) 1 EHRR 373 **190**
Verrall v Great Yarmouth Borough Council
   [1981] QB 202 **190**
Vilvarajah v UK (1991) 14 EHRR 248 **99**
W, X, Y and Z v Belgium (1975) 2 DR 110 **268**
Waddington v Miah [1974] 2 All ER 377 **92**
Webster v Southwark LBC [1983] QB 698 **190**
Weeks v UK (1988) 10 EHRR 293 *51*, 57
Welch v UK (1995) Series A, No. 307-A *54*
Whitehouse v Lemon [1978] 67 Cr.App.R 70 **172**
Williams v Home Office (No. 2) 1981 [1981] 1
   All ER 1211 **94**
Wills v Bowley [1983] AC 57 **189, 192**
Wilson v Associated Newspapers 1995 **214**
Winterwerp v The Netherlands (1979) 2 EHRR
   387 **57**
X v Belgium 4YB 324 **272**

Bibliography and Sources

References to all government papers and reports are contained in the text and are not repeated in the Bibliography. Parliamentary and committee stage debates, statements, Parliamentary Questions and Answers are all referenced in the text, according to a simplified system: HC Deb and HL Deb are references to the relevant Hansard; and the date and column number then follow. WA indicates a reference in the Hansard section for Written Answers. Documents used in compiling the Human Rights Index are contained in the Appendices: the texts of the International Covenant and Optional Protocol, and of the European Convention on Human Rights will be found in Appendices 2 and 3; a list of other instruments and documents drawn upon is contained in Appendix 4. Politicians' speeches have been obtained from the press office of the relevant political party or government department. Except where explicitly stated, the place of publication of books cited in the bibliography is London.

Allen, T.R.S. (1985) *Public Law*, 614
Allen, T.R.S. (1994) *Law, Liberty, Justice* (Clarendon Press, Oxford)
Alston, P. (1992) *The United Nations and Human Rights* (Clarendon Press, Oxford)
Amnesty International (1990–95) *Annual Reports* (Amnesty International)
Amnesty International (1994a) *Political Killings in Northern Ireland* (AI Index: EUR 45/01/94)
Amnesty International (1994b) *Asylum-Seekers Detained in the United Kingdom* (Amnesty)
Arblaster, A. (1984) *The Rise and Decline of Western Liberalism* (Blackwell, Oxford)
Archbold, J.T. and Richardson, P.J. (eds) (1995) *Criminal Pleadings, Evidence and Practice* (Sweet and Maxwell)
Article 19 (March 1993) *Press Law and Practice: a comparative study of press freedom in European and other communities* (Article 19)
Article 19 (August 1993) *Freedom of Expression Handbook: international and comparative law, standards and procedures* (Article 19)

Bailey, S.H., Harris, D.J. and Jones, B.L. (1991) *Civil Liberties: cases and materials* (Butterworths)
Barnett, S. and Curry, A. (1994) *The Battle for the BBC* (Aurum Press)
Barrie, Sir G. (1989) 'Regulation of Public and Private Power' *Public Law*, Winter

Beddard, R. (1993) *Human Rights and Europe* (Grotius, Cambridge)
Beetham, D. (1993) *Auditing Democracy in Britain*, Democratic Audit Paper no. 1 (Human Rights Centre, University of Essex and Charter 88 Trust)
Beetham, D. (1994) *Defining and Measuring Democracy*, Modern Politics Series vol. 36, sponsored by the European Consortium for Political Research (Sage)
Beetham, D. (1995) 'What Future for Economic and Social Rights?' *Political Studies* vol. 43 (special issue: *Politics and Human Rights*, ed. Beetham, D.)
Beetham, D. and Boyle, K. (1995) *Introducing Democracy* (UNESCO/Polity, Oxford)
Bentham, J. (1894) 'Anarchical Fallacies' in Bowering, J. (ed.) *Collected Works of Jeremy Bentham*
Bevan, V. (1986) *The Development of British Immigration Law* (Croom Helm)
Birkinshaw, P. (1990) *Government and Information* (Butterworths)
Blackburn, R. (1993) *Rights of Citizenship* (Mansell)
Boyle, K. (1995) 'Stock-taking on Human Rights: The World Conference on Human Rights, Vienna 1993' *Political Studies*, vol. 43 (special issue: *Politics and Human Rights*, ed. Beetham, D.)
Bracton, H. de (1968) *De Legibus et Consuetudinibus Angliae* 4 vols, 1915–1942 (Yale University Press, New Haven)

Bradley, A.W. (1989) 'The Judge Over Your Shoulder' *Public Law*, Winter

British Youth Council (1993) *Democratic Deficit: young people and the parliamentary process* (British Youth Council)

Brook, L. and Cape, E. (1995) 'Civil Liberties' in Jowell, R. *et al.* (eds) *British Social Attitudes* (Dartmouth, Aldershot)

Brown, D. and McColgan, I. (1992) 'Employment Law and the International Labour Organisation: The Spirit of Co-operation' *Industrial Law Journal*

Browne-Wilkinson, Lord (1992) 'The Infiltration of a Bill of Rights' *Public Law*, Autumn

Bunyan, T. (1995) *The Europol Convention* (Statewatch)

Burke, E. (1968) *Reflections on the Revolution in France*, Cruise O'Brien, C. (ed.) (Penguin, Harmondsworth)

Butler, D. (1963) *The Electoral System in Britain since 1918*, 2nd edn (Macmillan)

Byrne, P. (1976) 'Parliamentary Control of Delegated Legislation' *Parliamentary Affairs*, no. 29

Chapman, R. and Hunt, M. (eds) (1987) *Open Government* (Beckenham)

Clapham, A. (1993) *Human Rights in the Private Sphere* (Clarendon Press, Oxford)

Coliver, S. (ed.) (1992) *Striking a Balance: hate speech, freedom of expression and non-discrimination* (International Centre Against Censorship)

Collins, E. and Meehan, E. (1994) 'Women's Rights in Employment and Related Areas' in McCrudden, C. and Chambers, G. (eds) *Individual Rights and the Law in Britain* (Clarendon Press, Oxford)

Colville, Lord (1987) *Review of Emergency Legislation*

Colvin, M. (1989) *Section 28: a practical guide to the law and its implications* (National Council for Civil Liberties)

Commission on Social Justice (1994) *Social Justice: strategies for national renewal* (Vintage)

Costello, D. 'Limiting Rights Constitutionally' in O'Reilly, J. (ed.) *Human Rights and Constitutional Law. Essays in Honour of Brian Walsh*

Council of Europe (1993) *The Council of Europe and Human Rights* (report for the World Conference on Human Rights, Vienna), (Council of Europe, Strasbourg)

Cox, B. (1975) *Civil Liberties in Britain* (Penguin, Harmondsworth)

Crossman, R. (1977) *The Diaries of a Cabinet Minister* vol. 3 (Hamish Hamilton and Jonathan Cape)

Dahl, R. (1989) *Democracy and its Critics* (Yale University Press, New Haven)

Demos (1995) *Freedom's Children: work, relationships and politics for 18–34 year olds in Britain today*, by Wilkinson, H. and Mulgan, G. (Demos)

Denning, Lord (1949) *Freedom Under Law* (Butterworths)

Dicey, A.V. (1885, 1924) *Introduction to the Study of the Law of the Constitution* 8th edn (Macmillan)

Dickson, B. and Scarman, Lord (1990) *Civil Liberties in Northern Ireland: the CAJ handbook* (Committee on the Administration of Justice)

Dixon, D., Bottomley, K., Coleman, C., Gill, M. and Wall, D. (1990) 'Safeguarding the Rights of Suspects in Police Custody' *Policing and Society*

Donnison, D. (1991) *A Radical Agenda: after the New Right and the Old Left* (Rivers Oram Press)

Dorril, S. (1993) *The Silent Conspiracy: inside the Intelligence Services in the 1990s* (Heinemann)

Dunn, J. (ed.) (1992); *Democracy: the unfinished journey* (Oxford University Press, Oxford)

Dworkin, R. (1977) *Taking Rights Seriously* (Duckworth)

Dworkin, R. (1988) 'Devaluing Liberty' *Index on Censorship* vol. 17, no. 8

Dworkin, R. (1990) *A Bill of Rights for Britain* (CounterBlasts 16) (Chatto & Windus)

Erskine May (1989) *Treatise on the law: privileges, proceedings and usage of Parliament*, 21st edn, ed. Boulton, C. (Butterworths)

Ewing, K. (1994a) 'Freedom of Association' in McCrudden, C. and Chambers, G. (eds) *Individual Rights and the Law in Britain* (Clarendon Press, Oxford)

Ewing, K. (1994b) *Britain and the ILO* (British Institute of Employment Rights)

Ewing, K. and Gearty, C. (1990) *Freedom under Thatcher: civil liberties in modern Britain* (Clarendon Press, Oxford)

Feldman, D. (1993) *Civil Liberties and Human Rights in England and Wales* (Clarendon Press, Oxford)

Fenwick, H. (1994) *Civil Liberties* (Cavendish Publishing)

Fitzgerald, M. (1993) *Ethnic Minorities and the Criminal Justice System* (RCCJ Research Study no. 20) (HMSO)

Foley, C. (1995) *Human Rights, Human Wrongs: the alternative report for the UN Human Rights Committee* (Liberty, Rivers Oram Press)

Freedom House (1994) *Comparative Survey of Freedom* (Freedom House)

Freeth, S. (1994) *Compiling the Electoral Register 1993* (OPCS)

Ganz, G. (1987) *Quasi-Legislation: recent developments in secondary legislation* (Sweet and Maxwell)

Garrett, J. (1992) *Westminster: does Parliament work?* (Gollancz)

Gearty, C. (1995) 'After Gibraltar' *London Review of Books*, 16 November

Genn, H. and Genn, Y. (1989) *The Effectiveness of Representation at Tribunals* (Report to the Lord Chancellor)

Giles, M. (1992) 'Judicial Law-Making in the Criminal Courts' *Criminal Law Review*, June

Gilmour, I. (1992) *Dancing with Dogma* (Simon & Schuster)

Glidewell, Sir I. (chairperson) (1966) *The Asylum and Immigration Bill 1995: the Report of the Glidewell Panel*, Justice

Goldstein, R. (1986) 'The Limitations of Using Quantitative Data in Studying Human Rights Abuses' *Human Rights Quarterly* vol. 8, no. 4

Gregory, J. (1987) *Trial by Ordeal* (Equal Opportunities Commission)

Grief, N. (1991) 'The Domestic Impact of the European Convention on Human Rights as Mediated through Community Law' *Public Law*, Winter

Griffith, J.A.G. (1960) *Coloured Immigrants in Britain* (Oxford University Press/Institute of Race Relations)

Grigg-Spall, I. and Ireland, P. (1994) *The Critical Lawyers' Handbook* (Pluto)

Halsbury's Laws Statutes of England and Wales (1992) 4th edn, Brown, P. (ed.) (Butterworths)

Hampson, F. (1990) 'The United Kingdom Before the European Court of Human Rights' in *Yearbook of European Law 1989* (Clarendon Press, Oxford)

Hansard Society (1991) *Agenda for Change: the report of the Hansard Society Commission on Election Campaigns* (Hansard Society)

Hansard Society (1992) *Making the Law: the report of the Hansard Society Commission on the Legislative Process* (Hansard Society)

Harden, I. and Lewis, N. (1987) *The Noble Lie: the British constitution and the rule of law* (Hutchinson)

Heady, H., Bruce, S., Freeth, S. and Smith, S. (1995) *The Coverage of the Electoral Register* (OPCS)

Heath, A., Jowell, R., Curtice, J. and Witherspoon, S. (1986) *End of Term Report to the ESRC: methodological aspects of attitude research* (Social and Community Planning Research)

Held, D. (1987) *Models of Democracy* (Polity Press, Cambridge)

Heuston, R.V.F. (1979) *Essays in Constitutional Law* 2nd edn (Stevens and Sons)

Hewitt, M. and Thornton, P. (1989) *The Liberty/NCCL Guide* (Penguin, Harmondsworth)

Higgins, R. (1976–77) 'Derogations under Human Rights Treaties' *British Year Book of International Law* no. 281

Hilton, I. (1993) *Look Who's Talking: telephone metering*, Violations Paper no. 9 (Charter 88)

Hirst, P. (1995) 'Quangos and Democratic Government' in Ridley, F.F. and Wilson, D. (eds) *The Quango Debate* (Oxford University Press/Hansard Society)

Hodgson, G. (1993) *A Squinting Eye to Democracy: the electoral register*, Violations Paper no. 8 (Charter 88)

Hood Phillips, O. and Jackson, P. (1978) *Constitutional and Administrative Law* (Sweet and Maxwell)

Humana, C. (ed.) (1986, 1992) *World Human Rights Guide* (Oxford University Press, New York)

ICM (1994) *Poll on Democracy* for Channel 4, March

International Centre Against Censorship (1991) *Information, Freedom and Censorship: world report 1991* (Library Association Publishing)

International Centre Against Censorship (1993a) *The Article 19 Freedom of Expression Manual* (Bath Press)

International Centre Against Censorship (1993b) *Press Law and Practice* (International Centre Against Censorship)

Jabine, T. and Claude, R. (eds) (1992) *Human Rights Statistics: getting the record straight* (University of Pennsylvania Press, Pennsylvania)

Jellicoe, Lord (1983) *Review of Emergency Legislation*

Jenkins, S. (1995) *Accountable to None* (Penguin, Harmondsworth)

Jones, T.H. (1990) 'Common Law and Criminal Law: The Scottish Example' *Criminal Law Review*

Jones, T H. (1995) 'The Devaluation of Human Rights under the European Convention' *Public Law*, Winter

Jowell, J. and Lester, L. (1978) 'Beyond Wednesbury: Substantive Principles of Administrative Law' *Public Law*, Autumn

Justice; (1993) *Miscarriages of Justice: Defendant's Eye View* (Justice)

Kaye, T. (1991) *Unsafe and Unsatisfactory* (Civil Liberties Trust)

Kennedy, H. (1992) *Eve Was Framed* (Vintage)

Kinley, D. (1993) *The European Convention on Human Rights: compliance without incorporation* (Dartmouth, Aldershot)

Klug, F. (1993) 'Human Rights as Indicators of Democracy',Paper for the European Consortium for Political Research Workshop on Indices of Democratisation, University of Leiden, ECPR – Department of Government, University of Essex, March

Klug, F. and Starmer, K. (1995) *The Battered Shield: the system for protecting human rights in the UK* (Submission to the UN Human Rights Committee) Democratic Audit Paper no. 6 (Human Rights Centre, University of Essex, and Charter 88 Trust)

Klug, F., Starmer, K. and Weir, S. (1995) ' "The British Way of Doing Things": The UK and the International Covenant on Civil and Political Rights, 1976–94' *Public Law*, Winter

Laws, Sir J. (1993) 'Is the High Court the Guardian of Fundamental Constitutional Rights?' *Public Law,* Spring

Lawyers' Committee for Human Rights (1992, 1993) *Critique: review of the US Department of State's country reports on human rights practices* (Lawyers' Committee for Human Rights, New York)

Leigh, D. (1988) *The Wilson Plot* (Heinemann)

Lester, A. (1984) 'Fundamental Rights: The United Kingdom Isolated', *Public Law,* 46

Lester, A. (1993) *The Crisis Facing Human Rights in Europe,* Chartist Paper no. 2 (Charter 88)

Lester, A. and Bindman, G. (1972) *Race and the Law* (Penguin, Harmondsworth)

Lewis, N. and Birkinshaw, P. (1993) *When Citizens Complain: reforming justice and administration* (Open University Press)

Liberty (1991) *A People's Charter: Liberty's bill of rights* (Civil Liberties Trust)

Liberty (1992) *Broken Covenants: Violations of International Law in Northern Ireland (Liberty)*

Livingstone, S. and Morison, J. (1995) *In Place of Fear,* Democratic Audit Paper no. 5 (Human Rights Centre, University of Essex and Charter 88 Trust)

Locke, J. (1963) *Two Treatises of Government* (Cambridge University Press, Cambridge)

Lonsdale, S. and Walker, A. (1984) *A Right to Work: Disability and Employment* (Low Pay Unit)

Lopez, G. and Stohl, M. (1992) 'Problems of Concepts and Measurement in the Study of Human Rights' in Jabine, T. and Claude, R. (eds) (1992) *Human Rights Statistics: getting the record straight* (University of Pennsylvania Press, Pennsylvania)

Macdonald, R. St J., Matscher, F. and Petzold, H. (1993) *The European System for the Protection of Human Rights* (Martinus Nijhoff, Dordrecht/ Boston/London)

McConville, M. and Bridges, L. (1994) *Criminal Justice in Crisis* (Edward Elgar, Aldershot)

McCrudden, C. and Chambers, G. (1994) *Individual Rights and the Law in Britain* (Clarendon Press, Oxford)

McGoldrick, D. (1991) *The Human Rights Committee* (Clarendon Press, Oxford)

McKenzie, I., Morgan, R. and Reiner, R. (1990) 'Helping the Police with their Inquiries' Criminal Law Review vol. 22

Mark, R. (1978) *In the Office of Constable* (Collins)

Martin, R. (1993) *A System of Rights* (Clarendon Press, Oxford)

Michael, J. (1982) *The Politics of Secrecy* (Penguin, Harmondsworth)

Michael, J. (1994) *Privacy and Human Rights* (Dartmouth, Aldershot)

Mount, F. (1992) *The British Constitution Now* (Heinemann)

Norton, P. (1992) *The Constitution: the Conservative way forward* (Conservative Political Centre)

Norton-Taylor, R. (1995) *Truth is a Difficult Concept: inside the Scott Inquiry* (Fourth Estate)

Nowak, M. (1993) *UN Covenant on Civil and Political Rights* (N.P.Engel, Kehl/Strasbourg/ Arlington)

Oyediran, J. (1992) 'The United Kingdom's Compliance with Article 4 of the International Convention on the Elimination of All Forms of Racial Discrimination' in Coliver, S (ed.) *Striking a Balance: hate speech, freedom of expression and non-discrimination* (Article 19)

Paine, T. (1791) *The Rights of Man* (J. Johnson)

Partsch, K.J. (1993) 'Discrimination' in Macdonald, R. St J., Matscher, F. and Petzold, H. (eds) *The European System for the Protection of Human Rights* (Martinus Nijhoff, Dordrecht/Boston/London)

Pateman, C. (1970) *Participation and Democratic Theory* (Cambridge University Press, Cambridge)

Patten, J. (1991) in *Modern British Government* (European Policy Forum)

Pinto-Duschinsky, M. and Pinto-Duschinsky, S. (1987) *Voter Registration: problems and solutions* (Home Office)

Power, M. (1994) *The Audit Explosion* (Demos)

Rawls, J. (1972) *A Theory of Justice* (Oxford University Press, Oxford)

Richardson, G. and Genn, H. (eds) (1994) *Administrative Law & Government Action* (Clarendon Press, Oxford)

Robertson, A.H. and Merrills, J.G. (1993) *Human Rights in Europe* (Manchester University Press, Manchester)

Robertson, G. (1989) *Freedom, the Individual and the Law* (Penguin, Harmondsworth)

Robertson, G. (1993) *The Cure for the British Disease* (Charter 88)

Robertson, G. and Nicol, A. (1992) *Media Law* (Penguin, Harmondsworth)

Rosas, A. and Heligesen, J. (1990) *Human Rights in an East–West Perspective: facing a new reality* (Pinter)

Rousseau, J.-J. (1968) *The Social Contract* (Penguin, Harmondsworth)

Rowntree Reform Trust (1991, 1995) *State of the Nation.* Opinion polls, full data available from MORI, London. For commentary on 1991 poll, see Smith, T. 'Citizenship and the Constitution' *Parliamentary Affairs,* vol. 44, October 1991. For highlights of the 1995 results, see MORI newsletter, *Public Opinion,* June 1995

Ryan, A. (1991) 'The British, the Americans and Rights' in Lacey, M. and Haakonssen, K. (eds) *A Culture of Rights: the bill of rights in philosophy, politics and law* (Cambridge University Press, Cambridge)

Ryssdal, R. (1992) 'Human Rights Proceedings: European Provisions and Experience' in *Developing Human Rights Jurisprudence* vol. 4 (Fourth Judicial Colloquium on the Domestic Application of International Human Rights Norms)

Sanders, A. and Bridges, L. (July 1990) 'Access to Legal Advice and Police Malpractice' *Criminal Law Review*

Scarman, Lord (1974) *English Law: the new dimension.* The Hamlyn Lectures (Stevens)

Scoble, H. and Wiseberg, L. (1982) 'Problems of Comparative Research on Human Rights' in Nanda, V. *et al. Global Human Rights, Public Policies and NGO Strategies* (Westview Press)

Sieghart, P. (1983) *The International Law of Human Rights* (Clarendon Press, Oxford)

Sieghart, P. (1986) *The Lawful Rights of Mankind* (Oxford University Press, Oxford)

Silk, P. and Walters, R. (1995) *How Parliament Works*, 3rd edn (Longman)

Smith, J. and McLean, I. (1992) *The UK Poll Tax and the Declining Electoral Roll: unintended consequences?* (University of Warwick)

Spencer, M. (1990) *1992 and All That* (Civil Liberties Trust)

Standing Advisory Commission on Human Rights *Annual Reports* 1–20 (HMSO)

Stewart, J. (1992) *Accountability to the Public* (European Policy Forum)

Stone, R. (1994) *Textbook on Civil Liberties* (Blackstone Press)

Thompson, W. (1938) *Civil Liberties* (Victor Gollancz)

Thornton, P. (1989) *Decade of Decline: civil liberties in the Thatcher years* (National Council for Civil Liberties)

Townsend, P. (1979) *Poverty in the United Kingdom: a survey of household resources and standards of living* (Penguin, Harmondsworth)

United Nations (1994) *Human Rights and Elections* (UN Centre for Human Rights, Geneva)

Van Dijk, P. and Van Hoof, G. (1990) *Theory and Practice of the European Convention on Human Rights*, 2nd edn (Kluwer)

Wade, E.C.S., Bradley, A.W. and Ewing, K.D. (1993) *Constitutional and Administrative Law*, 11th edn (Longman)

Wadham, J. (1994) *Your Rights* (National Council for Civil Liberties)

Walker, C. (1992) *The Prevention of Terrorism in British Law* (Manchester University Press, Manchester)

Walker, C. and Starmer, K. (1993) *Justice in Error* (Blackstone, Oxford)

Wallington, P. (1985) 'Policing the Miners' Strike', *Industrial Law Journal* vol. 14, 156

Weir, S. (1993) 'Auditing Democracy: Subjective and Political Elements', Paper for the European Consortium for Political Research Workshop on Indices of Democratisation, University of Leiden, March

Weir, S. (1994) *Democracy in the Balance: how Britain compares with five other democratic nations,* Democratic Audit Paper no. 3 (Human Rights Centre, University of Essex, and Charter 88 Trust)

Weir, S. and Hall, W. (eds) (1994) *EGO TRIP: extra-governmental organisations in the United Kingdom and their accountability* (Human Rights Centre, University of Essex, and Charter 88 Trust)

Woodhouse, D. (1994) *Ministers and Parliament: accountability in theory and practice* (Clarendon Press, Oxford)

Wright, P. (1987) *Spycatcher* (Heinemann)

Young, H. (1990) *One of Us* (Pan)

Index

Figures and tables appear in *italic*.

absolute privilege 169
Access to Health Records Act (1990) 147
Access to Personal Files Act (1990) 147
Ackner, Lord 84; on the European Convention and the courts 98
Act of Settlement (1700) 69
Act of Union with Scotland (1707) 69
activities: prejudicial to interests of state 147–8
affirmative action 131–2
'affirmative instruments' 67
aggravated trespass 200, 202, 203, 299
Alderson, John (Chief Constable of Devon and Cornwall): destroyed files 231
American Convention on Human Rights 41
Amnesty International 256; Damien Austin case 262; examples of deportation methods 263; human rights reports 15; ill-treatment in Ireland 262–3; and shoot-to-kill policy 242
Animal Rights Index 228
anti-discrimination instruments 112–15
anti-discrimination laws 101, 120, 123–8, 136–7, 296, 313; in Northern Ireland 129–31; not applied uniformly throughout UK 137; permitting affirmative action 131; weaknesses and gaps in 125–8
Anti-Nazi League 198
armed forces 220; not disciplined in NI 310; restrictions on freedom of association 218, 219, 223, 301; and use of lethal force 241, *see also* security forces
Army Act (1955) 219
arrest 247–8, 264, 301; concept of 239; international requirements 239; international rules 245–6
arrest and detention powers: misuse of 249–50
Association of Electoral Administrators 279
Asylum and Immigration Bill (1955) 311
asylum seekers 102; rights of further curtailed 311
Atkinson, Lord: on equal pay for Poplar council employees 121
Austin, Damien: alleged ill-treatment of 262
Austria: broadcasting monopoly challenged 142, 166

bail 299, 306; applications, secrecy of in Crown Court 160, 297; concern about new restrictions 256–7; granting of presumed 239; not granted under certain circumstances 254–5; refusal of 84
Bail Act (1976) 199, 254, 256, 302
Bail (Amendment) Act (1993) 78
bail conditions 199–200; and international standards 201–2
Baker, Kenneth: and non-disclosure 162
Balcome, Lord Justice: Derbyshire County Council v Times Newspapers, (1992) 106
'band of reasonableness': allowed by European Court 22
banning: of organisations 208, 223
banning orders 193–5, 203, 298; broad scope of 195–8
Barnes, Harry MP: on under-estimates of non-registration of voters 283, 285
'basic interests' 104, 295, 312; distinguished from political rights and freedoms 91; and equality before the law 102; equality not among 116; not 'presumptions' 100
BBC: government interference in 180, 182, 183
Bermingham, Gerald MP: and Prevention of Terrorism Bills 56; on restriction of right to silence 87
Bill of Rights 9, 11, 46
Bill of Rights (1689), Britain 4, 37, 69, 94, 165
Bill of Rights (1791), America 5; 1968 amendment concerning voting rights 271
bind-overs 199, 201, 248, 299
blanket bans 187, 194, 196
blasphemy 172, 184, 308–9; law of discriminatory 173–4, 297
Blatch, Baroness: spoke against Human Rights Bill 39
bodyguards 240
breach of contract 214
breach of copyright, law against 149
breach of the peace 199, 201, 239, 248, 251–2, 299
Brent (London): fall in number of registered voters 289
Bridge, Lord: broadcasting ban case 98; on executive administrative discretion 97
Britain *see* United Kingdom

British Citizenship 12
British constitution 81
British courts: tasks of 38
British political system: constitutional and legal
    flexibility 314
British Social Attitudes (BSA) surveys 78, 79–80,
    82; suggest public opinion now less tolerant
    and anti-reformist 135
British subject 12
The British Way of Doing Things 133–8;
    challenged by international human rights
    instruments 313–14
Broadcasting Act (1990) 180
broadcasting media: ownership and control of 180
broadcasting, television and cinema enterprises:
    licensing of 166
broadcasting voice ban 97, 183, 184, 298;
    circumvented 183
Brown, Lord Justice Simon: and homosexuals in
    the armed forces case 98, 121
Browne-Wilkinson, Lord 91
brutal violence: and obscenity 173
buildings, privately owned: activities unregulated
    191
buildings, publicly-owned: no general right of use
    for meetings 190–1; use of by political
    candidates for meetings 190
Burke, Edmund: influence on British political
    thought 5
byelaws, local 103; and equality 121; restricting
    public assemblies in open spaces 189–90
Byers, Stephen MP: need for more time for
    standing committee on Criminal Justice Bill
    88; on right to silence in N Ireland 87

Callaghan, Jim (Home Secretary): postponement
    of boundary changes 69
Camden, Lord: and 'presumption of liberty' 100
Campaign Against the Arms Trade (CAAT):
    conditions imposed on 198
The Campaign for the Homeless and Rootless
    (CHAR) 285
Campaign for Nuclear Disarmament see CND
canvassing: for the electoral register 288–9
Caravan Sites (Amendment) Bill (1993) 120
Castlereagh Holding Centre: internationally
    condemned 263
censorship by 'prior restraint' 146
Census Validation Survey (1991) 283
CERD see UN Convention on the Elimination of
    All Forms of Racial Discrimination
Channel Island dossiers 152–3
Charles Humana World Human Rights Guide 14,
    15
Charter 88 77, 135
'the chattering classes' 77
Child Care Act (1980) 51
citizens 9; assuming democratic rights 111; extent
    of political activity 324; individual and
    minorities, ill-protected by public opinion

75–6; the law and their rights 80; no universal
    right to equality 116; right to privacy
    compromised in UK 236–7
citizenship: British 12; criteria for 323; equality of
    320; rights of, democratic criteria 322–3
civil liberties xii; limitations on protection of by
    judicial review 95–6, 98; not explained 81; not
    well served by parliamentary process 89
civil rights see political and civil rights
Civil Rights (Disabled Persons) Bill 1994: blocked
    by government 128–9
civil servants: behaviour determined by ministers
    65; drafting misleading replies to PQs 65; and
    freedom of association 219–20; responsible
    only to ministers 64–5; senior, concealing
    truth on arms to Iraq 150
Civil Service Pay and Conditions of Service Code
    219
civil society 323–4
Claim of Right (1689) 37
Clapham Common 190
Clark, Alan MP 160
Clarke, Kenneth MP 161
closed shop 213, 300; a violation of the
    Convention 93
CND: convictions and sentences upheld 153;
    police ban on marches 8
Coffey, Ann MP 88
Colin Wallace affair 153–4
collective action 212, 214, 300
Colville, Lord: review of 1984 PTA 252
Commission for Racial Equality 60, 124;
    complaints to 176; on the Race Relations Act
    126
Committee on the Administration of Justice in
    N Ireland 130; assault allegations 262–3
Committee of Experts (European) 211, 212, 213,
    218
Committee of Experts (ILO) 32, 33, 60, 212, 215,
    216, 217, 218
Committee of Ministers 32, 32, 141;
    Recommendation on the Access to
    Information Held by Public Authorities 144;
    on the rights of prisoners 275
common law 295; applied and developed by the
    courts 91; and autonomy of voluntary
    associations 214; blasphemy an offence under
    172; and the citizen 80; conspiracy to corrupt
    public morals 173; contempt of court rules
    'not necessary in a democratic society' 159;
    created by courts 38; deliberate contempt 157;
    and discrimination 116; does not and cannot
    give equal protection under the law 119;
    failures of 100–1; flexibility argument 104–5,
    138; and human rights obligations 136;
    interests protected by 99–101, 103;
    judge-made developments 104; offence of
    outraging public decency 173; prisoners and
    civil rights 276; protects basic rights rather
    than positive rights 136, 312; recognises

autonomy of associations 208, *see also* basic interests; bind-overs; breach of the peace; criminal law; statute law

Commons select committees: Select Committee on Procedure 62; unable to obtain facts in sensitive cases 65

Commons standing committees: 'crafted to favour government' 63; for Criminal Justice Bill (1994) 88; role of 61–2

Commonwealth Immigrants Act (1968) 47, 55–6, 306; inspired by mass panic 76

communication of information: state's obligation not to interfere with 144

Companies Act (1985) 87

Comparative Survey of Freedom, Freedom House 14, 15

Conference on Security and Cooperation in Europe: Copenhagen document 204, 267, 271, 272; public entitlement to information on human rights 144–5

confidence and copyright 148–9

confidence, obligation of 145

confidentiality: and the *Spycatcher* case 155–6

Conservative government 64; exploited fear of crime and 'moral panics' 79

conspiracy law 207, 208, 223, 300; concerns about 208

constitutional convention: significance of 68–9

constitutional and legal safeguards: necessity for 135

constitutional rights: British tradition of a double-edged legacy 3–4

Consultative Assembly *32*, 33

contempt of court 156, 157

Contempt of Court Act (1981) 47, 157, 158–9, 164, 181, 297

Convention on Discrimination in Employment and Occupation (ILO) 115

Convention on Equal Remuneration (ILO) 115

Convention on the Participation of Foreigners in Public Life at Local Level (Council of Europe) 272

Convention on Transfrontier Television (Council of Europe): Preamble 142

'conventions': lack of respect for 69–70; unwritten 38

Copenhagen document (CSCE) 204, 267, 271, 272

Copyright Act (1988) 149

cordless (mobile) phones: tapping of 234–5, 237, 299, 308

coroners' courts: defects of, Northern Ireland 244–5, 264, 301

Coroners (Practice and Procedure) Rules (1963) 244

correspondence: protection afforded to 226, 227

corruption and indecency in schools 179

Council of Europe 9, 31, 144, 258; Parliamentary Assembly on press monopoly and concentration 182; resident foreigners and the vote 272; Social Charter 17, 33, 211, 212, 213, 218

counter-terrorism 228

Court of Appeal 99; and breach of the peace 199; broadcasting ban case 97; and Derbyshire County Council v Times Newspapers, (1992) 105–6; homosexuals in the armed forces case 121; Miller, Paris and Abdullahi case 261; and peaceful picketing, Hubbard v Pitt case 191–2; prevention of Channel 4 TV broadcast 159; use of European Convention 93

court hearings and documents: regulation of access to 145

court orders: magistrates', restricting access to court 158

courts 128, 156–9, 294–5; 'balance of convenience' test 163, 164, 297; failures of 120–1; hearings in public 157–8; interpret statutes in conformity with notions of fairness and justice 294; interpreting Acts of Parliament 91–2; justice equated with necessity 127–8; openness of 160–4; and overriding rule of parliamentary sovereignty 312; and protection of journalists sources 181; restriction of public access to 297; sitting in private 157; trials under Official Secrets Acts 157; unable/unwilling to embrace wider notion of equality 116; vital functions of 90–1, 135–6, *see also* Court of Appeal; High Court; judicial review

Courts and Legal Services Act (1990) 118

crime: prevention of by force 241

Criminal Code Commissioners 80

criminal contempt: a new invention 159

Criminal Justice Act (1967) 51, 57

Criminal Justice Act (1988) 106; section 159 procedure 160

Criminal Justice Act (1991) 78, 118

Criminal Justice Act (1993) 78

Criminal Justice and Public Order Act (1994) 78, 83–9, 251, 302, 307B, 313; additional stop and search powers 247; and age of consent 118; blanket bans 194; complaints about Parliamentary process 88–9; designed to exploit fear of crime and 'moral panics' 79, 87; discriminatory impact on gypsies 119; government attitude to amendments 83–7; new offence of aggravated trespass 200; new offence of 'intentional harassment' 118; opposition attempts to amend 84, 85; opposition remained silent 87; removal of right to bail for certain offences 254–5, 256, 302; section 134 (torture) 259–60; special powers to prevent 'raves' 194–5

criminal law: and conspiracy 207; and highways 192

Criminal Law Act (1967) 241

Criminal Law Act (1977) 173, 207

Criminal Law (Northern Ireland) Act (1967) 241; 'absolute necessity' amendment recommended 242

'criminal libel' 169, 171, 184, 297, 308–9
criminal proceedings: initial detention in 254–5; rights of defendants 145–6
Crossman, Richard 55; compares British constitution to a rock 78–9; distinguished two publics 76–7; on Edmund Burke 5; government wished to stop publication of memoirs 152
the Crown: and democracy 110; government information property of 141, 146
Crown Service: discrimination by allowable 126
CSCE *see* Conference on Security and Cooperation in Europe
culture of freedom 185
'culture of liberty' 38, 68, 74–82, 134–5, 311
Cunningham, John: evidence to Hansard Commission 64
Currie, Edwina MP 88

data protection: and Europol 68
death: through lethal use of force 241
Declaration on Freedom of Expression and Information (1982) 141, 144
defamation 167, 168, 169–71, 184, 297, 306; by innuendo 169; McDonald's case 102, 171; no legal aid for defence against or initiation of actions 102; Tolstoy case 170–1
Defence Regulation 18B 76
degrading treatment: defined 258
delegated legislation 66, 293; not well scrutinised 66–7
democracy 309; appeal of xi; development of in UK 110–11; and freedom of association 204; human rights view of 9; implications of treatment under detention/restraint 239; and social equality 11
democracy-human rights links 8–10
Democratic Audit xi, xii, 317–18; auditing criteria 13–14; carrying out the audit 20–3; role of derogations and reservations 23–4; using Lexis facility 106
democratic criteria xi, xii, 13, 16, 24, 25, 319–25
democratic protection 44–5
democratic rights 304; audited by Human Rights Index 8; ensuring and securing 41–3; and equality 110; fundamental, probably safe in UK 82; protected by legislation 46; which to be audited 10–12
democratic society, notion of 22B, 43, 167, 206, 323–5
Denning, Lord 199; in Ahmed v Inner London Education Authority (1978) 93; and the European Convention 92–3; in Hubbard v Pitt case 191–2; on law of blasphemy 173–4; on the Magna Carta 3; unable to award compensation to sacked worker 93
deportation 307B; forced, and removal of immigrants 263–4
'deprave and corrupt': meaning of 172, 174, 297
derogations and reservations, role of 23–4

detention 239, 246, 264, 302; and breach of the peace 252; derogation from international standards 255–6, 302; international standards 252–3; pending trial 239, 253, 254–5; prohibition on torture and ill-treatment during 258–9; special powers of 239
Dicey, A.V. 70, 82; on constitutional law 38–9; identifies three pillars of liberty and the rule of law 40; principle of equality before the law 102; on protection of individual liberties 5; quoted 100
'Diplock Courts', N Ireland 70, 241
Diplock, Lord: on criminal libel 171
Disability Discrimination Act (1995) 129, 136, 296
disabled people: discrimination against 114–15, 128–9, 286
Disabled Persons (Employment Act) (1944) 71, 117, 125, 128, 296
'discovery' process, civil proceedings 158
discretionary powers: for ministers 66, 310
discrimination 176; and absence of right to equality 116–20, 295; against the homeless through disenfranchisement 285–6, 303; anti-union 211, 215; by public officials 126; direct 114, 123; and disabled people 114–15, 128–9; and EU law 116; indirect 114, 123, 124, 128; positive 296; in private relations, not prohibited 113; prohibition of and protection against 112–13; still not fully ended 101; and stop and search powers 251, 265; though Public Order Act 178, *see also* anti-discrimination laws
discriminatory conduct: unintentional 127–8
disenfranchisement 290; inequalities in the process of 283–6, *see also* voter registration
disinformation: concerning former prime ministers 153–4
dismissal: for failure to join a union 219, *see also* unfair dismissal
dissent: suppression of 170
domestic law: does include European Union law 38; does not include human rights treaties/conventions 37–8; EU law prevails over 116; must provide effective remedies if human rights are violated 40; nothing to gurantee equality and outlaw discrimination 116; and strikes 214
Donaldson, Lord 3, 97; on reporting restrictions 160; *Spycatcher* litigation 105
Drug Trafficking Act (1994) 78

economic and social rights 322
The Economist: on the doctrine of ministerial responsibility 64
Education Act (1944): and freedom of religion 93–4
Education (No. 2) Act (1986) 190–1
elections 303; by secret ballot, trade unions 214; candidates misleading voters 281–2, 290, 303; constitutional protection of 268; and

democracy 10; democratic criteria for 319–20; democratic elections, notion of 267; European, registration of resident EU citizens 289; indirect government interference in 270–1; local, vulnerable to interference 269; state obligations to ensure freedom and fairness of 278–9; suspension of 269, 271; to European Parliament 275; UN pre-requisite rights for 10–11; who may vote or stand for election 273–8

Electoral, Civil and Social rights of prisoners (Council of Ministers) 272

Electoral Court: exposed problem of naming of 'political parties' 281; petitions to 280

electoral register: effect of poll tax on 270; registration system obsolete 290; structural inequalities in procedures 290; those missing from 283, *284*, 285–7, 303

electoral registration officers 279; discretion re 'permanent residence' 285; work of 280, 287–9

electoral rolls 280; fall in 282–6, 303

Emergency Provisions Act (1991) 264, 301, 302, 313

Employment Act (1988) 214, 216–17

Employment Act (1989) 125

Employment Act (1990) 213, 215

employment law 116, 300; 'adjusted' by government 118–19

Environmental Information Regulations (1992) 147

Environmental Protection Act (1990) 147

Equal Opportunities Commission 60, 124, 128

Equal Pay Act (1970) 117, 124

equal pay for equal work 124

equal pay legislation and case law: EU influence 108

Equal Pay (Remedies) Regulation (1993) 124

equal protection of the law 113, 117–21

equality 110–11, 136–7, 295–6, 301, 308, 322; absence of right to 116–17; limits of before the law 102–3; no general right to in UK 137, 313; not a basic interest 101; of opportunity 130; primacy of 112–15; in right to vote and stand for election 279; and weakness of 'presumption of liberty' 103–4, *see also* political equality

equality before the law 113, 116, 119, 137, 295, 313

EROs *see* electoral registration officers

Erskine May 61

ethnic minorities 307B; affected by inequalities 122–3; and criminal justice 122, 132; discrimination against 301; disenfranchised 283, 284, 285, 303; public support for anti-discrimination laws 80

EU Directives: Equal Pay Directive 124; Equal Treatment Directive 116, 124, 126; Pregnancy Directive 124

EU European Commission 12

EU law 295; and discrimination 116; influence on domestic rights 108–9; influence on sex discrimination law 124; inter-state control of justice and home affairs 109; protection afforded by 107–8; scope of justifiability defence 127

Euro-MPs: people disqualified from being 275B

European Commission *see* European Commission on Human Rights

European Commission on Human Rights 12, 17, 31, 305; and blanket bans 196; favours extension of voting rights to long-term residents 278; found violations in Commonwealth Immigration Bill 55–6; and GCHQ employees 107, 221; Harman and Hewitt case 229, 229–30; individual complaints to 17; and ownership of the media 181–2; 'right to fair and public hearing' 128

European Committee for the Prevention of Torture and Inhuman or Degrading Treatment or Punishment 15, 101, 263, 306

European Communities Act (1972) 38, 45, 107

European Convention *see* European Convention on Human Rights

European Convention on Human Rights xii, 6–7, 8, 13, 16, 17, *31*, 32, 136, 267, 336–42Ap; Article 2 (right to life) 239; Article 3 (torture) 258; Article 5 (arrest) 246, 250, 252; Article 8 (privacy) 225, 229, 235; Article 10 (freedom of expression) 142, 144, 145, 155, 164, 166, 167; Article 11 (freedom of association) 205, 208, 210, 221; Article 13 (surveillance) 229; Article 14 (discrimination) 112; Article 60 ('catch all' Article) 222; can be used to solve ambiguities in legislation 105; and conflicting rights 18; democracy-human rights links 9; equality and prohibition of discrimination 112; lethal force requirement 242; Parliamentary references to *86*, 87; Preamble 266; Protocols (1, 4, 6 and 7) 342–8Ap; ratified by UK 58; requires ensuring or securing of rights 41; and restrictions on state employees 218; The European Human Rights Umbrella 31–3; UK prison conditions violation 15; UK violations of 7, 47, *48–54*, 55–7, 310–11; use of in British courts 93–4, 106; violations through secondary legislation 134; on voting 271–2

European Convention for the Prevention of Torture and Inhuman or Degrading Treatment or Punishment 258

European Convention for the Protection of Human Rights and Fundamental Freedoms 31

European Court *see* European Court of Human Rights

European Court of Human Rights 9–10, 12, 17, 18, 22B, *31*, 32, 43, 70, 210, 217, 234, 305; freedom of expression 142; Gibraltar killings decision 243; Immigration rules breached European Convention 56; interpretation of European Convention 22; judgments

compliance with International Convention 61; reluctant participation in human rights treaties 57–9; supremacy of in Parliament 313; trade union policies breach international obligations 217; willing to accept amendments in the Lords 63, 64

government information: and Code of Practice on Access to Government Information 146, 151; and law of confidence and copyright 148–9; no 'public interest' defence for unauthorised disclosure 153; public access to 149–51

government institutions: democratic criteria for 320–1

Governmental Social Committee 32, 33

Greater London Council: elections for cancelled 269

Griffiths, Jim 58; on strong government 314

Guardian: Spycatcher articles 155, 156

Guidelines on the Use of Equipment in Police Surveillance Operations 232, 234

gypsies: adequate site provision for 88; discrimination against 119–20

habeas corpus 239, 253, 255; failing power of 257; a right reduced 70

Habeas Corpus Act (1641) 69

Halsbury, Lord: on refusal of access to court for public and press 157

Halsbury's Laws of England 74, 311

Hansard Society: Commission on Electoral Campaigns 279; report on legislative process 62–3

Harman, Harriet 229, 229–30, 306

Hattersley, Roy: on the European Convention 13

Helsinki Watch: found abuse of children by security forces in NI 263

Henderson, Paul: in Matrix Churchill case 160–1

Heseltine, Michael (President of the Board of Trade) 161, 162, 164

Hewitt, Patricia 229, 229–30, 306

Higgins, Professor Rosalyn: on doctrine of the margin of appreciation 23

High Court: homosexuals in the armed forces case 121; limitations on in judicial review 95–6; in Salman Rushdie case 179

highways 309; and freedom of assembly 188–9, 298; freedom of assembly a matter of 'good grace' 191, 192, 193, 203

Highways Act (1980) 188, 192, 202

HMSO: does not publish human rights reports 60, 61

Home Office 287; and the electoral register 288–9; Electoral Registration of Mentally Ill or Learning Disabled People, Code of Practice 276; Guidelines on Special Branch Work in Great Britain (1994) 228, 230

Home Secretary: can prohibit transmissions by BBC 180

homeless people: disenfranchised 285, 303

homosexual law reform 77

homosexuality 77, 114, 116, 177, 208, 298; and the armed forces 98, 121; and discrimination 117–18, 121; growing intolerance of 178; and Local Government Act (1988) 119; and right to privacy 178

Hong Kong: International Covenant incorporated into law 47

House of Commons: dominated by government 133–4; Home Affairs Committee's dissatisfaction with application of Race Relations Act 176, *see also* government; Parliament

House of Lords (judicial): on admissibility of illegally obtained evidence 234; cases of direct discrimination 123; on conformity of UK legislation with international human rights obligations 92; equal pay lacked 'rational proportion' 121; on executive powers and the European convention 97; on free speech 165; House of Lords judgements and international human rights 105; judgement on Sinn Fein media voice ban 97; on judicial review and national security 96; prisoners no right to sue over prison conditions 101; refused to remove injunction on *Spycatcher* publication 155–6; review of ministerial powers and human rights 95

House of Lords (revising): amendments to bills inserted here 63; amendments to Criminal Justice Act (1994) reversed by government 84, 87; complacency of 56; complaints about procedural shortcomings, Criminal Justice Bill (1994) 89; defender of constitutional principle 45; and European legislation 67; lacks democratic legitimacy 134, 293; Lords Committee on a Bill of Rights 64; restricted ability of acts to combat discrimination 127; Select Committee on the Scrutiny of Delegated Power 67; supposedly a revising chamber 89, 293

Howe, Lord: to Scott inquiry 150

human rights: in democracies 9; discharge of Britain's reporting obligations 60–1; effects of Orders in Council on 71; international, awareness of Britain's obligations 86, 87–8; no widespread or systematic violations 304; Parliament as pillar of 46–55; positive, new tradition of xii; previous attempts at auditing 14–16; protection by court interpretations 90; qualitative and quantitative approaches to auditing 14–16; universal, development of 5–7; violations, by individuals or organisations 19, *see also* UN Human Rights Committee

human rights auditing: qualitative approach 15–16; quantitative approach 14–15

Human Rights Index xi, xii, 7–8, 13–25, 40; compiling and presenting data for audit 19; how it works 16–18; inapplicable to social and economic rights 11; includes but does not represent international law 18–19; an index of human rights standards 19; and principles of equality and non-discrimination 111; reconciling conflicts between instruments and rights 18–19; to represent best practice 18, 24; use of primary materials and secondary sources 17–18

human rights instruments: contain allowable restrictions 310; gaining influence in UK courts 136; Parliamentary references to 86; permitting affirmative action 131–2

human rights obligations, international: attempts to introduce, failure of 96–7; courts' approach to 92; need to adjust UK law and practice to 58–9; relevance to common law 105–6; UK governments indifferent to 133

human rights standards 16; questions of UK compliance with 81; state obligations to ensure free and fair elections 278–9; universal standards 24–33, 41–3

human rights standards, evolving 16, 143–6, 221–2, 305; arrest and detention 245–6; detention pending trial 253; freedom of assembly 187–8; freedom of expression 167–8; freedom of information 143–6; ill-treatment in detention 258–9; for life and liberty 240–1; and the poll tax 270–1; and restrictions on freedom of association 207; right to form and join trade unions 211–13; rights to vote and stand in elections 268; surveillance and the right to privacy 226–7

human rights standards, international: allow for restrictions on freedom of association 209; British infringements of 306–10; influence of on courts 105–7; and the Public Order Act (1986) 195–8; and restrictions on public protest 201–2; UK law and practice does not measure up 117–21

human rights treaties: government participation in reluctant 57–9; no effective influence on domestic courts 294, *see also* European Convention on Human Rights; International Covenant on Civil and Political Rights

Hurd, Douglas: and the broadcasting ban 97, 183

'husband rule' 56, 60

Hyde Park 190

ill-treatment: by police of suspects in custody 260–2; evidence of, Northern Ireland 262–3

illegality: and the courts 95, 135, 312

ILO *see* International Labour Organisation

immigrants: forced deportation and removal of 263–4, 303

Immigration Act (1971) 76; and *habeas corpus* 255; and retrospective penalties 92, *see also* Commonwealth Immigrants Act (1968)

Immigration Rules: 'husband rule' 56, 60; and laws, sexual discrimination in 59; standard of living of immigrants not relevant 121

'incitement to racial hatred' offence 123

indecency, concept of 173

indecency laws 174–5, 184, 297

Independent: published allegations in *Spycatcher* 159

Independent Television Commission (ITC) 180

individuals: and freedom of assembly 198–201; right to petition not accepted by UK government 58

industrial action, obligation to ballot before 215

inequality(ies): caused by ban on some legal aid 102; and the judiciary 120; significant, in British life 122–3, 132

information: access to, importance of 164; seen as property 148, *see also* freedom of information; government information

inhuman or degrading treatment 302; deportation enforcement 263–4

inhuman treatment: defined 258; Northern Ireland 262–3

injunctions: a backdoor route to prior restraint 163–4; use of 162–3

'innocent until proved guilty' principle: still believed 79

inquests: no legal aid for 102, *see also* coroners' courts

Intelligence Service Commissioner 228

Intelligence Services Act (1994) 227, 228; secretive regulatory measures 229

Intelligence Services Tribunal 229, 231

'intentional harassment': a new offence 119

intercepted communications: disclosure an offence 148; warrants for 232, 233

Interception of Communications Act (1985) 47, 60, 224, 232, 237, 299, 300; does not regulate metering 236; reasons for introduction 234; tribunals to investigate warrants 232

interceptions: concerns about regulation of 234–5; unlawful, safeguards against 232–4

International Bill of Human Rights 17

International Covenant on Civil and Political Rights 9, 13, 16–17, 26, 94, 136, 205, 217, 267, 295, 305, 326–34Ap; Article 2 (discrimination) 112; Article 3 (equal rights) 112; Article 6 (life and liberty) 238–9; Article 7 (torture) 258; Article 9 (arrest) 246, 252, 252–3; Article 17 (right to privacy) 224–5, 235; Article 19 (freedom of expression) 142, 145, 165–6, 168; Article 20 (prohibits propaganda) 168, 175; Article 22 (freedom of association) 205, 210, 221; Article 25 (participation in public life) 268, 271; Article 26 (equality) 112, 113, 117, 125, 132, 313; absence of anti-racial discrimination legislation, N Ireland 72; and conflicting rights 18; equality and prohibition of discrimination 112, 113; Optional Protocol 26, 28, 58, 106, 256–7, 334–5Ap; reference to in UK courts 106; require ensuring or securing of rights 41; and restriction of right to silence in N Ireland 72; and restrictions on state employees 218–19; signed by UK 58, 175; United Nations: the Human Rights Umbrella 26–30 international instruments: limitations on exercise of 20

International Labour Organisation 27, 29–30, 107; Convention on Freedom of Association violated 29, 95–6; conventions 87 and 98 29, 95–6, 210, 211, 212, 215, 216, 218, 219, 222; covenants protect trade unionism 204; Declaration of Philadelphia 29; machinery to deal with freedom of association issues 210–11, *see also* Committee of Experts (ILO); Convention on Discrimination in Employment and Occupation (ILO); Convention on Equal Remuneration (ILO); Freedom of Association Committee (ILO)

international relations: disclosure of information concerning an offence 154–5

internment: use of, UK 252

interpretations 23

invasion of privacy 224

irrationality principle 312; and challenge to discrimination 117; and control of government decisions 95; and protection of civil liberties in judicial review 97–8; seen as not sufficiently robust 135–6

James I, and judicial independence 90

Jefferson, Thomas: on equality (Declaration of Independence) 110

Jellicoe, Lord: on proscription 209–10

Jenkins, Roy (Home Secretary): introduction of 1974 Prevention of Terrorism Act 76; on our criminal law 80

Jews: and the Magna Carta 4

journalism: investigative 75; protection of sources 181, *see also* National Union of Journalists

journalistic privilege: absence of 180–1

Jowitt, Lord: warned of need to review UK law and practice 58

'judge-made law' *see* common law

judges/judiciary: areas of non-intervention 95–6; creative development of the law 104–5; and discrimination 120–1; failures of 120–1; higher court, as custodians of fundamental rights 91; independence of 90, 320; interpretations conform with notions of fairness and justice 92

judicial review 38, 46, 90, 94–9, 158, 294–5, 312; and banning orders 197; constraints on judges' 'constitutional raid' 95–9; expansion of 91; and GCHQ problem 220; on grounds of illegality, irrationality and procedural impropriety 94–5, 116–17, 312; homosexuals in the armed forces 121

jury trial, immutable right to 69, 322; withdrawal of 70

Justice 89, 117; and allegations of physical abuse 262

Kaye, Gordon: and invasion of privacy 101

Kinley, David: study of government sensitivity to European Convention 57, 65

Kirby, Justice Michael: on freedom of information legislation in Australia 152

Knorpel, Henry 66

Labour government 151, 315; Commonwealth Immigrants Bill 55–6; major role in establishment of human rights treaties 57–8

Lady Chatterley's Lover, D.H. Lawrence 173

law: Acts of Parliament should prevail over European Convention 93; flexibility argument 104–5, 133, 138, 295; no distinction between 'public' and 'private' law 37, *see also* common law; criminal law; judicial review; legislation; statute law

Law Commission: and codifying the criminal law 80; on law of blasphemy 174

The Law of the Constitution, A.V. Dicey 38, 40

law enforcement: and the use of force 240

law lords: and irrationality principle 97–8

Law Society 89; on delegated or secondary legislation 66, 67

Laws, Mr Justice 91; on judicial review proceedings 99

League of Nations 6

legal advice, right to 59

legal aid 295; eligibility for 102–3, 137; not available for defamation cases 169; not available for industrial tribunals 128; reduction in availability of 102, 137

Legal Aid (Scotland) Act (1986) 54

legal rights: positive, need for 315

legal system, English 4

legislation: affecting human rights, little explanation offered 81; in breach of human rights obligations 133; by Order in Council 71; designed to placate or exploit public 'fear and prejudice' 76; discriminating against groups without parliamentary majorities 119; European 67–8; and human rights 46–7; 'instant' 311; judicial interpretation of 90, 92–4; and other measures addressing discrimination 118–19; and proscribed organisations 208–9; relevance of European Convention to 105–6; and residue of liberty 103, 312; scrutinised and amended by Parliament 45; secondary, not adequately checked by Parliament 134, 310; should not act retrospectively 92; timetable controlled by government 62; violating European Convention 47; weight of and lack of clarity 63, *see also* delegated legislation; law; quasi-legislation

Lester, Lord QC: on adequate provision for gypsies 88; arguing on broadcasting ban case 97; checked on Britain's reporting to specialised human rights authorities 60–1

lethal force 264, 308; 'absolute necessity' justification 241–3; outlawed by law 241, 301

libel 169; and Derbyshire County Council 105–6

New York Times 156
Newspaper Libel and Registration Act (1881) 180
newspapers: ownership of and take-overs 180, 298
The Noble Lie, Harden and Lewis 64
Nolan Report: on open government 146
non-governmental organisations (NGOs): in Britain 75
Northern Ireland 175, 296, 303, 304; anti-discrimination laws in 129–31; banning of public processions and meetings 298–9; broadcasting ban case 97; Chief Electoral Officer 279–80; democratic deficit 71–3; Diplock Courts 70, 241; emergency powers contravening European Convention 57; evidence of ill-treatment 262–3; excepted, reserved and transferred matters 71; extra-judicial killings in 241–5, 301; and homosexual law reform 77; law of obscene libel 172; media reporting restrictions 8; not included in Race Relations Act (1976) 117; political and civil rights in 71; proscribed organisations 209; public order law 197; restriction on political and civil rights 42, 143, 309–10; restrictions on right to silence 72, 87; shoot-to-kill policy 242, 243, 264; stop and search powers 248; Ulster TV declined to relay 'shoot-to-kill' documentary 159, *see also* Fair Employment (Northern Ireland) Acts (1976 and 1989); Public Order (NI) Order (1987)
Northern Ireland Committee 71
Northern Ireland Constitution Act (1973) 71, 117, 129, 130
Northern Ireland Court of Appeal: quashed convictions because of fabricated evidence 26
Northern Ireland (Emergency Provisions) Act (1991) 209, 247, 251
Northern Ireland Human Rights Assembly 262–3
Norton, Philip: on constraints on government 74
Norton, Professor: speaking to Hansard Commission 63
nuclear weapons: developed under secrecy 151

O'Brien, Mike MP: need for research and reflection in standing committees 88
Obscene Publications Act (1959) 172, 174; 'public good' defence 173
obscenity 172–3, 184, 297
The Observer: on judicial independence 87; *Spycatcher* articles 155, 156
obstructing the police 200–1, 202, 299
obstruction of highways: criminal offence and civil wrong 188–9
Office of Population Censuses and Surveys (OPCS) 282
official information: access to 146; concealment of by many governments 150–1; liberalising regime of secrecy 151–2; release of 141
official secrecy/secrets 145, 147–8
Official Secrets Act (1911) 76, 141, 147, 153

Official Secrets Act (1920) 157
Official Secrets Act (1989) 141, 147, 154, 164, 296; Colin Wallace affair 153–4; *Spycatcher* saga 154
Official Secrets Acts 220
officials *see* civil servants
open government: Britain's record on 152–3; trend towards 149
Open Government white paper (1993) 146, 147; Code of Practice on Access to Government Information 146, 151
open justice: and reporting restrictions 157–8, 160
open spaces: holding meetings in 189–90; not freely available for public assemblies 193
Orders in Council 66; and GCHQ staff 95–6; for Northern Ireland 71, 129–30
organisations: banned or proscribed 208–9
'Osmotherley rules' 65
'other status': defined 114; includes disability 129

PACE *see* Police and Criminal Evidence Act (1984)
PACE Code of Conduct 250–1
PACE Order *see* Police and Criminal Evidence (Northern Ireland) Order
Paine, Thomas: *The Rights of Man* 5
Parks Regulation Act (1872) 190
Parliament: ability to deny public what it wants 79; as a buffer (Crossman) 79; deals ineffec-tively with European legislation 67–8; failure to legislate to protect rights of free expression and privacy 47; failure to protect individual rights 310; failure of as watchdog 61–4; as indifferent to or ignorant of Conventions provisions as government 65; legislative process 45; ministerial responsibility/account-ability to 45–6, 149; 'Osmotherley rules' 65; as pillar of human rights 46–55; 'Ponsonby Rules' 68; power of 37, 46, 116; powers conferred by may be challenged in court 90–1; powers to control the executive 64–6; presumed not to intend to breach interna-tional law 92; protection of political rights and freedoms 293; role as forum for scrutiny and amendment easily negated 83–7; role of 44–5, 133–4; scrutiny of legislation by is largely ineffective 62–3, 134, 293; structures failing MPs 70–1; violations of European Convention 47, *see also* executive; government; House of Commons; House of Lords; ministers; MPs
Parliament Acts (1911 and 1949) 69
parliamentary oversight: ineffective 134
Parliamentary Questions: deliberately misleading replies in arms to Iraq and Iran case 65; scope limited by rules 65
parliamentary sovereignty 310; and the courts 90, 294, 312; and protection of basic rights 313
parliamentary supremacy 313; and control of government 95; curbed by European Union 107; means lesser role for courts 38

parliamentary terms 280

Patten, John: on a Bill of Rights 45; on 'culture of liberty' 74

'Patten's law' 69, 70; broken by Criminal Justice and Public Order Act (1994) 83

'payroll vote' 62

peaceful assemblies: no right to in UK 193; protection for demanded by international standards 192–3

peaceful protest, right to: public now less in favour of 80

Permanent Court of Justice: requires legislation modification to fulfil obligations 41

permanent injunctions 163

personal freedom: a basic interest 100

personal liberty: a basic interest 91

picketing: lawful 191; peaceful, protection for 189

plurality voting 266–7

police 220; allegations of ill-treatment by in NI 262–3; arrest and detention by 246–7, 249; and banning orders 194; and breach of the peace 199, 251–2; conscious or unconscious racism by 127; ill-treatment of suspects in custody 260–2; imposing conditions on processions and assemblies 195; obstruction of 200–1, 202; and peaceful protest 198; restrictions on freedom of association 218, 219, 223, 301; stop and search powers 111, 239, 247, 250–2, 265, 301–2, 307B, 312; surveillance by 79, 228, 237, 299, *see also* security forces; Special Branches

Police Act (1964) 219

Police Complaints Authority: Govell case 231; limited powers of 231

Police and Criminal Evidence Act (1984) 59, 246, 248, 250, 264; Code C 259; detention under 254, 302, 303; effect on ill-treatment in custody 260–2

Police and Criminal Evidence (Northern Ireland) Order 247, 250

Police Federation 220

Police and Magistrates' Court Act (1994) 78

Police Regulations 1987 219

political activities: limitations on permissible 272–3

political and civil rights 322; and common law flexibility 104–5; and the Democratic Audit 10–12; entrenched in law, need for in UK 137–8; failure by UK to adopt 305–6; main criteria for measurement of 13; protection afforded by judicial interpretations not clear 92–4; restriction of 143, *see also* civil liberties; human rights; political rights; political rights and freedoms

political convention: fading power of 69–71

political equality 266, 322; missing in quantitative surveys 15; principle of 11

political parties: need for registration of (UK) 281–2

political rights 136, 219; and 'band of reasonable-ness' 22; equal access to 110–38; freedom of

association as 204; protection by the courts 90–109, 295; restrictions assessed by Three-Part Test 20–3

political rights and freedoms 309; little formal legal protection for 304, 305; protected by 'force of public opinion' 74

political values: protection of 74–5

politicians: criticisms of 168

poll tax 270–1; popular revolt against 75, 82

polling stations: many inaccessible to the disabled 286

'Ponsonby Rules' 68

Ponting, Clive 154; jury refusal to convict 148

population: changes in 282

'populist anti-reformism': shift towards 77, 78–80

positive rights 80; conferred by international instruments 20; need for 314–15

postal votes 280–1, 286, 290, 304

pre-requisite rights, UN: ensuring free elections 10–11

prerogative powers 66, 68, 133, 227; used to ban trade unions at GCHQ 66

pressure groups and associations 77; campaigned for reforms 77–8; lobbied for amendments to Criminal Justice Bill (1994) 89; protecting and promoting political and civil rights 75

'presumption of liberty' 100; weakness of 103–4

'presumptions' 38, 91–2; further 92; giving some protection to political rights and freedoms 99–100

Prevention of Terrorism Act (1964) *51*

Prevention of Terrorism Act (1974) 56, 76

Prevention of Terrorism Act (1984) 23, 255

Prevention of Terrorism Acts: violation of European Convention and International Covenant 72, *see also* Emergency Provisions Act (1991)

Prevention of Terrorism (Temporary Provisions) Act (1989) 209, 239, 254, 255, 264, 301; and detention at port of entry 248–9, 302; misuse of powers of arrest and detention 249–50; people detained, excluded and charged under 246–7, *247*

prior restraint 155–6, 210, 297; censorship by 146; injunctions a backdoor route to 163–4

prison conditions 307B; legal challenges to impossible in UK 101; violating European Convention 15

prison rules *48*; campaign for reform of 77; changes to regarding right to legal advice 59

Prison Standing Orders: 1982 changes *49*

prisoners: convicted, denied right to vote or stand for election 276; voting rights of 272, 275–6, 303

privacy: invasions of 100–1, 226; no right to unless 'basic interest' is involved 136; not a basic interest 100; protection of 104, *see also* right to privacy

private nuisance: and striking miners 104

'privilege'; defence in defamation cases 169
procedural impropriety 135, 312; and control of government decisions 95
prohibited places 147–8
prohibition: of organisations 208, 209
Prohibitions del Roy (1607) 90
proscription 209, 223, 300; legal challenges to 209–10
Protestants: and the Magna Carta 4
proxy votes 276, 278, 280–1, 286, 290, 304
PTA *see* Prevention of Terrorism (Temporary Provisions) Act (1989)
public: need to know and understand rights 80–2; 'right to know' 142
public access: to court hearings and documents 158–9, 297; to government information 149–51; to public records 147
public assembly: no positive right to 189–90, 191–5, 298
'public' duties: excluded from discrimination acts 127
public interest 243
public interest defence: lack of 153, 154, 308
public interest immunity 158
public interest immunity certificates 149, 160–2, 164, 297, 308; given by Northern Ireland Secretary 244; often used for government convenience 150, 161–2
public law: and equality 121; inequality not grounds for judicial review 116
public morality: laws on scrutinised 173–5
public morals 173; allow for changing conception of 168, 174
'public nuisance': obstruction of the highway as 188–9
public opinion 311; force of 74, 75–6; may sanction violations of basic political rights and freedoms 135, 311; role of 134–5; shift towards 'populist anti-reformism' 77, 78–80, 294, 311–12; varying strands of 76–8
Public Order Act (1936) 194, 208
Public Order Act (1986) 175, 177, 200, 297–8; and banning orders 194, 197; falls short of international standards 184; imposing conditions on processions and assemblies 195; restricting freedom of expression 178
public order legislation 123
Public Order (NI) Order (1987) 188, 194, 197
public order offences 176–7
public protest: relying on good grace or common sense 309; residual right of 185–203
Public Record Acts (1958 and 1967) 147
public records: access to 147; government seeks to liberalise regime 151–2; retention for 100 years 147
Puddephat, Andrew (Liberty): consequences of human rights not inscribed in law 80–1

qualified privilege 169
'quasi-legislation' 66–7, 134, 293, 310; almost

entirely outside parliamentary control 67; and Special Branch Activities 228, 230
Questions of Procedure for Ministers: and 1996 Scott report 149; commits ministers to open government 146

Race Relations Act (1965) 101, 175
Race Relations Act (1976) 117, 123, 125, 126, 131; national security exclusion seen as deficient 126; not extended to N Ireland 130; provides civil remedies 124; subordinate to other statutes and statutory instruments 125
Race Relations Bill: Conservative attitude to 79
racial discrimination 123, 296, 311; no prohibiting legislation in N Ireland 130; not contrary to Treaty of Rome 108
racial harassment 307B
racial hatred 123, 175–6, 297
racial inequality: and the judiciary 120
'reasonable suspicion', arrest and detention 246, 247, 248, 249, 265, 302, 312
'reasonable' use of force 241, 242, 259
Recommendation on the Access to Information Held by Public Authorities 144
Redgrave, Vanessa: complained about secret listening devices 235
Reducing the Risk of Legal Challenge, Cabinet Office 56–7
Reid, Lord 64, 175
religious discrimination 296; in employment 72–3
reporting: of hearings in public 157–8
reporting obligations: British government's discharge of 60–1
reporting restrictions: and open justice 157–8, 160
Representation of the People Act (1983) 190, 269, 279
Representation of the People (Amendment) Bill (1994) 283
reservations: covering immigration and nationality 23
residency: and voter registration 280
returning officers 279
Rifkind, Malcolm (Defence Secretary) 161
right of assembly *see* freedom of assembly
right to bail 256
right to equality: absence of 111, 116–17; bizarre effect of absence of 117–20
right to a fair trial 145
right to form and join trade unions 213–14
right to free speech 136, 163, 312
right to freedom of assembly 136, 185–203, 312
right to freedom of association 205–10
'right to know' laws 149
right to life: non-derogable 239
right to life and liberty 136, 238–41, 301–3, 312; violations of and political equality 238
Right to Organise and the Collective Bargaining Convention 29, 210
right to peaceful protest: public now less in favour of 80

right to privacy 178, 224–5, 295; a derogable right 226; not recognised in UK 230, 232; restrictions imposed on surveillance 226–7
right to a 'public hearing' 145
right to receive information 142, 144
right to silence: and Criminal Justice and Public Order Act (1994) 83, 84; public opinion influenced by politicians 79; restrictions to 87
right to stand in elections 267–8, 303; restrictions on 271–2
right to strike: absent in UK 216–17; restrictions permitted 212
right to vote 267–8, 303–4; absence of constitutional protection 269; in European Convention 267–8; people to whom right denied 275–7; protection of 269; restrictions on 271–3
right to worship 93–4
'rights': in the UK 3
rights and freedoms, individual: in Britain 4–5
Rights of Man (1789), French Declaration 4–5
Rights of Man, The: Thomas Paine 5
rights, restriction of 21–2B, 42–3, 137, 186–7; by Parliament 44; compliance with recognised aims 21–2B, 42, 43; freedom of association 205–6; freedom of expression 166–7; freedom of information 143; necessary in a democratic society 22B, 42; prescribed by law 21B, 42; and privacy 225–6
Rix, Lord: and voting rights of mental health patients 277
RPA *see* Representation of the People Act (1983)
Ryssdal, Judge (President of the European Court) 23

Scarman, Lord 38, 56, 311; argued for constitutional restraint on instant legislation 76; dissenting in Ahmed v Inner London Education Authority (1978) 93–4
Schengen Information System 68
Scotland: and homosexual law reform 77
Scott inquiry: civil servants' deliberately misleading answers to PQs 65; and public interest immunity certificates 160–1; and reports 70; to review Matrix Churchill prosecution 161
Scott report: Commons debate on 149; failure of ministers to give full information 149–50, 311; misleading of Parliament 308
Scottish Council for Civil Liberties 60
secret listening devices 232, 235, 299
security forces: limited surveillance of 228–30
Security Service Commissioner 228, 235
security services: withholding documents 162
Security Services Act (1989) 47, 227, 229; secretive regulatory measures 229
Security Services Tribunal 229, 231, 235
sedition 177, 179, 184, 298, 309

seditious libel: Thomas Paine indicted for 5
Sedley, Mr Justice 91, 99; on expansion of judicial review 95
self-defence: as murder defence 241
sex discrimination 108, 136
Sex Discrimination Act (1975) 117, 123, 125; provides civil remedies 124
Sex Discrimination (Amendment) Order (1988) 126
Sexual Offences Act (1967): and homosexuality 118
shoot-to-kill policy 242, 242–3, 243, 264, *see also* Gibraltar killings
Simon, Lord: on common law and discrimination 116
slander 169
social and economic right: freedom of association as 204
social security benefits: denial of to married women 125
society: traditions and culture of 324
Speakers' Conferences 281–2; way of reviewing electoral law and practice 280
Special Branches (police) 228, 299; failure to control activities of 230–2; intelligence gathering activities 231, 237
Spycatcher case 53, 105, 154; and confidentiality 155–6
Squires, Robin MP 179
Stalker/Sampson inquiry: shoot-to-kill policy 243, 320
Standing Advisory Commission on Human Rights in Northern Ireland 71–2, 129, 256, 309; concern about legislation by Orders in Council 72; draws attention to government violation of international human rights 72; recommended amendment of 1973 Constitution Act 130–1; recommended anti-discrimination legislation to protect 'Travellers' 119–20; report on Bill of Rights for NI 72; reports on political discrimination and equality of opportunity in NI 130; and the use of lethal force 242, 245
State Department Country Reports: critique by American Lawyers Committee for Human Rights 16; selectivity and lack of objectivity of 15
state employees: restrictions on free association 219–20, 223; right to form and join associations restricted 218–19; and trade union membership 220–2
State of the Nation surveys (Rowntree Reform Trust) 4; show fall in public support for right to silence 79; show public know little about their rights 81
state secrets: disclosure a criminal offence 148
state surveillance 224–37, 299, 308; rules for 224–7
state surveillance agencies 230; activities of 227–8

statute law 103, 138, 295; and the citizen 80; judicial interpretation of 91–4; and protection of civil and political rights 46, *see also* common law; criminal law; freedom of assembly

statutory instruments 66; cannot be amended by MPs 67

stop and search powers 111, 239, 248, 265, 301–2, 307B; arbitrary use of 250–2, 312

Street, Harry: *Freedom, the Individual and the Law* 16

strikes 212–13; as breach of contract 214; no right to in UK 216–17

Summary Jurisdiction (Isle of Man) Act (1960) *48*

Sunday Times: *Spycatcher* extracts 155, 156

surveillance *see* police: surveillance; state surveillance

suspects: police ill-treatment of in custody 260–2

tabloid press: and privacy 15

Taylor of Gosforth, Lord (Lord Chief Justice): amendments to Criminal Justice Bill (1994) 84

telephone metering 227, 232, 234, 236, 300, 308; 'not in accordance with the law' 60, 236

telephone tapping 80, 104, 105, 229, 232, 235

temporary injunctions 163, 164, 198, 297

terrorism: and government interference in the media 182–4, *see also* Northern Ireland

terrorist suspects: detention of 59, 249

Thatcher, Margaret 154; on our belief in freedom 3; Prime Minister, and the GCHQ problem 95–6, 220

third parties: protection for 208

'30-year rule' 147, 151, 164; and Three Part Test 152

Three-Part Test 97–8, 186–7; and the broadcasting ban case 97; check on restrictions on political/civil rights 10, 21–2B, 22–3, 162; freedom of assembly 192; freedom of association 205–6; freedom of expression 166–7; privacy 225–6; and restriction of rights 143

The Times: editorial on disquiet about crime 78

Tocqueville, Alexis de 38; on liberty in English customs 74

Tokyo Rules 253, 256

torture: a criminal offence 259, 302; defined 258

Town Police Clauses Act (1847) 189, 192, 202, 298

Trade Union and Labour Relations Act (1974) *48*, 218

Trade Union and Labour Relations (Consolidation) Act (1992) 189, 213, 214

Trade Union Reform and Employment Rights Act (1993): selective pay rises 215

trade union rights law 125

trade unions 204, 205, 210–23, 322; autonomy of 214, 215, 300; discipline 216; gaps in protection for members 214–16, 300; reductions of immunity for consequences of strike action 217; right not to join 218, 223

Trafalgar Square 190, 193

Trafalgar Square Regulations (1952) 189

treason 177, 179

Treaty of European Union (Maastricht): recognition of fundamental rights 108

Treaty of Rome: Article 19 124

trespassory assemblies 186, 193; and banning orders 194, 195–6

UN Basic Principles on the Use of Force and Firearms by Law Enforcement Officials 240, 242

UN Commission on Human Rights 26, 30, 43

UN Commission on the Status of Women 26, 30

UN Committee Against Torture 26, 28–9

UN Committee on Economic, Social and Cultural Rights 6, *26*, 29

UN Committee on the Elimination of Discrimination Against Women *26*, 28, 60

UN Committee on the Elimination of Racial Discrimination *26*, 28, 60, 127, 130

UN Committee on the Rights of the Child *26*, 29

UN Congress on the Prevention of Crime and the Treatment of Offenders: Resolution 17 (Pre-trial Detention) 256

UN Convention Against Torture and Other Cruel, Inhuman or Degrading Treatment 27, 28–9, 258; Article 10 (ill-treatment) 259

UN Convention on the Elimination of All Forms of Discrimination Against Women 27, 28, 30, 115, 267

UN Convention on the Elimination of All Forms of Racial Discrimination 27, 28, 115, 168, 176–7, 207, 267; violation by UK 126–7

UN Convention on the Political Rights of Women 30, 267

UN Convention on the Rights of the Child 26, 29, 115

UN Covenant on Civil and Political Human Rights 6, 8

UN Covenant on Civil and Political Rights xii, 27

UN Covenant on Economic, Social and Cultural Rights 6, 17, 27, 29, 211

UN Declaration on the Elimination of all Forms of Intolerance and of Discrimination Based on Religion or Belief 115

UN Declaration on the Rights of Disabled People 114–15, 129

UN Declaration on the Status of Women 30

UN Draft General Principles on Freedom and Non-Discrimination in the Matter of Political Rights 268

UN Framework for elections 267, 278, 293–6

UN Human Rights Committee 3, 6, 7, 17, 22B, 43, 56, 92, 144, 268, 304, 314; and affirmative action 131–2; British infringements of International Standards 306–10; concerns about political freedom in UK 307B, 307–8; on control of the media 181; and Criminal

Justice and Public Order Act (1994) 83; definition of discrimination 114; an disability 129; and discrimination 113, 125; emphasises wider duty 41–2; and evolving human rights standards 167; found British system a failure 39; General Comments of 18, 28; importance of education in human rights 42; individual petitions direct to 28; individuals should know their rights under the Covenant 81–2; no UK right of petition to 7, 58, 106; 'other status' defined 114, 129; on quality of liberty in British society 75; reports to 17–18, 27, 28; on UK legal system 306–7; UK refuses to ratify Optional Protocol 23; UK report (1995) 117; UK report (1st: 1977) 202–3; UK report (3rd: 1989) 105, 119, 241; UK report (4th: 1994) 105, 118, 119, 122, 176, 276; UK reports to 60, 133; voting rights of convicted prisoners 276; women, equality in society and protection of the law 122; work of 26, 27, 28

UN Human Rights and Elections 268, 278, 279, 286

UN human rights instruments: conflict between 18

UN Principles 267

UN Principles on Detention 259; Principles 10 and 12 (arrest) 246, 252

UN Principles on the Effective Prevention and Investigation of Extra-Legal, Arbitrary and Summary Executions 240–1, 244

UN Standard Minimum Rules for Non-Custodial Measures 253

UN Standard Minimum Rules for the Treatment of Prisoners 94, 239

UN Standard Rules on the Equalisation of Opportunities for Persons with Disabilities 115, 129

unemployment: N Ireland 130

UNESCO Commission on Human Rights 256

UNESCO Convention against Discrimination in Education 115

unfair dismissal 214, 300

United Kingdom 29; absence of right to strike 216–17; candidates for national elections 273, 274B; complacent about political freedom 315; contributed to International Covenant and European Convention 6–7, 7–8; criteria for eligibility to vote 273B, 273; derogation from international obligations on detention 255–6; discrimination in 116–20; effectiveness of law in eliminating torture, inhuman or degrading treatment 259–64; elections, rules for and conduct of 279–81, 303; European Convention and International Covenant not incorporated in British law 7; failure to adopt internationally recognised civil and political rights 305–6; failure to comply with CERD 176; failure to meet obligations under the Covenant 42; failure to review law, regulation

and practice 305; freedom of assembly regulated by law 186–7; full civic rights for Commonwealth and Irish citizens 278; and human rights treaties 304–5; infringements of international standards 306–10; legislation to restrict expression of racist ideas 175–6; life and liberty guaranteed 238; the missing voters 266–90, 303; no constitutional right of equality 110; no freedom of information statute 146; no positive right of assembly and protest 203; no public land with unrestricted right of access exists 188; no right of peaceful assembly anywhere 193; no right to privacy 230; no statutes to protect freedoms 70; political freedom in 3–12; political rights and freedoms not well protected 137; protection of human rights 37–40; record on open government 152–3; record of systemic failure 310–15; rights protected from interference by others 20; rights protection and enforcement, duality of 7; society less libertarian in the 1990s 78; state surveillance 224–37; use of reservations, interpretations and derogations 23–4; violations of international human rights 72

United Nations: Economic and Social Council 29, 30; General Assembly 26, 115, 141; the Human Rights Umbrella 26–30; Secretary General (1991) on democracy 266; Universal Declaration of Human Rights 6, 16, 27, 110, 112, 205, 213, 224, 238, 245

United Nations Charter 27

United States: Declaration of Independence (1776) 110; outlawing prior restraint 156; *Pentagon Papers* case 156; State Department Country Reports 15

Universal Declaration of Human Rights, UN 6, 16, 26, 110; Article 1 (equality) 112; Article 3 (life and liberty) 238, 245; Article 5 (torture) 258; Article 9 (arrest) 245; Article 12 (interference with privacy) 224; Article 20 (freedom of association) 205, 213; Article 21 (right to take part in government) 267; Article 23 (freedom of association) 205; quoted 112

universal suffrage: recognition of 268

university/college authorities: positive duty to secure freedom of speech for visiting speakers 190–1

'unreasonableness', test of 95

'the usual conditions' *see* bail conditions

voluntary associations, lawful: determine own membership and rules 207–8

voter registration 280; decline in 282–6; duty to promote actively 286–9; impact of poll tax 270; non-registration rising 282–3

voters: unregistered 283

voting rights: position of aliens living in Britain 277–8; restrictions on 271–2 voting systems 266–7, 279

Waddington, David (Home Office minister) 236
Waddington, Lord: paramount nature of
government's business needs 64
Walker, Bill MP 104; on protection of citizens'
rights 45
Wallace, Colin *see* Colin Wallace affair
Wardle, Charles: (Home Office minister) on
unregistered homeless people 285–6; on
judicial review as a safeguard 91
warrants: of further detention 254; for surveillance
agencies 228; for telephone tapping and mail
interception 232, *233*; to intercept
communications 234
Washington Post 156; published extracts from
Spycatcher 155
Wedderburn, Lord: on absence of right to strike
216–17
Wednesbury principle 95
'well-informed public' 76, 77

West Midlands Crime Squad: working practices,
non-compliance with PACE 261
Whitelaw, William: and 'husband rule' 56
Williams Committee: on obscenity and film
sensorship 174
Wilson government: plot to destabilise 229
The Windlesham Rampton Report 183
Windscale nuclear accident 150–1
women: in British society 308; participation in
public life 122, 132; and slow/complex
procedures of equal pay legislation 128
worker-employer consultation 212
World Human Rights Guide, Charles Humana
14, 15
World Programme of Action Concerning Disabled
People 115
Wright, Peter 229, *see also Spycatcher* case

Young, Hugo 90–1
young people: missing from electoral register *284*,
285